The Transition to Capitali
in Modern France

Historians, since the 1960s, argue that the French economy performed as well as did any economy in Europe during the eighteenth and nineteenth centuries thanks to the opportunities for profit available on the market, especially the large consumer market in Paris. Whatever economic weaknesses existed did not stem from the social structure but from exogenous forces such as wars, the lack of natural resources or slow demographic growth.

This book challenges the foregoing consensus by showing that the French economy performed poorly relative to its rivals because of noncapitalist social relations. Specifically, peasants and artisans controlled lands and workshops in autonomous communities and did not have to improve labor productivity to survive. Merchants and manufacturers cornered markets instead of being subject to the market's competitive imperatives.

Thus, distinctive features of capitalism—primitive accumulation (the dispossession of peasants and artisans) and the competitive obligation faced by merchants and manufacturers to reinvest profits in order to keep the profits—did not prevail until the state imposed them in a process lasting for a century after the 1850s. For this reason, it was not until the 1960s that France caught up to (and in some cases surpassed) its economic rivals.

Xavier Lafrance, Professor of Political Science at UQAM (Université du Québec à Montréal), is the author of *The Making of Capitalism in France* (2019) and coeditor, with Charles Post, of *Case Studies in the Origins of Capitalism* (2018).

Stephen Miller, Professor of History at UAB (University of Alabama at Birmingham), is author of *State and Society in Eighteenth Century France* (Revised updated edition, 2023), *Feudalism, Venality and Revolution* (2020) and, co-authored with Christopher Isett, *The Social History of Agriculture* (2017).

Routledge Studies in the Modern History of France
Series Editor: Rachel Utley
University of Leeds, UK

Titles in the series:

French Soldiers' Morale in the Phoney War, 1939–1940
Maude Williams and Bernard Wilkin

Edmond Fleg and Jewish Minority Culture in Twentieth-Century France
Sally Debra Charnow

The Man Who Murdered Admiral Darlan
Vichy, the Allies and the Resistance in French North Africa
Bénédicte Vergez-Chaignon
Translated by Richard Carswell

The Making of the Citizen-Worker
Labour and the Borders of Politics in Post-revolutionary France
Federico Tomasello

For more information about this series, please visit: https://www.routledge.com/
Routledge-Studies-in-the-Modern-History-of-France/book-series/FRENCHHISTORY

The Transition to Capitalism in Modern France

Primitive Accumulation and Markets
from the Old Regime to the post-WWII Era

Xavier Lafrance and Stephen Miller

Routledge
Taylor & Francis Group

LONDON AND NEW YORK

First published 2024
by Routledge
4 Park Square, Milton Park, Abingdon, Oxon OX14 4RN

and by Routledge
605 Third Avenue, New York, NY 10158

Routledge is an imprint of the Taylor & Francis Group, an informa business

© 2024 Xavier Lafrance and Stephen Miller

British Library Cataloguing-in-Publication Data
A catalogue record for this book is available from the British Library

ISBN: 9780367553005 (hbk)
ISBN: 9780367553043 (pbk)
ISBN: 9781003092896 (ebk)

DOI: 10.4324/9781003092896

Typeset in Times New Roman
by codeMantra

Contents

Introduction

Most accounts of economic growth in France (and elsewhere) treat markets, trade and capitalism as a single phenomenon. From this perspective, all forms of commercial exchange in search of a profit, no matter how restrained or embryonic, represented capitalism. They existed long before, and eventually brought about, an industrial economy. Rising opportunities for wealth, tied to expanding commercial exchanges, eventually led to specialized production, innovation, reinvestment and growth. The expansion of markets propelled development. What needs to be explained—a capitalist civilization—is simply assumed, and historical enquiries focus on the removal of barriers to the natural propensity to maximize productivity and profits and to accumulate capital.[1]

The foregoing summarizes the "commercialization model" of economic history, which was elaborated in Adam Smith's analysis of *The Wealth of Nations*. Smith famously explained how the division of labor occasioned a "universal opulence which extends itself to the lowest ranks of the people" by causing the "improvement of the dexterity of the workman," "saving of time" and ensuring "the application of proper machinery" in production. The extent of the division of labor, he went on, is determined by the extent of the market, stressing that "it is the power of exchanging that gives occasion to the division of labor." The growth of output per capita occurs through the expansion of the market—the larger the market, the deeper the division of labor, the greater the nation's wealth.[2]

For Smith, the same factors producing "universal opulence" in contemporary society also propelled the historical development of humanity through different modes of "subsistence," culminating with a transition to a "commercial society" (capitalism). While "the accumulation of stock must, in the nature of things, be previous to the division of labor," once wealth has been amassed, the subdivision of production "is the necessary, though very slow and gradual, consequence of a certain propensity [...] to truck, barter, and exchange." This division of labor, and the sustained growth it supports, is not "originally the effect of any human wisdom," but the result of an "invisible hand"—the unintended aggregate effect of self-seeking individual actions. It is by pursuing self-interest and profits that humans specialize and trade, leading not only to rising efficiency and labor productivity, but also to the historical appearance of "commercial society" (capitalism) and its characteristic pattern of self-sustained growth.[3]

DOI: 10.4324/9781003092896-1

This book departs from Smith's commercialization model and offers an analysis of France's transition to capitalism understood as a distinct civilization. We conceive of capitalism as a mode of exploitive production characterized by the generalized market dependence of socioeconomic actors. Under capitalism, workers and employers depend on markets to secure goods necessary for their economic survival. Historically specific dynamics—rising labor productivity and sustained economic growth—ensue, we will show, from market imperatives to specialize, innovate and accumulate. Contrary to Smithian assumptions, however, the historical advent of these capitalist dynamics is not the natural result of self-interested rational behavior per se. We must refrain, in other words, from depicting the rise of capitalist societies as the inherent and unproblematic response to the prospects for gain in a context of rising trade opportunities.

As this book shows, of all the leading capitalist countries, the French case offers one of the clearest illustrations of rational self-seeking economic behavior, to seize market opportunities, which avoided market dependence and competitive imperatives. The existence of a socioeconomic setting in which rational behavior leads to capitalist dynamics of accumulation and growth cannot be assumed—its historical emergence must be explained. Capitalist patterns of economic growth result from a specific social structure. This social structure had to be built, often imposed, through a process that, as this book demonstrates, was contentious, protracted and nonlinear.

In contrast to our perspective, influential historical works, analyzed in the first two chapters of this book, track the economic development of France by assuming that it followed the expansion or contraction of market exchange. William Sewell's *Capitalism and the Emergence of Civic Equality in Eighteenth-Century France* is the most recent contribution to this body of work. Sewell's book, based on impressive historical breadth, and brimming with insights, mobilizes a Marxist framework similar to ours, but ultimately reverts to Smithian assumptions. Sewell's thesis is that the spirit of civic equality promoted by Enlightenment philosophers and put forward by the revolutionary regime was fostered by the "French experience of capitalism" during the eighteenth century. This was "commercial capitalism," but capitalism nonetheless, according to Sewell, since it entailed "sustained dynamism [...] powered by the widespread and ever-increasing production of commodities for sale on the market." Commercialization promoted "abstract commodity-based social relations," tied to the logic of monetary equivalence and the anonymity of market exchanges. This anonymity and monetary equivalency instilled an egalitarian civic spirit, as the "abstract character of commodity exchanges" came to be reflected in the notion of the formal equality of citizens.[4]

Agrarian producers near urban centers, especially in the Paris Basin, specialized and innovated as they produced for exchange in response to rising demand. The capitalist restructuring of industry, Sewell argues, was even more pronounced. While a significant part of urban manufacturing moved to *faubourgs* exempted from guild regulations, growth mostly took a "proto-industrial" form, in response to expanding international trade, as textile merchants tapped the reserves of cheap labor for spinning and weaving in the countryside.[5]

Sewell's historical reading of the transition to capitalism builds on Marx's critical analysis of capitalism, advanced in the *Grundrisse* and *Capital*.[6] Marx understood that "the emergence of capitalism constituted a sharp break from previous types of economic and social life." This transition required "the universalization of commodity production" which, "crucially, entailed that human labor be made into a commodity to be exchanged in the market like any other." Workers had to be dispossessed of means of production, causing labor to become "abstracted" and "alienated." Workers, to be specific, had to sell their time to capitalists in exchange for a wage. Labor-power constituted a special type of commodity capable of producing a surplus of value above what it cost for the worker to survive. Employers appropriated "absolute" surplus value by lengthening and intensifying work or "relative" surplus value by reorganizing production and investing in new tools and machinery. It is the latter form of surplus value extraction—relative surplus value—which Sewell (correctly) identifies as the "distinguishing feature of capitalism" and the cause of its specific dynamism. Absolute surplus typified noncapitalist feudal and slave economies. Capitalism, by contrast, led to labor-productivity enhancing technology in production, so employers could decrease unit costs and outcompete other capitalists who had to adopt similar technologies or find alternative ways of reducing their own costs to stay afloat.

Sewell, however, proposes an amendment to Marx's theory. The latter was developed through an analysis of mechanized factories employing "fully proletarianized workers" in nineteenth-century England. According to Sewell, Marx wrongly inferred from this experience that capitalist production and dynamic growth required the employment of dispossessed waged workers. Eighteenth-century French commercial capitalism, he explains, did not work that way. The relationship between employers and direct producers was not mediated by a wage contract but by credit, since merchants advanced the material transformed by spinners and weavers, and often also the tools necessary to perform their labor. As part of this relationship, workers were compelled by "unequal debt relations" to create absolute as well as relative surplus value appropriated by the traders who hired them.[7]

Sewell thus urges us to give up Marx's "ultimately futile search for a moment of primitive accumulation," an historical event that made people juridically free and in need of paid work to survive. Sewell maintains that "the fully proletarian condition" was an "outcome," not a "prerequisite" of the early phase of capitalist development. As cogent as Sewell's rethinking of the transition seems, it begs the question: where did this early phase of capitalist development come from? What caused its emergence in the first place? Sewell's answer is straightforward: "commerce was the keyword and driver in the eighteenth century." Capitalism was pushed forward by "expanding markets" and "improved market access," which "as Adam Smith and all economists since tell us, gives rise to increased division of labor and hence greater efficiency."[8]

In spite of his Marxist inclinations, Sewell thus reverts to the Smithian framework. Marx, Sewell recognizes, did not believe the expansion of opportunities for profit through trade could turn feudal or slave economies into capitalism. Marx maintained that the development of "commercial capital [...] taken by itself, is

insufficient to explain the transition from one mode of production to the other."
He explained that, as a rule, "the less developed production is, the more monetary
wealth is concentrated in the hands of merchants." He added that:

> the independent and preponderant development of capital in the form of
> commercial capital is synonymous with the non-subjection of production to
> capital, i.e., with the development of capital on the basis of a social form of
> production that is foreign to it and independent of it. The independent de-
> velopment of commercial capital thus stands in the inverse proportion to the
> general economic development of society.

Marx thus argued that commerce, far from bringing about capitalist social relations, actually had a solvent effect on noncapitalist social formations. Whether or
not a "new mode of production arises in place of the old, does not depend on trade,
but rather on the character of the old mode of production itself."[9]

Each mode of production had its own specific "laws of motion," and any analysis of the transition to capitalism, Marx argued, must include an examination of the
society out of which it emerged. The class structure, economic logic and forms of
sociopolitical conflicts of that society determined the consequences of commerce.
The author of *Capital* consequently stressed that one must look for an alternative
to explanations of the transition single-mindedly focused on trade. He offered his
alternative explanation in Part Eight of the first Book of *Capital*, titled "So-called
Primitive Accumulation," to critique Smith's thesis that capitalism arose out of a
prior piling up of wealth. This wealth, according to Smith, would inevitably be
invested in production, unproblematically fueling the social division of labor and
self-sustained growth. Marx explained that in themselves, money and commodities
are no more capital than the means of production and subsistence are. They need to
be transformed into capital …. Capital is not a thing, but a social relation between
persons which is mediated through things, and for wealth to become capital, a
transformation of class relations must take place.[10]

The "secret" of so-called primitive accumulation is "the historical process of
divorcing the producer from the means of production." Marx explained that regarding England, "the expropriation of the agricultural producer, of the peasant, from
the soil, is the basis of the whole process." The expropriation of the peasants, turning them into market dependent free laborers, simultaneously involved the breakup
of peasant communities. Some peasants took up commercial leases from landlords
and became capitalist tenants. Others, through expropriation or as a consequence of
economic competition, joined a proletariat detached from means of subsistence and
production and compelled to seek employment from capitalist farmers. This epoch-
making transition created England's classic tripartite class structure: *landlords* reliant on an economic form of surplus appropriation, a competitive market in leases
supported by the commercial profits of capitalist *tenant farmers* who employed
wage laborers and who maximized efficiency because of the pressure to compete
applied by their peers, the other capitalist tenant farmers. Marx recognized the
sustained growth generated by this capitalist structure: "the revolution in property

relations on the land was accompanied by improved methods of cultivation, greater co-operation, a higher concentration of the means of production and so on, and because the agricultural wage laborers were made to work at a higher level of intensity."[11] "Primitive accumulation," then, entailed both the commodification of labor and the extension of market dependence to capitalist tenant farmers compelled to develop the productivity of the labor they employed.

This historical process of expropriation—the reduction of direct producers to a commodified labor force and the generalization of a market dependence to the employers—is the source of the abstraction of social relations that Sewell correctly identifies as a core dimension of capitalism. In a market economy, producers can only coordinate their private activities through the exchange of commodities and the fluctuation of their prices. What lies behind the exchange-value of their products is not their concrete labor (which creates the use-value of their products), but "abstract" labor. By selling commodities on the market, capitalists "validate" the labor they employed. Their ability to sell in a competitive context depends on their capacity to produce according to the "socially necessary labor time"—the productive standards of their society—which sets the value of their product. They have, in other words, to abide by the "law of value." To do so, employers must be able to treat labor just as they would any other commodity, reducing its cost and maximizing its productivity.

Contrary to Sewell's belief, the expropriation and commodification of labor is indeed a *prerequisite* of the formation of "abstract" labor in production, under the supervision of competing employers. As such, it is also a precondition of generalized commodity production and of the value-form of labor that makes it possible. Marx demonstrated that labor-power had to be abstracted from peasant communities, which mediated its relationship to the means of production (most importantly land), in order to become a variable component of capital wielded by employers to extract surplus value. Put another way, for the abstraction and alienation of labor to operate in the daily functioning of capitalism, a prior moment of "abstraction," or separation, must have taken place.

That said, once established, market exchange and competition itself became a factor of expropriation, as producers became insolvent and joined the class of wage laborers. Marx did not perceive the transformation of class relations entailed by "primitive accumulation" as a "sudden" historical moment, as Sewell would have us believe. He presented it as a *process* entailing physical coercion, economic compulsion, legislative initiative and state intervention. Marx depicted the English case as a "classic form" and used it to present his general conception of the transition to capitalism.[12] Given that, as Marx emphasized, the form taken by the emergence of a new mode of production depends on the "character of the old mode of production itself," subsequent transitions to capitalism were bound to vary in accordance with the characteristics of the societies in question. What remains general to all transitions, however, are processes that led to market dependence, compelling people to develop new strategies of reproduction (or economic survival). What Marx described as "primitive accumulation" was the historical emergence of new "social property relations."

Social Property Relations and Rules for Reproduction

The conceptual framework guiding our analysis of the transition to capitalism in France was developed by Robert Brenner and Ellen Meiksins Wood from Marx's theory of primitive accumulation.[13] Brenner presents a critique of the "commercialization model," discussed above, as well as the alternative reading of European economic history known as the "demographic model." This latter reading undermined the former model's assumption that expanding trade led to sustained economic growth. The demographic model showed instead that population growth caused recurrent Malthusian cycles of stagnation and decline, as population outgrew available resources. Proponents of the commercialization and demographic models, however, both assume that either commerce or demography acted as independent variables to which the economy was responsive. Both models are consequently incapable of explaining how cross-European patterns of trade expansion, from the eleventh century, and the population collapse and feudal crisis of the fourteenth century, led to divergent paths of economic development.

In Eastern Europe, peasants lacked robust communities and were unable to resist the imposition of a "second serfdom" in the wake of the fourteenth-century crisis. In western continental Europe, including France, the solidarity of village communities allowed peasants to capitalize on the demographic collapse of the period, which made lords vulnerable to peasants interested in farming lands abandoned in the crisis. Even before the fourteenth and fifteenth centuries, the lords had to accept the abolition of serfdom (unpaid forced labor and restrictions on freedom of movement). They also accepted unvarying monetary (not in-kind) dues for the lands farmed by the peasants. As the lords lost, in this way, major sources of income, they reconstituted their authority and wealth, in a contradictory and convulsive process, through the formation of absolute monarchy. Peasants kept possession of their plots and prioritized "safety first" agriculture, covering household needs before marketing their surpluses. Nobles, under the aegis of absolute monarchy, secured a part of their revenues by taxing the peasantry. This political and economic configuration, like serfdom in Eastern Europe, did not stimulate economic development.

England, in sharp contrast to the rest of Europe, embarked on a course toward agrarian capitalism—an unintended consequence of feudal class conflict. Peasants liberated themselves from serfdom during the fourteenth century. They obtained freedom of movement to farm fields abandoned during the demographic collapse of the fourteenth century. The lords, however, retained the power to raise fees charged for land transfers (in contrast to the unvarying monetary dues in western Europe) and thus undermined the peasants' possession of farms. In the following centuries, the lords morphed into a class of gentry landowners able to raise these fees as high as the market would bear (like commercial leases) and force the tenants to farm competitively for the market to earn the money needed to pay for the use of the land. Successful tenant farmers, with the help of the landed gentry, broke up village communities, expropriated peasants and created a class of wage laborers. The centralized (relative to other feudal monarchies) Plantagenet and Tudor states enforced the gentry's control over this system of agrarian capitalism, in which tenant farmers specialized, innovated and accumulated to extend, or at least, preserve, their access to leases.[14]

This dynamic led to a historically unprecedented process of sustained growth. England broke the Malthusian demographic ceiling that continued to constrain development on the Continent. The gentry obtained surpluses through private property and economic relations and did not rely on the absolutist form of government, which buttressed noble privilege and power in France. The expropriation of the peasants, at the heart of English capitalism, included the formation of a consumer market, in addition to the market for labor, as the inhabitants had to purchase items of subsistence, which they had formerly been able to produce in communities. The competitive dynamics of labor and consumer markets forced farmers to work more productively, thereby bringing down food prices—even though agriculture began to require less labor relative to output—and laying the basis for the growth of manufacturing and eventually industrial capitalism.

Brenner's comparative analysis of these historical patterns of development exposed how commerce and demography were mediated by specific balances of power between lords and peasants, which varied according to the relationships of conflict or solidarity within these classes. He showed how these conflicts, as well the economic dynamics that emerged out of them, were shaped by specific "social property relations" and "rules for reproduction."

Brenner's concept of social property relations echoes the Marxist "modes of production." Both have specific "laws of motion," which orient economic dynamics, as well as specific forms of class conflict and historical evolution. As Marx explained, "the innermost secret, the hidden basis of the entire social edifice," as well as "the entire configuration of the economic community," emerge out of the "the specific economic form in which unpaid surplus labor is pumped out of the direct producers," which "determines the relationship of domination and servitude, as this grows directly out of production itself and reacts back on it in turn as a determinant."[15]

Social property relations, or modes of production, thus give rise to what Brenner described as specific "rules for reproduction" for the people living under them. Put another way, structures of surplus appropriation define the strategies that individuals can be expected to follow to reproduce themselves and their families. What is more, "in aggregate," rules for reproduction, followed by the mass of the population, "give rise to certain corresponding developmental patterns."[16]

To concretely illustrate these points, we can see, for instance, how in the feudal context, of autonomous sovereign manors, the rivalry among lords, to control lands and peasants, required to take wealth, compelled them to "accumulate" means of coercion. Feudal social property relations entailed a mode of exploitation mediated by political power, in which moments of coercion and appropriation were fused. The lords faced rules for reproduction that constrained them to systematically build up their coercive capacities to force the peasants to work on their behalf and to protect (or expand) their feudal domains vis-à-vis other predatory lords. As feudalism declined on the European continent, in the 1200–1500s, and as absolutist states re-configured the political and economic authority of the nobles, these states followed this same process of building coercive capacities (in relation to peasant subjects and other monarchies) in what has been called "geopolitical accumulation."[17]

As Brenner puts it, "the drive to *political accumulation*, to *state-building*, is the *precapitalist analogue* to the drive to *accumulate capital*."[18] Under capitalism, exploitation takes place through the "dull compulsion of the market." Moments of appropriation and coercion are separate. Appropriation entails production privately controlled by capitalists subject to market imperatives. Coercion is monopolized by states which protect the private property of the capitalists. Workers and employers must successfully compete on the market to reproduce themselves. This implies rules for reproduction, which compel employers to accumulate capital, since they are legally prohibited from privately accumulating the means of coercion. Capital accumulation requires investments to cut costs and maximize labor productivity.

It should by now be clear that, contrary to the Smithian assumptions of the commercialization model, and following Brenner, our theoretical framework rejects "any notion of trans-historical individual economic rationality." It puts forth the idea that "the specific forms of socio-economic behavior that individuals and families will find to make sense and will choose will depend on the society-wide networks of social relationships – society-wide constraints and opportunities – in which they find themselves." In short, people live in societies with rules for reproduction, which appear natural to them. Their economic behavior does not arise out of a natural human propensity or automatic response to expanding market demand.[19] Indeed, capitalism has arisen out of class conflicts that involved the coercive reduction of a typically recalcitrant society to a condition of market dependence.

The Role of the State in Overcoming this Recalcitrance and Facilitating the Transition to Capitalism

A central distinctive characteristic of capitalism is the "operation of the capitalist market as imperative rather than as opportunity."[20] Capitalism emerges historically when both producers and appropriators come to depend on the market for their reproduction and when the relation of exploitation between the two is mediated by the market, that is, when entrepreneurs appropriate surplus value created in production on the condition of successfully selling their products on competitive markets.[21] The market, under capitalism, is never simply a set of opportunities to buy, sell and make a profit. It is compulsory: workers must sell their labor-power on competitive markets to ensure their survival, while employers have to optimize their price/cost, selling price relative to costs of production, to stay afloat against competitors.

Commercial exchange, of course, existed long before the emergence of capitalism. Markets often supported the growth of production, and sometimes technical improvements. Yet this growth and improvement resulted from opportunities arising out of the expansion of the market—not out of market imperatives—and tended to be "once and for all" innovations, not systematic improvements.[22] Precapitalist merchants made profits through "arbitrage between markets," and this type of profit-making entailed "strategies of its own," and had "nothing to do with transforming production in the sense required by capitalist competition."[23] French merchants, we demonstrate in Chapter 2, thrived on cornering, managing and intermediating between fragmented markets.

Capitalist markets, by contrast, imply not simply production for exchange, or even for profit, but rather production aimed at maximizing profits as a requirement for economic survival—competitive reproduction through market relations. The ownership class, under capitalism, does not simply produce to sell on markets. Owners are compelled to attain the socially necessary rate of productivity and profitability to remain in business. They must, put simply, "compete or go under." Precapitalist merchants certainly sought to make a profit, attempting to buy at the cheapest and sell at the highest price possible, but capitalist producers and traders are "subject to price/cost pressures in a wholly new way" and are constrained to "cost-effective production."[24]

Humans, given the chance, avoid this capitalist market dependence. Although they readily profit from market opportunities, they avoid allowing their very economic existence to be determined by them. This is certainly the case for peasants, as we explain in Chapter 1. Farmers, who specialize output for the markets and forgo the production of subsistence, put themselves at the risk of hunger in three potential scenarios: the absence of demand for their specialized commodity, bad harvests and insufficient output of this commodities or unaffordable prices for the food, which they must buy once they specialize their farms for the market. Peasants have direct experience with dearth or know about it from ancestors, and therefore opt, whenever possible, for safety-first agriculture. They market surpluses *after* they meet the needs of their households and communities. Such a strategy—adopted not out of cultural conservatism but out of material self-interest—explains the perpetuation, described by Fernand Braudel, of France as a "peasant society" until after the Second World War.[25]

Against the liberal narrative, which equates capitalism with the rise of the bourgeoisie, we argue that this tendency to avoid market dependence is also true for entrepreneurs, merchants and manufacturers. Entrepreneurs seek profits, not aggregate and sustained development. The unintended consequence of their quest for profit leads to development only under specific circumstances. Entrepreneurs, as a rule, avoid capitalist market dependence—the obligation to competitively reproduce themselves through markets. They adopt strategies ranging from exclusive trade networks to outright military control over trade routes. They develop their individual and collective market power to control prices, minimize risk and maximize income. While they might depend on the market for profit, they build capacities to shape the market and escape competitive imperatives. Businesses, in other words, avoid the type of market dependence that compels them to compete to ensure their reproduction. As we explain in this book, French manufacturers were not exceptional, nor were they poor entrepreneurs enmeshed in an incapacitating "Malthusian" culture. They seized market opportunities and invested according to their individual interests but not in ways that promoted national economic development.

Smith, for instance, in the *Wealth of Nations*, presented the historical process that led to the emergence of "commercial society" as the unproblematic consequence of self-interested individual actions and the natural propensity to trade, which advanced the division of labor. Yet, he also, contradictorily, decried the proclivity of merchants and manufacturers to distort the law of the market. Thus, while assuming, rather than explaining, the emergence of capitalism, Smith correctly stressed that the self-seeking action of entrepreneurs only served economic growth in a distinct setting.[26] Smith was appalled by "the mean rapacity, the monopolizing spirit of merchants and manufacturers." He explained that

> the interest of the dealers… in any particular branch of trade or manufactures, is always in some respect different from, and even opposite to, that of the publick. To widen the market and to narrow competition is always the interest of the dealers. To widen the market may frequently be agreeable enough to the interest of the publick; but to narrow the competition must always be against it, and can only serve to enable the dealers, by raising their profits above what they would normally be, to levy, for their own benefit, an absurd tax upon the rest of their fellow-citizens.[27]

As David McNally explains, Smith believed that the normal functioning of the capitalist economy lowered the rate profit and led merchants and manufacturers to react by conspiring to maintain prices artificially high, thus propping up profits at the expense of the public interest. Smith showed that entrepreneurs "have become formidable to the government, and upon many occasions intimidate the legislature." He consequently called for barriers against the influence of traders and industrialists on the legislature. The state could then subject merchants to market competition and thus apply downward pressure on profits until they reached their "lowest ordinary rate." A fall of commodity prices and rise of real wages would ensue, ensuring a "higher level of consumption of the average member of society, of the working poor," which was Smith's fundamental indicator of the wealth of a nation. The state, then, had to preserve the institutional setting that guaranteed opulence and served the public—that is, impose competition—and only then would laissez-faire function effectively, and self-seeking behavior lead to growth.[28]

We recognize the importance of Smith's intuition regarding the propensity of entrepreneurs to maximize their market power and the role of the state in enforcing competition to ensure the functioning of the market. We stress, however, that the tendency to avoid market dependence and competition is not simply a reaction to capitalist markets once they have been established—or to a transhistorical law of the market—but is, in fact, inherent to the functioning of precapitalist economies. Breaking this tendency is thus part of the very transition to capitalism. The emergence of a capitalist society implies the imposition of market dependence upon recalcitrant peasants and entrepreneurs in a way that leads to the proletarianization of direct producers, the establishment of capitalist farming and the development of productivity-maximizing industrial firms with the overall result of self-sustaining growth. The transition to capitalism did not involve the removal of obstacles, which constrained the natural predisposition to seek profit. It involved the creating of structural imperatives that compelled people to engage in strategies of ongoing accumulation.

Following the pathbreaking work of Alexander Gerschenkron, economic historians have questioned Walt Rostow's linear stages of development and have been attentive to the diversity of routes taken by late-developing countries. Historians associate this diversity with the distinct forms of government industrial policies.[29] Studying late industrializers such as France, Germany and Russia, Gerschenkron showed that they each forged a distinct pattern of economic development, varying in accordance with their level of "economic backwardness," by establishing institutions and policies that acted as "substitutes" for the dynamics and resources of advanced industrial countries.

In Gerschenkron's view, the state acted to compensate for backwardness and lack of resources (raw materials, entrepreneurship, capital or labor force) by facilitating the formation of the banking sector, squeezing scarce capital out of the population, investing in large-scale factories or supporting imports of advanced technologies. One of Gerschenkron's influential ideas is that late developers did not replicate Britain's pattern of development focused upon light industries such as textiles, but rather developed large-scale industries using the latest technology. Capital-intensive, in contrast to labor-intensive, industrialization required state support to concentrate and direct financial capital. The acquisition of technology and its labor-saving effect allowed late-developers to form an abundant and disciplined labor force and compensate for the slow uprooting of the peasantry from the land.[30]

Like Gerschenkron, Alice Amsden emphasizes the role of the state in the late-developing countries of East Asia and the Global South. She departs from Gerschenkron by noting that late developers often began with labor-intensive industries. She recognizes, however, that further development required a combination of relatively advanced technologies with relatively cheap labor to compete with earlier developers and penetrate world markets. This required limits on mass consumption, protectionist policies and subsidies to industry conditional on performance standards.[31] Studies of the "developmental state," since the original theorization of the concept by Chalmers Johnson in the early 1980s, have focused on its institutional configuration, its economic functions and how it shapes patterns of development.[32]

Naturally endowed, or institutionally provided, resources certainly matter. Gerschenkron was right to direct our attention to the role of the state in supporting the modernization of banking and in making the technologies of advanced economies available to industrialists. On their own, however, resources do not lead to sustained growth unless they are mobilized by private investors. Gerschenkron stated that the Cobden-Chevalier Treaty of 1860, the reduction of tariffs and abolition of quotas, which exposed French industry to international competition and contributed to industrial development to "a not inconsiderable extent," amounted to "negative policies." He contrasted these policies with the "powerful positive impetus" provided by the restructuring of finance, under the auspices of the state, which led to the rise of industrial banking under the Second Empire (1852–1870).[33]

As we show, however, while industrial firms in some sectors were compelled by international competition—as well as other dynamics such as the consolidation of a national market and the erosion of customary regulations of production—to engage in capitalist processes of accumulation after the 1860s, they did so by mobilizing newly available financial resources to a remarkably underwhelming degree. This failure to use the newly developed financial system, we argue, stemmed from an incomplete transformation of the socioeconomic structure and, specifically, from the consolidation of the peasantry and traditional agriculture, or the slow proletarianization of the population, for which no labor-saving technology could compensate on its own.

The identification of entrepreneurial values as a condition for the efficient usage of resources and capitalist growth is frequent in the literature on economic development and industrialization, especially in the literature on France. Clive Trebilcock, for instance, argues that the productive or unproductive use of resources depends on noneconomic variables, namely the "climate of opinion" affecting "the behavior of entrepreneurial groups." Trebilcock thus appropriates not only Rostow's and Gerschenkron's work, but also Talcott Parsons's theory of the "social value systems" and "role expectations" of a given society, which provide entrepreneurs with the "social approval" to launch economic development. Trebilcock also adopts Raymond Aron's "slight refinements" of Parsons's theory, namely a consideration of the attitudes fostering entrepreneurial forces. Trebilcock applies these models to explain the transfer and use of technologies facilitating the industrialization of continental Europe, which depended not only on "factor endowments" but also on appropriate "value systems."[34]

The first problem with explanations of growth based on entrepreneurial values is that they generally cannot explain the provenance of attitudinal dispositions. The presence of a capitalist spirit is often assumed to be present in precapitalist societies but depicted as constrained or repressed by traditional values. More fundamentally, this approach fails to grasp the connection between values and structures. While social institutions and structures are reproduced through the meaningful social actions of agents guided by values, this is not the case for social property relations, since the latter directly "relate to the actor's economic viability and, in this capacity, they set the rules for what actors have to do to reproduce themselves."[35] Because it pertains to their reproductive needs, individuals are compelled to adapt to social property relations by forsaking goals and values that conflict with rules for reproduction tied to these relations. These rules for reproduction thus become the common sense of society. We therefore insist that peasants or entrepreneurs stuck to noncompetitive and economically suboptimal practices, not out of conservative values, but out of self-interest, which appeared obvious to the people in question.

That said, social property relations involve relationships of exploitation and of competition within the exploiting class over access to surplus labor, and are therefore inherently unstable. Crises and resistance compel exploiters to deploy strategies and build institutions to ensure the reproduction of the means of surplus appropriation. As Brenner explains, "the critical condition for the reproduction of the property relations is the existence of a community of economic actors which sees the reproduction of these relations as its conscious purpose."[36] Just as peasants and workers often develop solidarity to resist exploitation, surplus appropriators build political institutions to defend, and reproduce, the prevailing class structures.

It follows that the basis for the reproduction of social property relations, or mode of production, is political, and the same goes for the *transition* from one mode to another. States proved instrumental to the creation of capitalist social property relations.

Once states pursue a capitalist restructuring of the economy and society, the central issue becomes their capacity to accomplish this goal. But both parts of the process—the emergence of a capitalist orientation and the building of capacity to enact the transition—must be explained historically. Such an explanation is precisely what is lacking in the institutionalist approach, dominant in the developmental state literature, which focuses on governmental autonomy, the creation of appropriate state agencies and coherent bureaucracies.[37] These institutional phenomena certainly matter. Yet their evolution and impact can only be understood by situating them in class relations.[38] One must consider the logic by which elites and the lower classes reproduce themselves economically, as well as the conflicts pitting elites against one another and all elites against the lower classes.

In precapitalist societies, members of ruling classes competed against one another for the rank and wealth obtained through the state. They also worked together within these states to wage war against the ruling classes of other predatory states. After the consolidation of capitalism in England at the end of the 1600s, this state could effectively tax the self-sustaining growth of the economy and raise the resources to establish itself as the global hegemonic power. Geopolitical pressures then played a crucial role in leading other ruling classes to pursue capitalist reforms. Such reforms, however, undermined the social bases, economic reproduction and political domination of the ruling class. State reformers threatened not only nobles, who depended upon state-offices and noncapitalist forms of land tenures and rents, but also merchants, who relied on noncompetitive markets. Attempts to engage a transition to capitalism created intra-ruling class conflicts between administrators, intent on overhauling the economy to cope with geopolitical pressure, and elites whose means of reproduction were threatened by the overhaul. These conflicts between "modernizing" and traditional forces took place both within the state and between the state and anti-reformist elites. Forces attempting to accomplish a transition to capitalism therefore sought to build the autonomy of the executive and administrative apparatuses of the state vis-à-vis elite factions.

To these inter-elite conflicts, we must add a consideration of class relations between the elites and working population. Processes of capitalist restructuring also threatened the material interests of, and provoked resistance from, peasants and artisans. Factions of the ruling class opposing reforms could then attempt to forge cross-class alliances with peasants and artisans against capitalist restructuring. Alternatively, pro-capitalist reformers tapped into popular discontent toward rent-seeking merchants and notables to forge a cross-class alliance in favor of pro-development reforms.

As Benno Teschke puts it, the form taken by the transition to capitalism in a given country emerged out of the "clash of external imperatives and internal responses, formulated against the background of nationally pre-existing and distinct class constellations."[39] A successful transition to capitalism hinged on the ability of government coalitions to develop a coherent program and state apparatus, in a specific context of class conflict and cooperation, to impose social property relations and rules for reproduction conducive to market competition.

Using this framework, we analyze the protracted transition to capitalism in modern France. We contend that despite pressures to modernize its economy, France remained noncapitalist throughout the Old Regime and long after the Revolution. A transition toward capitalism began first in the industrial sector during the 1860s. Capitalist industrialization, however, was severely constrained by the absence of agrarian capitalism. We maintain that the transition to capitalism was finally completed during the post-World War II period.

To demonstrate this protracted transition to capitalism from the 1860s to the 1960s, Chapter 1 takes up the question of how agricultural production grew to accommodate the doubling of the population from about 1700 to 1900 in the absence of capitalist social property relations and of gains in labor productivity. In Chapter 2, we ask a similar question: under what political, social and market conditions did France industrialize in the eighteenth and nineteenth centuries and what is the proper way to measure this industrialization? We inquire, in Chapter 3, into policies pursued by the Second Empire and Third Republic (1870–1940), in particular, in what ways did they promote economic development, what resistance did they face and to what extent did they succeed? Chapter 4 takes up the issue of "primitive accumulation," or dispossession of the peasantry, and examines whether it can be applied to the period after the Second World War. In a word, how do we explain the unprecedented burst of agricultural productivity in the 1960s? Lastly, in Chapter 5, we ask how the state ultimately overcame the efforts of industrialists to control and manage markets and what was the economic outcome of this final transition to capitalism from the 1950s to the 1970s?

Notes

1 We use the term civilization in the spirit of Fernand Braudel, not to evaluate societies relative to an ideal of human refinement, but as the cultural orientation of an entire era and the social structure of a long duration; Braudel 1980, p. 180–81, 204–05, 207, 209–10, 213–14.
2 Smith 2003, p. 14–16, 19, 27.
3 Smith 2003, p. 22, 24–25, 350. Smith offers his historical narrative of the rise of capitalism in Book III of the *Wealth of Nations*.
4 Sewell 2021, p. 5–8.
5 Sewell 2021, p. 5–6, 44–48, 51, 57.
6 Sewell appropriates Marx's work through the lens of Moishe Postone.
7 Sewell 2021, p. 57–58. We offer a detailed critical response to Sewell's capitalist reading of eighteenth-century proto-industrialization in Chapter 2.
8 Sewell 2021, p. 46, 56, 65.
9 Marx 1991, p. 444–445, 449.

10 Marx 1990, p. 874, 932.
11 Marx 1990, p. 876, 908.
12 See Brenner 1989, p. 293–94.
13 Brenner 1977; 1985; 2007; Wood 1995; 2002.
14 Spencer Dimmock describes the transition from feudalism to capitalism, in the four-teenth and fifteenth century, in historiographical and empirical detail; Dimmock 2014.
15 Brenner 2007, p. 58; Wood 1995, Chapter 2; Marx 1991, p. 927.
16 Brenner 2007, p. 59.
17 Teschke 2003.
18 Brenner 1986, p. 31–32.
19 Brenner 2007, p. 57–58.
20 Wood 2002b, p. 7.
21 Wood 2002a, p. 70.
22 Brenner 1977, p. 36–37.
23 Wood 2002a, p. 67.
24 Wood 2002a, p. 64, 68, 77.
25 Braudel 1986.
26 Smith's position is problematic and contradictory in so far as he criticized monopolizing behaviors as they manifest themselves in a capitalist economy and distort the function-ing of the competitive market of commercial society—the natural law of the market— once it has been established. He did not recognize that the law of the market remained inoperative so long as capitalist social property relations had not been established, and that this establishment required precisely the eradication of the cornering of markets by merchants and manufacturers that he denounced, and that has been the norm in precapi-talist societies.
27 Quoted in McNally 1988, p. 221.
28 McNally 1988, p. 210, 221–222, 225, 252.
29 Gerschenkron 1962; Rostow 1960.
30 Gerschenkron 1962, p. 9.
31 Amsden 1992; 2001. Kasza 2018; Mathews 2016, offer good synthetic discussions and comparisons of the works of Gerschenkron and Amsden.
32 Johnson 1982; 1999.
33 Gerschenkron 1962, p. 11–12.
34 Trebilcock 1981, p. 12, 14–16, 18.
35 Chibber 2017, p. 35.
36 Brenner 1986, p. 48–49.
37 Haggard 2015.
38 On this point, our framework overlaps with, and is in part inspired by, Chibber's (2003) contribution to the theorization of late industrialization. We come back to these issues in more details in Chapter 5.
39 Teschke 2005, p. 9.

1 French Agriculture in the Eighteenth and Nineteenth Centuries

Growth without Development

Historians long believed that the economy of France stood still. Productivity hardly increased from about 1000 to 1720. The population reached at least 17 million in 1320 but then plummeted to a mere nine million in 1440 after famine, plague and war. Peasants subsequently reoccupied the deserted countryside, cleared the scrubland and resumed grain production. Their numbers grew to those reached prior to the Black Death. However, in about 1520, and continuing until 1740, the economy suffered frightening fluctuations, as the population kept coming up against ceilings in cereal production. The saturated countryside experienced unemployment, seigneurial and state levies, poverty, malnutrition and late marriages. Peasant debts—contracted for grain, implements, services and cash—led to insolvency and the abandonment of lands to seigneurial agents, merchants, office holders and other townspeople, especially to Parisian nobles. The population mounted to about 27 million in 1789 and over 40 million by the end of the 1800s, as villagers made minor improvements without an agricultural revolution, rescuing themselves from long-term dearth but without eliminating poverty.[1] In this chapter, we examine how the rural population expanded and sustained itself without a transition to capitalist agriculture in the eighteenth and nineteenth centuries.

Revisionist historians, by contrast, have argued over the last several decades that urban market demand, mainly from Paris, awakened capitalist predispositions, spurred farmers to abandon feudal customs and fueled economic growth. Tenant farmers in northern France consolidated fields and acquired horses to reduce the labor costs of carting, plowing, shepherding, harvesting and preparing grain. Farmers specialized in wheat, fodder and wool to gain income from the market. They brought back manure from horses in Paris, combined it with what they collected from their penned sheep and thus fertilized more acreage and improved yields. The farmers of northern France in the eighteenth century, and those of central France in the nineteenth century, adopted the system of mixed husbandry—extending cropland at the expense of fallow fields through the cultivation of nitrogen-restoring artificial prairies—to obtain fodder and nourish animal power for agricultural work. In the nineteenth century, agriculturalists also invested in improved farm buildings and implements, such as plows, to increase productivity.[2]

The foregoing advances made total factor productivity (TFP)—production (measurable in lease prices) minus the costs of taxes, wages and implements—equal,

DOI: 10.4324/9781003092896-2

if not superior, to what agriculturalists achieved in England, especially in per capita terms, from 1750 to 1914. If crop and animal yields, output per worker and growth lagged behind levels attained elsewhere in western Europe, it was not because of the social structure of France but because of exogenous forces, namely insufficient incentives offered by weak economic demand, especially from the urban industrial sector.[3]

In what follows, we refute these arguments, demonstrating instead that a structure of peasant plots and communities on the one hand and landowning urban notables on the other, a structure forged in the feudal era, put agriculture on a noncapitalist path, perpetuating stagnation and slow growth. Rural households and communities, throughout the country, diversified crops, livestock and money-making work and relied on common lands to assure their subsistence. Had they followed the opposite course and focused their land and labor on a single commodity for the market, then a bad harvest, frequent in the eighteenth and nineteenth centuries, could have imperiled their very existence. The price of non-cereal commodities, in which they might have specialized, collapsed in years when grain scarcity increased bread prices. All the way into the twentieth century, peasants continued to farm parcels of land scattered over the territory of a community to prevent crop failures on one or more of the fields from putting their livelihood in danger.[4]

Of course, most members of communities did not have enough strips of land to cover their needs. They therefore turned fields over to high-yielding subsistence crops, such as chestnuts, potatoes, maize and rye, to facilitate cultures on other parcels of flax, dyes, garden vegetables, fodder, livestock, mulberry trees for sericulture and other money-generating lines with the purpose of supporting their households. Peasants had family members to put in the intensive labor for these lines and consequently could outcompete proprietors obliged to pay workers. Many peasants worked for remuneration on landed estates, as well as in rural manufacturing, and thus further subsidized their households, making their market lines even more competitive. For these reasons, over many decades after about 1740, rural households purchased parcels and extended peasant agriculture.

One should not, however, regard this expansion of peasant agriculture and market lines as a sign of capitalist development. The goal was to reproduce peasant households and communities, not to accumulate capital. The peasants did not invest earnings to make their labor more productive of profit. The peasants, rather, limited outflows of income on implements for tasks that could be done by family members. Indeed, they would not have subjected themselves to the drudgery of high-yielding subsistence crops like maize and potatoes, or labor-intensive cash crops such as vines, had their plots been large enough to cover household needs. For this reason, although output per hectare increased, per capita production grew slowly, stagnated or even declined in many parts of the country.[5]

In England, conversely (see Introduction), the productivity of land and labor increased simultaneously. The lords had undermined peasant plots and communities in social conflicts of the feudal period. Thereafter, the inhabitants could only obtain land by having a plan to specialize in economic lines that would earn the money to cover the cost of leases. Tenant farmers consequently had to produce for

the market. They had to reinvest the gains from their farms in order to augment productivity, beat (or at least match) the market prices of their peers facing the same
competitive context and maintain their ability to fulfill the terms of leases. This
capitalist dynamic led to the consolidation of tracts of land amenable to horses,
artificial prairies, stables and other improvements of the early modern agricultural
revolution.[6]

In France, where rural communities held on to plots through negotiation, liti-
gation and outright revolt from the 1100s to the 1300s, the peasants continued to
practice safety-first subsistence agriculture and resorted to market lines only when
necessary to reproduce their households, not to accumulate money. For this reason,
the peasants did not face large proprietors and seigneurs (referred to in this chapter
as the landed classes or notables), and their tenant farmers and stewards, as variable
capital (to use the Marxist terminology). Peasants did not represent labor power
(a free, rootless cost of production) for the landed classes to purchase on the market
with the purpose of increasing capital. Members of communities did not embody
an adjustable expense on balance sheets, an expense that constantly had to fall,
relative to income, under the pressure of price competition against other producers.
In other words, the rural community had not disintegrated, and the peasants had not
become deracinated individual components of capital.

Given this context, the landed classes, rather than invest in agriculture to increase productivity, developed three means of taking income from their properties
and the peasants. First, the lords and their stewards, we will see in what follows,
carefully calculated seigneurial rights to capture as much peasant production as
possible. Second, they collected extractive rents, which increased over the course
of the eighteenth and nineteenth centuries, as the population in rural communities
grew and the peasants needed additional land. In England, where the lords and
their tenant farmers had broken up peasant communities in depopulating land en-
grossments and evictions from the late 1300s to the 1500s, the gentry only could
obtain value from their land through the investments of their tenant farmers. The
gentry offered decades-long leases so that the tenants could see their investments
fructify. Labor productivity and the value of leases increased over the long term. In
France, the notables offered leases of three to four years, never longer than nine, so
that they could revise the terms, as the growing communities of petty proprietors
put family members to work generating additional resources. Short leases, however, led sharecroppers and tenants to shun investments from which they would
not benefit.

Third, because of the historic pattern of landholding—with parcels scattered
over the territory of villages to prevent adverse weather and crop disease from ruin-
ing entire harvests and causing dearth—the notables and their tenant farmers found
it rational to maintain common crop rotations for all village landholdings and to retain fallow on large areas of the fields. They used this untilled land to graze sheep,
which yielded wool and fertilizer. But this husbandry of grain farming, common
field rotations and sheep herding made it impossible to even contemplate the fencing off of fields for artificial prairies and thus blocked the path followed in England
to an agricultural revolution.

The Growth of Peasant Agriculture and Its Limits
in the Eighteenth Century

To substantiate the foregoing argument—that a noncapitalist structure of peasant plots and communities on the one hand, and rentier elites on the other, held back economic development in France—we begin with the period of recovery from the depression of the seventeenth century. Revisionists argue that the leaseholders of the landed estates consolidated fields into productive farms. Studies of the land market, however, concur that from about the 1740s to the 1800s, the nobles lost ground and the bourgeoisie found itself on the defensive, as the peasants acquired parcels of land. The extent of peasant property varied from one region to another and overall amounted to 30 or 40 percent of the total in the decade before the Revolution.[7]

In Lyonnais, where the population grew in the eighteenth century into one of the densest concentrations in the realm, the peasants of the mountainous region of Forez warded off dearth by clearing scrubland and purchasing plots from well-to-do townspeople. They farmed potatoes—a labor-intensive crop which yielded more sustenance per hectare than did grains—to make space for animal rearing and thereby obtain cheese and milk for the market. Closer to Lyon, the peasants put in indefatigable work converting woods and stony soils to vineyards of fewer than five, often fewer than two, hectares with the aim of complementing their holdings in rye and wheat for bread, hemp for cloth and oats for animals. Viticulture filled the calendar year with hewing, layering to multiply the base of the vines, plowings with hoes, putting in stakes for vine shoots, preparing vessels and basins, harvesting, fermenting, pressing and many other tasks. Viticulture required little monetary investment and allowed households to put their labor reserves to use augmenting the income from their plots. The Lyonnais countryside buzzed with tiny vineyards around the arable fields of the landed classes.[8]

The peasants of Poitou possessed anywhere from 2 percent of the land around Poitiers to 25 percent in areas of the Vendée and 70 percent in remote areas of the eastern part of the province. They had a much greater percentage of the land in hemp and vines. Hemp required much labor soaking the stems, grinding the dried ones a month later, cleaning and combing, spinning and then putting the hanks on winders for making cloth. Artisans typically worked a quarter of the year in rural cloth workshops, the rest on their parcels of land. They planted turnips after the hemp to bring nutrients to the topsoil and prepare it for rye. This crop, which predominated on the peasants' fields, did not fetch as high a price as did wheat but did better on land lacking fertilizer and helped assure their subsistence.[9]

Cereals covered at least 70, and usually 80–90, percent of Poitevin fields, especially those of the landed classes. They took up the main part of the peasants' work. Even so, peasant smallholders and sharecroppers cultivated fodder crops for commercial cattle in the wooded countryside with small irregular-shaped fields and many hedges and copses in western Poitou. They developed rotations of buckwheat to renew the soil and then broom, gorse bush, vetches, and sainfoin, along with barley and oats after the wheat harvest. The gorse bush on the heaths fixed lime and phosphorous in these acidic soils naturally deficient in nutrients. Peasants left the broom and gorse on paths to be saturated by rain and animal droppings and trampled by cattle and people. They obtained excellent fertilizer in this way and had fodder to rear about one draft animal per two hectares, a proportion superior to that obtained on the commercial cereal domains and open fields of northern France.[10]

This husbandry required the peasants to farm plots for several years, abandon them and later clear the unplanted land. The peasants used hoes to divide the broom and gorse and to break up the roots and take out the weeds. The hoes required more drudgery than did plows but ventilated and weeded the soil better and cost less to acquire. This land preparation required the toil of both sexes and all ages and appeared as time wasted to townspeople. To rural households, the work offered a way to apply otherwise idle labor to generating the resources needed to support the growing population.[11]

The peasants of Berry in central France reserved the best land for subsistence grains, but also grew fodder and reared oxen. Horses worked more rapidly than did oxen but cost more to buy and maintain, and seemed like a needless expense, when family members were on hand to work household farms with oxen. In any case, the peasants obtained more manure for their fields from the oxen than the landed classes of Berry did from the extensive sheep grazing on the fallow lands of their commercial cereal domains. The peasants used household labor intensively to farm peas, broad beans and turnips, which renewed the soil and raised yields. Fallow receded from their plots long before it did from the large domains. The peasants of Berry laid out gardens and vineyards and farmed hemp to make household clothing and maybe have a few surplus garments to sell. They used spades and hoes, which required more labor than did plows, but could be made with wood from the forests, and did not require expenditures on replacements and maintenance. The peasants saved instead for new parcels to assure their subsistence.[12]

In the Paris basin, the population grew 31 percent in the 1700s, making the region the second most densely inhabited of the realm. Historians have documented farms as large as 300 hectares in certain areas. Yet, peasant plots, mostly smaller than two hectares, existed in nearly every parish and covered anywhere from 5 to 45 percent of the farmland.[13] The peasant share expanded at the expense of the large farms, as rural inhabitants took on debts to buy plots in the hopes of attaining security and having land to distribute to offspring or to sell when too old to work and in need of means of support.[14] The expansion of peasant farming resulted from the income generated by the unpaid work of family members in labor-intensive lines such as market gardening in the parishes bordering Paris to the northeast. Peasants gardened with spades and sickles, even though these tools did not accomplish much work relative to the labor expended, because more efficient implements would not have augmented yields but would have depleted household income. Regional peasants also created vineyards, which, like the gardens, generated more income per hectare than did grain fields. They had far fewer prairies and woods than did the landed classes, but nearly all the vineyards of the Paris basin.[15]

In short, the peasants had plenty of labor in their households and communities and used it creatively to generate income. Their market lines did not, however, hail the advent of capitalist growth. Peasants turned to them not to accumulate profit, but to cover the needs of their households. To this end, peasants would have preferred to have more parcels to produce things useful to their communities and forego all the drudgery involved in viticulture and market gardening. Indeed, rather than infuse wealth into the countryside, the reliance on markets actually coincided with the poverty prevalent in rural areas. To be specific, peasants not only farmed cash crops, but also put family members to work on large estates in return for grain and wages. They used the money to purchase food and plots from their social betters. This trend increased the price of land and bread relative to the price of labor and other commodities. Most peasants did not have the surpluses to speculate on grain markets. They more commonly used the diminishing returns from the commercial line—market gardening, viticulture, wage work and cloth production—to cover the rising cost of land and bread. For this reason, the economic trends led to poverty and malnutrition, if not outright dearth, rather than to economic development.[16]

In the region of Lyon, for instance, the price of wine rose over the course of the eighteenth century, as consumption recovered from the crisis of the seventeenth century. Peasants, we have seen, capitalized on the rising price by creating vineyards. Yet, only a third of them carved out the two hectares necessary to support a family. The rest had to obtain income by laboring on the arable fields of the landed classes. The growing population and its reliance on labor markets for income and grain markets for food drove up the price of rye, the staple crop, faster than the agricultural wages. Meanwhile, the growing number of vineyards eventually expanded the grape harvest excessively and drove down wine prices from 1776 to 1785, as urban residents sacrificed wine purchases to necessities in years of high bread prices. The rural population thus found itself mired in precariousness.[17]

After 1770, rising land rents and rural poverty in Poitou diminished the market for nonessential goods and provoked a downturn in artisanal activity affecting all the households reliant on ancillary income from hemp. While the price of staples rose, those of wine and flax fell because of all the vineyards and hemp fields carved out of the hillsides and poor lands where cereals did not grow. The vintners of northern Poitou saw the value of their plots decline in the 1780s. Livestock sales increased in the fairs of western Poitou from 1758 to 1776 but then faced a brutal recession. The peasants did not have sufficient land for the fodder to sustain animal fattening and persistently sold amid falling prices for nonessential goods like cattle. The after-death inventories, measured against Poitevin grain prices, show a 20 percent decline in fortunes over the course of the eighteenth century and a particularly sharp decline among day laborers and tenants without much land. As the number of indigents swelled in western Poitou, the population growth of the eighteenth century reversed in the 1780s.[18]

The Landed Notables and the Peasants

The peasants, in a word, struggled to wring a livelihood from their plots. Yet, even if they did not own sufficient land or means of production to support themselves and thus had to seek remunerated employment, they differed from workers in a capitalist context because of the existence of the peasant community. Peasants did not offer themselves to the landed classes as a commodified labor force adjustable according to the ebb and flow of competition, investment and profitability. Proprietors and tenant farmers did not calculate peasant labor as one of the components of capital. They did not face a context in which competition for market share against other farmers incessantly compelled them to cut labor costs through investments in implements as the sole means of avoiding insolvency and preserving their land and equipment. As Max Weber discerned, "the ancient communist traditions of forest, water, pasture, and even arable land, which firmly united the peasants and tied them to the inherited form of husbandry, survived" in western Germany and France down to his day at the end of the nineteenth century. "The superabundance of the labor force" in rural communities "diminishes the desire to save labor by the use of machines."[19] Clergymen, nobles and the upper strata of the Third Estate had no thought of breaking up communities and evicting the smallholders. They instead maintained the age-old custom of pinning the peasants down to the soil through overlapping forms of tenancy, remunerated labor and seigneurial prerogative.[20]

In the Roannais-Brionnais region of Lyonnais, for example, grain fields continued to predominate over pastures and meadows into the nineteenth century, even though the monetary returns from meadows and cattle rearing proved far superior. Converting the arable land to pasture would have required the breakup of the peasant community. Urban landowners did not even contemplate this course of action, because they had at their disposal a mass of villagers lacking holdings sufficient to avoid working their arable fields of grains as tenants and laborers in the sclerotic sharecropping system characteristic of the province. Rental contracts stipulated corvée labor obligations with draft animals or manual work for peasants bereft of oxen. They stipulated carting obligations for harvests, manure, wood and construction materials, as well as compulsory fields of wheat, rye, barley or oats and always an expanse of fallow to prevent soil exhaustion. The proprietors, this way, obtained satisfactory incomes without having to relinquish wealth on farm improvements. Growth, needless to say, did not materialize. The records of three cathedral chapters of Lyonnais show that production grew slowly until 1760–1765 when it equaled the level attained before the crisis of the 1680s and then started to decline. The Lyonnais plain suffered "fevers" and high mortality rates.[21]

In Poitou and Berry, the rental agreements—offered by the merchants, office holders, nobles and ecclesiastics—contained provisions for seigneurial dues and for services carting goods to market or to the landowner's table in the towns. Rural inhabitants in need of land accepted onerous terms of tenancy, obliging them to cede more of the harvests over the course of the eighteenth century. Debts commonly bound tenants to the land, obliging them to accept leases, which restricted the extent of the seeded fields through compulsory rotations of grains and fallows to prevent soil exhaustion. In Berry, sheep yielded so much more revenue than did grains that proprietors maintained common fields and fallows for grazing and thus obstructed the development of artificial prairies and arable farming. From their point of view, limited harvests maintained high prices and acceptable profits. Compulsory rotations assured the availability at harvest time of the crops subject to seigneurial dues.[22]

These extractive feudal-like relations also prevailed in the Paris basin, where revisionists purport to show economic development. Jean-Marc Moriceau and Gilles Postel-Vinay argue that tenant farmers, prompted by the profit available in the urban market, grouped together compact farms and thus gained the flexibility to plant artificial prairies and fodder crops and reduce the extent of fallow land. The value of the fodder increased, thanks to all the horses used in Paris, and brought wealth into the countryside. With larger farms and additional horses, the tenants economized on the labor of shepherds, plowmen and carters. The application of fertilizer to all their fields, by using the droppings of penned sheep and the manure of the horses in Paris, raised yields. The foregoing sorts of improvements, Philip Hoffman calculates, increased TFP in the second half of the eighteenth century.[23]

If one unpacks this research, one notices that the large farms presented by Moriceau reached their maximum extent of about 200 hectares in 1675–99 but then contracted to 160–170 in 1775–99. This sequence resulted more likely from the vagaries of the peasant economy than from the consolidation of cost-effective farms. Urban notables were stuck with properties in the crisis of the seventeenth century—as the peasants abandoned the land amid war and falling prices—but then sold parcels to peasants willing to take on debts, deploy additional labor and wring more income from the land, as prices rose in the eighteenth century. The evidence on the agrarian structure, to be clear, does not demonstrate a drive to cut costs on farm labor and buildings through the eviction of peasants and enclosure of fields.[24]

The research of Moriceau and Postel-Vinay does not indicate that the tenants of the large farms faced the competitive pressure, intrinsic to capitalism, to constantly reinvest surpluses with the aim of increasing their price/cost ratio. It shows that a minimum of 26.3 percent of their arable fields remained fallow and usually about 30 percent. Moriceau and Postel-Vinay document nitrogen-restoring fodder crops on 31.8 percent of the arable land on one farm but on average a maximum of only 4.3 percent across the Paris basin. Nearly 40 percent of tenant farmers left no mention of artificial prairies in their after-death inventories.[25] The enduring expanse of fallow, along with this negligible presence of artificial prairies, demonstrates that the tenants did not pursue the ventures intrinsic to early modern agricultural revolutions. The tenants, that is, did not replace fallow land with nitrogen-restoring fodder crops, accumulate draft animals, build stables, amass manure fertilizer and expand the arable surface for the purpose of cutting costs and accruing surpluses.[26] Given the evidence from Berry and Poitou, it is likely that the slight reduction in fallow and increased acreage of nitrogen-restoring crops, recorded by Moriceau and Postel-Vinay, resulted from the peasants' efforts to apply family labor—to the additional land and meticulous work required of this husbandry—to scrape further income out of the land.

Indeed, peasant ingenuity, in labor-intensive farming, no doubt accounts for the yields documented by Moriceau and Postel-Vinay.[27] The proliferation of smallholders, and their need for income, permitted farm managers to wring labor from the peasants and profit from their expertise, discussed above, in weeding, renewing the soil, enhancing its fertility and raising yields. Tenant farmers extracted what Marx referred to as absolute surplus value: they appropriated additional hours of peasant labor intensively cultivating the soil. The tenant farmers thus obtained more output for the Paris market. They did not appropriate relative surplus value: additional value from a given amount of labor through investment in implements to improve labor productivity. Increased drudgery, rather than investments and labor-saving implements, surely accounts for the yields on the estates managed by the tenant farmers.

Analyzing the work of Moriceau and Postel-Vinay, Gérard Béaur points out that because of the abundance of peasant labor in rural areas, the focus was less on diminishing wage costs than on expanding output. Jean-Michel Chevet examined the evidence of Moriceau and Postel-Vinay and found that the farms in question would have required additional employees, not fewer, for the new economic lines of the eighteen and nineteenth centuries. Specifically, wheat and oats required additional laborers for harvesting and threshing. Ovines required additional shepherds. They required open fields, common and fallow land, which, according to Chevet, appear in the field maps displayed by Moriceau and Postel-Vinay. The tenant farmers must have used the additional horses, supposedly purchased to plow larger areas, and economize on labor, as alternates, since the improved plows, required to cover more ground, did not appear until after the 1850s.[28]

This issue of peasant labor has made George Grantham skeptical about using TFP in French agricultural history. The problem with measuring productivity through production and cost functions is that most work was not remunerated with a wage, and it is therefore difficult to determine its true cost. Families valued labor differently than did the market, because it allowed them to retain their plots or climb the agricultural ladder. Members of peasant families labored on their plots at odd intervals and in conditions not economical for employers to hire them. The true cost of household labor does not appear in the recorded wages.[29]

Béaur has also criticized the use of TFP in French economic history. Specifically, land rents amount to the principal means used by Hoffman and other historians to estimate production. The problem is that the terms of leases reflected the relative bargaining power of proprietors and tenants and lead to deceptive conclusions for the decades after 1750, when grain and lease prices rose, and wages remained constant.[30] In the previous century, for example, grain and lease prices stagnated for an extended period. In England, where a capitalist context prevailed, this fall in prices did not depress the value of leases like it did elsewhere in Europe. Tenant farmers invested in agriculture to increase productivity and offset the fall in prices. Competition for market share, to obtain the money to lease land from the gentry, constrained tenants to increase output despite the disincentive of falling agricultural prices.[31]

In France, abundant evidence indicates that, toward the end of the eighteenth century, leases became favorable to proprietors because of their bargaining power rather than agricultural productivity. Arthur Young noticed that although "the soil of France is, for the most part, better than that of England, the average produce of the former" is "so much inferior." Young found that "18 bushels of wheat and rye, and miserable spring corn, afford as high a rent in France, as twenty-four in England with the addition of our excellent spring corn." Young attributed the difference to "the poverty of the … tenantry" in France, to a system that "depresses the lower classes," blending the farmers "with the peasantry," and making them "hardly superior to the common laborers."[32] As the number of smallholders grew, property owners had leverage to add stipulations of a feudal character to leases obliging tenants of the Paris basin to pay seigneurial dues, in addition to the money lease, and deliver fruit from gardens and chickens or other animals on Christmas Day. Leases often indicated debts obliging the tenants to submit to all sorts of burdens, such as unpaid carting services, hardly distinguishable from the medieval corvée.[33]

Some tenant farmers of the Paris basin had the cash to lease the domains of seigneurs and proprietors, and, in doing so, collected dues from the numerous class of smallholders and rural laborers with the aim of amassing funds, purchasing a royal office and leaving behind rural life and agriculture. They threw their weight around in the lord's name, hired local laborers and stored grain for charity, wages and other means of influence. They often held the peasantry in debt and benefited from the lord's tax privileges. Béaur's examination of the evidence shows that the tenant farmer of the plains of the northern rim of Paris, studied by Moriceau and Postel-Vinay, behaved like the ones he studied in the Beauce. The tenant squandered profits in a fierce quest for land. In contrast to the capitalist disposition to accumulate cash reserves, the tenants of the Paris basin took on risk, depleted revenue, even went into debt and sterilized investment to purchase land. They followed the traditional wisdom of assuring the social respectability of landholding for their sons.[34]

Many tenants therefore maintained common pasture and fallow land with the purpose of continuing to collect the sure profits from the wool of sheep. The tenants only conceived of looking after the herds through crop rotations conserving fallow fields for grazing. In the economically depressed conditions of Louis XIV's reign, proprietors generally believed that intensive farming, without fallow, exhausted the soil. They believed that it caused overproduction and lowered the prices of farm products and leases. Proprietors and tenants eschewed innovations based on the replacement of fallow fields with artificial prairies. For these reasons, tithe records demonstrate that cereal output lagged behind demographic growth in the Paris basin from 1715 to 1789. Across France, output per farmer stagnated over the course of the early modern period and amounted to less than half of the rate of agricultural labor productivity attained in England at the end of the eighteenth century.[35] If rents and TFP increased in the Paris basin, this trend must have resulted from the conjuncture, after 1750, of population and prices, which tilted the feudal-like relations in favor of property owners and their agents and allowed them to dictate the terms of leases and extract additional work from the peasant small holders.

The French Revolution and Agricultural Growth in the Nineteenth Century

The continued existence of the peasant community, to which rural labor was rooted, made possible the revolts of the Revolution against the foregoing forms of exploitation. The peasants banded together in innumerable uprisings, which resulted in the definitive abolition of feudalism in 1793. They laid hold of property belonging to the king and émigrés and cleared and cultivated lands held on a communal basis. They had hesitated to farm this land prior to 1789 for fear that the lords would assert feudal claims to it and foist burdens on the cultivators. For decades after 1789, peasants purchased church and émigré property acquired by speculators with the intention of reselling it to land-hungry rural inhabitants. The peasants' portion of the land varied from region to region but probably increased from about 30 percent or 40 percent of the national total to about 50 percent after the Revolution.[36]

These land acquisitions, together with the elimination of feudal dues during the Revolution, permitted the peasants to augment production even more than they had in the eighteenth century. There is thus some truth to Guy Lemarchand's argument that the Revolution cleared the way for economic growth. In the Pays de Caux of Normandy, as the population grew from the eighteenth into the nineteenth centuries, poor peasants farmed clover and green fodder after the plowing to have the feed to build up stocks of cows and other farm animals, accrue manure and improve yields. Farmers replaced some of the fallow land with colza seed, which they sold to oil producers and which, with hoeing and fertilizer, prepared the soil for other crops. They also labored in the textile industry, growing madder and laboring in workshops to gain extra income for their households. Town notables captured much of this growth by raising rents and adding clauses to leases requiring the delivery of chickens, fabrics and candles to their residences. They scrupulously watched over their accounts to prevent outlays on implements and to collect as much income as they could from their tenants' labor.[37]

To the east, in the Calvados part of Normandy, the use of lime, pitch sand, ashes from washing powder and dried deodorized night soil mixed with various substances facilitated a revolution in yields, especially on the marly and clay soil of the Bocage and Bessin. These fertilizers permitted farmers to increase the area of cereals, colza and artificial prairies and nearly eliminate fallow fields during the nineteenth century. The Bocage changed from a backward region at the end of the Old Regime to an area with diverse crop production. This intensive agriculture obliged farmers to raise salaries to attract workers after 1850, a cost partially offset by the increase in profits and labor-saving devices such as steam-powered threshers and the replacement of sickles with scythes. Farmers replaced some arable fields with grasslands toward the end of the 1860s, as the rural population began to thin. They thus concentrated wheat on the soils suited to it and improved average yields.[38]

In the Pays de France region of the Paris basin, farmers brought back fertilizing muds and manure from the city, eliminated common grazing and fallow and developed the cultivation of oats, straw, fodder and sugar beets prior to 1840. Farmers added 69–123 percent more nitrogen, phosphoric acid, potassium and lime to the soil of the Paris basin. Thanks to these fertilizers, as well as to additional plowings, 100 hectares of arable land, able to feed 205 people in 1800, could feed 240 in 1900. What is more, stronger draft teams—as well as improved plows, grubbers, scarifiers, stubble cultivators and even mechanized mowers/combine-binders for both fodder and cereal crops—augmented labor productivity. Departments around Paris had the highest yields and output per worker in France in the middle decades of the nineteenth century.[39]

The surface of artificial prairies in Loire-et-Cher, southwest of Paris, more than doubled in the 1840s and continued to grow in the 1850s amid a continuous decline in fallow until 1892. In the 1850s, farmers in the valleys perfected crop rotations of diverse cultures, one after another, on the same ground without any fallow in five- or six-year cycles. They commonly used lime and marl fertilizer by the early 1860s. These years also saw a growing use of improved plows, seeders, harvesters, horse-pulled rakes, mowers, presses and threshing machines, though few steam-powered implements. The number of hectoliters harvested per hectare grew from a little under 100 in Loire-et-Cher in 1840 to about 170 in 1910 for wheat and from about 68 to 230 for oats. Previously, weak yields had threatened subsistence in 1847 and 1855. However, between 1871 and 1885, the building of railroad stations and thousands of kilometers of roads opened access to markets. Roger Price argues that market access not only made commercial fertilizer available, and thus allowed farmers to improve yields and eliminate fallow, but also made food prices more reliable and thereby allowed farmers to specialize in cash crops suited to their areas. In Loir-et-Cher, insufficiency gave way to conditions in which farmers sold a growing volume of production for the highest possible returns.[40]

In these ways, farmers capitalized on the observable opportunities offered by new crops, methods, implements and markets. The educated classes knew about the English agricultural revolution since the publications of the Physiocrat school of economic thought in the eighteenth century. The notables and their land managers also observed the intensive techniques used by peasants to augment yields on smallholdings.[41] The obvious benefits of these new crops and methods permitted noble landowners and tenant farmers of the Charolais-Brionnais region of Burgundy to extend, close off and improve the quality of pasture, thus raising its monetary value. They reared additional animals to sell to merchants interested in taking advantage of the demand for meat in Lyon from the 1750s to the 1800s.[42]

Even sharecroppers in the Allier department in central France began to fertilize the soil with lime and use faster-working plows in the 1850s and 1860s. Wages increased for agricultural workers. The improvement of mills permitted the inhabitants to eat higher-quality bread. They had better clothes to wear and a higher overall standard of living. In the still poorer Aveyron department further south, lime became available thanks to the building of railway lines after the 1870s, and the peasants began to correct the acidity of the soil, making it better suited to cereals, potatoes and hay. Farmers began to rear more sheep and cattle and sell cheese on the national market. Poverty and disease dissipated by the end of the century.[43]

In the southeastern departments of Var, Gard and Vaucluse, the rural population grew nearly 15 percent from 1821 to 1851. Peasants continued to farm with traditional pickaxes and ard plows. Large proprietors introduced improved plows. Farmers also created artificial prairies of nitrogen-restoring fodder for horses and mules. New strains of wheat helped diminish harvest fluctuations. Transportation enhancements allowed more wheat to enter the region. Bread prices stabilized and fears of famine dissipated. Peasants could then switch parcels from subsistence grains to dye plants for the textile market. They also increased the output of vineyards. Though olive trees remained central to the regional economy, official statistics of the Gard show that sericulture augmented nearly four times over from the 1830s to 1850. Women and children cultivated mulberry trees and put in long hours using the leaves to nourish silkworms.[44]

As the rural population grew, farmers across France cleared untilled areas after the 1820s, with a peak of 34,000 hectares a year from 1851 to 1879. The area in wheat, potatoes and oats expanded at the expense of fallow. Wheat yields grew by an average of 80 percent, with the highest rates in central France, between 1815–1820 and 1902–1912. The cultivation of oats spread from the Paris basin to the south and west, as farmers switched from biennial to triennial rotations to gain income from the market demand generated by the greater numbers of livestock, particularly horses. Grass output—above all from hay meadows and herbages in Normandy, Ile-de-France and the southern Loire valley in central France—increased 127 percent from the 1830s to 1912. Farmers of the Paris basin, as well as the Vienne, Seine-et-Marne, Charente-Inférieure and Isère departments, increased the output of clover, lucerne, sainfoin and other artificial meadows 166 percent by 1912. Oats, grasses and artificial prairies allowed them to feed more draft animals and use heavier plows. Industrialists offered employment to poor villagers displaced by the spread of these crops onto common land formerly used by villagers to graze their cows. Farmers, for the first time, had to compete for workers. Better transportation infrastructure, however, opened up distant markets, raised prices locally and gave them the income to pay higher wages. The standard of living thus increased in rural areas from around the 1840s to the early 1870s.[45]

The Limits to Growth in the Nineteenth Century

Despite this undeniable progress, the productivity of the agricultural population grew only 0.25 percent per year in France, as opposed to 1 percent in Britain from 1815–1824 to 1905–1913. Wheat yields were 69 percent higher (54 percent for barley, 57 percent oats and 84 percent for potatoes) in Britain in 1902. While French farmers no doubt improved animal husbandry, British farmers devoted far more acreage to cattle rearing and thus concentrated grains on the soils best suited to them, obtained more manure fertilizer and acquired more draft power to replace human labor. Productivity in French agriculture remained close to the bottom of the western European average, considerably lower than levels in Denmark, Belgium, the Netherlands and Germany. In these countries, in 1912/1913, the average yield (qx/ha) of wheat ranged from 33.5 in Denmark to 23.6 in Germany but amounted to only 13.8 in France. Output annually grew 0.76 in France, 1.31 in Germany and 2.07 in Denmark from 1880 to 1930. The slow rate in France, the country with perhaps the best agricultural resources, stands out.[46]

To account for these facts, revisionists argue that slow demographic growth dampened demand and diminished incentives to augment output. In France, demand for food grew 0.9 percent a year from 1815–1824 to 1875–1884, a modest rate at the time. Prices received by farmers further declined after 1880. The rate of growth of demand lagged behind the rate of growth of output. Revisionists posit that until 1930, peasants provided the urban industrial sector with more food per capita and at lower real prices, and did so without agricultural research, extension, credit systems and subsidies from the state common in Denmark, Germany, Japan and the United States. If French peasants had expanded the rate of growth of output, declining prices, attributable to inelastic demand, would have punished them.[47]

It is true, we will see in the next chapter, that France industrialized and urbanized more slowly than did its European neighbors, Japan and the United States. It is not true, however, that farmers adequately supported the urban industrial sector, which grew slowly after the 1850s. Although farmers added seven million hectares to the arable surface after 1882, cereal production did not cover national needs. Farmers annually produced 10–12 million tons of cereals between 1905 and 1913, and the country imported 600,000–1,000,000, with a peak of 1.5 million in 1910–1911, despite the increase of customs barriers on several occasions.[48]

The reason for the slow rate of growth was that it took place in the absence of capitalist social property relations. Producers exploited the available opportunities of new crops, livestock, implements and markets but did not face the structural imperative of competitive markets.[49] Peasant households and communities oriented agriculture primarily to local uses, not the accumulation of money. In a capitalist structure, farmers must produce for the market to build up surpluses. They must reinvest gains to improve production, lower costs relative to revenues and thus beat or match the prices of other growers. Failure to do so means ruin. For this reason, capitalist agriculture—which prevailed in France in the 1960s (see Chapter 4)—does not merely respond to, or arrive at, the economic demand of urban and industrial populations. Price competition leads it to overrun such demand, create gluts, reduce prices and enhance discretionary spending across the economy. Thus, in southern Brazil, the northern United States, Canada, Japan and England, capitalist agriculture preceded and facilitated industrialization and urbanization rather than result from these processes.[50] Although the slow rate of agricultural growth in France, we will see in Chapter 3, did not preclude capitalist restructuring and substantial progress in manufacturing, it limited industrial expansion and diversification in comparison to other European countries, Japan and the United States.

England, for example, had fewer city dwellers than did Belgium, Germany, France, Italy and Spain at the beginning of the sixteenth century. In spite of the lack of incentive offered by urban demand, English farmers, owing to the capitalist context (see Introduction), produced sufficient food supplies and raw materials to minimize the upward movement of wages and input costs. By the beginning of the eighteenth century, wheat prices had fallen 25–33 percent below levels of the 1660s. Cheap bread and a lower cost of living made per capita real income rather high, facilitating not only the expansion of domestic linen, cotton, glassware, stoneware and pottery manufacturing but also large-scale imports of tea, sugar, tobacco, printed calicoes and linen. Urban demand did not entice and beget this rise in agricultural output. Farmers generated a surplus beyond national needs, exported grain, yet still faced sagging prices.[51]

Subsequently, from 1750 to 1840, the demands made on English agriculture could hardly have been greater. The population grew rapidly, increasing by a factor of three. Moreover, the proportion of the population/labor force out of agriculture increased from about 55 percent to 75 percent. Despite these trends toward the increase of population and of nonagricultural employment, as well as the enormous upward pressure on grain prices that resulted from a run of bad harvests and full-scale war from 1793 to 1815, nominal wages still managed to keep up with the cost of living and then increased by about 30 percent from 1815 to the mid-1850s. What made all this possible could not be clearer: a continuing rise in agricultural labor productivity. Between 1750 and 1850, output per agricultural worker grew by about 60 percent, while output per unit of land (yields) rose, at a minimum, by 40–50 percent. Up until the early 1820s, wheat imports were negligible despite a 100 percent population increase since 1750 and the proportion in non-agrarian pursuits having grown from 55 percent to around 65 percent.[52]

Extraordinary harvests first appeared on the light soils of southern and eastern England, which growers had left under sheep pasture for centuries but then, after 1650, found especially responsive to mixed husbandry with fodder crops, cereals and cattle rearing. These soils were free draining and had a long working season and low traction costs. The excess grain and fatstock from the south and east put pressure on farmers of the wetter elevated parts of the north and west and of the heavy Midland clays. These ill-drained vales had long been one of the country's granaries but could not support the new fodder crops as readily. Elites in the north, west and Midlands sought to have the crown suppress the planting of clover in the South in the 1680s but ultimately had to give up arable farming and focus on dairy-ing and rearing store beasts, leaving fattening to plowmen with the forage crops in the south and east. The loss of work among rural inhabitants in the north, west and Midlands, dispossessed by the enclosure of parishes laid down to pasture for dairy and store livestock, led them to concentrate on cloth-making, hosiery, leatherwork and nail-production. The Honiton lace industry spread into the countryside in East Devon, and other manufacturing into districts of the north, in the late seventeenth and early eighteenth centuries. These areas saw the emergence of Birmingham, Manchester, Leeds, Liverpool and other towns, which turned England from the least urban country in Europe in 1500 to the most urban one in 1800. Manufactur-ing meanwhile withered away in southern England and East Anglia.[53]

France did not experience this sort of regional specialization. Farmers did not produce excessive volumes of cereals and animal products, make prices unbear-ably low for less productive growers and thus force them into alternative economic lines better suited to their areas. Neither low nor high prices could shape or alter economic behavior, because production for local use remained the common sense of country dwellers. Most of them produced the things they needed, marketed sur-pluses and bought whatever they could not produce. The spread of potatoes in Brit-tany, Auvergne and Provence and maize in the south of the Paris basin and Rhône valley, both high-yielding crops, permitted the rearing of livestock and the market-ing of previously consumed cereals. Peasants, in this way, farmed more cash crops yet still grew their own food. As they used the cash to acquire more land, much of the country reverted to subsistence farming. For peasants, land meant social status, the possibility of economic independence, an improved standard of living and a secure future for children. The possession of at least some land cushioned against seasonal unemployment and disruptions of food markets. Harvest failures, spikes in prices and threats of unrest—in 1816–1817, 1837, 1839–1840, 1846–1847, 1854–1856 and 1867–1868—must have left the impression that security lay in the soil.[54]

In Calvados Normandy, for example, the peasants' desire to own land and divide it among offspring led to an extreme division of nearly 75 percent of the soil into medium and small plots in the 1830s. Most of the peasants farmed wheat, oats, buckwheat and barley for their subsistence, worked on larger farms, reared a few animals, occasionally sold crops and engaged in weaving and lace-making during down times in the agricultural year. They had to seek employment to scratch out a living and always sought to buy land with their earnings. Even a small piece of land could help prevent misery.[55]

Agriculture improved and the cultivated area expanded 25 percent in western France from 1820 to 1860. Farmers devoted most of this new farmland to subsistence grains and, to a lesser extent, livestock for butter and other commercial products. In the 1870s, agronomists sought to create model economic units run by dairy farmers, but the peasants did not contemplate full specialization, a reduction in grain fields, changes to their methods of cultivation and modifications to their way of life until well into the twentieth century.[56]

Peasants in the Perche and Sologne regions of Loire-et-Cher tended to live from their own crops and paid little attention to price fluctuations. They achieved high yields and assured their subsistence with just a few hectares on the fertile soil of the Beauce region of Loire-et-Cher. In the parts of Beauce fragmented into even smaller parcels, the peasants supplemented the grain grown on their farms by working as day laborers or paying high prices to rent land.[57]

Sharecroppers in Allier and Gironde in central and southwestern France ate black bread of coarse-ground rye with the husk left in and mixed with the flour. They ate baked potatoes, sometimes a stew of pumpkin or beans, and most commonly onion or potato soup with haricot beans and tiny dots of butter. Families, livestock, swine and fowl consumed the bulk of the grain grown on the farm. The sharecroppers used corn and barley, two of the main grains in the southwest, as their animal feed. They took calves, their best vegetables, fruit and other surpluses to the towns for sale. The farmers thus obtained a little money to purchase clothes, shoes, headgear, groceries, haberdashery and other things they did not produce themselves.[58]

Improvements in transportation, by the mid-nineteenth century, removed the need for self-sufficiency in the southeastern departments of the Gard, Var and Vaucluse. The growing village populations produced wine, olives, dye-plants and silk for the market. All the same, peasants still relied on common land for pasture, wood, fruit and herbs. The poor sometimes used common land to clear a small arable plot. Peasants continued to devote land to subsistence grains as a form of disaster insurance. In the event, severe storms, crop disease and industrially produced dyes wiped out the market lines and led about 20 percent of the rural population to migrate elsewhere in the 1870s and 1880s. The remaining villagers, who had never abandoned subsistence production, returned to the traditional husbandry of wheat and sheep rearing to assure their existence.[59]

Of course, many peasants, like those of the Southeast, perceived that with the attenuation of price fluctuations around mid-century, they did not have to plant grains at all costs and could instead make the most of advantageous prices for pastoral farming or viticulture. The improvements detailed above meant that they could assure their existence on less land and free up parcels for market lines. The improvements required little capital investment, only intensive labor. The peasants, for example, perfected tillage and used row cultivation to increase the cleanliness of fields, substituted planted meadows for fallow, added nitrogen to the soil, fed more livestock on a smaller space and gained manure. Weeding boosted crop yields 20–50 percent. Farmers in the Southwest frequently clod beetled manually— working ten days by hand, as opposed to a day or two with a harrower or roller. Hoeing, sickling and hand threshing gave greater yields per hectare than did labor-saving tools. Whenever peasants completed a task with family labor, they saw it as a matter of more work at no expense. They paid little mind to the inconvenience as long as it did not cost anything. Hired hands drained income, required supervision and did not shift as quickly from task to task in response to idle time or weather changes.[60]

Holding down costs in this way, the peasants could sell their market lines at lower prices than could large proprietors dependent on hired labor. Rural wages rose because of the declining birth rate, urban and manufacturing job offerings, intensive farming and the consequent demand for agricultural workers. Peasants used the cash to acquire land and join the ranks of small farmers, further depleting the supply of agricultural laborers. Large farmers thus saw their costs rise. Small farmers, by contrast, relied on family labor. Some bourgeois proprietors, during the depression in prices of the 1880s, perceived an advantage in selling strips from their estates to land-hungry peasants instead of managing or leasing their properties. Small holders also bought parcels from other peasants, who pursued nonagricultural means of making a living. Thus, between 1862 and 1882, while the agrarian structure hardly changed, both the number of farms above 30 hectares and the number of workers classified as landholders declined. Many of these former workers no doubt made up the 300,000 new owner-occupiers enumerated in the census of 1882. France saw the consolidation of peasant agriculture at the same time as marginal rural workers, smallholders and sharecropper emigrated to urban and industrial areas.[61]

Consider the northern areas of Picardy, Artois, Cambrésis, Beauvaisis and Hainaut, where the quality of the soil made for the highest yields in France. Farmers began to acquire more and better tools to hoe and fertilize artificial prairies of rapeseed, clover and alfalfa, further enhance the quality of the soil with manure and prepare it for other crops toward the end of the eighteenth century and especially in the first half of the nineteenth century. Although these improvements allowed the peasants to bring new lands under cultivation at the expense of extensive sheep rearing, the strong continuous demographic growth in the first half of the nineteenth century meant that most farmers had fewer than five hectares, leased most of their farmland and had to work for the tenants of the large farms in return for money or the use of draft animals. The new tools, fertilizer and crops, by raising agricultural output and bringing income into rural communities, facilitated the growth of the number and area of small farms at the expense of larger holdings, which had grown at the expense of peasant agriculture until the 1780s. Empirical studies show that because the improvements coincided with the clearing and tilling of marginal lands, average yields remained about the same from the end of the 1600s to 1840. The population tripled across these northern regions in the eighteenth century and grew substantially thereafter. Wheat production per person went from 7.8 hectoliters per hectare at the beginning of the eighteenth century to 4.6 in 1778 and 2.57 in 1840. Growth thus followed a complex process involving the consolidation of peasant farming and deterioration in the standard of living.[62]

The standard of living increased in these northern departments after mid-century thanks to improvements, land clearances, new remunerative crops and cottage industry, though not an agricultural revolution. Many large farms divided into smaller ones, particularly around 1880, as the expense of laborers, fertilizer and other agricultural material made rental income less remunerative. In 1789, 70 percent of the land of Artois/Pas-de-Calais consisted of holdings of 70 hectares or more, whereas only 21 percent did in 1859 and 15 percent in 1898. In the region around Dunkerque, farms of 0–5 hectares had made up around 40 percent of all holdings in the eighteenth century, 55 percent from 1852 to 1892, and 63.8 percent in 1892. The number of hectares seeded and farmed remained stable from about 1620 to 1820 but then increased from 20,000 hectares to 28,000 hectares from 1820 to 1902. Small holders using family labor accumulated fertilizer, cultivated artificial prairies and industrial plants, tilled labor-intensive high-yielding subsistence crops such as maize and potatoes and raised yields by as much as 75 percent from 1820 to 1882. They outcompeted large farmers obliged to hire workers. Peasants exchanged labor services with other members of the rural community or worked on the remaining large farms in return for grain, for plowing their small holdings or for the use of implements. Smallholders had family members work for remuneration on beet farms, which appeared after mid-century and required many laborers for weeding. Rural inhabitants also made ends meet by working in rural manufacturing, which disappeared in some cantons of Picardy but hung on in many others. Manufacturers continued to locate tile and cloth workshops in rural areas at the end of the nineteenth century—despite the development of mechanized industry in northern France—because of the abundance of available laborers in the countryside.[63]

The Aude department, at the opposite end of France in the southwest, saw a similar sort of labor-intensive growth, which accommodated an expanding rural population without an agricultural revolution. Audois peasants mainly farmed grain in the first decades of the nineteenth century, as they had for centuries. Since few members of rural communities had enough land to cover their subsistence and avoid periods of idleness for family members, many of them turned some of their strips of land over to viticulture or worked on the fields of farm managers in return for potatoes, beans or meals. By the 1860s, railway construction and trade treaties with Great Britain and other countries raised the price of wine and lowered the cost of bread. Households capitalized on these trends by converting fields to vineyards, though they did not cease to grow wheat. They used cost-free methods and age-old hand tools, such as wooden swing plows and spades, to cultivate the vineyards. Peasants relied on family members to avoid the cost of the labor needed to prune and cultivate, place grapes in cisterns to ferment, draw off batches of wine, plant new vines, fertilize, gather and bundle fallen branches, cut unproductive and woody shoots from the base to encourage more prolific growth of fruit in the sunshine, apply pesticide, prepare winemaking vessels, equipment in the wine cellar and material for the harvest and finally to perform the most time-consuming task of all, the harvest.[64]

The peasants' competitive advantage, thanks to unpaid family labor, led urban residents to divide their large grain farms and sell tiny parcels. Landownership increased among vineyard workers, artisans and traders, as plots became smaller and smaller in the Aude in the last decades of the nineteenth century. These trends, however, did not raise the standard of living, because they contributed to an increase in land prices and encouraged the large proprietors to loan funds to peasants for the purchase of vineyards. The townspeople collected interest payments, as the peasants worked to pay off debts. Most peasant viticulturists, to make ends meet, had to send family members to work for the managers of the large vineyards belonging to townspeople. As owners of plots and members of communities, the peasants were not going anywhere. This immobile labor force allowed vineyard managers to keep wages low. The low wages and community bonds, however, created a propitious context for strikes. Labor unrest wracked the Narbonnais region of the Aude in January 1904.[65]

The fundamental reason why commercial viticulture, cattle rearing and beet growing did not result in rural development is that far from representing a leap into specialized growing, their purpose was to support the subsistence obtained from household plots and protect the village community from full market dependence. The cash crops allowed peasants to ward off dearth at a time when the countryside became more populous than ever. Farmers did not grow cash crops on compact tracts of land. Peasants, rather, had parcels scattered over the village. Each parcel contained a different crop—grains, vines, beets or fodder—in line with community rotations. Marc Bloch revealed the extreme division of the soil in his field maps of the 1930s. The layout of the narrow strips made fencing them off seem absurd. It would have been costly for villagers to reach their holdings solely from the nearest path. Villages therefore did not restrict the right of access to the plots. It is doubtful that village livestock would have found the fallow for grazing without a compulsory system of crop courses and common pasture. Under these conditions, the advantages of coordinating field rotations appeared so obvious that the practice remained. Only a closely knit society, composed of people who thought instinctively in terms of the community, could have created such an agricultural regime.[66]

Seeing this obvious opportunity for reform and the example of other industrializing countries, the Chambers of Deputies of the July Monarchy, Second Empire and Third Republic took up bills to wind down common rights and consolidate dispersed landholdings. Most peasants, however, rejected the idea. The notables, who dominated the legislatures, opposed the principle of forcing "proprietors to do things for the general interest against their will." Thus, in Meaux, Pays de France and Seine-et-Oise (areas of the Paris Basin, the most productive region of France), scattered smallholdings still remained prevalent even after the Second World War.[67]

With an infinity of small plots, France had the highest percentage of people working in agriculture in western Europe, apart from the Mediterranean countries, on the eve of the First World War. Notwithstanding the rise of wages in earlier decades, 33 percent of rural workers remained dependent on charity and 43 percent of them ate only one plate a day, often potatoes or toast with lard in a soup. Crowded villages suited the notables, who, despite profitable sales of parcels to peasants, continued to draw much of their wealth from land rents. According to the statistics of 1882, tenants and sharecroppers made up 20 percent of farmers and tilled 40 percent of the land. Notables complained about rural depopulation despite the enduring presence of dense village populations and micro proprietors dependent on wages, sharecropping and leasing. Because of the high percentage of the population in rural areas, the age-old custom remained of short-term leases regularly adjusted in ways beneficial to the landowners. Tenants, for this reason, invested little in roads, deep plowings, wells, drainage, lime applications and other improvements, which would only pay off after a decade or more.[68]

Between 1848 and 1889, the Chambers of Deputies debated bills to have the surplus value of capital divided equally among proprietors, farm managers and workers. The legislatures, however, never went forward with any laws. Founded in 1867, the *Société des Agriculteurs de France*, less an organization of agriculturalists than a league of proprietors, reacted to the debates by advancing the principle of the inviolability of property written in the Rights of Man. The *Société* maintained that the legislature had no right to interfere in conventions between proprietors and farmers. After conservatives and Catholics rallied to the Third Republic in 1892, the rentier attitudes of the landed classes further tightened their grip on the political establishment. The Third Republic imposed tariffs on imports in the 1880s and 1890s. In 1911, agricultural prices were much higher in France than they were in the United States, Britain and Belgium. Politicians did not see these prices as incentives for investment and productive agriculture. Rather, they touted protectionism as a means of preserving small farms, a numerous population on the land and the preeminence of agriculture in French society. Their discourse presented all landowners, large and small, as a single group with a united lifestyle and interests. It mixed references to a professional activity and territory and posited rural life as the essence of the national identity.[69]

The notables thereby benefited from the peak of the rural population at the time of the 1890 census. Every job, farm and strip of land on the market attracted numerous applicants. In the Allier department in central France, leases required up-front payments, obliging sharecroppers to begin their tenancies in debt. Some masters forbade their sharecroppers to trap or shoot game or obstruct their pursuit of animals, even if the tillers had to stop working and look on as hunting parties damaged the crops. Sharecroppers had to do a host of jobs, helping the house cleaner with washing, looking after the master's horse, washing his carriage, harnessing and unharnessing it whenever he made calls, working in his garden and cutting his wood.

These jobs tediously distracted the sharecroppers from farm work. Bourgeois land-owners economized on everything, refusing outlays on phosphates, nitrates and other fertilizers. They thought the sharecroppers should make do with the farm manure. The proprietors often kept the sharecroppers under surveillance to make certain they did not eat chickens or sell farm products. In bad years, sharecroppers were left with a tiny share of the harvest and fell further into debt. If they disputed the master's calculations, he could allude to the large number of people looking for work and threaten eviction. In such cases, the master could enforce every condition in the lease and dismiss the sharecroppers with nothing to their name. They feared going to court, where the master presented well-ordered accounts and where the downtrodden were always wrong. After a number of good years, the master could raise the rent, leaving the sharecroppers with the choice of remaining poor on the farm or leaving and seeing the master usurp their improvements.[70]

Notables preferred this secure status of master to the capitalist alterative of sub-mitting to competitive markets and the relentless compulsion to increase surpluses by reinvesting gains and improving agriculture so as to beat or match the prices of other proprietors and avoid insolvency. In the wealthier Calvados department in Normandy, for instance, leases long remained restrictive, because the advantages to modifications to farming methods did not seem apparent to the property own-ers. Agriculture stagnated or developed slowly over the course of the nineteenth century because of high rents, which left tenants with little money to spend on im-provements. For these reasons, across France, rates of investment did not show any periods of rapid increase between 1871 and 1939, even though the Crédit Agricole made funds available to proprietors at the end of the nineteenth century.[71]

In conclusion, members of peasant communities, we saw in the Introduction, had fought together in the feudal period to secure hereditary rights to the land. They regarded their plots as the foundation of their households and communities and continued to farm for subsistence in the eighteenth and nineteenth centuries. Of course, most of them did not have sufficient land to cover their needs amid the population growth in rural areas during this period. Peasants therefore farmed more intensively, improving their processes for harvesting maize, potatoes and grains on their parcels. The peasants devoted other parcels to grape vines, dye-plants, fod-der for livestock and mulberry trees to nourish silkworms with the leaves. They thus obtained income on the market for their households. Family members worked for wages in rural workshops and in the harvests of various crops, and, with the earnings, subsidized the market lines grown on their parcels of land. Using unpaid household labor, rather than depleting family resources on implements, allowed peasants to outcompete large growers. For this reason, as agricultural prices de-clined in the late 1870s and 1880s, many notables found it more profitable to sell parcels of land to peasants rather than compete with them on the market.

In England, by contrast, the lords and their tenant farmers broke up village com-munities, attacked common lands, evicted peasants and demolished cottages to make way for parks and pasture in the Midlands, southern and eastern England after the 1440s. It became increasingly apparent to the lords by the second half of the fifteenth century that they best assured their wealth and power by requiring market-based rents on large economically competitive farms. By the late sixteenth century, the gentry and their tenants engrossed their holdings, enclosed fields, removed traditional rights of way and depopulated villages. The replacement of subsistence production and village manufacture with competitive leasehold forced tenant farmers to constantly improve labor productivity and brought about an agricultural revolution in the seventeenth and eighteenth centuries. An increasing number of people lived outside of agriculture supported by farm production. The rate of urbanization in England between 1500 and 1800 was not matched anywhere else in Europe. The separation of manufacturing from the peasantry represented the indispensable foundation for dynamic industrial development and ultimately an industrial revolution.[72]

In France, the peasants' ability to intensively till the land, raise output and gain income facilitated economic growth but did not subject the population to the foregoing capitalist imperatives. Peasants continued to grow subsistence crops all over the country. The market lines brought in the extra income needed to supplement what the peasants obtained from their parcels in grains, maize and potatoes. The market lines thus rounded out the peasants' subsistence and shielded them from the price competition faced by English tenant farmers. Capitalists must obtain the highest returns for their land and labor or face economic elimination at the hands of competitors. French peasants, by contrast, did not relentlessly strive to augment income relative to expenses with the purpose of beating or matching the prices of other farmers. They did not face a capitalist context creating constant pressure to augment output as the sole means to maintain their standard of living.

The agricultural sector, for this reason, did not generate overabundance. Farmers did not force counterparts, in locations less suited to a given commodity, to focus on a different product or abandon husbandry in favor of manufacturing. When farmers specialize, and give up growing subsistence grains in their communities, the agricultural sector as a whole concentrates cereals, as well as other crops and livestock, on the areas most suited to these lines and thus raises average yields and productivity. When farmers concentrate on wheat production in the regions most suited to it, they leave more space for animal husbandry to develop. French peasants, however, did not make this change and thus did not have as many productive farm animals as did agriculturalists in other countries of western Europe at the turn of the twentieth century. French growers thus did not obtain as much manure or have the traction power to cut labor costs.

The reason for this lag in labor productivity and output was not the absence of economic demand from the urban and industrial centers. The capitalist conditions, described in the preceding paragraphs, do not lead farmers merely to fulfill the economic demand of consumers. Capitalism leads them, through the coercive laws of competition, to constantly increase output, saturate markets with foodstuffs, drive down prices and export surpluses. This dynamic took place during the agricultural revolution in seventeenth-century England, as well as in France during the 1960s (see Chapter 4). In contrast, at the end of the nineteenth century, French farmers did not generate enough output to meet the needs of the domestic market. France imported grain despite successive increases in protective tariffs.

This situation did not trouble the dominant classes of the time, made up mostly of townspeople with landholdings in the countryside. They controlled the legislatures of the revolutionary era and subsequent regimes of the nineteenth century. The notables preferred to see a large population of small holders in the countryside. Most peasants did not have enough land to support their households and therefore relied on the notables for employment and tenancies. The notables could impose terms on the peasantry. They extracted profits from the peasants, as the rural population grew in the eighteenth and nineteenth centuries, without having to submit to the coercive laws of capitalist competition. The notables, that is to say, did not have to relinquish much of their revenue in investments in their properties. They instead obliged peasants to bring agricultural products to their residences, respect their hunting rights and treat them as masters. For all these reasons, French agriculture remained mired in slow growth throughout the nineteenth century.

Notes

1 Le Roy Ladurie 1981, p. 11–13, 22, 25, 99, 105–106, 227–28; 1974, p. 5, 227, 247, 295, 311; Bloch 1966, p. 4, 17, 95–96, 141–42, 241–42; Jacquart 1974, p. 623, 626, 636, 733, 737, 753–54, 756; Brenner 2005, p. 219.
2 Moriceau and Postel-Vinay 1992, p. 191–95, 197–98, 209, 212, 217–18, 289, 318, 322; Moriceau 1994a, p. 33–34, 38, 50–51, 53, 58; 1994b, p. 72, 618–22, 635, 640–43, 659–60, 779–80; Newell 1973, p. 697, 699, 710, 721–23; Grantham 1996, p. 41, 52–53, 56; Sutherland 2014, p. 152–53; Chevet 2014, p. 160–61, 164, 167, 169.
3 Hoffman 1996, p. 82, 84, 91, 102–103, 125, 132–33, 144–46, 148–52, 159, 162, 171, 191, 201–202; Sutherland 2014, p. 150–52, 156; Ruttan 1978, p. 714–16, 720–21; Heywood 1981, p. 360, 369–70; Grantham 1997.
4 Brenner 1997, p. 18; Antoine 2006, p. 36; Gaveau 2021, p. 280–81, 289.
5 Brenner 2001, p. 287.
6 Dimmock 2014, p. 91–92, 118–19, 143, 272.
7 Meuvret 1987, p. 76, 124; Lefebvre 1962, p. 329–30; Berenson 1984, p. 9–10, 18, 20, 22–23; Brennan 2006, p. 183, 186, 189–90, 193, 197–98; Labrousse 1966, p. 48–51; 1970, p. 485; Bodinier, Teyssier, and Antoine 2000, p. 368; Price 1975, p. 260–61, 264; Grantham 1975, p. 295–98, 317, 323; Béaur 1984, p. 270, 336, 339; Tulippe 1934, p. 110, 161–63, 241, 318–19.
8 Fournial and Gutton 1974–1975, p. 10; Lugnier 1962, p. 109, 112, 119, 121–22, 129, 227, 240; Berger 1985, p. 183–84; Tomas 1967, p. 409–10; 1968, p. 381, 389–90, 395; Gutton 1971, p. 172; Jomand 1966, p. 230, 291–92, 447, 507–508; Brenot 1980, p. 235; Dupâquier 1999, p. 53.
9 Peret 1998, p. 43–44, 98; Guillemet, Pellegrin, and Peret 1981, p. 11, 14–15; Merle 1958, p. 40–41, 64; Bossis 1972, p. 132–33, 135–36; Elie 2003, p. 238; Pichon 2004, p. 149, 152, 154; Pellegrin 1987, p. 380–81; Martin 1988, p. 64.
10 Benoist 2005, p. 120, 184–85, 294–95; Benoist 1985, p. 163–65, 167; Bossis 1980, p. 143; Tilly 1964, p. 33; Gérard 1990, p. 42–44.
11 Antoine 1999, p. 121, 124–26, 128–29, 131.
12 Gay 1967, p. 159–60, 162–63, 169, 184–85, 308.
13 Loutchisky 1933, p. 121, 123, 134; Brunet 1960, p. 284; Vovelle 1980, p. 85, 217, 202; Dupâquier 1956, p. 145–46, 214, 255; 1995, p. 76; Jacquart 1974, p. 104–105, 107, 117; Tulippe 1934, p. 110; Béaur 1984, p. 128.
14 Herment 2013, p. 362–63, 367; Béaur 1991, p. 285, 287.

15 Peru 2003, p. 68–69, 71; Dion 1959, p. 32, 466–67; Labrousse 1944, p. 554, 558; Baulant 1979, p. 96; Bianchi 1999, p. 53.
16 Aymard 1988, p. 235; Bouton 1993, p. 57–59; Labrousse 1984, p. 362, 437–40, 509, 599, 612, 616.
17 Durand 1979, p. 41–42, 291–92, 507–508; Gutton, 1971, p. 71.
18 Dehergne 1963, p. 23, 28, 54, 70; Peret 1998, p. 47, 157; Martin 1988, p. 71–72; Bossis 1972, p. 136; Gérard 1990, p. 55; Labrousse 1970, p. 540–41.
19 Weber 1958, p. 366.
20 George Comninel provides a good analysis of the noncapitalist agriculture of the eighteenth century; Comninel 1987, p. 183–93.
21 Garnier 1982, p. 363, 381; Vignon 1978, p. 451–52; Dontenwill 2003, p. 123, 127; 2006, p. 278–79, 282, 289; Fournial and Gutton 1974–1975, p. 10; Tomas 1968, p. 381, 389–90, 395; Gutton 1971, p. 71.
22 Couturier 1909, p. 74–76; Massé 1956, p. 24, 28; Autexier 1947, p. 85, 147–48; Peret 1976, p. 101, 132–33, 194, 225; Legal 1995, p. 331–32, 348–49; Dehergne 1963, p. 28, 117–18, 177–78; Guillemet, Pellegrin, and Peret 1981, p. 12, 14; Elie 2003, p. 236; Surrault 1990, p. 197; Menault 1991, p. 118; Gay 1958, p. 409–10; 1955, p. 36, 38–39, 42–43; 1967, p. 276.
23 Moriceau and Postel-Vinay 1992, p. 191–95, 197–98, 204–206, 209–12; Moriceau 1994a, p. 33–34, 38, 50–51, 53, 58; 1994b, p. 640–43, 659–60, 779; Hoffman 1996, p. 82, 102, 133, 144–46, 150–51.
24 Meuvret 1987, p. 88–89; Jacquart 1975, p. 362–65, 373–75; Moriceau 1994b, p. 631; Labrousse 1970, p. 484–85.
25 Moriceau and Postel-Vinay 1992, p. 191–95; Moriceau 1994a, p. 50–51.
26 Grantham 1978, p. 332–33.
27 Moriceau and Postel-Vinay 1992, p. 210–12; Moriceau 1994a, p. 33–34.
28 Chevet 1994, p. 118–19, 123, 125–27, 130–32, 136, 138–39; Béaur 2000, p. 158. Micheline Baulant makes the same point as Béaur that landowners and tenant farmers did not calculate or economize on labor inputs; Baulant 2006, p. 147, 155, 157, 159.
29 Grantham 2000, p. 38–39.
30 Béaur 2000, p. 159; Labrousse 1970, p. 454–55, 462, 495.
31 Jones 1967, p. 20; 1968, p. 60; Wrigley 2006, p. 467; John 1965, p. 19–20, 22–24.
32 Young 1969, p. 285–86.
33 Lejosne 1989, p. 61–62; Venard 1957, p. 72–73, 83; Mireaux 1958, p. 40–41, 45–46, 103–104, 112–15, 117–18, 120–21; Jacquart 1975, p. 359, 362–63; Loutchisky 1933, p. 141–42; Aymard 1988, p. 222, 225, 239; Tulippe 1934, p. 107–108, 110, 163, 241, 316, 318; Dupâquier 1956, p. 145–146, 172–74, 207, 214, 255.
34 Parker 1996, p. 116; Béaur 1996, p. 381–83, 385; 2000, p. 120; Meuvret 1987, p. 132, 134, 201; Bouton 1993, p. 44–45; Labrousse 1970, p. 483.
35 Allen 2000, p. 20; Clarke 1999, p. 211; Goy 1987, p. 5; Ado 1996, p. 57–58; Ganiage 1988, p. 37, 41, 54, 61; Mireaux 1958, p. 112–13, 117–18, 120–21; Loutchisky 1933, p. 139, 141–42; Jacquart 1974, p. 272–74, 317, 757–58; Meuvret 1987, p. 37, 42–43; Labrousse 1970, p. 463.
36 Nicolas 2002, p. 76–77; Miller 2008, p. 193–94; Bloch 1966, p. 169; Vivier 1998, p. 58–59, 164–66.
37 Lemarchand 1989, p. 264–65, 268, 289–93, 324, 328–29, 365–66; 1988, p. 171–207.
38 Désert 2007, p. 38–39, 193, 196–97, 307–308, 312–13, 347, 530, 588.
39 Pautard 1965, p. 46–47, 113; Vidalenc 1970, p. 80; Paris 1975, p. 238–39; Chevet 1994, p. 105, 108–109, 113; 2014, p. 160–61, 164, 167, 169, 174–75.
40 Dupeux 1962, p. 203, 210–13, 220–21, 233–34; Price 1981, p. xii, 66–67, 71–75, 84–85.
41 Lafrance 2020, p. 71, 75, 85; Jones 2016, p. 14–15, 17–19, 217.
42 Dontenwill 1973; 2006, p. 289, 291–92.
43 Guillaumin 1983, p. 112–14, 126; Le Roy Ladurie 1981, p. 203–204.

44 Agulhon 1979, p. 27–29, 44–45; Rivoire 1842, p. 73, 256, 297; Wylie 1974, p. 17, 19.
45 Clout 1983, p. 49–50, 76, 79–81, 100, 102, 150–51; Price 1975, p. 271–73; Pataud 1965, p. 100.
46 Keyder and O'Brien 1978, p. 102, 107–108, 116–19, 121–22; Dormois 1996, p. 335, 348; Clout 1983, p. 152; Ruttan 1978, p. 714–16; Price 1983, p. 394–95.
47 Ruttan 1978, p. 718, 720–21; Heywood 1981, p. 369–71; Grantham 1997.
48 Haine 2000, p. 150; Moulin 1991, p. 92; Dormois 1996, p. 332–33; Price 1983, p. 63–64, 336, 339.
49 Lafrance 2020, p. 71, 75, 85.
50 Brenner 1987, p. 213–27; Isett and Miller 2017, p. 74–92, 145–68, 257–67; Evans 2019, p. 191–213; Carlson 2019, p. 239–63; Dormois 1996, p. 359–60.
51 Wrigley 1985, p. 707; 2006, p. 20; Jones 1967, p. 20; 1968, p. 60; John 1965, p. 19–20, 22–24.
52 Brenner and Isett 2002, p. 643–44; Levine 1976, p. 107–22; 1977; Wrigley et al. 1997, p. 134, Table 5.3; Wrigley and Schofield 1981, p. 260, Table 7.28; Feinstein 1998, p. 642–43; Overton 1996, p. 84–88, Table 3.11; Mokyr 1999; Clarke 1999, p. 211, Table 4.2.
53 Brenner 1987, p. 311; Jones 1967, p. 9, 31, 36–37; 1968, p. 60–62, 70; Wrigley 2006, p. 467; 1985, p. 690, 707.
54 Kemp 1962, p. 339; Moulin 1991, p. 49–56, 144–45; Grantham 1975, p. 297, 310; Berenson 1984, p. 3, 22; Meuvret 1987, p. 215; Clout 1983, p. 152.
55 Désert 2007, p. 119–20, 145–45, 152, 348.
56 Cocaud 2016, p. 65, 73, 75.
57 Dupeux 1962, p. 110, 114, 501.
58 Amann 1990, p. 201; Guillaumin 1983, p. 6–7, 73–74, 151.
59 Pitié 1971, p. 125; Plack 2005, p. 52, 56–57; Wylie 1974, p. 16–17, 19–20, 33; Agulhon 1979, p. 27–29, 44–45.
60 Grantham 1975, p. 301, 303–306, 308; Berenson 1984, p. 3, 7; Moulin 1991, p. 49, 93.
61 Jessenne 2006, p. 212; Berenson 1984, p. 3, 22; Grantham 1975, p. 295–97, 317, 323; Heywood 1981, p. 362; Moulin 1991, p. 57, 61, 93, 109, 114; Gaveau 2021, p. 278–79, 289.
62 Demangeon 1905, p. 227–28, 243–44, 248–49, 290, 347, 399, 401–402; Vidalenc 1970, p. 58, 60; Labrousse 1970, p. 444; Morineau 1976, p. 436–37; Vandewalle 1994, p. 129, 132–33, 135–36, 179, 209, 214, 224, 290–91, 299, 308.
63 Demangeon 1905, p. 298–99, 302–303, 356–57; Pinchemel 1957, p. 57, 75, 86–87, 90, 92–93, 95–96; Pataud 1965, p. 46–47, 77, 86, 100; Vandewalle 1994, p. 129–31, 179, 214, 224, 290–91, 305–306.
64 Levine Frader 1991, p. 16, 19, 22, 30–31; Heath 2014, p. 19, 162–63.
65 Levine Frader 1991, p. 22–27, 35; Heath 2014, p. 22, 195, 205.
66 Grantham 1980, p. 522; Bloch 1966, p. 39–41, 43–45, 180–81, 232–33, 240; Vivier 1998, p. 176; Jones 2016, p. 92–93.
67 Grantham 1980, p. 528–31; Bloch 1966, p. 39–40, 241–42; Brunet 1960, p. 284; Gaveau 2021, p. 246, 278–79, 289, 296–97.
68 Augé-Laribé 1950, p. 97–98; Jessenne 2006, p. 214; Amann 1990, p. 183; Vidalenc 1970, p. 81; Pitié 1971, p. 292; Pinchemel 1957, p. 95; Gaveau 2021, p. 246.
69 Jessenne 2006, p. 204–205; Augé-Laribé 1950, p. 93–94; Heath 2014, p. 84; Pautard 1965, p. 139–40; Price 1983, p. 331, 337, 339.
70 Weber 1983, p. 81; Guillaumin 1983, p. 38, 45, 47–48, 91, 140–41, 147, 152, 154.
71 Désert 2007, p. 309–310, 708; Jessenne 2006, p. 215; Price 1983, p. 394–95.
72 Dimmock 2015, p. 27, 28, 104, 143–44, 155, 272; 2019, p. 47–51.

2 Industrialization from the Old Regime to the Postrevolutionary Era

For a long time, scholars of France viewed industrial growth, like the agrarian economy, as weak and slow from the mid-eighteenth, through the nineteenth, and well into the twentieth centuries. From the 1930s to the 1950s, historians largely accepted what François Crouzet named the "retardation-stagnation" thesis.[1] This perspective claimed that France lagged far behind British industrial performance and was eventually overtaken by continental competitors. Ernest Labrousse, the most influential social and economic historian of his generation, explained that France remained an "ancien régime economy" until the mid-nineteenth century, while others, like Stanley Hoffman, spoke of a "blocked society."[2] France did not undergo an industrial revolution, as the country stayed mostly agricultural and reluctant to mechanize production.[3] This industrial backwardness tended to be explained by sociocultural factors, namely the country's national character and "Malthusian" and conservative entrepreneurs reluctant to innovate.[4] In an influential article, David Landes asserted that entrepreneurs "lacked drive, initiative, and imagination," which explained the underwhelming industrial performance.[5]

Key characteristics of the economy of the eighteenth and especially the nineteenth centuries support this reading of the country's industrial development. Historians tend to divide French economic growth over this period into long cycles. France underwent industrial growth during the second half of the eighteenth century and again from 1815 to 1840, this time accompanied by mechanization even as it remained mostly labor-intensive. Economic growth accelerated from 1840 to 1860 and included the construction of railroads. France was then hit particularly hard by the "great depression" of the 1870s and 1880s, before rapid industrialization from the mid-1890s to the First World War.[6] Over the whole period, however, levels of output remained relatively low—far behind Britain's—while the United States and several European countries caught up to, or outstripped, France. Many economic resources were still concentrated in agriculture, and large-scale mechanized production remained scant.[7]

If, however, one looks at growth per capita, one gets a different picture. During the 1960s, cliometrics, which combine neoclassical economic theory with historical analysis, led to the publication of national income estimates by Jean Marczewski and his collaborators. These, and other quantitative estimates produced over the following decades, proposed a more optimistic take on the economic record.[8]

DOI: 10.4324/9781003092896-3

While the French gross domestic product (GDP) declined significantly relative to Britain's and fell behind that of Germany by the end of the nineteenth century, calculated per capita, French GDP growth remained more or less on par with these countries.[9] Notwithstanding the publication of works underlining the languor of French industry,[10] a robust "revisionist" challenge emerged in the 1960s and eventually gained dominance, using the close parity of France's growth rate per capita with its competitors as the cornerstone of its argument.[11]

Revisionists recognize that France did not undergo the structural change that took place in Britain after the end of the eighteenth century. This, however, did not stem from entrepreneurial deficiencies but from a distinct national context, defined by the turmoil of the Revolution and Napoleonic Wars, low coal endowment, slow demographic growth, a large agricultural sector and a limited home market, all of which brought a distinct mode of industrial development.[12] In this national context, businesses found it rational to develop labor-intensive enterprises capitalizing on artisan skills to produce high-quality goods as an alternative to the coal-powered mechanized production of British factories. "French businessmen" had to make do with a distinct set of opportunities and, in fact, "exploited their more limited markets more effectively."[13] They innovated in their own way, developing new products and fashions instead of labor productivity enhancing technologies. This, according to revisionists, was a model of industrialization that should not be judged inferior to its British counterpart, since there is no unique "definable and optimal path to higher per capita incomes" and no "simple equation of material progress with mechanization."[14] It was, rather, an alternative and, in the end, equally efficient and more humane model. So much so that, according to O'Brien and Keyder, "labor productivity in French industry [was] above British levels until the 1890s."[15]

In this chapter, we will rebut this revisionist reading of French industrialization by analyzing the class structure and mode of surplus extraction—the social property relations—that oriented patterns of industrial development in the eighteenth and nineteenth centuries. This analysis will define the range of strategies that economic actors found rational to adopt to reproduce themselves and their communities. Over most of this period, it was Britain that offered a distinct model of development, while France remained close to European norms. Britain outperformed France because the former country undertook a capitalist process of industrialization, while the latter did not. In other words, arguing that, as revisionists do, France embarked on its own distinct path of industrialization does not take us very far and is largely beside the point. The French economy remained noncapitalist, and this explains the absence of structural economic change as well as the relatively poor economic performance. The point is precisely that to compete with other industrializing powers and reach modern standards of development, France eventually had to undergo structural changes like those experienced by Britain and, later, by countries such as Germany and the United States.

French manufacturing developed in an environment stamped by the absence of agrarian capitalism. As we saw, agriculture was characterized by the prevalence of peasant proprietors oriented toward production for subsistence, with significant numbers in possession of plots so small as to force them to seek wage labor on larger farms and in rural workshops. The agrarian structure forestalled a process of expropriation like the one that had taken place in England over previous centuries. The entrenchment of peasant property and the absence of competitive market imperatives in the countryside constrained the progress of productivity (larger outputs for given inputs) that could have reduced food prices and increased purchasing power. Stagnant levels of agricultural productivity due to traditional methods and implements restricted the growth of a home market (for both consumer and capital goods) already severely constricted by the preponderance of subsistence-oriented production in the countryside.

The limitations of the home market, and reserves of cheap rural labor, biased merchant manufacturers toward investing in cottage workshops. Manufacturers, moreover, adapted to noncompetitive, protected and fragmented markets. They seized opportunities in these markets, investing to a certain extent in factories and mechanization over the first half of the nineteenth century. Since, however, they did not face interfirm competition imposing cost-cutting and profit maximization as a matter of survival, entrepreneurs were not compelled to *systematically* invest in productivity-enhancing technologies. Industry therefore retained a preponderance of petty producers and small workshops and a restricted number of mechanized factories. Gains in productivity were too small for firms to compete with British rivals on the world market. Many firms therefore focused on elite consumption at home and abroad, and excluded competitors, through the quality and reputation of artisanal expertise. In a context where businesses faced no compulsion to impose a capitalist division of labor, workers retained control over the labor process and, building on new rights gained in the Revolution of 1789, consolidated and extended the customary regulation of their trades, which remained in place until the closing decades of the nineteenth century.

Industrial Development Under the Old Regime

Industrial production grew over the early modern period. France, together with the Low Countries, northern Italy and England, had the biggest industrial base in Europe in 1600. After a sharp downturn in the second half of the seventeenth century, "proto-industrial" production became widespread across the realm in the 1700s. Most growth concerned textiles and secondarily construction and public works. Spinning and weaving developed in rural areas long before the crown's authorization to circumvent urban guilds in 1762. The metallurgic industry was still feeble despite the appearance of a few large mills. Chemistry, paper mills and glassworks hardly affected the industrial structure. Whereas commercial manufacturing had concentrated in urban settings in medieval times, a division of industrial labor subsequently emerged between town and country. Preliminary stages of production such as washing, combing, and grease removal generally took place in towns. Peasant households, often the women, did much of the spinning. Urban artisans did much of the weaving. Skilled urban laborers took care of the finishing steps of industrial processes, a way to ensure the quality of the commodities. Though a few large factories began to emerge, in urban and in rural settings, small artisan workshops remained the rule for all trades and scattered cottage manufacturing dominated in the countryside.[16]

Commerce was the most dynamic element of the Old Regime economy and the major engine of growth.[17] City-based and wealthy merchants, known as *négociants*, imposed oligopolies and monopolies to manage the interregional and international trade of manufactured goods, while their agents coordinated the circulation of production materials between towns and villages. Merchant-manufacturers, known as *fabricants*, often themselves direct producers, also engaged in trade, especially where larger *négociants* had not fully taken control of trading activities. Merchants—whether *négociants* or *fabricants*—provided raw materials and credit to spinners, weavers and other artisans and bought back finished goods. They devoted much of their capital to managing markets by monopolizing information and building exclusive networks.

The whole commercial-industrial structure was based on credit chains, with bills of exchange and traders' notes as their links. *Négociants* acted as bankers, simultaneously financing trade and engaging in lending activities with states and other rich individuals. A merchant or trading agent would sell on credit raw material to a spinner, buy back the yarn and sell it again to a *négociant* to obtain the liquidity to pay back the workers. Manufacturing processes were lengthy—it often took a year and a half to manufacture printed cotton cloth. Merchants invested very little in industrial equipment. Their circulating stock was much more important than their fixed capital.

Guilds controlled by master-artisans or *négociants* had the crown's endorsement to coordinate trades in urban areas. They set norms of quality and apprenticeship, sought to protect their members against outside competition and attempted to regulate prices, wages and quality standards. Guilds, however, did not exist in certain towns and crafts. Some manufacturing and trading escaped their direct control, including in faubourgs on urban peripheries or when powerful *négociants* traded independently from merchant corporations and attempted to encroach on product design. *Négociants* sought to monopolize commercial activities and set prices. Large merchants formed their own guilds or sometimes worked with guilds controlled by master-artisans to organize trades and subcontract labor. But they also often circumvented guilds by putting work out to impoverished peasants in need of supplementary income, whose labor was 20–50 percent cheaper than its urban equivalent. Peasants spun, knit and wove at home, drove merchandise carriages around the countryside, made whitewash, bricks and roof tiles and worked in nearby mines and forges. Much of this production was for local consumption and executed on demand. Textile production fit into the downtime of agricultural cycles when family members were not tilling the fields and could spin the loom.[18]

The main antagonism of the Old Regime commercial and industrial world opposed merchants to direct producers.[19] While conflicts over pay within urban and rural units and local networks of production occasionally broke out, they were experienced as ruptures in normally reciprocal relationships. Workers received pay, moreover, from merchants who bought their products, not their labor-power. Employers and direct producers entered credit rather than wage relations. Direct producers, whether urban artisans or rural workers, often depended on large merchants for credit to get raw materials or tools, as well as for access to markets for their products. Many producers were indebted and stuck in relations of dependence with merchants. This dependence on credit, which was difficult to access, was used by merchants to extract surplus labor as workers struggled to pay interest and clear debts.

Contrary to Sewell's assertions, however, this surplus labor was appropriated by employers through *unequal exchange* and did *not* take the form of surplus value. Labor takes a value form under capitalism because workers are deprived of means of productions and must sell their labor power to employers who are compelled by competitive imperatives to produce commodities according to standards of "socially necessary labor time." To do so, employers must control means of production and organize labor activities. Workers are alienated from their activity (their "concrete labor"), which is controlled by their employer, who oversees the production of "abstract labor," giving labor a value form. This abstract labor appears in market exchange as value. The ability of employers to abide by the "law of value" and ensure that production is done according to socially necessary labor time is validated by his capacity to sell commodities on a competitive market, thus receiving a share of socially produced surplus value. Crucially, this surplus value is created in production, not circulation—workers freely sell their labor power to employers *at their value* (exactly what the labor commodity costs on the market), but employers gain the ability to compel workers to produce more value than necessary to reproduce their labor power. Workers submit to such exploitation because they have no choice. They do not have independent means of subsistence.

In the Old Regime commercial economy, by contrast, merchants extracted surplus labor through unequal exchange in circulation, not production. Merchants profited at the expense of producers and consumers. Workers were independent producers. Guillaume Daudin stresses that there was "no concentration of the means of production" by employers.[20] Moreover, as Sewell explains, workers "were juridically independent petty contractors, not wage earners." They "were exploited as effectively as wage laborers would have been, but *via the putter-out's manipulation of prices and interest rates* rather than by low wages and long working days."[21] The fact that merchant profited by manipulating prices—which implied unequal exchange—shows that markets were not competitive and that employers were not constrained by the law of value and could use their market power to accumulate wealth.

Indeed, to gain a structurally dominant position and extract commodities from direct producers at the most advantageous price, *négociants* relied on the monopolization, not of the means of production, but of exchange. Merchants wielded "external" and indirect yet real power over artisans and industry by controlling the commerce and exchange of products. Artisans and smaller merchant-manufacturers (*fabricants*) responded by attempting to enforce customary regulations of trade and just prices on open marketplaces and fairs where they could more easily short-circuit the secretive and monopolistic trading operations of *négociants* and their agents. They also routinely resorted to public protests or outright violence to limit the arbitrary power of merchants over commercial exchange.

Whatever power imbalances existed between producers and merchant employers, the former did not sell their labor-power on the market and were not wage laborers of the sort found in a capitalist society. "Labor markets" were highly segmented and did not organize the social division of labor according to supply and demand in response to freely fluctuating wages. The price of a product bought by a merchant and the amount of pay disbursed by a master to a journeyman were fixed within a framework of multiple and often intertwined layers of customary, guild, judicial and political regulations, the effects of which depended in the last analysis on the balance of power between producers and merchants. The income of direct producers, in other words, was much more the result of social and political relationships than of economic transactions. Most producers, moreover, manufactured in rural settings and had access to parcels of land and to livestock in a way that shielded them from full market dependence. They were not fully responsive to market demand for labor, as agriculture remained their main activity. This was even true for part of the urban workforce, which seasonally migrated to towns between harvests to work in trades and supplement their agricultural income.

In fact, Daudin explains that most townspeople were involved in agriculture in one way or another. In a large number of towns, most families were landowners, often of parcels situated in the town itself. Peasants often lived in towns and tilled plots in the nearby countryside. In Dauphiné, nine towns out of ten produced more than half their needs in cereal. Gardens and orchards were present in towns throughout the country.[22]

Even in the case of landless urban workers, extra-economic regulations of all sorts sheltered them from the "labor market." Specifically, rural and urban workers kept control over labor activities not subject to capitalist discipline. Neither smaller merchant-manufacturers nor *négociants* were interested in imposing such discipline and in any case, were not compelled to do so by competitive market imperatives. Peasants—who possessed insufficient land to support their families and were forced to engage in manufacturing activities within their household or nearby—were not thereby reduced to a pure and malleable commodity by those who employed them and to whom they sold, not their labor-power but the product of their labor.[23]

Workshops were active in parallel to, or often as part of, large and complex enterprises, most of which persisted in using traditional and unmechanized production methods. The *fabrique* was a common way to coordinate production by a multitude of small units, federating the workshops of a town and peasant households of a region. Lyon's silk industry represented one of the largest such networks, with a few hundred master-artisans and an even smaller number of merchants and clerks after a 1744 ruling granted them a monopoly over commercial activities. Lyon's silk industry employed some 30,000 workers in dispersed small workshops. In middle-sized towns such as Sedan, in Champagne, and Elbeuf and Louvier, in Normandy, the production of fine wool sheets tended to concentrate in urban, and sometimes quite large, workshops and factories, but much of the spinning was done by thousands of rural inhabitants. In Champagne, Languedoc and Dauphiné, drapery manufacturers hired tens of thousands of spinners in hundreds of villages.

Similar patterns were true for mining, where enterprises hired thousands of peasants to extract coal on their own, and for metallurgy, where merchants contracted work to forges employing a handful of workers. The same applied to most papermaking and glassmaking.[24]

Large factories emerged during the late eighteenth century and the following century. They remained exceptional even in "modern" sectors. Cotton spinning penetrated the countryside in the late seventeenth and early eighteenth centuries, beginning to displace other textiles such as linen and hemp in Pays de Caux and Picardy and wool in Languedoc. Cotton production involved putting-out networks to rural cottages, though factories (*manufactures concentrées*) also emerged. The factories housed printing, as merchant-industrialists continued to import cotton cloths from India and later in the eighteenth century, from England. Concentrated cotton spinning only took off in France in the first decade of the nineteenth century, as the Napoleonic Wars and custom policies curbed imports. A few printing factories were built in Normandy in the 1740s and 1750s, and dozens more were established in the region after production was authorized in 1759. Cotton factories were also founded in Alsace and in other regions and some around Paris, the largest being Oberkampf, founded in 1760 to supply fine printed calicoes to the court in Versailles and the Parisian market. Over 170 such factories could be counted across France in the 1760s.

Concentrated manufacturing, using wool and other textiles, also developed during this period, though not nearly as much as for cotton. Much metal production was still undertaken by small units using traditional techniques, though several larger forges developed in the late seventeenth century—such as iron making complexes in the Loire Valley, in Alsace, and in Lorraine—largely to supply the royal army and navy. Le Creusot, a monumental foundry, which began production in 1785, was the first to import the English coke-smelting technique to refine iron. The coal mining enterprise of Anzin in northern France employed around 4,000 miners in some 27 pits in 1789, extracting half of all coal production. The coal pits of Littry in western Normandy required the labor of about 3,000 miners, while the Norman and Languedocian mining concessions of Pierre-François Tubeuf hired around 2,500 miners. The glassworks of Saint-Gobain, established in 1695, were another industrial emblem of the Old Regime that grew steadily in the eighteenth century.[25]

If they concentrated workers—often a few hundred, rarely more than a thousand—factories did not concentrate machines. They were not built with an eye on mechanization to improve labor productivity—their main purpose was to collect workers under one roof to supervise them, assure quality and curb the embezzlement of materials common in putting-out production. Workers did not work together but next to each other. Cotton spinning and ordinary weaving were put out in domestic production, whereas later steps of fine weaving were completed in workshops. While a factory producing steam engines was established in the Parisian faubourg of Chaillot in 1778, the use of such engines remained exceptional. English spinning jennies and mull jennies began to be built in Hargreaves, Rouen and Sens after the 1750s and in Paris after the early 1770s, but their use and diffusion remained scant. Factories and workshops were mostly powered by water and wood, whereas coal, though increasingly present, was used much less. Merchant-manufacturers were aware of technical innovations, but few of them rushed to adopt the new techniques.[26]

For industry as a whole, productivity remained low and appears to have barely improved. It was not capitalist techniques and management that sustained the industrial growth of the eighteenth century but the intensive employment of rural labor, which yielded stagnant or declining returns per unit. The use of old looms and techniques was still the rule in textiles. In metallurgy, most furnaces functioned without any modern technical knowledge, and the distinction between iron and steel was ambiguous. Furnaces operated in rural settings in accordance with the harvest rhythms and often stayed idle three years out of four and sometimes as many as nine out of ten years. Textile production, employing a mass of peasant-spinners and weavers, was likewise in tune with, and secondary to, agricultural work.

The management and accounting of industrial enterprises—whether dispersed or concentrated in factories—were a far cry from modern capitalist standards, and in fact remained fully rooted within a merchant accounting logic that had much more to do with tracking credit flows than with calculating profits. Balance sheets were produced only rarely and erratically, mingled the agricultural and industrial assets of owners and only considered earnings and expenditures while ignoring capital depreciation and interest. Prosperous merchants sought to join the nobility and mimic its lifestyle, buying offices and landed property, while several aristocrats engaged in commerce, especially after the lifting of the derogation penalty for wholesale trading by a royal edict in 1701.[27]

Large cotton printers like Oberkampf acted, and considered themselves primarily, *négociants* rather than industrial entrepreneurs. For them, profits resulted from "gains on exchange, on the difference between buying price and selling price," even "for ... highly capitalized branches such as calico factories." Oberkampf claimed that "the key to success was his ability to buy unbleached cloth cheap and sell it printed at the highest price, wherever demand was highest," and he explained that his job

> was to collect information efficiently, through a network of informants, to find out where there was a large offer at given levels of quality and prices, buy there, and at the other end find expanding markets on which marketing his products would bring in the best results.[28]

Industrial manufacturing, whether rural putting-out networks or large mills, was self-financed by merchants, who acted simultaneously as traders, financiers and insurers. Modern banking and credit institutions, mobilizing the savings of the public to fund economic activities, were nonexistent—this was still a period dominated by *banquiers* (private banking) functioning as closed and mutually co-opting inner circles rather than by institutionalized and impersonal banks. These private bankers saw themselves primarily as *négociants* and were more interested in trade or lending to states and rich rentiers than in funding industry. Merchants resorted to trade bills within tight networks for short-term credit. Though already emerging in the seventeenth and eighteenth centuries, bill discounting by bankers was rare in the absence of a modern baking system. Merchants interested in industrial activities and acquiring mills generally sought to avoid resorting to credit and, when lending did take place, it was *intuitu personae*, between individuals with trust relationships. Industrial enterprises were family businesses and capital was raised within family networks and often involved alliances formed through weddings between merchant clans. This amounted to what Pierre Léon has called an "aristocratic mobilization of capital." General partnership companies predominated, and only a handful of capital companies, dividing funding and management responsibilities, had been established by the end of the 1780s. Mills and commercial assets were part of the broader family holdings. Richer merchants sought to live off the land and other forms of rent and often sought ennoblement. Very few merchant-manufacturers sought to become entrepreneurs like their British counterparts.[29]

It is true that successful merchants, like other rich members of society, obtained an increasing number of private long-term loans (often in the form of obligations, life annuities or other types of rents) from strangers through the intermediary of Parisian notaries who acted as expert brokers based on their knowledge of the finances of borrowers and lenders. The fact that notaries helped individuals to establish financial relations beyond their family and inner circle, however, did not amount to the progressive rise of the impersonal economic logic that characterizes capitalism, as Philip Hoffman, Gilles Postel-Vinay and Jean-Laurent Rosenthal would have us believe.[30] The growing sums lent through these notaries were not directed toward productive investments of a *capitalist* type aimed at productivity gains as part of the ongoing processes of capital accumulation driven by impersonal market competitive forces.

Indeed, as Hoffman and his colleagues show, while notaries raised and circulated impressive amounts of financial capital, the unwillingness about "putting it to productive use" persisted "well into the nineteenth century."[31] Lenders, as a rule, were older rentiers, who provided loans to younger individuals eager "to purchase a government office, construct a glorious new residence, or pay what was due their siblings in order to settle their parents' estate"[32]—in short, to become rentiers themselves. Moreover, the vast number of state rents and government loans (nearing "half of what the crown owed") peddled by notaries and marketed to investors in provinces by the end of the Old Regime, which is discussed by the authors,[33] had less, if anything, to do with a capitalist logic than with the debts of an Old Regime state entering its final crises and desperate for revenues as it grappled with the growing geopolitical power of capitalist England.

Finally, let us note that the brokering role played by notaries can be described as "impersonal" only in the sense that it connected parties unknown to one another. This had nothing to do with the impersonal and coercive forces of market imperative of a capitalist economy. Notaries and their clients were, in fact, very much embedded in interpersonal relationships facilitated by their close acquaintance with discrete individuals. These relationships actually conform to the broader commercial dynamics of the time, which led merchants to routinely engage in "impersonal" exchange and credit relations with partners outside their immediate circles with the help of formal and informal partners acting as brokers.[34] As we will see below, merchants focused on building networks that structured markets and protected them from the impersonal market dynamics of capitalism.

While private investment in mills and machinery remained limited, the expansion of industrial activities was still largely, as Denis Woronoff explains, a "state affair" under government tutelage. Jean-Baptiste Colbert, while serving as Louis XIV's controller general of finances after 1661, built on previous state policies and systematized the mercantilist doctrine by limiting purchases of foreign goods and selling on foreign markets. The goal was to retain and accumulate wealth on French soil to support the monarchy's military power. This mercantilism amounted to import substitution. State officials, that is, supported imports of foreign industries, technologies, engineers and workers. Technical knowledge was introduced into the realm from other European countries, as in the case of Dutch papermaking, Venetian glassmaking, and German smelting. Most efforts, however, were focused on Britain where, at an accelerating pace over the course of the eighteenth century, the French state sent agents to bring back machines and skilled workers. To promote domestic industry, many enterprises were granted the status of "royal manufactories," which came with privileges such as subsidies, tax exemptions, protective duties or monopolies in producing specific goods in a region or the entire realm. To support foreign trade, especially of lucrative luxury goods for which high quality standards were key, the crown established restrictive systems of regulation and inspection of manufacturing processes, while it also supported the extension of guilds to as many trades as possible.[35]

State voluntarism, however, came up against an unfavorable socioeconomic context. France possessed a large population of 28.6 million in 1790, up from 22 million in 1700. Large in absolute terms, this growth was weak relative to the rest of Europe, where the French population went "from … 18 percent of the … total … to just 16 percent." [36] Paris was home to 450,000 in 1680 and 750,000 in 1789, and Lyon, Bordeaux and other large cities also grew at an impressive pace over the early modern period. Yet, the proportion of the population living in cities of over 10,000 accounted for about 9 percent in 1789 and barely changed over the course of the eighteenth century. The growth of luxury goods consumption in urban markets, especially in Paris and nearby Versailles, encouraged industrial production. Below this apex of elite consumption, the realm was home to some six million households whose market purchases also played a role in propelling industry—a role that must nevertheless be kept in proper perspective. Stagnant agricultural and industrial productivity limited real incomes, which are, in fact, estimated to have decreased by around 25 percent during the eighteenth century. Much popular consumption was also subject to the hazards of a traditional agrarian economy, with cyclical bad harvests leading to sudden and severe increases in agricultural and food prices, which limited the consumption of manufactured goods.

Moreover, most of the population consisted of peasants who possessed land, were not market dependent and did not have to specialize in single lines of production. They opted for diversified subsistence production, hence limiting their market purchases. Most of the clothes, shoes, pots and utensils, furniture and home appliances needed by peasant households were produced at home or purchased from local artisans. Peasants used these items with parsimony and repaired them to prolong their use or reused and swapped them within villages. Thus, while the French consumer market grew and sustained manufacturing output over the course of the eighteenth century, this was due to incremental demographic growth and expanding luxury consumption by elites, not to change in the consumption habits of the vast majority of the realm's inhabitants, whose purchasing power actually declined over time.[37]

Meanwhile, the impact of foreign markets on French industry increased during the eighteenth century. The extension of foreign trade allowed merchants to reach wealthy consumers in different parts of the globe. The markets of northern Europe, along the North and Baltic Seas, as well as in Italy, the Iberian Peninsula and South America, offered them outlets. Merchants sold fine textile products and other luxury goods in the Levant, which received 40 percent of exports in 1787. Trade with this region remained stable, while market shares were lost on the Iberian Peninsula during the second half of the century due to foreign competition. This loss, however, was more than compensated by a spectacular tenfold growth in the value of the Atlantic trade, with Antillean commerce contributing to most of this expansion. Colonies were an important dimension of Colbert's mercantilist policy. Following in the footsteps of Richelieu and Mazarin, Colbert developed the merchant fleet. Trading posts were secured on the Indian Ocean and colonies were captured in North America and the Caribbean. The seizure of Canada secured access to fishing zones and the fur trade, but followed mostly military and geopolitical motivations. The capture of Martinique, Guadeloupe and, most importantly, Saint-Domingue was tied to commercial ambitions. Coffee, cotton and, above all, sugarcane plantations were established and a soaring African slave trade provided the workforce. Trade with these colonies gave access to lucrative resources, did not cause precious metals to leave the country and allowed for the acquisition some of these metals, as tropical commodities were exchanged with other European countries.[38]

These developments were part of the logic of the French monarchy, which needs to be distinguished from the English model of colonial expansion. The English Empire was the product of agrarian capitalism, which fueled rapid population growth and settler colonialism.[39] The latter was aimed at reproducing capitalist property forms abroad, while Britain had a mass domestic market, which served as an outlet for exotic goods like coffee, tobacco and sugar. The exploitation of resources and slave labor in the American South and the Caribbean did not cause the emergence of British capitalism but contributed to its development by providing cheap raw material as well as profits to reinvest in Britain. The French empire, by contrast, continued the feudal-absolutist logic of expansion and led to the projection, on the Atlantic world (and beyond), of the military and commercial competition of the noncapitalist ruling classes of Europe. Monarchs sponsored colonial ventures to secure economic resources they could not amass at home. Much of the trade and colonization was undertaken by state-sanctioned companies enjoying monopolies over imports and exports, as was the case, for instance, of the French East India Company until its dissolution in 1769. As a rule, the wealth violently extracted from colonies was spent on feudal-absolutist pursuits, such as war, empire and the conspicuous consumption of ruling classes, not on capitalist investments. As was the case for other aspects of its mercantilist policies, the goal of the crown's colonial policy remained improving its fiscal affairs and geopolitical status.[40]

By the end of the seventeenth century, "new merchants" in Britain, who could foreclose on planters, supplanted the "company merchants" and undertook the colonization of the English Caribbean and North America. State-chartered companies no longer restricted trade in the colonies. In the French case, Colbert at first granted a privileged company the exclusive control over the Antilles trade, but merchants protested and made sure that the colonization of the islands would be assumed by independent entrepreneurs. Trade with the Antilles, however, continued to be the exclusive domain of French merchants, and most importantly, laws forbade the seizure of the planters' land and slaves to cover debts, meaning that capitalist market imperatives remained absent from the colonies. Planters and their managers, that is to say, did not have to produce competitively under the threat of losing access to the means of production.[41]

Sugar plantations in Saint-Domingue, Martinique and Guadeloupe were often semi-industrial ventures that required heavy investments in rolling mills and boiling houses, not to mention the constant import of slaves. By the end of the Old Regime, these agro-industrial complexes in Saint-Domingue allowed the island to produce around 40 percent of Caribbean sugar. Plantations were deeply integrated in the Atlantic triangular economy of the time, importing goods from Europe, slaves from Africa and selling exotic crops on metropolitan markets. Yet, they were also "organized to promote certain forms of enclosure and self-sufficiency," producing "subsistence crops" and "growing food stores" of their own to be "hedged against climatic or market disruptions" while "minimizing purchases outside the household."[42] The heavy investments required for sugar production represented "once and for all" costs. Not facing market pressures, absentee metropolitan sugar barons—often aristocrats—and their property managers did not have to continually reinvest and develop their means of production.[43] Domain management was often lacking, a large proportion of plantations approached a state of decrepitude and boiling mills were idle half of the year. Planters did not take advantage of new boiling techniques, equipment or improvements in cane processing in the second half of the eighteenth century. They drove their slaves harder as land fertility declined, especially after the 1760s.[44] While planters extracted great wealth exploiting their slaves, they did not do so in a capitalist way by continually improving labor productivity.

The value of foreign trade grew about five times from 1716 to 1788, as the prices and volume doubled. The growth of foreign trade was much faster from 1720 to 1750, approximately 3 percent per year, against a little more than 1 percent between 1750 and 1780, suggesting a phase of recovery during the first half of the century following a sharp slowdown in the seventeenth century. Moreover, the growth of imports was much higher than that of exports, and France went from a commercial surplus to a deficit. Still, the development of foreign trade was considerable, and some of this increase was attributable to soaring commercial exchange on the Indian Ocean after the end of the French East India company after the 1760s, though most of it was tied to the Antilles trade.

Atlantic commerce involved the trading of some 60,000 slaves per year toward the end of the Old Regime. The number of slaves in the Antilles increased from 40,000 at the end of the seventeenth century to 500,000 in 1789. Plantations in the French Antilles produced mostly sugar (over 80 percent of their agriculture in 1756), coffee (around 12 percent) and, to a lesser extent, cotton, indigo and cacao for European markets. French demand for sugar was, however, limited, as its consumption per capita was ten times less than England's. Sixty percent to eighty percent of the sugar was reexported to other parts of Europe. French colonies in the Antilles consumed wheat, wine and manufactured goods produced in France. The ports of Bordeaux, Marseille, Nantes and Le Havre shared 90 percent of the Atlantic trade and the regions surrounding these cities experienced considerable manufacturing development and were among the most industrialized in the country. Shipbuilding and textile manufacturing soared in and around these cities. Sugar refineries, distilleries and tobacco mills were also established, especially around Bordeaux. France actually took market share from England, as its portion of world trade rose from 8 percent in 1720 to 12 percent in 1780.[45]

As impressive as Atlantic commerce was, it scarcely modernized French industry.[46] Around 1789, the value of foreign trade per capita was two-and-a-half times lower than it was in Britain. More to the point, only a limited proportion of the profits of colonial ventures ended up as investments in the metropolitan industrial economy, and these investments did not change industrial techniques.[47] In other words, French and British colonial trades were integrated into their respective metropolitan industrial economies in fundamentally different ways. Silvia Marzagalli thus concluded that:

> colonial imports only gave a modest stimulus to the French economy as a whole, in contrast to the British economy, characterized by the importance of exporting manufactures. The growth of French overseas trade, with its strong colonial component, did not on the whole benefit the rest of the French economy, and was only a sort of 'bubble' depending on special conditions laid down for a time by the French state.[48]

Commercial balance sheets demonstrate that French manufacturing was already falling behind the British. As P.M. Jones explains:

> if we take figures for the export of manufactured goods as broadly indicative of the extent to which trade drove the dynamo of industrialization, the position of France is revealing. Between 1715 and 1787 the percentage of manufactured articles (essentially fabrics) in the total volume of French exports scarcely altered, whereas the quantity of manufactured imports,

again measured in percentage terms, rose significantly. Britain, by contrast, mainly imported raw materials and by the 1780s her exports consisted over-whelmingly of manufactured goods.[49]

Because of France's relatively low industrial productivity, it lost ground in international trade outside its colonial preserve to a much more vibrant British economy. Industrial producers were much less efficient than their British counterparts and largely unable to compete on international markets, except in luxury goods. French merchants, to take a case in point, proved incapable of moving into the considerable market of the former British 13 Colonies during the second half of the 1780s. The dynamism of Britain's economy allowed it to sell a value of an average of 103 million *livres tournois* (l.t.) per year in the newly independent United States from 1786 to 1790, while French exports to this country averaged a value of only 1.4 million l.t. per year from 1787 to 1789. Britain also dominated other markets, including South America. As Guy Lemarchand puts it, "on the eve of the Revolution, Britain was already in the process of winning the global commercial and modern industrial battle against France."[50]

British industrial capacity owed much of its edge to the quantitative and qualitative characteristics of its domestic market. Social property relations and rules of reproduction created the context for, and expansion of, English agrarian capitalism and laid the foundation for a domestic market and subsequent emergence of industrial capitalism. With the development of economic leases, fixed competitively on the market, tenant farmers had to sell their output. They had to specialize, compete and adopt labor-saving techniques, not only to sell their products to consumers, but also to access the means of production—land itself.[51] As growing numbers lost this economic war and access to their land—through enclosures and the use of force to accelerate the process of dispossession—a growing labor force was "freed up" from subsistence farming, making it increasingly available for wage labor in factories. The population also had to buy its basic subsistence items on the market.[52]

Improving labor productivity, due to a steady stream of investments in agriculture, propelled the growth of both labor and consumer markets by sustaining demographic growth of approximately 280 percent in England from 1550 to 1820. Productivity gains allowed the country's urban population to go from just over 10 percent of the total to almost a quarter in 1800, while only around 36 percent of English adult males remained primarily engaged in agriculture.[53] Even though the population grew rapidly, Britain's agricultural productivity fueled a fall in food prices and an ensuing substantial rise of real wages, which were about a third higher than in France by the 1780s.[54] As food became cheaper, much broader sections of the British population were able to purchase an ever-growing volume of factory-produced basic necessities such as cutlery, pottery, candles and printed fabrics.[55]

Far larger than its European counterpart, the British market was also qualitatively different and uniquely integrated—not just geographically, but also because of the unprecedented way it partook in the integration and circulation of production. The emergence of a unified competitive national market was a consequence of economic and political transformations in post-feudal England—"not a cause, of capitalism and market society."[56] The Norman conquest of the eleventh century turned an already unified country into one of the most centralized states in Europe. Much of the autonomous power of lords, municipal entities and other corporate bodies were increasingly monopolized by the central power during the fifteenth century. The English aristocracy was the first ruling class to be demilitarized in Europe. It was integrated into a monarchy that used its coercive powers to protect the private property of landlords wielding the "economic" powers tied to their landed property as their main tool for extracting surpluses from market dependent tenants. This new division of political and economic powers between the monarchical state and landlords—which was definitively settled when the 1688 Glorious Revolution eclipsed the crown's absolutist pretensions—consolidated a centralized power and eliminated the parcellized sovereignty of feudal times.[57]

The corollary to this centralized state was an increasingly integrated economy. "Already in the sixteenth century, England had an impressive network of roads and water transport that unified the nation to a degree unusual for the period."[58] The country developed a "single national market, the largest, free trading zone in Europe,"[59] and thanks to the further development of roads, waterways and ports, "by the end of the eighteenth and early nineteenth centuries, ... had ... the most advanced transport and communication infrastructure in the world."[60]

Within this economic space, industrial producers faced consumers that were not only increasingly numerous, but also dispossessed and therefore *compelled* to buy everyday basic commodities on the market. The specific nature of the domestic market was largely determined by the primary needs of its consumers, and consequently differed greatly from the relative price inelasticity of the luxury trade for wealthy consumers in other countries. While productivity gains propelled real income growth, the budget of most British inhabitants remained limited and compelled manufacturers, active within an integrated economic space, to engage in cost-effective production.[61]

Market exchange no longer acted as an external force connecting separate and heterogeneous spaces of production and consumption from the outside. While being integrated and subsumed to a new capitalist mode of production, circulation took an unprecedented hold on production and oriented its organization, as producers had to engage in cost-sensitive manufacturing and to attain efficiency standards imposed by market competition.[62] The market operated less and less on the basis of age-old merchant "profit on alienation" (buying cheap somewhere and selling dear elsewhere) and increasingly on the basis of competitive production. A new trading and banking system, which had its roots in agrarian capitalism and grew along with industrial capitalism, departed from the ancient "carrying trade" system of commercial arbitrage between separate markets.[63]

The competitive logic of this new integrated domestic market "eventually extended its reach beyond Britain's national boundaries to create a new system of international trade"[64] that replaced "the infinite succession of arbitrage operations between separate, distinct, and discrete markets that had previously constituted foreign trade."[65] Eventually, after the 1760s, as productivity increased in textile manufacturing, the largest cotton producers from Lancashire and woolen producers from Yorkshire began to bypass traditional merchants and export their products directly. According to R. C. Nash, these developments resulted from a "constant rise in output, especially in cotton, and a continuous fall in prices" that "created the most intense competition ever seen in Britain's domestic and foreign markets." As Nash explains, "manufacturers, faced by excess capacity at home, were forced to export a growing proportion of output on low profit margins but found the existing mercantile structure inadequate to the task." Few "merchants vigorously promoted exports on the manufacturers' behalf," and many "were unwilling to take the financial risks of pushing exports in an aggressive manner."[66] But by the end of Napoleonic Wars, old commercial structures had been swept away, and the merchant houses in Liverpool, Leeds and London, which did not adapt to the new competitive system, went bankrupt.

Commerce in France did not share these characteristics. As we have seen, the peasantry retained access to the land and was embedded in traditional relations of surplus extraction, and so agrarian capitalism and its imperatives of productivity improvement were absent from France. As a consequence, there was no mass of landless and market dependent wage laborers of the kind that emerged in England. Limited gains in productivity meant that French agriculture, in any case, did not sustain as much demographic growth as did England. As discussed above, French demographic growth remained below the European average and its urbanization was very modest. The agrarian economy did not yield the workers and consumers needed to support capitalist industrialization.

The evolution of France's social property relations also obstructed political and economic integration. In France, there was no division of political and economic powers of the kind that developed in England. Elites used extra-economic means to obtain wealth. State taxation emerged as a form of surplus extraction during the early modern period. Rents obtained from landed property, moreover, preserved quasi-feudal characteristics. France "remained a confusing welter of competing jurisdictions, as nobility and municipal authorities clung to the remnants of their autonomous feudal powers, the residues of feudal 'parcellized sovereignty.'"[67] Even as the crown was increasingly able to concentrate political authority and channels of surplus appropriation and to co-opt the aristocracy into the state apparatus, this same process entailed a new form of pulverization. Specifically, state power was redistributed and privatized, as venal offices and other forms of privileges and sinecures were bought by, or granted to, aristocrats and members of the bourgeoisie.[68]

Just as state integration led to economic integration in Britain, political fragmentation maintained the economic fragmentation of France. Over 2,500 internal custom posts were still in place, despite the crowns' efforts to reduce their number, in the final years of the Old Regime. Improvements were made to transport infrastructure over the course of the eighteenth century, but the quality of roads and of waterways remained too poor to eliminate the interregional price disparities and enforce price competition.[69] "France had nothing like England's unified internal market, where goods passed freely"[70] and, as David Parker puts it, "there was no such thing as the French economy; only a number of regional ones and, within these, many local ones."[71]

Merchants profited from these segmented economic spaces by mediating between interregional and international markets and capitalizing on price differentials. The sphere of exchange—the circulation of goods—was the key to this political economy (since it was where prices, profits and all important economic factors took shape), and it was shaped by merchant intermediaries active at its core.[72] Merchants reproduced themselves within an economy shaped to serve their interests and made profits not by way of continuously innovating production, but by developing new products and fashions, for which maintaining quality reputation was essential, and, crucially, by monopolizing access to market segments. Put another way, merchants did not have to adjust to independent price pressures—rather they actively shaped prices and market structures.

As Robert DuPlessis emphasizes, "structural characteristics of early modern markets obliged [merchants] to develop modes of analysis and business strategies appropriate to their environment."[73] Pierre Gervais' work provides insights into these strategies.[74] Given the numerous, unpredictable, yet recurrent, shocks to markets (war, bad weather, loss of ships, bad harvests, bankruptcies breaking chains of credit, etc.), merchants avoided specializing in a narrow set of commodities and instead diversified their activities and products to minimize risk and maximize gain. Since commodities were not standardized and imitation and fraud were pervasive (hardly curbed by official and guild regulations), quality and price levels had to be continually reassessed. Reliable information on taste, demand and prices for the distinct and heterogeneous markets was key. Likewise, merchants routinely engaged in short-term credit exchange and accepted, endorsed and gave large amounts in payment notes, letters of exchange and trader's notes, not to mention dubious metallic currencies, the quality of which, along with the trustworthiness of multiple creditors and debtors, had to be assessed and validated. All of this called for expertise on a wide variety of products, markets and financial papers—an expertise impossible for merchants to acquire on their own.

Merchants therefore developed a network of trusted suppliers and selling agents—expert correspondents with specialized knowledge on what, and where, to buy and sell—with whom the merchants would partner in the different markets. A key point, here, is that the building of this network of expertise on a particular market segment represented "a first step which would also turn the group of allied peers [...] into a formidable tool for market control."[75] Indeed, the same process that allowed some to share market information with trusted peers also served as a means and strong incentive to monopolize this knowledge within a closed network of insiders, thus making market segments opaque to outsiders. Trust relationships among a select club of partners were used to exclude competitors and control markets.[76]

Deprived of access to these networks, an isolated merchant would act blindly, face considerable risk and trade inferior products to satisfy tastes he could only imperfectly perceive. Price indicators necessary to guide profitable buying and selling remained inaccessible to outsiders or were in any case very poor guides, since "prices were never used as public signals on an open market on which demand and offer faced off." Merchants strove to ensure that "prices would not ... be reached through an open, transparent bidding process," but instead by "secret negotiating," despite resistance from producers interested in selling their products at public marketplaces and from consumers interested in more choices, higher quality and lower prices. Moreover, even at the lowest level of the merchant world, that of the village grocer or urban hawker, prices were never set through a straightforward confrontation of offer and demand, but rather as the local manifestation of complex battles between competing oligopolies within a customary and sometimes official framework of regulations. Using their closed networks, "merchants constantly traded information on prices in the markets they were familiar with" and, as Gervais stresses, such information "was not public, and constituted insider information which could be exploited for profits."[77]

Merchants built networks to manipulate market segments and control supply and demand. They formed cartels or peer groups to establish oligopolistic control over buying and selling of particular products in particular spaces. Consequently, "in these markets, insider trading, buyer and seller cartels, price-fixing, speculation, market cornering – in short virtually unbreakable barriers to entry and imperfect information reserved for the privileged few – were not bugs, they were fixtures."[78]

Daudin insists that the very nature of the commercial economy, necessarily based on intermediaries, collusion and monopolistic strategies, indicated that markets were not competitive.[79] Merchants thus did not face market imperatives to systematically maximize profits. Supply and demand did not determine economic decisions. Gervais finds that "the only risks incurred were ... logistical, relating to time and transportation issues."[80] Prices fixed by oligopolies were ultimately "a negligible topic, because any extra cost could and would be passed to consumers as long as it did not shift the demand curve significantly."[81] Merchants hardly considered profit rates. Market structures made such calculations unrealistic. Shipments consisted of different bunches of products bought at different prices hardly traceable through interregional and international trade. Each product and market deviated radically from the ones previously encountered. Profit depended, above all, not on quantifiable productivity rates or other calculable factors, but on knowledge of quality scales and consumer tastes, all of which were accessible through trust relationships among peers. The aim of merchant accounting was to track credit flows, not profit rates. Accounting was necessary to provide a sound picture of assets and liabilities—to preserve the confidence of creditors and to weed out bad debtors—and maintain the trust of the allies crucial to the merchants' reproduction and prosperity.[82]

If Philippe Minard is right to say that "competition, in truth, cannot be much more imperfect" than it was in France at the time,[83] it is because this "competition" was fundamentally different from the one that exists in a capitalist economy. Put another way, we are not simply dealing with an embedded form of utilitarian, capitalist rationality, but rather with an altogether different form of rationality. Economic agents occasionally adopted "once and for all" new (and often foreign) techniques to access a market for a given product. But they did not seek to outcompete economic rivals through efficient managerial practices, together with cost-cutting, productivity-enhancing techniques and machinery, in the way that their British counterparts did.[84]

The economic advantage that England built over France through the constant revolution and improvement of techniques, first in agriculture, and later in industry, was translated into a military superiority increasingly manifest over the eighteenth century, especially after Britain's victory in the Seven Years' War cost France most of its North American colonies. French political elites saw the urgency of economic and political reform. Pamphlets emphasizing the innovations and improvements, which explained English agrarian superiority, emerged in the 1720s. These reflections were taken over and systematized around mid-eighteenth century by Physiocrats eager to emulate English agrarian capitalism and restore the geopolitical standing of France. In the late 1740s, a group of liberal state servants began to meet, under the intellectual influence of Vincent de Gournay, and insinuate themselves into the corridors of power. During the 1760s, followers of Gournay influenced the crown to liberalize the grain trade and lift the prohibition of printed calicos. These policies, however, produced widespread discontent and were withdrawn. The influence of liberal reformers within the state apparatus reached its zenith with Anne Robert Jacques Turgot's tenure as controller general from 1774 to 1776. Turgot's most controversial edict abolished artisan guilds but was rapidly retracted after it ignited insubordination among artisans and strong dissatisfaction among elites. Jacques Necker, Turgot's successor, pursued policies informed by a much milder liberalism.[85]

As McNally explains, facing opposition from the dominant classes, the Physiocrats knew that they "had ... to look at a state-directed social transformation towards agrarian capitalism. Agrarian capitalism was the key to state building; the state was key to agrarian capitalism." They "looked to the state to undertake a revolution from above which would wipe away feudal rights and privileges, unify and centralize political power, and establish the social and political framework for an English-style transformation of agrarian economy." Turgot, after the failure to abolish the guilds, knew, like the Physiocrats, that the capitalist restructuring of industry could only be accomplished by a "despotic monarch." Reformers "required an *absolute autonomy* of the state from civil society."[86]

In the absence of such an autonomous state authority, the liberal reforms attempted after 1750 did not transform the economy. The reforms promoted by Gournay, Turgot and others had revolutionary implications in a society that had, as its basic units, not atomized individuals connected by market exchange but rather bodies (*corps*) interwoven under the crown's authority.[87] Liberal reformers not only endangered specific privileges but also threatened to erode the very "substance of privilege ... and [to] gnaw at the corporatist heart of the ancien regime."[88] Gournay's liberal vision clashed with the logic of the merchants' socioeconomic reproduction. Merchants may have contested specific regulations but, as a social class, did not call for the elimination of corps and privileges, since they had an interest in state and guild regulations ensuring the quality and reputation of their goods.[89] As Gervais explains, merchants excluded from markets and privileges might call for

> an end of privileged positions, for better freedom of entry into a market, and for the destruction of tariff and non-tariff barriers, but they would quickly change their tunes as soon as they themselves had consolidated a cartelized

position. The tug-of-war between militants of the free market open to all and defenders of traditional market management by a privileged few was thus constantly reborn with new actors, and should not be seen as reflecting any deep-seated opposition between political economies.[90]

Ultimately, the freedom sought by merchants was embedded in the extent system of privileges. Freedom, under the Old Regime, was the privilege to organize as a body (as a *corps intermédiaire*) with the concurrence of the crown. This was the institutional terrain on which merchants operated, and, again, it was totally different from the competitive market imperatives that propelled British capitalist enterprises.[91]

The state's efforts to support industry, by either liberal reforms or by sticking to the established privileges, brought disappointing results. France was still among the mightiest industrial economies in the 1780s, but, as François Crouzet explains, its economic development

> took place in a framework that, in its organizational aspects and in terms of methods, remained very much traditional …. On the eve of the Revolution, the French economy was not fundamentally different than what it had been under Louis XIV: it only produced more.[92]

The diffusion of technological innovations had been significantly more important in Britain than in France. On the eve of the Revolution, in its cotton trade, England had 260 spindles per 1,000 inhabitants, France 2 per 1,000. There were 900 spinning jennies in France, 20,000 in Britain and no more than a dozen mull jennies in the former country, 9,000 in the latter. Eight French establishments used Arkwright's water frame compared to 200 in England. There were ten times as many steam engines in use in Britain as in France, where only a few dozen could be found. The Parisian factory producing these engines, established in 1778 by the Périer brothers, had only built 40 by 1790, some of which had been sold abroad. Finally, the proportion of iron produced in blast furnaces using coke reached 30–40 percent in Britain but stagnated at 2 percent in France.[93] Overall, change had only taken place at the margins of the industrial economy and, "for the most part, manufacturing technology in France remained what it had been at the outset of the eighteenth century."[94]

The relative frailness of the economy was abruptly revealed by the Anglo-French commercial treaty of 1786, the immediate effects of which were nothing short of "catastrophic" for the industrial economy. The major hub of cotton production in Haute-Normandy collapsed almost overnight. As cheaper English yarn entered French markets, merchants reacted by decreasing the prices paid to their middlemen, who, in turn, passed this price reduction on to the spinners. This reduced the peasant-spinners' revenues by some 30–40 percent, and most of them, therefore, abandoned the trade altogether. Other industries such as metallurgy, pottery and paper production were also hit. While French exports to Britain grew by 75 percent between 1786 and 1789, British exports to France rose by 360 percent over the same period.[95] Clearly, the first attempts of the state to emulate the capitalist development of its British rival had failed. A second serious attempt would have to wait several decades. In the meantime, France experienced substantial development in a context that remained essentially non-capitalist in nature.

The Noncompetitive Economic Context of the Postrevolutionary Era

As we explained in the Introduction, an emerging capitalist class did not lead the Revolution of 1789 and the Revolution did not introduce capitalism. Chapter 1 of this book explained how the Revolution consolidated and expanded peasant land tenure. This section now turns to the impact of the Revolution on the industrial sector which developed, until at least the 1860s, within the same social property relations of the Old Regime. Modes of surplus appropriation—revolving around land ownership, traditional forms of rent, oligopolistic commercial strategies (even as merchants invested in industrial production) and manipulation of state power—weighed on direct producers in the same way they had prior to 1789.

The Revolution abolished the fiscal immunities and legal privileges of the nobility. The Declaration of the Rights of Man, in stating that all men were equally admissible to public offices, formally ended venality of offices. The constitutional monarchy of the Restoration confirmed these principles. Nevertheless, the eradication of seigneurial rights, privileges and venal offices did not uproot old forms of exploitation.

Old Regime elites favored a "proprietary" kind of wealth embodied in land and urban property, venal offices, state bonds and annuities on private loans. These rentier patterns of investment guaranteed relatively low but secure revenues, and remained prevalent in postrevolutionary France. George Taylor explains that

> both before and after the Revolution, the social values of the old elite dominated the status-conscious men and women of the wealthy Third Estate. Avid for standing, they had little choice but to pursue it as the aristocracy defined it, and the result was a massive prejudice that diverted *roturier* as well as noble wealth into ... proprietary investments.[96]

We explained in the previous chapter that traditional, feudal-like leases continued to exist throughout the nineteenth century and allowed landlords to collect rents from peasants. Land remained a steady source of income for the ruling class under the Restoration and subsequent regimes, and "in 1840, of 57 men nationwide who paid over 10,000 francs in tax, 45 were landowners, six merchants or bankers, and three industrialists."[97] Lending to individuals also remained a lucrative and widespread investment practice. Needy peasants and workers resented the tyranny of usurers. *Trésoriers généraux*—state officials in charge of collecting taxes—"did more private than public business."[98] They offered a palpable example of state officials using government resources to secure private gains, and they were far from alone in this business. The material basis of the notability, composed of preeminent nobles and the high bourgeoisie, which emerged as the ruling class of the nine-teenth century, combined landholding and state power.

A tax quota strictly limited the franchise until 1848.[99] Widespread nepotism and patronage, at the apex of the administration, amounted in practice to venality of office. High-ranking state positions offered lucrative stipends. State bonds channeled revenue into the fortunes of the notables just as they had under the Old Regime.[100]

Theodore Zeldin estimates that, around 1848, rich families

> invested about 43 per cent of their wealth in land or houses (two-thirds of it in Paris, one-third in the provinces), they placed about 18 percent in state bonds, safest after houses, and they lent 15 percent to individuals. They put only 3.7 percent in company shares, and 4.5 percent in the shares of the Bank of France.[101]

Overall, this national pattern of investment did not fundamentally change until the last third or even the last two decades of the century. A striking characteristic of this investment pattern is how little was invested in commercial and industrial enterprises. Rich merchant-bankers, the grand *négociants*, who controlled financial capital, and most factory owners were part of, or aspired to join, the select club of notables, who kept the aristocratic way of life alive. Merchant-bankers, like notables, amassed land and sought state position for themselves and their offspring. Their capital did not stand apart from, but was, in fact, integral to, proprietary wealth.[102]

As will be discussed below, merchants began to invest in factories and machinery on an unprecedented scale over the decades following the First Empire. Industry, however, remained remarkably labor-intensive, as industrial entrepreneurs continued to rely on the reserves of cheap labor disseminated across the countryside. As had been the case under the Old Regime, vast numbers of agricultural laborers were also part-time industrial workers as a means to supplement their incomes, while most industrial workers toiled on the land during at least part of the year. The case of the thousands of Massif Central inhabitants, who left their region for a few months at the beginning of each year to be hired in workshops or on construction sites in Paris or Lyon, is illustrative of the broader pattern of seasonal migration common to agricultural workers.[103]

As Woronoff explains, the way in which the Revolution kept the peasantry on the land had a profound impact on the development of industry. The interpenetration of agriculture and manufacturing remained in place and, for most of the nineteenth century, industrialization took place through the extension of production in the countryside. This was the case for much textile production, which accounted for about 50 percent of the national industrial added value and in which about 60 percent of industrial workers were engaged. It was also true for metal production, which was scattered across the countryside among blacksmiths. For industrial workers in general, factory labor was a complementary activity, in which they engaged during the agricultural offseason and according to their needs. Miners were also, and primarily, peasants, who seasonally rotated between mining and farming. Most workers hired by large-scale industrial enterprises were peasants. Workers left the enterprises when hands were needed on the land. Factory production peaked after the harvests when workers no longer toiled on the land, and, as a result, the monthly labor force of factories fluctuated greatly, by an average of 38 percent, until the last decades of the nineteenth century.[104]

Factory workers sought to preserve access to the land and, as a rule, had a strong "hunger to buy land that industrial earnings helped to feed." As a result, "landownership among industrial workers actually increased over the century." Working in a factory "was not a permanent condition or one that separated industrial workers from the rest of the rural community as a ... 'working class.'" For most of the nineteenth century, women and men active as industrial workers

> were determined to preserve their ways of working that allowed them to keep their ties with the land ... Time and again, the offer of higher wages did not change their minds; nor did the threat of lay-offs or dismissal.[105]

As had been the case under the Old Regime, a capitalist labor market, distributing the labor supply in response to demand expressed by wage fluctuations, remained largely inoperative—a fact that was only hardened by the persistence of the customary regulations of labor that will be discussed below. Most industrial workers remained peasants first: peasants who continued to value multi-activity and to seek subsistence on the land to avoid market dependence. Put another way, industrial workers did not constitute a proletarianized class.[106]

Because of the avoidance of wage labor and market dependence by the majority, and combined with slow demographic and urbanization growths, the scope of the consumer market remained limited. As Roger Price explains, from the mid-eighteenth century all the way through to the second half of the nineteenth century, agriculture and population grew within the confines of a "traditional society."[107] Demographic growth was checked by the relatively low productivity of the agricultural sector and remained lower than that of other European countries.[108] The absence of a mass of proletarianized wage laborers limited popular consumption, in sharp contrast with the conspicuous consumption of the wealthy. The gap between elite and popular forms of consumption was partly filled by the moderate development of middle-class consumption of "semi-luxury" goods over the course of the nineteenth century.

Below this social stratum, the consumption of urban workers was strongly limited by real wages, which stagnated, or decreased, until at least the 1850s. The share of food expenditure within these workers' overall budget remained substantial. Workers typically bought their wedding suit from a tailor and subsequently turned it into their Sunday clothes. The rest of their wardrobe consisted of apparel bought from secondhand dealers and repaired at home multiple times. Women often sewed their own dresses and their offspring's apparel. Though cotton clothes became accessible to a part of the laboring population, peasants continued to make at home much of their clothing and the items for daily use. Part of the materials necessary to make clothes and other goods were bought outside the household as were some apparels. Yet, while most of the food consumed by peasants was produced on their land, 60–70 percent of the average peasant budget was dedicated to buying additional food products. The mass of poor peasants dedicated only around 13 percent of their budget to supplementary fabric and apparel, richer peasants (with incomes above 1,500 francs a year) around 20 percent.[109] This limited the consumption of manufactured goods and slowed industrial development.

The segmentation of the domestic market was also an enduring fact, one that had consequences for the development of industry. The Revolution and Napoleonic era abolished many commercial barriers, such as internal tariffs, and contributed to the formal integration of a national market. Yet, in practice, the absence of adequate transport infrastructure fragmented the economic space. Fluvial shipping was the most widely used means of transportation in the first decades of the nineteenth century. In this domain, France was much less favored than Britain or Germany. Only a few of the country's rivers were navigable all year round under all weather conditions. Principally for political and military considerations, the state engaged in the building of a canal network and the improvement of road infrastructure under the Restoration and the July Monarchy. Waterways tripled in length, but their development came relatively late and because of a lack of standardization (some canals being too narrow to accommodate watercraft coming from others), the impact of the canal system on transportation did not meet expectations. Navigability was made irregular by floods and droughts, and bulky transport remained slow and expensive in most of the country, and unreliable during parts of the year. The early phase of railroad building from the 1840s was insufficient to integrate the national territory. Railroads achieved substantial integrative affects only during the Second Empire and the completion of secondary rail networks only occurred under the Third Republic.[110]

In consequence, "France did not have the market integration in the middle of the nineteenth century that England had achieved by the end of the seventeenth century."[111] The French economic space remained segmented, composed of a mosaic of *pays* with different cultures and standards of living. Many regions were practically isolated for parts of the year, if weather conditions turned out to be unfavorable.[112] France still "consisted of a series of local and regional markets grouped around one or two country towns; such markets had only loose connections with each other and a national market scarcely existed."[113] Within these local spaces, village manufacturing turned out the textiles, tools and domestic utensils used by peasants.[114]

Economic continuities with the Old Regime can also be observed in the grand *négociants'* and other merchants' preference for the fragmented economy as well as in their enduring control over market exchanges and industrial activities. Most of the new industrial enterprises of the first half of the nineteenth century were founded by merchants, "either merchant-manufacturers already involved in an industry as organizers of cottage production or merchant bankers seeking new investment opportunities." Despite the establishment of industrial enterprises and the rapid growth of trade, these trends did not alter the organization and conduct of commerce: "trade – whether local or long distance – remained what it had been since medieval times: a personal process carried on by myriads of individual merchants, partnerships, or family firms, all arranged in a pyramidal hierarchy."[115] In 1850, as in 1750, merchants prioritized exclusive networks of mutual trust among privileged insiders. Notwithstanding the appearance of commercial instruments such as circular letters, *négociants* remained the central actors of trade, and the underlying structures of the circulation of goods stayed essentially the same. As had been the case under the Old Regime, there were no standardized goods on offer and no publicly available catalogues of prices.[116]

Négociants stuck to the tradition of diversifying their activities, and the goods they traded, to limit risk and maximize gain. They "typically combined commodity trading and merchant banking with currency speculation, government finance, industrial investment, and whatever else promised a profit. Like their forebears in earlier centuries, [merchants] remained generalists – jack-of-all-trades." Michael Stephen Smith describes great merchant family firms such as the Mallets, which "continued to trade in woolens, lace crystal, coffee, soap, and other luxury commodities in the early nineteenth century just as they had in the eighteenth century."

The richest of all merchant-bankers, the Rothschilds, traded cotton but also imported "tallow, lard, and sugar and, in the aftermath of the crop failures of 1846, became major importers of Russian grain." The Rothschilds liked to deal in high-priced commodities "that offered the possibility of monopoly profits, particularly nonferrous metals."[117] As will be discussed below, this kind of monopolistic behavior still characterized commerce until the profound socioeconomic transformation that began under the Second Empire in the 1860s. But until then, the industrial sectors of textile and metal producers made profits thanks to monopolies.

Merchants continued to engage in a diverse and wide range of commercial and financial activities, which required networks of expert partners to monopolize market segments. They acted as intermediaries at both ends of the production process—providing raw materials and marketing manufactured goods—to control prices. Merchants built networks of regional and international elites to make profits in circulation. Consumers continued to denounce the merchants as "parasites" who cornered markets by arbitrating between economic spaces. The merchants' activities and successes were dependent on but also constitutive of the fragmentation of the economic space.

Besides being fragmented, the French economy was also highly protected. The state maintained protectionist measures until the Anglo-French treaty of 1860 (though tariffs on coal, metal and machinery were reduced after the 1840s). The catastrophic impact of the 1786 treaty on the French economy led to the reintroduction of high tariffs in 1791. Napoleon pursued a protectionist policy, even before the continental blockade, in an attempt to stifle Britain's economy. The productivity gap between Britain and France grew even wider in 1815 than it had been in 1786. The end of the continental blockade following the downfall of Napoleon once again exposed the economy to British competition and threw many industrial branches into crisis with the sudden irruption of British iron products nearly eradicating the metal industry. A strong sense of economic inferiority and vulnerability became widespread. Protectionist views became the rule among large sectors of the political and industrial elite. In 1816 and 1817, the new regime adopted high and often prohibitive tariffs, including an outright prohibition on the import of cotton products, as well as tariffs of 50 percent on iron, hiked up to 120 percent in 1822. Consequently, on the eve of the 1860 treaty, imports of manufactured goods amounted to a mere 0.7 percent of the national industrial product. British competition was completely muffled, and industrialists mobilized against a growing liberal opposition to ensure that it would stay that way.[118]

In these fragmented and protected economic spaces, loosely connected by merchants via oligopolistic networks, employers did not face price competition. Workers, for this reason, were able to avoid capitalist discipline and preserve control of the labor process. It is often thought that a major step in the transition to capitalism came in 1791 with the D'Allarde and Le Chapelier laws, which abolished trade corporations and prohibited workers' and merchant-manufacturers' associations or coalitions. The same year, the Goudard decree abolished state-backed workshop rules and suppressed the royal inspectors that enforced them. Taken together, these decrees are assumed to have established private property in the means of production and to have paved the way for a capitalist restructuring of artisanal and industrial production.[119] Contrary to this account, we argue that the Revolution consolidated noncapitalist social property relations—and the regulations of production that they entail in urban and rural settings.

The Revolution not only helped peasants to safeguard and expand their landholdings but also had emancipatory effects for artisanal and industrial workers. It is first worth noting that the "moral economy" or *bon droit*, which had prevailed in industry under the Old Regime, did not depend on the guilds. Many trades had never established guilds, but nevertheless maintained customary regulations, often under the supervision of municipalities and through an intricate network of high and low courts, parlements, *bureaus de marque*, and police offices, not to mention popular mobilizations. Parallel to, but also often in competition with, guilds, one could find what Michael Sonenscher has named "bazaar economies"—spaces where normative regulations of economic activities prevailed. Even in areas where the state had authorized artisanal production outside the jurisdiction of guilds, such as in the Parisian *faubourg Saint-Antoine*, popular *bon droit* and artisan regulations remained strong.[120]

Moreover, the abolition of guilds "was not, as is usually thought, an outgrowth of the commitment of the revolutionary bourgeoisie to the principle of economic freedom."[121] The *cahiers de doléances* and the process leading to the eradication of guilds show that it arose out of resistance from journeymen and masters excluded from guild leadership. Relying on, and promoting, their *bon droit*, while borrowing and appropriating from Enlightenment philosophers, workers had long organized and struggled against the subordination imposed by guild masters. These popular struggles intensified with the Revolution, as assemblies sprouted, demonstrations multiplied and numerous petitions circulated. Workers interpreted the Revolution as an overthrow of the old labor regime. They were acutely aware of the emancipatory potential of the abolition of privileges by the Constituent Assembly on the night of August 4 and were determined to apply this revolutionary rupture to labor relations by rejecting subordination to employers. Growing numbers of workers overtly and unilaterally overlooked oppressive guild rules, left their masters and ignored the consequences. Guilds had been disintegrating well before their formal abolition in 1791.[122]

As Alain Cottereau explains, all the upheavals brought forth by the Revolution, from the abolition of privileges to the abolition of guilds, through the Declaration of the Rights of Man and of the Citizens,

> were intensely lived as a ... worker's emancipation, as a triumph of old moral struggles, and as the consecration of a ... capacity to fairly negotiate with employers. These were not only formal civil rights, but indeed new real possibilities, massively used.[123]

Before the Revolution, *louage d'ouvrage* and *louage de service* had existed as distinct forms of employment contracts. The former guaranteed that workers could retain their autonomy in the face of their employers and that they could organize their labor as they saw fit as long as customary usages were respected. As for the second type of contract, it was closer to a relation of domesticity and implied submission to a master's directives. The rights conquered by workers in the wake of the Revolution materialized through an immediate and widespread expansion of *louage d'ouvrage* contracts. Toward the end of the Second Empire, still about 90 percent of workers performed labor under the aegis of this type of contract.[124] The Civil Code, which had been in preparation since 1793 and was finally promulgated in 1804, recognized the difference between *louage d'ouvrage* and *louage de service* and how the former ruled out the subordination of employees to employers.[125] Accordingly, the jurist Charles Renouard insisted in 1854 that the Civil Code "clearly established that the renting of one's labor is not an alienation of the capacity to work, and that this faculty, inherent to human activity, remains the property of the worker."[126]

Article 1135 of the Civil Code specified that contracts—including labor contracts—"compel not only to what they express, but also to every follow-up that equity, usage or the law pose as an obligation according to its nature."[127] The equity and usage mentioned in this article referred in part to components of the moral economy of trades, which was administered and enforced, underneath and in spite of a spreading elite liberal discourse, by a set of local and regional institutions. Municipalities played a role in setting tariffs for worker pay or overseeing and mediating negotiations over tariffs. In 1790, the Constituent Assembly established *justices de paix*, which were local courts offering a simplified, rapid and free form of justice. Favoring a conciliatory approach, justices of the peace dealt with a wide range of day-to-day disputes, but also intervened in conflicts over labor relations and commercial exchanges. They arbitrated hundreds of thousands of legal conflicts in 1791 and between two and four million over the 80 years that followed. The establishment of justices of the peace signaled a durable institutionalization of *bon droit* in labor relations in postrevolutionary France.

The moral economy of trades was also supported by *conseils de prud'hommes*, which first appeared in 1806 in Lyon as an outgrowth of eighteenth-century and revolutionary struggles. Elected within trade communities, the officials of these

councils pronounced judgments and provided conciliatory advice on labor relations. They refused to grant arbitrary powers to employers or to let unfettered
market competition set wages and working conditions. *Prud'hommes* ensured that
manufacturing was conducted according to local and trade usages and cracked
down on attempts by employers to unilaterally encroach on such usages. Municipal
and regional authorities often backed the *prud'hommes*.[128]

These developments contrasted sharply with the erosion of customary regulations over manufacturing taking place in Britain at the time. As the British industrial sector experienced a capitalist restructuring, employers arrogated the power to
control labor processes through the appointment and training of managerial staff,
including wage-earning foremen responsive to hierarchical structures, and through
the deliberate design of mills, all to impose new minute divisions of labor and time
discipline.[129] This new industrial discipline emerged during the eighteenth century
in diverse industrial branches, including textile, pottery, metallurgy, engineering,
mining and other sectors like brewing, for which a book of instruction stated as
early as 1742 that in the factory system, "everything is to be considered that can
save labor of the people employed." Employers were backed by the state, which
strengthened the judicial repression and control of the labor force. Until the mid-
1870s, the Law of Master and Servant ensured that employees remained legally,
and practically, subordinated to their employers.[130]

In France, workers emancipated themselves from this kind of subordination and
were free to leave their employers at will.[131] Moreover, the forms of capitalist management spreading in Britain left no trace in French factories and workshops for
decades after the Revolution. Workers remained in control of their labor and preserved an employment relationship with factory owners like the one that artisans
and rural workers had with merchants. Rather than working as wage laborers, they
rented a spot in a mill, buying raw material and selling final products back to the
owner. Discipline was weak and hierarchical supervisory structures essentially absent.[132] Until approximately the last third of the nineteenth century, for merchants
and industrialists, "to organize work was not economically relevant.... In the end,
the idea of organizing work was not even envisaged."[133] As noted by Michelle
Perrot, factory owners "did not have ... a true productivity policy."[134] Philippe
Lefebvre argues that this lack of concern for the organization of production—the
norm until the last third of the nineteenth century—stemmed from the absence of
"sufficient competition to be forced to pay great attention to production costs."[135]

This context stood in stark contrast to Britain, where "precisely at the point at
which serious competition set in," most clearly from the second half of the eighteenth century in a growing number of industrial sectors, "firms began to calculate
their costs more seriously and more exactly." The cotton industry, for instance, had
by then "developed competitive market prices for the main ranges of quality and
weight" and firms were compelled to "accept the market price and endeavored to
keep costs below them." Out of this experience emerged "the first stirring towards
the use of accounts in aid of management decisions," which "included the estimates of costs and revenue, in order to establish which methods of production or

which departments to adopt, enlarge, reduce or wind up" and "attempt to calculate which [...] goods were, and which were not, producing their share of profits."[136]

While Sidney Pollard, in his pioneering research on the origin of industrial management, maintains that these accounting practices remained "embryonic" and "partial," compared to twentieth-century industrial accounting, different studies published since the 1990s have shown that fairly sophisticated cost calculation techniques were developed and adopted by British industrial firms throughout the eighteenth century (and sometimes even as early as the late seventeenth).[137] Pollard, in any case, mentions "how widespread were the efforts to find technical solutions, and how advanced certain techniques in *ex ante* estimating and in partial costing had become." Moreover, he stresses that one of the most significant developments in accounting practices during the industrial revolution in Britain was "the adoption of regular, periodic returns in place of the *ad hoc*, waste book or journal type of book-keeping, the forcing of the natural rhythm of work into a strait-jacket of comparable sections of time." As he concludes, "the regularity or periodicity of the account kept is the single feature which emerges most sharply from the evidence."[138]

Researchers have identified five French industrial companies that adopted industrial accounting and began to calculate cost prices during the 1820s and 1830s: the Saint-Gobain glass manufacture, the Decazeville mines and iron manufactures, the Baccarat crystal works, and the Allevard and Le Creusot ironworks. These were among the largest firms in France at the time, and some looked at their British counterparts for technological and managerial inspiration to ensure the profitability of the capital invested. Most French industrial firms, including textile manufacturers, however, did not bother to calculate costs until much later, as will be discussed in the following section.[139] Furthermore, even in the case of the five large companies mentioned here, reliable cost accounting was made years (often over a decade) after boards of directors formally adopted the practice, and the evidence shows that the cost calculation produced by these firms from then on was done in a more or less *ad hoc* fashion, "either semi-annually or annually or when the directors required specific information for making a particular decision." As Trevor Boyns and his colleagues explain, "there is no evidence, however, of the keeping of regular (e.g., weekly or monthly) cost sheets by individual departments before 1880."[140]

In a noncompetitive economic context, British accounting techniques and also mechanical technologies and productive methods were imported to France, but their diffusion was much less rapid than in their native country. We have seen that the main point supporting the revisionist account of nineteenth-century France's economic development is the country's high rate of growth per capita. This point, however, is deeply misleading. As stated by Crouzet, himself a "moderate revisionist," it was only because the demographic growth of France was comparatively much slower that its GDP per capita remained close to the European average.[141] The French demographic pattern, in turn, was directly related to the consolidation of peasant property and the absence of agrarian capitalism.

In the words of Denis Woronoff, France "industrialized without major rupture [...] mechanization was progressive, incomplete and growth not very much capitalistic."[142] During the first two-thirds of the century, the economy remained principally agricultural, and a major contrast existed between France's peasant majority and the absence of peasants in Britain. Already in 1811, nearly two-thirds of the British labor force belonged to the industrial, commercial and service sectors, while fewer than 35 percent remained in the agrarian sector. By 1850, the urban population reached 40 percent of the total, and the share of the population engaged in agriculture dropped to 25 percent in 1840. In France, in 1851, 64.5 percent of laborers were still primarily engaged in agriculture, the forest sector or fishing, while no more than 35.5 percent belonged to the industrial and service sectors of the economy (again, many were still attached to the land, though involved in industrial activities intermittently). In 1847, 44 percent of French national income was tied to agriculture against 29 percent for industry, while in Britain, agriculture (which was much more dynamic and productive than in France) contributed only 20 percent to the country's GDP in 1850. As late as 1870, 53.7 percent of the French labor force was primarily involved in agriculture and resource-extraction industries.[143]

French manufacturing was still scattered in the countryside and large factories represented isolated patches in an ocean of dispersed cottage labor. Overall, factory production remained the exception and industrial development largely took place within the framework already in place in the eighteenth century. Workplaces were remarkably small, and "as most ... economic historians now agree, mechanization played only a minor role in the French economy between 1815 and 1850."[144] Even in the towns, production was highly fragmented between large numbers of very small enterprises. In 1850, the industrial sector "was only slightly more concentrated than it had been in 1800" and as late as the mid-1860s, "industry had shown little movement toward consolidation."[145] The census of 1851 revealed that the majority of enterprises comprised fewer than five workers, while the Industrial Survey of 1860–1865 and the census of 1866 indicated that "95 percent of all industrial firms and about 80 percent of the labor force [outside of agriculture] belonged to the artisan sector."[146] Industrial enterprises remained small, with a national average of 14 workers per employer. It is estimated that in Paris, in 1860, out of around 100,000 bosses, only about 7,500 employed more than ten workers, 31,000 employed two to ten workers, while the remaining 62,000 had only one or no employee.[147]

The preponderance of artisanal and small-scale industrial production was in part due to the fact that consumer goods dominated the manufacturing sector. As we just saw, large-scale industrial production using machinery was still limited and until the 1840s, machines were mostly imported from Britain and Belgium. Moreover, the fragmentation of the French economic space, the small size of landholdings and the absence of imperatives to improve farming techniques precluded the development of a mass market for standardized manufactured agricultural implements and hardware. Farm implements were largely produced on demand for local or regional markets. Luxury commodities, by contrast, held a large place in manufacturing, as we will see in the following section.[148]

This duality of machine-powered production with less capital-intensive mechanized production existed between, but also within, manufacturing branches, and, in the absence of a competitive compulsion to adopt state-of-the-art technologies and techniques, remained strong until the last third of the nineteenth century. In Britain, where the coexistence of capital-intensive and labor-intensive production also existed but was much less salient and declining more rapidly, the industrial sector was much more mechanized and efficient. The number of power looms in the French textile industries went from 5,000 in 1834 to 31,000 in 1846. As impressive as this evolution may seem, it was outshone by the growth of power looms in England and Scotland from 14,150 in 1820 to 40,000 in 1825, 55,500 in 1829, 80,000 in 1830, 116,800 in 1835 and 250,000 in 1857. In France, the number of handlooms (and the attendant volume of traditional domestic production) remained "abnormally" high and was only overtaken by the number of power looms in 1875, where there were 85,000 power looms against 80,000 handlooms. In Britain, three decades earlier in 1845, there were already 225,000 power looms and only 60,000 handlooms. Already in 1831, over 77 percent of woven cotton goods were produced mechanically in Britain.[149]

The development of horsepower in French industry over the first two-thirds of the nineteenth century was also comparatively sluggish. In 1833, 1,000 steam engines could be found in France, producing a total of 15,000 horsepower, while Britain had 15,000 engines and a total capacity of 220,000 horsepower. In 1840, France, with a population of 35 million, possessed steam engines producing 34,000 horsepower, while Britain, with a population of 19 million, possessed steam engines producing 350,000 horsepower. In 1850, these figures had respectively increased to 67,000 horsepower against 544,000, and France had by then fallen behind Prussia. In 1870, the quantity of horsepower per industrial employee in France was equal to only 21 percent of the amount in Britain.[150]

A comparison of other power sources shows that in France, hydraulic energy remained dominant, while steam power played an auxiliary role in industry, including in metal and textile production. While steam power caught up with hydraulic power around 1880, in Britain, steam was already on a par with water by 1830 (both power sources reached 47.1 percent of the total, while wind power was at 5.7 percent). By 1870, 89.6 percent of total British power came from steam, whereas 10 percent was produced by water.[151] This cannot simply be explained by the relatively poor coal reserves of France, since (as will be discussed in Chapter 3) coal mining developed rapidly over the nineteenth century and its productivity improved exponentially in the closing decades of the century, while the usage of steam engines also multiplied.[152]

These technological gaps were reflected in productivity gaps between France and Britain. As we saw in this chapter's Introduction, O'Brien and Keyder make the rather intrepid revisionist claim that French labor productivity was superior to the British until the 1890s, a finding that the two authors themselves admit to be "certainly surprising."[153] But their claim is not simply "surprising"; as N. F. R. Crafts convincingly demonstrates, it is, in fact, invalid. Crafts explains that methodological errors led O'Brien and Keyder to underestimate the proportion of the

French labor force that was engaged in industrial production while also significantly overestimating the capital-labor ratio in the French industry. Taking this into account, Crafts suggests that French industrial output per worker was only equal to 51.1 percent of the equivalent output in Britain in 1855–1864.[154]

Eric Hobsbawm claims that the relatively weaker levels of investment and mechanization in France represented "one gigantic paradox." He reminds us "that the supremacy of French science" fueled a vibrant technological inventiveness. Moreover, the country was in possession of large capital reserves and Paris attracted capital and bankers from all over Europe, as "a centre of international finance lagging only a little behind London."[155] Technological innovations were available but not fully woven into the industrial fabric of the country. The large financial resources necessary to achieve this integration existed but were not channeled toward industrial investments to an extent that would have allowed France to compete with Britain and other emerging competitors.

In comparison to Britain's modernized financial sector, French banking institutions looked archaic in the first half of the century. Founded in 1800, the *Banque de France*, which was granted the privilege to issue the only paper money accepted for discounts in all cities, did not play an active part in promoting industrial development. It remained under the influence of the *Haute banque*, which grouped around 20 powerful family-based financial institutions, mostly concentrated in Paris. These large Parisian banks were privately owned by big merchant interests and were mostly involved in financing large-scale international commerce as well as in lending to French and foreign states, which they continued to prioritize until the Second Empire.[156]

Great Parisian bankers were involved in the funding of railway building from the 1840s, but their disinclination to invest was rapidly exposed, as two-thirds of capital came from foreign investors, mainly from Britain. Already in 1847, 60 percent of the capital invested in French railways was British. Bankers only timidly invested in French industrial development, judged too risky, and the *Haute Banque* was predominantly involved in a "business of a kind which had been practiced since the Middle Ages and which could grow in line with the expansion of the economy without fundamental change."[157] The *Banque de France* discounted bills of exchange, but only for a select number of merchants. It offered short-term loans to fund trade but as a rule, avoided long-term loans for industrial ventures. Jacques and other bankers helped create the *Société commanditaire du commerce et de l'industrie* in 1827 and the *Caisse générale du commerce et de l'industrie* in 1836, but both went bankrupt, in large part because of the hostility of the *Banque de France*. Investment banking did not really take root and mature until modernizing reforms of the banking system were undertaken under the Second Empire.[158]

The dominance of Parisian banking was accompanied by the feeble development of regional banks. Until the 1860s, much of France remained a monetary and credit desert. Following an arrangement between the *Banque de France* and the finance ministry, notes issued by provincial banks had no currency outside of their regions. Provincial bankers invested in commercial activities on a small scale. Financial transactions involving small loans to peasants were made under the aegis of provincial notaries in a way that would already have been familiar in the six-teenth century.[159]

Modern deposit banking practices were limited. The banking system was not designed to drain savings in a way that would allow for them to be channeled into industrial development. In 1850, deposits administered by banks were 50 times less than those in Britain. British banking was decades ahead. In Britain, limited-liability banking firms, and their elaborate branch networks, funded a myriad of industrial companies. This development prefigured transformations that only oc-curred in France at the end of the nineteenth century.[160]

The financial system could not support rapid industrial investment. But while these deficiencies certainly limited growth, they were first and foremost a reflection—rather than a fundamental cause—of the lethargy of industrial develop-ment.[161] Banks formed part of a larger noncapitalist infrastructure, in which entre-preneurs were not compelled by competitive imperatives to maximize profits by systematically investing in productivity-enhancing facilities and machinery.

Over the decades that followed the Revolution, then, one overserves manufac-turing in disconnected regional hubs and insulated from foreign (including British capitalist) competition. Within these regional hubs, most workers had direct access to their means of production and subsistence (most importantly, land). Workers engaged with institutions which afforded them individual and collective control over labor processes, and which contributed to an allocation of labor, across differ-ent industrial branches, resistant to the logic of a capitalist market. These regional hubs were connected with one another by the commercial activities of merchants or merchant-manufacturers enjoying monopolistic control. The absence of capitalist price competition meant that industrial enterprises invested to mechanize produc-tion at a much slower pace than their British counterparts did. The industrialization of France over the first two-thirds of the nineteenth century was not propelled by market imperatives, but rather by producers who seized market opportunities.

Market Opportunities and Manufacturing Development, 1815–1860

Put simply, it was market *opportunities*, not market *compulsion*, that stimulated the first phase of industrialization in France. This perspective allows us to explain both the substantial industrial development as well as the remarkable slowness of this development relative to Britain.

Manufacturing was driven by opportunities in two main ways over the first two-thirds of the nineteenth century. The first one was tied to the production of luxury and semi-luxury products sold to elite and wealthy consumers at home and, in-creasingly, exported for consumption by notables and swelling capitalist classes abroad. The second way in which market opportunities sustained manufacturing was through the introduction of mechanized production in a protected and noncom-petitive domestic market. This latter dimension of the process of industrialization was tied to the production of less expensive, mass consumer goods even though even here, as we will see, concerns over quality and reputation often continued to prevail. Industrialization took place in the context of an overall noncompetitive market space neighboring a highly dynamic British capitalist economy and emulated the latter's industrial and technological successes. These two patterns of manufacturing development, through noncompetitive market stimuli, were reflected in a divide between pro-free trade and protectionist factions of entrepreneurs, with the former concentrated in regions geared toward luxury goods exports and the latter prevailing mostly among manufacturers focused on production for the domestic market.[162]

We begin with an analysis of export-led luxury production. As industry began to grow more rapidly under the Restoration, a substantial part of French manufactured products was directed toward foreign markets. The value of total French exports increased by 60 percent from 1831 to 1846 and by a remarkable 241 percent between 1848 and 1868. Meanwhile, the share of exports of manufactured goods in the national industrial product nearly doubled from the late 1820s to the late 1860s, from 11.3 percent to 19.5 percent. Thus, a significant part of the growth in manufacturing from the Restoration was due to an insertion in an international division of industrial labor in which France opted for markets for luxury and semi-luxury goods. While luxury products like champagne were sold in great quantity to foreign countries, manufactured goods represented 71 percent of the value of exports in the early 1830s, a proportion that increased to 74 percent on average from 1837 to 1846 before declining to 60 percent during the 1860s.[163] British exports grew rapidly during the nineteenth century, thanks to mass consumer goods made cheaper through cost-cutting strategies tied to gains in labor productivity facilitated by rapid and sustained mechanization. By contrast,

> the structure of French exports is not explained by comparative advantages provided by differences in labor productivity by sector. The goods exported were not those manufactured in France with the highest productivity, nor the ones for which productivity differentials were the most favorable, compared with English goods.[164]

Since rising French exports were not caused by price reductions and grew out of branches that did not experience any acceleration of productivity gains, they did not depend on the seizing of market shares away from Britain. French industrialization and rising exports were complementary with, and in fact closely dependent on, the British process of capitalist industrialization. While British industrialists made fortunes manufacturing and exporting cheap goods, most notably cotton products, their French counterparts exported mostly luxury and semi-luxury commodities for conspicuous consumption. Aristocrats and notables in Europe, and in different parts of Asia, Africa and Latin America, continued to buy these commodities. Most of the growth in exports of manufactured luxury goods, however, reflected the mounting purchasing power of capitalist classes in Britain and in the United States and, to a lesser extent, of commercial and other bourgeois classes in other parts of the world. The capitalist process of industrialization, which was rapidly maturing in Britain over the first two-thirds of the century and was taking-off in the United

States, thus contributed to a major expansion of French luxury manufacturing until the turn of the 1870s. The share of French exports shipped to Britain increased from 11 percent in 1835 to 33 percent in 1865. Between 1855 and 1865, exports of French manufactured goods in the direction of Britain increased by 196 percent, from a value of 345 million to a little over one billion francs.[165]

Rather than a response to market imperatives to improve cost-price ratios, growing manufacturing tied to foreign demand for luxury products offered an opportunity to develop long-standing commercial and manufacturing practices centered on skilled labor, quality, reputation and other marketing tactics aimed at excluding potential competitors. Indeed, the growth of high-end manufacturing from 1815 to 1860 took root in the system of production based on refinement and reputation of the Old Regime.[166] This system relied on skilled labor and largely on a traditional organization of production, often in artisanal workshops and small firms using tooling and techniques perfected over long periods. This tended to severely constrain mechanical innovations and, in any case, the commercial success of this form of production did not depend on a mass market. As explained by Patrick Verley, the key to success was not labor productivity gains or lower labor costs (wages were often lower in Switzerland, Germany or Austria), but quality and a claim to setting good taste and fashion. This involved building reputation through technical expertise and constant product innovation so as to shape fashion and exclude counterfeit and competition.[167]

The exclusion of competitors also continued to be accomplished through interregional and international trading networks. These networks and the growth of the luxury manufacturing to which they were tied were supported by the development of practices of informal imperial domination from 1815 to the 1870s. David Todd has shown how the complementarity of French and British patterns of industrial and foreign trade over this period was reflected in the geopolitical convergence of the two powers. Whereas France had fought Britain over European and global hegemony from the War of the Spanish Succession to the Napoleonic Wars, French elites came to recognize the geopolitical superiority of their old rival during the nineteenth century. Bellicose Anglophobe discourses continued to rage in the press and parliament, and the state pursued and accelerated its efforts to build up its military capacities so as to limit, and hopefully fill, the power gap between France and Britain. Yet, a major reorientation toward the British hegemon took place in parallel. In a context shaped by the Vienna Congress, which deprived France of European allies, and by France's continuous drive for influence on the European continent (upon which the British had relinquished territorial aspirations), the French opted to become the junior partner of an overseas informal empire under Britain's leadership.[168]

This emerging geopolitical orientation was formalized when François Guizot, upon becoming minister of foreign affairs in 1840, developed a policy of Entente cordiale with Britain to advance France's overseas influence. Often with tacit or active British support, the French state used gunboat diplomacy to establish asymmetrical partnerships with local elites and to impose unequal commercial treaties and export products on people's of the Levant, East and Southeast Asia and Latin America. France, for instance, joined Britain's campaign to open up China and gain commercial concessions during the Second Opium War in an effort to secure access to the material necessary for its domestic silk industry. Loans to foreign states, which grew after the 1850s, were also used to intrude on their internal affairs and as means of financial exaction.

Parallel to the expansion of its territorial empire in Algeria, France thus engaged in a process of informal imperialism—secreting racist and orientalist discourses along the way—that culminated under the Second Empire with a military expedition to topple the Mexican Republic and replace it with a friendly monarchy. Through this informal empire, founded on a balance of military coercion, diplomacy and cultural prestige, the French state created new market opportunities and secured exclusive advantages for its manufacturers, which facilitated the import of raw materials at advantageous rates—frequently by making good use of British global trade infrastructures—and the export of luxury commodities to subdue local elites eager for French refinement.[169]

Benefiting from this foreign domination and influence, which created market outlets through extra-economic means, French manufacturers sold large quantities of fancy goods to elites abroad. Exports of champagne and other wines and alcohol went from a value of 88 million francs in 1849 to 319 million in 1865. *Prêt-à-porter* clothing exports quintupled from 1850 to 1860, to reach a value of 200 million Francs, while exports of *articles de Paris*, which included bibelots, kitchenware and other fancy household goods, quadrupled, reaching 118 million Francs in 1865. Toward the end of the 1860s, *articles de Paris*, jewelry, and artificial flowers amounted to 15.5 percent of industrial exports, while, taken together, metal tools, machinery and chemicals amounted to only 8 percent.[170]

Silk goods, including tissues manufactured in Lyon, and ribbons made in Saint-Etienne, were the main French exports until 1870, amounting to around 20 percent of the total between 1820 and 1870. The number of looms in Lyon, the main silk center, rose from 30,000 in 1825 to 120,000 in 1875, but this spectacular growth took place without any transformation toward factory production. The number of looms set up in the rural region surrounding Lyon increased during this period. Within the city proper, production was organized on a *fabrique* model. This entailed a myriad of small workshops mastering craft techniques and cooperatively developing and diffusing new fashions and technical innovations through an intricate network under the aegis of the local *prud'hommes* council and municipal government. Within this framework, mechanization remained remarkably limited. In the early 1870s, out of the 120,000 looms in the city, only around 5,000 were power looms. It was only as a consequence of growing international competition and evolving technologies that silk producers were later forced to mechanize their operations. Prior to 1880, however, silk production remained in the domain of arts and crafts, not mechanized factory standardization.[171]

Silk producers exported two-thirds of their production between 1820 and 1860. Part of it was shipped to European countries and the Levant or reexported to Latin America through the United States, but the main clientele for silk goods were wealthy British and North American consumers. The global reputation of French silk products had already been established during the eighteenth century. For the most expensive silk fabrics, or products of "true" luxury, price variations did not affect demand, but market outlets remained limited. As a silk ribbon maker explained in 1861, for high-end products, "the taste makes the price," and labor costs simply did not affect selling prices. Outlets were more important for less expensive luxury or semi-luxury fabrics, and grew rapidly in the United States and Britain. Even in this case, however, Lyon's silk producers did not face much competition on foreign markets. A silk fabric producer of Lyon explained in 1860 that

> since our products are made for luxury consumption, it appeared to us that the perfection of the fabric, the radiance of the colors, and all that could enhance the beauty of our raw materials, so expensive on their own, are conditions more desirable than low prices, which are rarely attained without impacting quality… we do not hesitate to say that the whole silk commerce and industry has arrived, in our great manufacturing region, to a degree of strength and perfection that puts it above all foreign competition.[172]

Lyon's producers escaped competition thanks to a reputation developed over a long period on the basis of their technical mastery and superior quality of their products. Other silk manufacturing centers, in England, Germany or Switzerland, attempted to copy French models, but always did so with a lag of several months, as producers of Lyon, Saint-Étienne and other towns in France constantly developed new fashionable fabrics and products. French producers were however incapable of penetrating external markets for low-cost goods, which were seized by foreign competitors thanks to lower labor costs and cost-cutting techniques, including mechanization.[173]

Similarly, while they abandoned low-cost cotton goods aimed at mass consumption to British manufacturers—and focused on the protected domestic market for this type of products—French producers successfully exported quality and luxury cotton products. An Alsatian manufacturer named Engel spoke, also in 1861, of "the great export markets supplied exclusively by England and that we were never able to penetrate, even at the cost of great sacrifices, by selling at prices that barely covered production costs." Alsatian cotton firms focused instead on luxury printed cloth. Sales were here again made possible by reputation, technical expertise, good taste and constant fashion innovation to avoid counterfeit.[174]

The priority given to quality also shaped the manufacturing of woolen textiles. During the opening decade of the nineteenth century and until the end of the Napoleonic Wars, demand remained too limited for mechanization. While spinning doubled the value of raw cotton, it only added 10–15 percent to worsted wool, and consequently, profitable opportunities tied to mechanized production remained too limited to pursue. A phase of accelerated investment in facilities took place between 1814 and 1834 and resulted from easier access to mechanical technologies (which had already been developed and adopted within the cotton trade), from growing demand in the context of a protected domestic market, and from access to foreign markets at the end of the Napoleonic Wars.[175] Mechanization, however, was comparatively very limited.

In the manufacturing center of Reims, for instance, the rapid installation of wool-combing machines only took off from the Second Empire under the whip of foreign competition, which obligated manufacturers to modernize their mills to safeguard the capital already invested in the equipment in previous decades in a less competitive context. The number of combing machines in Reims increased from just 63 in 1853 to 709 in 1878. Again, the contrast with England is stark. In this country, hand combing rapidly decayed after the mid-1820s and almost completely disappeared by mid-century. The same goes for wool spinning and weaving. Reims had a mere 577 spinning power looms in 1860, but this figure grew rapidly afterward to 4,000 in 1870 and 7,000 in 1875. Handloom spinning remained preponderant in Fourmies, another major woolen textile center, until at least the second half of the 1860s. In comparison, Yorkshire, the major wool manufacturing region in Britain, had at least 3,500 power looms in 1835. Hand spinning had already become rare in the region for over a decade, while mechanized weaving surpassed hand weaving during the 1840s.[176]

Exports contributed to more than half of the growth in wool manufacturing. Once again, quality and reputation were instrumental for sales to elites abroad and at home. Wool producers, setting fashions and constantly offering new products, made high profits in France, England and North American markets, before selling leftovers at discount prices—which, thanks to reputation, were still 8–12 percent above similar products made by foreign producers—on Latin American markets the following year.[177]

Verley explains how the significance of ruling class consumption relative to the meager consumption of the working classes, together with a foreign trade mostly focused on conspicuous consumption, pushed manufacturers to continue to think like merchants rather than industrialists and to prioritize quality over productivity. Verley quotes André de Neuflize, a wool manufacturer whose advice to his son, written in 1836, was "representative of the mentality of a manufacturer of his time, who was a merchant first and foremost." Neuflize praised his trade, which he described as among the most commendable industrial activities, since it made it possible to limit competition and ensure quality through skills and expertise. He was suspicious however of the cotton trade, which was spreading at the time, because it was conducive to "speculation" that lead producers to "multiply production endlessly" through mechanization in a way that created competition and dissolved the character of the craft.[178]

Notwithstanding Neuflize's fears, until at least the 1860s, most cotton producers, including factory owners, continued to regard themselves as merchants and focused on product quality. They made sure, in any case, to manage markets so as to maximize profits while avoiding risks tied to competitive imperatives. As such, cotton manufacturing, which was largely geared toward domestic consumption, is emblematic of the second dimension of market opportunity-driven industrial development mentioned above: mechanized production emulating British industry in a protected and noncompetitive home market. This was also largely true for metallurgy until the Second Empire.

It is noteworthy that Gervais identifies similar processes of opportunity-seizing by industrial firms in the United States, also during the opening decades of the nineteenth century. As he explains, some US textile manufacturers first adopted mechanized looms not as part of an ongoing and systematic process of productivity improvement, but as a "punctual choice" to enter a specific market by using a recent technological innovation. Industrialization progressed slowly, "with a rhythm of its own," characterized by only "sporadic" technical progress in the organization of labor. Gervais insists that this course differed radically from the capitalist process of sustained mechanization that began to emerge from around the 1830s in different parts of the country, when industrial firms became compelled by market competition to continuously adopt technological innovations providing productivity gains.[179] In France, capitalist industrialization came later, but in the meantime, the mechanization of certain firms arose out of similar "punctual" choices inspired by market opportunities.

At the beginning of the nineteenth century, the profits of British capitalists were plain to see and inspired opportunistic French entrepreneurs. Patently profitable British technological innovations were adopted, and "through the technical education it provided, sometimes unwillingly, Britain was in a real sense the parent of modern French industry."[180] Over the first half of the nineteenth century, almost all the new methods diffused in French industries were from Britain. The mechanization of the cotton industry was effectuated by constant imitation of the British model.[181] Commenting on this process of emulation, Charles Coquelin, author of a comparative study on the French and English linen textile industries, asserted in 1839 that

> most French manufacturers behave with regard to the British as pupils to masters, and seem not to aspire to any other kind of merit than that of repeating their lessons faithfully; they believe themselves skillful only in imitating and following; they do not yet dare to act and judge by themselves.[182]

Textiles were the driving force of French industrialization for most of the nineteenth century. From the fall of the First Empire until the 1870s, as we just saw, textile production developed in large part on the basis of high-quality manufacturing and retained a strong artisanal dimension. While factories and industrialists appeared, merchants (who represented many of the incipient industrialists) and their age-old practices continued to play a fundamental role.[183]

Cotton manufacturing played a key part in this development, and it was this branch that modernized most rapidly during the first decades of the century. The number of cotton-producing enterprises almost doubled from the mid-1810s to the mid-1820s, and value added by cotton producers grew six times over from the 1780s to the 1850s. In the early 1840s, over two-thirds of cotton production was concentrated in three departments, namely Seine-Inférieure, Nord and Haut-Rhin. The Alsatian department of Haut-Rhin was the most productive of the three, and many of its entrepreneurs built factories using English machines. By contrast, Seine-Inférieure in Normandy was the largest cotton-producing department in the country, with a turnover around 30 percent larger than that of Haut-Rhin. The Norman department had more handlooms and preserved many of its semi-rural putting-out networks.[184]

The expansion of cotton production was sustained by the growing demand of the first decades of the nineteenth century. Elite consumption continued to fuel much of this production of high-end cloth, apparel, lingerie and handkerchiefs. Noble and rich bourgeois consumption established fashion standards to which one had to conform in order to remain respectable. Elite consumption was constantly renewed, and its total increased steadily over the eighteenth century and into the nineteenth. Bourgeois families tried to mimic the outfits of the elites, and from the turn of the century, they were increasingly able to do so thanks to decreasing prices brought about by the labor-saving effects of new machines. Using productivity-enhancing technologies, cotton manufacturers had greater latitude to reduce prices. An average yearly fall of prices of around 5 percent was recorded from 1810 to 1845, before a sharp deceleration of this fall from the late 1840s until the early 1860s. Though certainly related to the mechanization of production, a good part of this fall also stemmed from the declining cost of raw cotton, which fell over 57 percent from 1820 to 1860. At any rate, falling prices fueled the expansion of popular consumption of coarse cotton products across the period.

Consumption of textiles (mainly cotton) increased at a rate of 3–4 percent a year between 1820 and 1840. From the Restoration to the end of the Second Empire, it increased approximately sixfold. Calicoes became increasingly popular, and by the end of the Restoration and during the July Monarchy, their consumption was well established among workers, though it remained limited, as secondhand consumption, household production and constant repairs remained the rule. The increased interest in cheaper cotton goods resulted in a reduction of the consumption of traditional textiles such as linen, hemp and wool among the rural and urban working classes, as these products were increasingly confined to luxury and semi-luxury production.[185]

The key point is that the development and spread of mechanized cotton manufacturing (printing, spinning and to a significantly less extent, weaving) only took place once the domestic market was shielded from British competition and, furthermore, that protectionism greatly contributed to the shape, and noncapitalist nature, of this industrialization process. From the early 1790s until 1815, war dislocated international trade, which was further disrupted by a series of governmental measures. A first initiative prohibited the import of many cotton and woolen cloth products in 1796. The list of banned lines was extended in 1799, and Napoleon's continental system, following lobbying efforts by cotton manufacturers, prohibited imports of British cotton goods in 1806. Britain retaliated with its own trade embargo in 1807. The impulse given by these measures to cotton manufacturing in Normandy, the North and Alsace was "spectacular."

Before the commercial treaty of 1786, cotton merchants had largely eschewed investments in spinning and weaving factories. Spinning and weaving were done in peasant households or in artisan workshops. Merchants bought cloth abroad before printing on it in French workshops or factories. It was from around 1800 that cotton printing, which had until then remained an artisanal industry, began to modernize and to mechanize, with the installation of cylindrical presses in a growing number of factories. The new technology was much more efficient than traditional manual block printing, and the growth of mechanized printing stimulated demand for unfinished white cotton cloth that could no longer be bought in Britain. Unable to order cloth from Britain and shielded from the latter's competition, French merchants and *fabricants* turned to mechanical spinning to supply yarn to a growing number of handloom weavers.[186]

The number of mechanical spindles grew from 300,000 in 1800 to close to a million in 1810, and eventually rose to more than four million in 1850. For entrepreneurs, these initial investments were often small but yielded large profits. Yet, because these were opportunity-driven investments, they remained less impressive and more irregular than the competitively driven developments taking place in English cotton facilities, where there were already five million mechanical spindles in 1810.[187] Consider the different ways British and French cotton firms reacted to the slump of the mid-1820s, which was caused by bad harvests that hiked grain prices and reduced demand for textile products.[188] Studies of manufacturers in the Nord department, for instance, show the high number of firms that paused activities—looms stopped spinning and factories that had just been constructed were sometimes disassembled in reaction to receding demand. In contrast, cotton manufacturers in Manchester were constrained by decreasing demand and increased competition "to seek every means possible to reduce the costs of production. This was done chiefly by speeding-up machinery and by adding power-loom weaving to spinning."[189]

The protectionism of the second half of the 1790s, renewed and stabilized by tariffs and prohibitions in 1816, spurred the industrialization of cotton production. Yet, it also gave this process a clear "dualist" character, as factories and mechanized production developed side by side with dispersed rural and traditional production of at least half of cotton goods in 1860.[190] The pace of mechanization differed from one region to another. Alsatian cotton industrialists proceeded with backward integration of mechanized production, from printing to spinning and more partially until the late nineteenth century, weaving. Meanwhile, Normandy and the North mechanized at a slower pace and less systematically. In Normandy, even as factory spinning grew, smaller workshops remained widespread in the first half of the nineteenth century. Norman manufacturers did not hurry to improve tools and output, nor to renew their installations once they had engaged in factory production. Likewise, production techniques evolved relatively slowly in the North even after mechanization had begun.

Alsatian manufacturers were more dynamic: they invested in new installations and frequently improved their equipment. Alsace also witnessed the parallel development of a chemical industrial branch and from the early 1820s, of machine building firms. These firms provided capital goods directly inspired by English engineering to textile manufacturers and contributed to replacing the machines that had been smuggled in from England during the previous decades. The concentration of production was much more advanced in Alsace than it was in Normandy: during the first half of the 1860s, the average number of workers per mill reached 280 in the Haut-Rhin while it remained a mere 80 in the Seine-Inférieure.[191]

Alsatian producers thus became more productive than their Norman counterparts. During the 1840s, the spindles of Norman mechanized looms could not pass 4,000 revolutions per minute, whereas the most advanced Alsatian mills often reached 5,500. Alsatian yarn prices decreased by nearly 75 percent between 1815 and 1837 (but decreased much less rapidly from the mid-1840s)—the highest fall of all cotton producing regions—in spite of the fact that Alsatian firms had to pay much more to buy raw cotton than did firms in Normandy and the North. These falling prices allowed Alsatians to sell yarn and cloth in Normandy, where it would be woven and printed.[192]

Yet, it is remarkable that while its mills and cotton trade were significantly less efficient, at least compared to Alsace, Normandy remained the largest cotton producing region in France. The percentage of spindles in Alsace, relative to the rest of the country, climbed from 7 percent at the end of the First Empire to 23.8 percent in 1844, a very substantial increase. Yet, after this date, the proportion stagnated until the late 1860s, "as if this industrial branch had exhausted its exceptional growth potential, from then on conforming to the average growth rate of other French regions."[193] This halt was, in fact, in large part due to the loss of foreign market shares from the late 1830s, and partially, but increasingly, to a turn to woolens from the 1840s. From 1812 to 1844, the number of new spindles put into use reached 745,000 in Alsace, whereas in Haute-Normandie that number reached 1,221,000. Haute-Normandie thus remained ahead of Alsace in terms of production volume, in spite of the fact that producers in the former region invested significantly less to mechanize their facilities and had lower levels of labor productivity.[194]

These regional disparities were related to the dissimilar types of cotton goods and clienteles. Normandy produced cheaper cotton clothes (that became increasingly popular as linen, hemp and woolen cloth receded) for the domestic (and protected colonial) market. Alsace, meanwhile, as we saw above, focused on high-end goods fashionable in rich social milieus at home, but mostly abroad, with much of its output directed toward London for local consumption and reexport elsewhere. In Mulhouse, the main industrial town of Alsace, manufacturers abandoned cheaper common cloth and concentrated on costly fashions. One should bear in mind that while Norman producers manufactured cheap cloth and apparel for the mass market, they remained farthest from the British capitalist model. Put another way, though they also produced for consumers with tight budgets, Norman manufacturers, unlike their British counterparts, did not have to aggressively and continuously reinvest profits to improve equipment, nor to adopt modern hierarchical modes of labor management so as to maximize productivity gains.[195]

The Alsatians were more dynamic and invested more rapidly to mechanize part of production, yet their workforce costs remained much higher than in other regions, representing a larger proportion of total value added. This apparent paradox is explained by the fact that the success of Alsatians firms, as we saw, was largely based on the production of printed luxury fabrics, manufactured with quality yarn and cloth and sold to wealthy consumers—more so than on their ability to cut the costs of manufactured yarn and cloth. In Mulhouse, the major cotton center of the region, "the finished product was of high quality" and therefore "competitive in foreign markets." Mulhousien firms penetrated foreign markets not so much through price competition, but rather thanks to superior quality and reputation, manufacturing "finer fabrics" and "what the French call *tissue de fantaisie*." As David Landes explains, following fashions (and trying to set trends), "the enterprise aimed at diversification and flexibility rather than specialization; the result was short runs that helped raise unit costs substantially above those of comparable mills in Britain."[196] Put simply, Alsatian manufacturers capitalized on growing opportunities to mechanize stages of production while preserving the technical expertise and artisanal character of stages that ensured their reputation and sales among elites at home and abroad.

Michel Hau explains that it was the mastery of "delicate" craft printing techniques, often performed by hand, combined with advanced dye chemistry, that allowed Alsatian firms to make profits on the domestic and, especially, on foreign markets. The fine printed cloth of the large Schlumberger firm, for example, made profits, which, after the 1850s, compensated for losses occasioned by the firm's spinning and weaving departments in times of crisis. Alsatian industrialists, including textile and mechanical - equipment - producing companies, concentrated on quality and product reputation rather than on competitive prices for their success. This emphasis on the collective reputation for quality of Mulhouse's firms becomes obvious when one considers that the town's industrialists did not seek to keep industrial secrets from one another. During the 1820s, industrialists founded the Société Industrielle de Mulhouse as a tool of cooperation to develop new techniques, to compare individual firm experiences and to diffuse and share scientific and technical knowledge.[197]

Because cost-efficiency was not the fundamental condition for the success of its firms, even as the most dynamic cotton manufacturing region in France, Alsace still lagged far behind Britain in terms of mechanization in the first half of the nineteenth century. While most British cotton clothes were woven with mechanical looms around 1830, the number of handlooms used for weaving continued to grow in Alsace, reaching 31,000 in 1834 against 3,090 power looms. The number of handlooms decreased during the 1840s, while the number of power looms increased, but the former still predominated in 1847. British spinning mills, moreover, had twice the number of spindles per worker. Even when mechanized weaving became prevalent in Alsace, the region's average productivity lagged behind that of foreign competitors. In the wake of the free trade agreements of the 1860s, as prices set in Manchester and in Zurich became prevalent in France, Alsatian spinning and weaving mills were unable to match the production costs set by English and Swiss competitors, and only high-end printed Alsatian goods remained competitive on French and international markets thanks to their quality and reputation.[198]

Alsace's firms did not fundamentally break with traditional commercial strategies prioritizing quality and reputation, and did not engage in systematic price competition, until France lost the region to Germany in 1871. Alsace was then introduced into the most dynamic economy of Continental Europe, which was experiencing rapid capitalist industrialization. The nature of the "French economic space had for a long period accustomed Alsatian industrialists to prioritize product quality over production costs," but "the characteristics of the German market compelled them to completely reverse their order of priority." In this new context, cheap mass consumption prevailed, and once confronted with "customers who had low expectations regarding product quality, industrial producers were in permanent competition over prices." Alsatian firms then relinquished hand printing and increasingly mechanized, since "they ran up against competition from southern Germany and Saxony and were forced to engage in a sustained price war."[199]

In spite of disparities between them, all French cotton manufacturing regions developed according to opportunity-driven strategies over the first half of the nineteenth century. From the first decade of the century, cotton industrialists, *"sought out new opportunities presented by the fervent demand for cotton and by the technological innovations available."*[200] Even though the capitalist competition from Britain from 1786 to the early 1790s came to an end, the new British "mode," as William M. Reddy puts it, "of production continued to make its influence felt on thinking but not on prices." Indeed, French cotton producers were shielded from British price competition while, within France, the market "was not well organized enough to provide that stable competitive pressure that one usually supposes to be the chief virtue of the market system." Markets were not "price-forming" and did not force producers to engage in "cost-conscious management," as "most profits were taken immediately out of circulation." Yet, the higher productivity and profits that could be gained from English looms were easily perceived. Even if markets did not impose competition, to quote Reddy again, "it does not take great efficiency for prices to reflect a 20-fold advantage in productivity."[201] Industrialists discovered the new opportunities offered to them, and it was this awareness, rather than competitive imperatives, that drove industrialization.

In short, French merchant and manufacturers could learn from the British experience without enduring, thanks to protectionism, the impact of British competition, and it was only in this context that it became rational for them to engage in mechanized cotton production. In this safer setting, "if one could just get a set of the new spinning machines into operation, one was assured a handsome profit."[202]

As prices declined due to labor-saving machinery, demand improved and cotton manufacturers obtained further opportunities, which stimulated additional mechanization. What is truly striking, however, is how much permissiveness cotton industrialists were granted by "how weak the force of competition was and how much real diversity the price-clearing mechanism of the yarn markets tolerated."[203]

Cotton spinners could decrease selling prices to enlarge sales just as they could raise them if they perceived that this could lead to higher profits. The reduction of production costs, brought about by the new mechanical technologies, often fueled enormous profits rather than result in price cuts for consumers. A report produced by a state official in the early 1860s following years of inquiry showed that Norman cotton producers had been

> only preoccupied by retaining or accumulating unbelievable profits, main-
> tained or increased yarn and fabric prices, while they obtained raw materials
> for almost nothing ... This or that manufacturer earned two million francs per
> year while people did not pay a dime less for the clothing that they bought.[204]

In an inquiry produced in 1855, Jean Dollfus, a leading Alsatian manufacturer, declared that spinning enterprises were at times generating profits that were 25–40 percent higher than those of foreign firms.[205]

Claude Fohlen argues that costs represented a "peripheral" concern for cotton industrialists. Looking at reports from the mid-nineteenth century:

> one is struck ... by how little the notion [of cost price] is present in employ-
> er's declarations. Never do they provide the slightest information concerning
> production in their firms, not by omission or out of discretion, but because
> the prosperity of their business was measured by earned money, not by quan-
> tities being produced.[206]

Entrepreneurs produced annual or biannual balance sheets in which "production did not enter into consideration."[207] The market in which they evolved was such that cotton producers made profits without having to pay attention to the way that their facilities and the labor power they hired were organized. As Charles Noiret, a handloom weaver in Rouen, put it in 1836, "the profits of the producers were such that they did not bother to count them: they bought, they produced, and sold according to habit and their capital quintupled in a single year ... They got rich without knowing why."[208]

Manufacturers made most of their profits in circulation, not in production. They made no sustained efforts to take control of production, impose labor discipline or optimize their labor/output and cost/price ratios. Spinners and weavers retained their autonomy at work and capitalist entrepreneurial control of the type existing in the British factory system remained absent. Efforts by some mill owners to develop new factory rules were only half-hearted, and in the end completely unsuccess-ful.[209] These new measures were, in fact, "not aimed at increasing productivity so much as at ensuring quality and uniformity of an article whose success depended heavily on appearance."[210]

This focus on quality and reputation was related to the fact that the industri-alization of the cotton trade had been undertaken by merchants who continued to rely on monopolies over segmented markets. Manufacturers were for the most part traders, either larger merchants or *fabricants* organizing local putting-out networks, and retained traditional business practices in an economic context not fundamentally different from the Old Regime. Merchants acted as intermediaries between isolated producers and consumers. Their central economic function endured in Rouen, Lyon, Lille, Roubaix-Tourcoing, Mulhouse and other major industrial centers.[211]

A number of *fabricants* were in fact *sans fabrique*—merchants without mills. They began to invest in factories only gradually, and once they did, old habits endured. The industrial environment of Lille, a major cotton manufacturing center of the North, allowed merchants to maintain their commanding position. Productive tasks and interest in technical matters remained embedded within a commercial outlook focused on exchange and trade networks.[212]

In the nearby town of Roubaix, another industrial center, manufacturers similarly persisted in traditional commercial practices. They formed a consultative chamber of manufactures in 1805, and in addition to actively agitating against tariff reductions on foreign goods, they fought for the restitution of official regulations that had ensured the quality of products under the Old Regime. Similar demands were presented to the authorities on several occasions during the following decade with the support of Lille's chamber of commerce. In 1816, Roubaix's industrialists sent a missive to the Minister of the Interior, claiming that their "cotton mills had made great progress over the last years" and that their mills now "only needed to sustain their reputation ... in order to retain access to *négociants* and consumers." In 1821, unable to convince the state to reset industrial regulations abolished during the Revolution, manufacturers from Roubaix and neighboring Tourcoing formed an organization to establish its own quality seals and police manufacturing standards for cotton goods. These seals of regional quality, together with the help of a restricted circle of trusted and privileged traders, became the basis on which manufacturers sold clothes.[213]

Moreover, like the merchants of the previous century, manufacturers preserved a *rentier* outlook toward their firms, which they saw more as interest-bearing investments than as productive industrial endeavors. Though Alsatian manufacturers tended to own and manage their enterprises more steadily from one generation to the next than did their counterparts in other regions, they mostly saw these enterprises as a means of social ascension to an aristocratic lifestyle and high-status public functions.[214]

Crucially, textile manufacturers did nothing to surmount the fragmented markets, which allowed them to secure high profits without having to systematically improve their mills' productivity. Fragmentation and oligopolistic cornering were still deeply entrenched in the first half of the nineteenth century. Mohamed Kasdi shows that *négociants*—who were also often manufacturers—from the North manipulated the prices of cotton products by flooding the region with credit granted to shopkeepers or by drying up credit when trade did not allow them to secure expected revenues.[215] As Jean-Pierre Hirsch explains, for the period stretching from 1780 to 1860,

> the logic of an ongoing decompartmentalizing of circulation, of a levelling of costs and prices did not exist in the attitudes of the vast majority [of] merchants, or even in the declarations of their representatives. Above all, as

years passed, nothing indicated an evolution toward a less 'imperfect' market, nor a will to reduce the number of filters through which supply and demand were at play.[216]

Merchants and manufacturers happily adopted technologies developed by British firms but eschewed the British economic strategies based on cost-cutting. Lille's chamber of commerce, active in one of the main industrial centers of the country, "did not have words harsh enough to describe the industrial policy practiced by English producers, the 'progressive debasement' of their prices, their 'bankruptcy prices,' a 'state of overproduction that had become the normal state of the country.'"[217]

Because of the prevailing social property relations,

> the French cotton industry continued to lag far behind that of Britain. Plants were smaller; machines were older, less efficient... It profited in the first half of the century from growing wealth and population at home and the opening of overseas markets like Algeria. But its expansion, which rested on the exclusion of competition, was paid for in slower overall economic growth.[218]

Linen production, which did not benefited from protectionist measures like cotton manufacturers did, collapsed after 1815 as a result of English competition. Investment in manufacturing returned during the 1830s but remained limited until a substantial tariff on linen yarn was adopted in 1842, allowing the trade to develop in the following years. The number of spindles rose from 40,000 in 1840 to 472,000 in 1857. The return of English competition after the 1860s compelled manufacturers, who had established facilities under a protectionist shield, to mechanize and concentrate production in order to stay afloat. In England, however, this process of mechanization had already been well underway since the 1820s.[219]

Metallurgy developed in market conditions, and following a logic, similar to those prevalent in the textile trades oriented mainly toward the domestic market. Annual production of pig iron grew from 100,000 to 600,000 tons from 1815 to 1847, a level of output still far behind the British level of five million tons. French metallurgy, moreover, trailed behind the British in technological innovations. Demand for farm implements and industrial equipment, together with the competitive nature of the British market, fueled the speedy diffusion of productive techniques. Coke smelting was one of the key technical novelties of the period and greatly improved iron making. Its use to produce pig iron became universal in Britain at the beginning of the nineteenth century.[220]

French metallurgy began to use pig iron and other British technologies in a quest for "global innovation" in the 1820s and the following decades.[221] These developments were fueled, albeit relatively weakly, by demand for equipment tied to the mechanization of the textile trades and more significantly, by canal building and other infrastructure projects. These technological transfers were undertaken, thanks to protectionism following the implementation of high tariffs for metal imports in 1822. Yet, as Bertrand Gille explains, beyond the impetus of market demand, another vital stimulant for investments in large factories was "the English example, the existence of a developed industrial world."[222] As was the case for cotton production, the French metal trade was modernized through market opportunities and attempts to emulate British achievements in a protected economic and noncompetitive space, where state policies played a role in sustaining demand, especially by supporting railroad building.[223]

Large firms corresponding to the "global innovation" model were founded in Alais, Decazeville, Le Creusot and Terrenoire during the 1820s. But they were badly hit by the economic crisis of that decade and except for Terrenoire, went bankrupt by 1829–1830. Before the onset of the first phase of railroad building during the 1840s, demand for metal products was still too narrow to support the "global innovation" strategy of the most ambitious entrepreneurs, and it was impossible for these companies to compete with British producers on foreign markets.[224]

In 1830, only 9 percent of pig iron was produced using coke fuel. Most foundries remained small operations using traditional techniques and tools. In 1840, little more than 40 blast furnaces used coke against 462 fueled by charcoal. In 1845, 60 percent of pig iron was still produced using charcoal. The boom in railway construction of the second half of the 1840s accelerated the development of large enterprises appropriating English technologies. Yet, traditional metal consumption, mostly for local agricultural purposes, remained dominant, and small foundries scattered across the countryside continued to eschew modernization. Traditional smelting methods using charcoal reached their highest volume in 1856.[225] Hence, even as modern metallurgy was emerging, and

> in contrast to English iron making, which put the emphasis on producing large quantities of a relatively low-quality, low-priced commodity, [French] steelmaking remained in … a quasi-artisanal industry in which skilled workers produced small quantities of high-quality products at correspondingly high prices.[226]

The end of tariff protection contributed to the formation of capitalist imperatives, under the Second Empire, and had a deep transformative impact on metallurgy. Up to that point, firms were shielded from foreign and domestic competition, and this reined in the modernization of the sector. Markets for metal goods were fragmented and regionally isolated—and producers responded to ad hoc demand for traditional domestic and agricultural needs within a protected economic space. High transportation costs and long distances insulated producers from price competition, and this situation often endured even as large-scale modern production was emerging. In the early 1830s, transportation could amount to as much as a third or a half of the costs of manufacturing coke pig iron.[227]

As was the case for other industrial sectors, markets were here again structured by commercial interests. Parisian metal traders cornered and mediated between segmented markets. They built networks to secure privileged access to distinct markets and, even as large-scale and modernized metallurgy was consolidated after the 1830s, price fixing and dividing up of markets remained the rule. As contemporaries observed, "competition was only a fiction."[228] Émile Pereire—whom we will meet again in the next chapter for his role in forging modern financial institutions under the Second Empire—was one the prominent developers and administrators of railroad companies from the 1830s to the 1850s. Based on his rich entrepreneurial experience, he asserted that the rail production market, which was instrumental to the growth and modernization of French iron foundries, had continuously been the theater of price fixing, a generalized practice from at least 1845 to 1858.[229] In the second half of the 1850s, railroad companies doubled their efforts to curb these practices and to submit metal producing firms to competitive imperatives that would compel them to accept market prices and to maintain production costs below these prices. Until then, however, in the absence of the efforts of the railroad companies to break monopolies and forge an integrated national market, and of free trade and foreign competitive pressures, "the rail market was not free and competitive."[230]

Conclusion

This chapter has shown that neither early modern nor the postrevolutionary France provided fertile terrain for an industrial revolution. Old Regime France did not undergo agrarian capitalism and therefore did not develop mass-consumer and labor markets without which industrialization could only proceed slowly. The productive sphere of the economy was still subsumed under a commercial sphere controlled by closed networks of merchants in charge of monopolies over market segments and thus able to turn supply and demand to their advantage. Industry did not face price competition or the obligation to systematically develop the productive forces.

As the geopolitical power of capitalist Britain led to French military defeats, especially after the mid-eighteenth century, liberal intellectuals and state officials attempted to reform the economy. Their policies, however, challenged the deep-seated interests of the ruling classes—including those of large merchants—and were either retracted or had limited impact. Industry continued to lag its British counterpart toward the end of the Old Regime. While eliminating formal barriers to trade and industry, the Revolution did not alter economic structures. As was described in the previous chapter, the Revolution consolidated peasant property and, as explained in the current one, strengthened customary regulations of industrial trades. The Revolution thus delayed the formation of labor and consumer markets. Markets, at any rate, remained noncompetitive and beholden to oligopolistic merchant networks. Market opportunities, rather than competitive imperatives, continued to propel industrialization from 1815 to the 1860s. This pattern of growth entailed sales to notable and capitalist consumers, facilitated by informal imperialism and territorial expansion in Algeria, as well as sales on a protected domestic market. In this context, investment in machinery guaranteed high profits and minimal risks. The upshot was an industrial sector that grew on its own terms, but also remarkably poorly compared to British industry.

As this chapter has made clear, this contrast was not due to a novel French model of industrial development as revisionist historians claim. France's economic pattern was different from that of capitalist Britain—however much the former borrowed from the latter's technological innovations—which was for a significant period the unique developmental model. Far from being original, France remained like other continental European economies (at least until they engaged in capitalist restructuring processes of their own). In other words, the reason why French industry performed poorly compared to Britain (though it outperformed several continental countries before falling behind new competitors over the course of the 1800s) was because of the absence of capitalist social property relations and rules for reproduction. As we have insisted, industrial firms evolved not under the compulsion of competitive imperatives, but rather by seizing opportunities to profit from fragmented markets over which they and merchants (who were often simultaneously industrial agents) held sway.

The capitalist development of industry only began in the last decades of the nineteenth century. Even then, however, it still faced profound obstacles, and its maturation did not occur until much later in the twentieth century.

Notes

1 Crouzet 2003. Crouzet provides an excellent overview of historiographical debates on French economic growth in the nineteenth century; see also Barjot 2012; Grantham 1997; Heywood 1992.
2 Labrousse 1954–1955; Hoffman 1963.
3 Clapham 1921; Fohlen 1973; Léon 1960; Morazé 1946; Sée 1942.
4 Clough 1946; Dunham 1951; Palmade 1972.
5 Landes 1949, p, 61.
6 Asselain 1984, p. 129–32; Bairoch 1965; Barjot 2014, p. 94; Beltran and Griset 1994, p. 7–17; Broder 1993; Caron 1995, p. 30–31; Lévy-Leboyer 1968; Rioux 1989, p. 105, 115.
7 Bairoch 1976, p. 283; Beaud 2010, p. 132; Grantham 1997, p. 370–71; Heywood 1992, p. 13–14, 16–22; Maddison 1982, p. 44–45; Rioux 1989, p. 105.
8 Marczewski 1965; Lévy-Leboyer and Bourguignon 1985; Markovitch 1965; O'Brien and Keyder 1978; Toutain 1961; 1965.
9 Crouzet 2003, p. 224; Grantham 1997, p. 370–71; Heywood, p. 13–14.
10 Asselain 1991; Crafts 1984; Dormois 1997; Kemp 1971; Salomon 1991.
11 In the most influential revisionist contribution published in English, Patrick O'Brien and Calgar Keyder (1978, p. 22–23) assert that "growth rates of real per capita output" represent "the best single measure available" to assess France's economic record.
12 Bergeron 1978; Bouvier 1987; Crouzet 1964; 1966; Fohlen 1978; Horn 2006; 2010; 2012; Lévy-Leboyer 1964; Marseille 1997; O'Brien and Keyder 1978.
13 O'Brien and Keyder 1978, p. 12.
14 O'Brien and Keyder 1978, p. 18.
15 O'Brien and Keyder 1978, p. 90.
16 Asselain 1984, p. 85; Lemarchand 2008, p. 53: Léon 1993[1970], p. 218; Smith 2006, p. 18–19; Woronoff 1994, p. 76–79, 82, 103, 184. Guillaume Daudin estimates that yearly nominal industrial growth averaged 1.7–1.8 percent between 1701–1710 and 1781–1790; Daudin 2011, p. 28, 49–50. However, using 1701–1710 as a base biases the result. These were years of severe depression, even famine. If the measure started in 1730 or 1740, average annual growth rates would be much lower than 1.7–1.8 percent a year.
17 Daudin 2011, p. 22.

18 Appleby 2010, p. 59; Chassagne 1981, p. 36; 1991, p. 21–22, 25; Cheminade 1994; Daudin 2011, p. 52–53, 55–59, 120–21, 146, 149–50; Léon 1993[1970], p. 219, 252; Lévy-Leboyer 1997, p. 357; Liu 1994, p. 49, 57; Smith 2006, p. 19; Woronoff 1994, p. 13–14, 35, 36, 79–81, 83–88, 104.
19 Chassagne 1981, p. 37–40, 46; Liu 1994, p. 70; Gervais 2004, p. 26–27, 32, 35–36, 45–47; Grenier 1996, p. 21, 420.
20 Daudin 2011, p. 30. Our translation.
21 Sewell 2021, p. 43, 50–51, 57–58. Emphasis added.
22 Daudin 2011, p. 23.
23 Chassagne 1981, p. 52; Gervais 2004, p. 25–26, 28; Grenier 1996, p. 21, 241–68; Liu 1994, p. 57–58; Verley 1997, p. 96.
24 Belhoste 1994, p. 460–62; Gayot 1985, p. 430–38; Koulischer 1931, p. 38; Léon 1993[1990], p. 250–51, 257–59; Smith 2006, p. 18; Woronoff 1994, p. 88–89.
25 Daudin 2011, p. 43, 46; Chassagne 1979, p. 104; 1981, p. 49; Léon 1993[1970], p. 260–61; Liu 1994, p. 82; Smith 2006, p. 19–21, 132; Woronoff 1994, p. 78, 91–98.
26 Daudin 2011, p. 38, 44; Jones 1995, p. 90; Lemarchand 2008, p. 53–63, 110–11; Léon 1993[1970], p. 243, 260; Parker 1996, p. 214; Smith 2006, p. 18; Woronoff 1994, p. 104, 143, 184.
27 Boyns, Edwards, and Nikitin 1997, p. 408; Cheminade 1994; Cheney 2017, p. 22–23; DuPlessis 2016, p. 172; Lemarchand 1995; Léon 1993[1970], p. 235, 264–65.
28 Gervais, Lemarchand, and Margairaz 2016, p. 5, 7; Chassagne 1981, p. 49–50.
29 Asselain 1984, p. 67; Chassagne 1991, p. 208–209; Daudin 2011, p. 147; Léon 1993[1970], p. 207–12, 254–55; Plessis 2001; Woronoff 1994, p. 37–39, 94–95.
30 Hoffman, Postel-Vinay, and Rosenthal 1999; 2001; 2019.
31 Hoffman, Postel-Vinay, and Rosenthal 1999, p. 92.
32 Hoffman, Postel-Vinay, and Rosenthal 1999, p. 90.
33 Hoffman, Postel-Vinay, and Rosenthal 1999, p. 88.
34 Lemarchand, McWatters, and Pineau-Defoi 2016, p. 31.
35 Ballot 1978, p. 11; Beaud 2010, p. 59–61; Harris 1998; Léon 1993[1970], p. 218, 221–24, 239–41, 245, 251; Minard 2007a; Smith 2006, p. 14, 19; Woronoff 1994, p. 184.
36 Parker 1996, p. 211.
37 Daudin 2011, p. 22, 24; Kasdi 2014, p. 22; Parker 1996, p. 211; Smith 2006, p. 17; Woronoff 1994, p. 22, 27–28, 40, 180.
38 Asselain 1984, p. 62; Léon 1993[1970], p. 197, 229–30; Meyer 2016, p. 15, 33, 35.
39 English American colonies were 10–15 times more populous than the French around the mid-eighteenth century; see Meyer 2016, p. 99.
40 Post 2017; Wood 2003, p. 89–117.
41 Blackburn 2010, p. 444–45; Brenner 2003; Smith 2006, p. 16–17.
42 Cheney 2017, p. 4, 7, 43, 46–47, 50.
43 Brenner 1977, p. 36–37.
44 Cheney 2017, p. 33, 45, 54, 61, 65, 69; Meyer 2016, p. 127–28.
45 Asselain 1984, p. 55–56, 64–70; Cheney 2017, p. 16; Léon 1993[1970], p. 196, 198, 229; Meyer 2016, p. 103–104, 192; Parker 1996, p. 210.
46 Daudin 2011; Todd 2022, p. 108.
47 Asselain 1984, p. 56–57, 67–68, 95; Smith 2006, p. 17.
48 Marzagalli 2012, p. 262.
49 Jones 1995, p. 99–100. Léon (1993[1970], p. 229) also stresses that the absolute value of industrial goods sold on foreign markets increased while the proportion of total exports of these sales stayed the same.
50 Lemarchand 2008, p. 119: "À la veille de la Révolution, la Grande-Bretagne est déjà en passe de gagner contre la France la bataille planétaire du commerce et celle de l'industrie moderne."
51 Wood 2002b, p. 100.

52 Brenner 1977, p. 60.
53 Appleby 2010, p. 80; Brenner 1987b, p. 318; Parker 1996, p. 211; Wrigley 2000, p. 118, 122.
54 Parker 1996, p. 211.
55 Brenner and Isett 2008, p. 635, 648–49.
56 Wood 2002b, p. 105.
57 Wood 2002b, p. 98–99.
58 Wood 2002b, p. 99.
59 Appleby 2010, p. 83
60 Zmolek 2014, p. 265. See also Marzagalli 2012, p. 255.
61 Wood 2002b, p. 139.
62 Brenner 1977, p. 51.
63 Wood 2002b, p. 134–35.
64 Wood 2002b, p. 136.
65 Kerridge quoted in Wood 2002b, p. 135.
66 Nash 2005, p. 118.
67 Wood 2002b, p. 104–105.
68 Teschke 2003, p. 173–77.
69 Jones 1995, p. 92, 95; Léon 1993[1970], p. 174; Minard 1998, p. 280; 2008, p. 84; Margairaz 1986; Woronoff 1994, p. 32. Léon (1993[1970]) notes that in this context, characterized by poor means of commodity transportation, merchants had a conception of space-time that was sharply different from ours and that they did not valorize time as we do.
70 Appleby 2010, p. 51.
71 Parker 1996, p. 32; see also Woronoff 1994, p. 40.
72 Grenier 1996, p. 417, 420.
73 DuPlessis 2014, p. 172.
74 Gervais 2004; 2008; 2014; 2020.
75 Gervais 2014, p. 23; DuPlessis 2014, p. 174–75.
76 Gervais 2020; Marzagalli, 2012, p. 259.
77 Gervais 2014, p. 22, 24. Duplessis 2014, p. 171–73 and Grenier 1996, p. 424, 427; Margairaz 1986, p. 1225–32; Minard 2008, p. 84.
78 Gervais 2014, p. 22, 24. See also Daudin 2011, p. 125, 133–34, 152–53, 164–72; Grenier 1996, p. 417–18.
79 Daudin 2011, p. 184–85.
80 Gervais 2020, p. 10.
81 Gervais 2020, p. 12.
82 Duplessis 2014, p. 173; Gervais, Lemarchand, and Margairaz 2014, p. 9; Lermarchand, McWatters, and Laure Pineau-Defois 2014, p. 31.
83 Minard 1998, p. 281.
84 Pollard 1965, p. 51; Woronoff 1994, p. 70, 73, 76–77, 80.
85 Crouzet 1985, p. 112; McNally 1988, p. 90–131. For a discussion of the reform attempted by Gournay and his supporters, see Deyon and Guignet 1980 and Jones 1995.
86 McNally 1988, p. 89, 145, 151, 265.
87 Minard 1998, p. 318.
88 Jones 1995, p. 111.
89 Daudin 2011, p. 60–64.
90 Gervais 2014, p. 24.
91 Minard 1998, p. 117. See also Deyon and Guignet 1980, p. 626.
92 Crouzet 1966, p. 271–72. Our translation. Woronoff 1994, p. 183.
93 Asselain 1984, p. 98; Démier 2000, p. 40; Léon 1993[1970], p. 249–50; Parker 1996, p. 214; Reddy 1984, p. 53.
94 Smith 2006, p. 21.
95 Asselain 1984, p. 107; Lemarchand 2008, p. 112; Reddy 1984, p. 57; Walton 2014, p. 49.

96 Taylor 1967, p. 472; see also Zeldin 1993, p. 113.
97 Tombs 1996, p. 281.
98 Zeldin 1993, p. 80–81; see also Pinaud 1990.
99 Charles 1991, p. 27; Tombs 1996, p. 99, 102–103. The electorate was again extended in the late 1840s and reached 248,000.
100 Chagnollaud 1991, p. 66, 96, 103; Charles 1980, p. 12, 27–31, 34–35, 39, 44; Daumard 1993b, p. 832–33, 837, 883; Zeldin 1993 p. 116–18.
101 Zeldin 1993, p. 60.
102 Barjot 1995, p. 121–22; Daumard 1993c, p. 884; Démier 2000, p. 48–49; Zeldin 1993, pp. 59–62. By contrast, in Britain, investment related to the development of industrial capitalism became dominant during the second third of the century; see Beaud 2010, p. 144.
103 Marchand and Thélot 1991, p. 136; Noiriel 1986, p. 51; Woronoff 1994, p. 216–17, 291.
104 Marchand and Thélot 1991, p. 45, 136–39; Noiriel 1986, p. 33–35, 39, 49, 52, 65; Guicheteau 2014, p. 191, 196; Tombs 1996, p. 269–70; Woronoff 1994, p. 224, 290–92.
105 Tombs 1996, p. 270–71.
106 Chassagne 1981, p. 52; Noiriel 1986, p. 61–62; Woronoff 1994, p. 202.
107 Price 1981, p. 183.
108 Asselain 1984, p. 134.
109 Daumas 2018, p. 16, 21–31, 80–82, 98, 101–103; Woronoff 1994, p. 202, 326.
110 Broder 1993, p. 42–61; Caron 1995, p. 120; Price 1981; Rioux 1989, p. 84, 113; Woronoff 1994, p. 227.
111 Appleby 2010, p. 80.
112 Bergeron 1978, p. 39–41, 61–62; Lambert-Dansette 1991, p. 154; Verley and Mayau 2001, p. 8–9.
113 Kemp 1971, p. 113.
114 Perez 2012.
115 Smith 2006, p. 33.
116 Bartolomei et al. 2017, p. 431–33, 453, 458–59.
117 Smith 2006, p. 34, 55–56.
118 Asselain 1984, p. 136; Barjot 2014a, p. 92–93, 97; Caron 1995, p. 136; Kemp 1971, p. 130; Stearns 1965, p. 50, 57; Todd 2008.
119 The most influential proponent of this account is Sewell, 1980.
120 Cottereau 1993, p. 113; Sonenscher 1989, p. 5, 28–30, 33, 280; Thillay 2002.
121 Vardi, quoted in Fairchilds 1988, p. 691.
122 Guicheteau 2014, p. 62, 99–105; Vardi 1988, p. 708, 712.
123 Cottereau 2006, p. 104. Our translation.
124 Cottereau 2002, p. 1530, 1546; 2006, p. 113–14.
125 Sonenscher 1989, p. 367. Cottereau (2002; 2006) discusses this issue at length.
126 Quoted in Cottereau 2002, p. 1553. Our translation.
127 Cottereau 2002, p. 1553. Our translation.
128 Cottereau 1987; 2002, p. 1545, 1547–55; 2011, p. 10; Delsalle 1987, p. 69; Guicheteau 2014, p. 173.
129 Pollard 1965, p. 255–56, 260–70.
130 Steinfeld 2001, p. 47–48; Zmolek 2014, p. 451–55.
131 The *livret ouvrier*, which workers presented to employers on being hired, was reinstated by Napoleon in 1803. It is sometimes presented as a tool used by bosses to disci pline workers. In fact, the *livret* had by then lost all disciplinary powers that it formerly retained and acted mainly to facilitate the workers' mobility; see Cottereau 2006, p. 108; Fombonne 2001, p. 58–60; Guicheteau 2014, p. 172; Sonenscher 1989, p. 368.
132 Jarrige and Chalmin 2008, p. 47–60; Lefebvre 2003, p. 16, 65.
133 Lefebvre 2003, p. 65. Our translation.
134 Perrot 1974, p. 275. Our translation.

135 Lefebvre 2003, p. 131. Our translation.
136 Pollard 1965, p. 219, 221, 225, 245, 247.
137 Pollard 1965, p. 248; Boyns, Edwards, and Nikitin 1997, p. 404–405.
138 Pollard 1965, p. 215, 226.
139 Boyns, Edwards, and Nikitin 1997, p. 408; Lemarchand 2016, p. 357.
140 Boyns, Edwards, and Nikitin 1997, p. 410; Lemarchand 2016, p. 357, 361, 363.
141 Crouzet 2003, p. 237.
142 Woronoff 1994, p. 343–44. Our translation.
143 Asselain 1988, p. 1239; Barjot 2014a, p. 121; 2014b, p. 378; Beaud 2010, p. 134–35; Brenner and Isett 2002, p. 643; Crafts 1984a, p. 55; Hobsbawm 1987, p. 343; Stokey 2001, p. 62.
144 Berenson 1984, p. 29.
145 Berenson 1984, p. 26, 28.
146 Berenson 1984, p. 26–27.
147 Beaud 2010, p. 142; Woronoff 1994, p. 220.
148 Asselain 1984, p. 143–45; Barjot 2014a, p. 98; Beltran and Griset 1994, p. 93; Smith 2006, p. 199–201.
149 Beltran and Griset 1994, p. 96; Broder 1993, p. 67; Caron 1995, p. 116; Hills 1989, p. 117; Lévy-Leboyer 1964, p. 66; Taylor 1949, p. 117.
150 Beltran and Griset 1994, p. 96; Broder 1993, p. 67; Crafts 1984a, p. 65; Fureix and Jarrige 2015, p. 63; Lemarchand 2008, p. 256; Rioux 1989, p. 72; Woronoff 1994, p. 210.
151 Chassagne 1991, p. 659; Hills 1989, p. 235.
152 Fureix and Jarrige 2015, p. 63–65; Smith 2006, p. 170–76; Woronoff 1994, p. 202–11.
153 O'Brien and Keyder 2011, p. 90.
154 Crafts 1984a, p. 64–66.
155 Hobsbawm 1996, p. 117; see also Beltran and Griset 1994, p. 121; Broder 1993, p. 15.
156 Barjot 2014a, p. 105, 112, 118–19; 2014b, p. 398–400; Bouvier 1968; Hobsbawm 1996, p. 177; Kemp 1971, p. 117, 124; Rioux 1989, p. 94.
157 Barjot 2014a, p. 104; Kemp 1971, p. 120, 127; Woronoff 1994, p. 232.
158 Barjot 2014a, p. 119; Plessis 2001; Smith 2006, p. 60.
159 Barjot 2014a, p. 117, 121; Broder 1993, p. 32; Hautcoeur 2011, p. 24–25; Kemp 1971, p. 121–22.
160 Asselain 1984, p. 135; 1988, p. 1242; Barjot 2014a, p. 93, 116; Plessis 2001; Sée 1926, p. 156.
161 Kemp 1971, p. 121.
162 Todd, 2008; 2022, p. 14–15.
163 Verley 2013, p. 695; Todd 2022, p. 109.
164 Verley 2013, p. 715. Our translation.
165 Verley 2013, p. 719; Todd 2022, p. 106–107, 131, 139.
166 Todd 2022, p. 114–15.
167 Verley 2013, p. 717.
168 Todd 2022, p. 18–20, 140.
169 Todd 2022, p. 14, 16, 21–22, 51, 55–56, 61, 106, 138–39, 147, 149–52.
170 Todd 2022, p. 113; Woronoff 1994, p. 323–25.
171 Caron 1995, p. 133–35; Frobert 2009, p. 17–19; Cottereau 1997, p. 78, 81, 89–93, 109, 127–28, 137, 142; Guicheteau 2014, p. 69–70, 135; Lambert-Dansette 1991, p. 173; Verley 1989, p. 70; Smith 2006, p. 154–58.
172 Verley 2013, p. 700, 702, 704, 706. Our translations.
173 Verley 2013, p. 706–708.
174 Verley 2013, p. 710, 716–17. Our translation. Todd 2022, p. 129.
175 Lévy-Leboyer 1964, p. 96–99.
176 Asselain 1984, p. 145; Broder 1993, p. 71; Caron 1995, p. 132–33; Hudson 1986, p. 43–44; Lipson 1921, p. 188, 204–205 Smith 2006, p. 150–51.

177 Verley 2013, p. 711–14.
178 Verley 2013, p. 742–43. Our translations.
179 Gervais 2004, p. 276, 279. On the transition to capitalism in the United States, see Charles Post 2012.
180 Stearns 1965, p. 52.
181 Chassagne 1991, p. 387–95, 657; Stearns 1965, p. 54; Woronoff 1994, p. 247.
182 Quoted in Stearns 1965, p. 56.
183 Caron 1995, p. 125–27, 136.
184 Caron 1995, p. 129; Kasdi 2014, p. 241; Kemp 1971, p. 115; Smith 2006, p. 144.
185 Beltran and Griset 1994, p. 100; Caron 1995, p. 128; Fohlen 1956, p. 54; Hau 1987, p. 2; Kasdi 2014, p. 23–33; Reddy 1984, p. 91, 99.
186 Kasdi 2014, p. 156–57; Liu 1994, p. 82; Smith 2006, p. 127, 133; Woronoff 1994, p. 193.
187 Bergeron 1978, p. 57; Crouzet 1989, p. 1197; Reddy 1984, p. 75.
188 Broder 1993, p. 25; Hau 1987, p. 70; Reddy 1984, p. 101. Alsatian firms produced mostly luxury goods and were much less affected by this weakening of popular consumption.
189 Collier 1964, p. 12; Engrand 1981, p. 244; Kasdi 2014, p. 249–50.
190 Chassagne 1979, p. 104.
191 Caron 1995, p. 129; Hau 1987, p. 77, 88, 98–101, 371–72; Lévy-Leboyer 1964, p. 90–95; Smith 2006, p. 138.
192 Hau 1987, p. 76–77, 371, 375; Lévy-Leboyer 1964, p. 95.
193 Hau 1987, p. 87–88. Our translation.
194 Asselain 1984, p. 145; Beltran and Griset 1994, p. 96, 100; Hau 1987, p. 87, 98, 371; Lévy-Leboyer 1964, p. 81, 87; Smith 2006, p. 138; Woronoff 1994, p. 234.
195 Lévy-Leboyer 1964, p. 79, 95; Hau 1987, p. 234, 380; Smith 2006, p. 137.
196 Landes 1969, p. 160, 163; Hau 1987, p. 240; Lévy-Leboyer 1964, p. 78.
197 Hau 1987, p. 380–87.
198 Chassagne 1979, p. 107; 1981, p. 52; Hau 1987, p. 232–33; Lévy-Leboyer 1964, p. 87; Milward and Saul 1973, p. 319.
199 Hau 1987, p. 241. Our translation.
200 Liu 1994, p. 87. Emphasis added.
201 Reddy 1984, p. 61, 74, 77, 79, 83.
202 Reddy 1984, p. 74.
203 Reddy 1984, p. 100.
204 Fohlen 1956, p. 91. Our translation, emphases added.
205 *Ibid.*
206 Fohlen 1956, p. 90. Our translation.
207 *Ibid.*
208 Quoted in Reddy 1984, p. 113. Noiret added to this: "Once their fortunes were made … they bought land and retired" (*Ibid.*); see also Liu 1994, p. 95–96.
209 Reddy 1984, p. 76–77, 99, 106, 111.
210 Reddy 1984, p. 99.
211 Chassagne 1991, p. 661; Bergeron 1978, p. 56; Hirsch 1985; Lambert-Dansette 1991, p. 169; Woronoff 1994, p. 263.
212 Hirsch 1991.
213 Kasdi 2014, p. 160–63, 165–66, 179–80; Woronoff 1994, p. 197.
214 Bergeron 1978, p. 52–54; Chassagne 1991, p. 94, 253, 629; Hirsch 1985, p. 28; Lambert-Dansette 1991, p. 155–56, 170.
215 Kasdi 2014, p. 192.
216 Hirsch 1991, p. 392. Our translation, emphasis added.
217 Hirsch 1991, p. 396. Our translation.
218 Landes 1969, p. 164.

219 Caron 1995, p. 131–32; Lévy-Leboyer 1964, p. 111; Liu 1994, p. 131–33; Smith 2006, p. 145.
220 Barjot 2014b, p. 404; Beltran and Griset 1994, p. 108; King 2006, p. 264.
221 Gille 1968, p. 48.
222 Gille 1968, p. 47. Our translation.
223 Smith 2006, p. 177.
224 Beaud 2010, p. 134; Caron 1995, p. 136–37; Gille 1968, p. 50; Smith 2006, p. 179, 181.
225 Asselain 1984, p. 144; Caron 1995, p. 136–37; Gille 1968, p. 51, 59, 62; Perez 2012, p. 5; Sée 1926, p. 158; Woronoff 1994, p. 211, 224, 318–19.
226 Smith 2006, p. 187.
227 Gille 1968, p. 56.
228 Gille 1968, p. 66–67. Our translation.
229 Gille 1968, p. 67.
230 Gille 1968, p. 53–54, 56, 66–67, 75. Our translation.

3 The First Transition to Capitalism

French Industry from the 1850s to the 1920s

In their influential contributions of the early 1970s, Jean-Jacques Carré, Paul Dubois and Edmond Malinvaud asserted that sustained economic growth began in France in the late nineteenth and early twentieth centuries and accelerated again after the Second World War. Likewise, in his sweeping economic history of France, François Caron questions those who draw a clear demarcation between a stagnant prewar economy and postwar economic miracle. Caron, like Richard Roehl, emphasizes an early period of dynamic industrialization beginning before World War I and accelerating during the 1920s. Other historians, such as Jean-Pierre Dormois and Jean-Charles Asselain, have challenged this optimistic reading of pre-World War II industrialization.[1]

A key thesis of our book helps explain such drastic differences in appreciation of French industrial development. We argue that capitalist social property relations and rules of reproduction were first introduced in France under the Second Empire, at the initiatives of state leaders, as a reaction to intensifying geopolitical pressures and with the intention of diffusing class struggles through a policy of industrial growth. We explain in this chapter that the imposition of competitive imperatives compelled industrial firms to invest and develop labor productivity, which translated into higher rates of mechanization than during earlier periods of market-opportunity-led development. As we will explain in Chapter 5, however, employers still had means to limit competitive imperatives, the absence of which slowed the pace of industrial growth and brought it to a standstill in the 1930s. Uninhibited capitalist industrialization did not occur until a more thorough proletarianization of the workforce and mass consumer market took hold. Both of these developments were closely tied to a capitalist restructuring of agriculture, which will be addressed in Chapter 4.

In what follows, we begin by discussing the reasons for the establishment of capitalist rules of reproduction in industry and the ways in which new competitive imperatives were imposed on investors and workers. We then turn to the new patterns of industrial development that ensued.

DOI: 10.4324/9781003092896-4

The Making of A Competitive Market

We saw in Chapter 2 how, in the face of geopolitical and military pressure from capitalist Britain during the eighteenth century, the French crown pursued liberal reforms aimed at modernizing the economy. Seeking to strengthen the state, in competition with foreign ruling classes, the modernizing faction of the elite was also caught up in conflicts with other elites and with the lower classes. While fighting over state control and economic policies against socioeconomic conservatives, modernizers also contended with popular resistance from below that endangered structures of surplus appropriation and sociopolitical stability, and thus had a chilling effect on the efforts to restructure the economy and state.

The capitalist transformation of the agrarian sector, together with the reform of the fiscal-military state apparatus, provided early modern Britain with a decisive edge in geopolitical competition and forced competing powers to attempt to develop self-expanding agrarian economies. The maturing capitalist industrialization of the second third of the nineteenth century added to Britain's international advantage, and made it increasingly clear to rulers of rival states that they had to emulate their rival's capitalist mode of production and pursue political and economic renewal. The international context was consequently marked by the unification of powerful and modernizing polities—Germany, Italy, the United States and Japan—and, crucially, by the emulation of British industrial capitalism in Europe, North America and Japan.

We saw in Chapter 2 how, after 1815, France became the junior partner in a strategy of informal imperialism led by the British hegemon. Yet as Britain's wealth and power developed, French leaders grew anxious about falling further behind their imperial ally. This is the context in which a naval arms race emerged between the two countries, even as they collaborated in various parts of the world between 1840 and 1870. An informal imperial alliance, however, became difficult to maintain, and clashes became frequent, as France and other European powers turned to colonial expansion in the Global South after the 1870s.

Prussia, nevertheless, became France's main geopolitical concern. Prussia had reached the status of great power in the eighteenth century and increased its influence during the following century. Prussia, allied with the newly unified Italian kingdom, defeated Austria in 1866 to assert its leadership over German unification to the distress of French leaders. The Second Empire's (1852–1870) efforts to assert geopolitical might through military campaigns in Crimea and Italy had met with success. Signs of decline soon followed, however, as the United States helped Mexico prevent France from extending its influence in the western hemisphere. Then came the fateful defeat to Prussia, which led its capitalist transition more effectively than did France, unified the German state and crowned its emperor in occupied Versailles in 1871. The defeat undermined French prestige and led foreign elites, notably in Japan and Latin American countries, to instead take the German Empire as a model for modernization.[2]

Yet, long before France's defeat in 1871, the leaders of the Second Empire had understood that the geopolitical context compelled them to initiate a transition toward a more dynamic form of industrialization. For Napoleon III and his collaborators, "the nation's greatness depended – no less than on military victory – on the success of an industrial revolution, in the broadest sense, that would hoist France to the level already reached by England." To safeguard the regime's position "in relation to foreign powers," the emperor understood "that national power was bound up inextricably with industrialization" and the imperative "to impel manufacturers into improving their technical efficiency in the cause of national power."[3]

The emperor and his political and administrative staff, however, remained aware of popular threats from below that had reined in their modernizing predecessors. The regime therefore adopted two parallel strategies to secure social stability vis-à-vis the popular classes. The first was to turn a major pitfall of modernizing socioeconomic structures—the expansion of a wage-earning working class—into an advantage by seeking to promote real income growth through industrial development. Bonaparte planned to improve popular consumption (without threatening elite wealth) and reduce unemployment through a "Saint-Simonian" class alliance forged through a modernizing industrial economy. Michel Chevalier, a close collaborator and economic advisor of the emperor, summarized the idea in the early years of the Second Empire: "one of the essential conditions for the stability of the state and society is growing social wealth, so that the objects and services which respond to the various human needs increase more rapidly than the population."[4]

Bonaparte had already formulated his intentions in his work *The Extinction of pauperism*, published in 1844. This policy became more urgent amid the democrat-socialists' electoral agitation during the Second Republic. Also decisive were the June Days uprising of 1848, when Parisian workers protested the closing of the National Workshops, which the provisional revolutionary government had established to provide work and income to the unemployed. The workers, whose uprising was violently repressed, had fought to imprint a social dimension on the democratic republic later overthrown by President Louis-Napoléon Bonaparte's coup d'état in December 1851. After becoming emperor by plebiscite in November 1852, Napoleon III hoped to assuage popular disaffection by offering economic growth and improved material conditions as a substitute for the loss of political participation and freedom. In a letter to minister of State Achille Fould, published in January 1860 by the journal *Le Moniteur Universel*, the emperor insisted on promoting industrial dynamism to keep prices low and consumption levels high, and "expand affluence among the working class" to a level "reached in a neighbouring country."[5]

The regime's second strategy to ensure stability—a strategy which dominated and ultimately undermined its first strategy—was to preserve and secure the support of the peasantry. The effort to secure peasant support was a direct response to the threat of renewed working-class discontent against which the peasantry was to serve as a bulwark. The peasants did not uniformly support Louis-Bonaparte. They sometimes acted collectively, departing from the political passivity of a class that Marx compared to a "sack of potatoes."[6] This was shown, for instance, in the electoral support for democratic socialists in a minority, yet a substantial number, of rural regions in the 1849 legislative elections and the insurrectionary peasant resistance in several regions to the coup of 1851. This turbulence reinforced Napoleon's conviction about the need to safeguard the support of the conservative peasants who had first elected him as president and later consolidated his imperial position in several plebiscites and legislative elections. Reciprocally, many peasants saw the Bonapartist regime as a dam protecting them against a restoration of the Old Regime.

The imperial regime hoped to limit contact between the urban republican and socialist working class and the peasantry—a task that proved increasingly challenging in a context of rapid development of transport and communication systems. The government acted to favor the peasants' interests in rural departments where republican ideas seemed to be gaining popularity. Yet, despite subsidies to develop vicinal paths and highways, agriculture retained a secondary position within the overall economic strategy of the regime. State initiatives in agriculture remained rare, and no general economic plan was designed for this sector. As was made clear in our preceding chapter, the regime showed no intention of uprooting the peasantry to implement agrarian capitalism.

When the liberalization of the regime led to electoral gains for the republican opposition in 1863, the Duke of Persigny, Interior Minister, praised the peasantry as the backbone of the regime. Persigny explained that the progression of the republican vote, from 2.5 percent in previous elections to 11.3 percent which swelled their number of seats from 7 to 17, stemmed from the irrational political behavior of the "isolated" and socially dislocated individuals in urban areas, ones easily "agitated" and "misinformed." Peasants, by contrast, were embedded in communities that nurtured mature, informed and rational electoral choices and did not easily lend themselves to manipulation by agitators. Peasant votes explain the regime's ability to retain a solid majority of 251 Bonapartists elected to the Corps Législatif. Persigny's analysis spouted the regime's self-interested political discourse yet clearly identified the peasantry as its social base and showed mistrust toward urban proletarians.[7]

The political will to uphold the peasantry was related not only to the emperor's interest in maintaining sociopolitical stability and therefore his own imperial standing, but also to the presence of conservatives among the elite, which shaped the overall economic posture of the Second Empire. This conservatism appeared in the discomfort displayed by the Council of State toward the liberalization of company law initiated by the regime. Much of the dominant class criticized the speculation, parasitism and economic instability associated with liberalizing company law. Many sitting in the Corps Législatif also sought to rein in the expansion of business banking, typified by the Crédit mobilier (on which more below), and did so in alliance with the traditional and dominant faction of the financial sector. Deputies branded as *budgétaires* leaned toward fiscal austerity, economic conservatism and limits to public expenditures. Issues of state credit and expenditures led to conflict within the executive branch between Saint-Simonian modernizers and partisans of a more conservative political economy.[8]

However, the coup of December 1851, the enactment of the new constitution and the formal restoration of a hereditary Empire by plebiscite in November 1852 provided Bonaparte and his entourage with the powers to override much of this

resistance. Male universal suffrage introduced by the Second Republic was maintained to elect deputies to a *Corps législiatif*—which stood next to an unelected
Senate—and played a key legitimizing role for the regime. The head of state selected and supported official candidates and carefully managed elections (and plebiscites). Ministers were responsible not to the legislature but to the emperor who
appointed them, and the powerful departmental prefects answered to the central
administration. The emperor had the power to authorize public works and extraordinary expenditures, and to wage war and to negotiate not just military but also
commercial treaties—a measure designed to short-circuit the expected opposition
to trade liberalization. The Council of State played a decisive role in the legislative
process. Its members, no longer elected by the legislature, as had been the case
under the Second Republic, were now named and revoked by the emperor, who
controlled legislative initiatives. Restrictions on civil liberties and freedom of the
press were severe and public opposition muzzled, at least until the liberalization of
the regime after 1860.[9]

The regime thus functioned as a personalized dictatorship despite the democratic shell. It was largely freed from the parliamentary control over monarchs
after the Restoration and, *a fortiori*, over the executive during the Third Republic
after the Second Empire. Indeed, "one of Napoleon's original objectives had been
to weaken considerably the authority of parliament, which he perceived to be a
divisive forum for political dispute and party particularism."[10] Popular sovereignty,
providing legitimacy to the regime, was to be expressed directly through plebiscites and embodied by the emperor's persona, allegedly situated above private
and class interests.

The regime thus had the executive power to initiate a capitalist restructuring of
industry. This executive power, to be sure, resulted from the revolutionary threat
of popular classes eager to impose a democratic social republic. This threat had
led panicked monarchists, divided in deeply hostile factions, to concede power to
Bonaparte. Bonaparte, from the monarchists' perspective, also prevented the rival
faction from crowning its leader king. That said, matters were not as simple as
Marx would have it when he depicted Louis-Napoleon as an arbitrator of a conflict between Legitimists and Orleanists. This conflict, Marx argued, expressed a
more fundamental "rivalry between capital and landed property."[11] Most owners
of "capital," however, whether financial or industrial, were conservatives not just
politically but also economically.

The French ruling class was still generally attached to the ideal of an age-old
rural France. This attachment, it is crucial to note, was not just ideological—it
was rooted in material interests and social relations. The notables, formed of nobles and the upper echelons of the bourgeoisie, lived off traditional land tenure
and rents—and the intricate system of annuities and other private rents built upon
the redistribution of these landed revenues—but also from state positions largely
funded by the taxation of the peasantry. Land and offices were sought after as
sources of income and social standing not just by conservative Legitimists, but also
by Orleanists and liberals, including industrial entrepreneurs, once their fortunes
had been made. The state was not just an instrument of class domination. It was

also a direct tool of "extra-economic" class *exploitation*, since offices offered a means of private enrichment as had been the case since the rise of the absolutist state. France remained very much still a "state-class"—the exploitive conduit of a ruling class that reproduced partly *in and as* the state—and indeed its parasitic character reached its apex under the Second Empire, as the number of state positions increased. This represented an impediment to the development of capitalism, since the ruling class had a material interest in preserving a large peasantry that it exploited directly through landed property, and indirectly, through state offices.[12]

The emperor, we have seen, also had an interest in preserving the peasantry: to stabilize the regime. Election campaigns, labor disputes and salons acted as mediums of politicization and fueled a growing republican opposition. Monarchists had welcomed Bonaparte's coup to stop the revolutionary threat in 1851, but opposition among notables grew during the 1850s and 1860s. The regime depended on the social clientele of elite opponents, on office-seeking notables recruited from opposition factions to staff the state apparatus, and was therefore eventually compelled to concede liberal reforms demanded by the oppositions, such as freedom of the press and assembly in the 1860s. The legislature gained new powers, making ministers more accountable and deputies able to exercise legislative initiatives, budgetary controls and overview and approval of custom treaties.[13]

Overall, the liberalization of the Empire "was a concession not to republicans, but to ... conservatives" intent on using parliamentary powers to curb the state's economic reforms and, crucially, to reinstitute strong protective tariffs—a key issue in the capitalist restructuring of industry, discussed below.[14] As the leading banking and merchant dynasty of the land, the Rothschilds stated publicly that they sought political liberties and "the unrestrained and rigorous control provided by legislative assemblies" as a stick with which to beat an economically irresponsible government. One thus sees the contradictory character of the state (in terms of economic policy) and can also understand the mixed results of the capitalist industrialization initiated during the Second Empire.

Yet, even as the Corps Législatif obtained new powers to control the ministry, Napoleon III, whose political discourse retained an authoritarian tone, continued to appoint his cabinet in the closing years of the Second Empire. Underlining the limits of the "Liberal Empire," Eugène Rouher, Bonaparte's faithful collaborator, acting as Ministre d'État, declared straightforwardly in a debate on freedom of the press in 1869 that "there was no question of a return to parliamentarism." In any case, time ran out, and the curtain fell on the Second Empire before the opposition could make much use of its newfound levers to alter economic policy.[15]

The postrevolutionary state, and even the Second Empire, was not autonomous (nor even "relatively" autonomous) from the ruling class. Rather, the ruling class reproduced itself, at least in part, in and as a state in which political and administrative positions were monopolized as means of private appropriation by a section of this class, while much of the rest of the upper classes aspired to these positions. Yet, what made the state under the Second Empire different was the fact that insurrectionary class struggles from below, combined with intra-ruling class divisions, provided the *executive* branch with room for maneuver in an otherwise constraining political and social environment. Moreover, this executive was wielded by a group of men who saw the imperative of competing with foreign ruling classes, through the modernization of industry, and also of mitigating popular mobilization from below. However, this group also had to consider, and cope with, elites who continued to hold state functions. Many of these elites saw the modernizing project as a threat to their social reproduction and to social stability.

For nearly two decades, in spite of growing opposition, Napoleon III benefited from executive and legislative power that he used to launch modernizing reforms of the financial and industrial sectors. He used this power against the immediate interests and will, not just of the class of notables described above, but also of those of traditional bankers and industrial entrepreneurs who wished to preserve a noncompetitive, protected domestic market that they could divide among themselves. The emperor could only count on the support of the most "advanced," and overall limited, sections of finance and industry against refractory bankers and businessmen.

Before coming to power, Bonaparte had spent years in exile in London, visited booming industrial cities such as Manchester and Birmingham and developed an interest in railways, steam engines and the dynamism of private enterprises. He read Jean-Baptiste Say and Adam Smith, and was introduced to the ideas of Claude-Henri de Rouvroy, count of Saint-Simon, who promoted the reform of finance, railway building and free trade in support of industrial development. Upon becoming head of state, Louis-Napoleon established close ties with the business community. Rich bankers, entrepreneurs and economists penetrated the legislature and state administration, thus gaining influence within the government. Saint-Simonians such as Michel Chevalier, the Pereire brothers, Eugène Rouher and others played key roles in the reforms introduced under the Second Empire. Though they participated in the intellectual debates of their times—Michel Chevalier became professor at Collège de France while Émile Pereire was a collaborator at the journal *Le Globe*—these were practical men and technocrats, often educated at the École Polytechnique, who aimed to transform their society.[16]

Napoleon III's "was the first regime in France to have given such distinct priority to economic objectives."[17] The emperor made this priority clear in his 1852 Bordeaux speech and again in his 1860 letter to Interior Minister Achille Fould. The emperor and his allies adhered to the Saint-Simonian policy of "productive expenses," which implied the use of credit to invest in public work in the hope of stimulating economic development and generating profits. The government would then have more fiscal resources to sustain a growing line of credit. This policy could divert France from the road to capitalist industrialization. Indeed, it tended to drain capital into speculative investments and unproductive public works such as the monumental urban renewal of Paris by Haussmann. Individual investors made fortunes and urban landscapes changed, but much of these public works did not develop basic infrastructure or facilitate industrial development.

Productive expenses nevertheless became crucial to the emergence of capitalism in France. Such state intervention represented a rupture with the budgetary austerity of previous regimes. Conservative politicians and businessmen demurred.

But in the absence of parliamentary control, the regime had a free hand to spend until the public debt, which grew steadily from around 6.4 to 13.9 million francs from 1853 to 1865, led the opposition to mobilize within the government and press for parliamentary control over the budget. The upshot was that for all the regime's boasting about productive expenses and the vocal opposition of pro-austerity deputies, public expenditures remained relatively low compared to the July Monarchy. Outside of railway building and urban public works, its direct interventions in favor of industry remained sparse and subsidies to industrial firms were rare, apart from the period following the 1860 commercial Treaty with Britain when the state helped firms cope with more efficient foreign competitors. Military expenses amounted to the largest part of public budgets and represented another heavy drain on capital markets away from productivity-enhancing investments.[18] All in all, productive state expenditures proved unpopular outside of Saint-Simonian circles and did not become policies to sustain capitalist industrialization for nearly a century.

That said, the state did act decisively to initiate capitalist development. It created a competitive economic context. "Free of all parliamentary control," the "government adapted legislation to the rise of capitalism, enacting numerous laws and decrees on economic matters," removed "non-indispensable constraints" on industry and allowed growing corporate firms to stifle traditional noncompetitive entrepreneurs.[19] Beyond simply allowing firms to act freely and compete with each other by adjusting the legal framework, the government actively built an environment that coerced an increasing number of private firms to constantly make reinvestments in productive technologies. The Second Empire forged an integrated and competitive domestic market, inserted into and subject to the imperatives of an emerging world market.

Modernizing the financial system was among the first undertakings of the regime, and a fierce struggle was waged to develop a new banking system during the 1850s. As discussed in Chapter 2, up until the Second Empire, banking had been a "rigid, incomplete, and uncertain system."[20] The period before the 1850s had been an era of bankers rather than institutionalized and bureaucratized banks. Most *maisons de banque* were family affairs or limited partnership companies, and respectability was a necessary attribute for co-optation into this restricted world. The *Haute Banque*, an informal network of banks, controlled the *Banque de France* under the leadership of banking dynasties such as the Rothschilds. These banks, historically tied to grand *négoce*, continued to be involved in traditional commercial activities and loaned to states more than to industrial firms.[21]

The state facilitated the establishment of new banks after the early 1850s to break with old practices and the omnipotent influence of the Rothschilds and other dynasties, some of which had been strongly tied to the previous Orleanist regime. In supporting the formation of new financial institutions, the emperor sought to expand the regime's capacity to tax, spend and borrow. In addition to these political and fiscal considerations, the goal was also to transform banking, to support sustained economic growth and, in turn, stabilize the regime, both geopolitically and socially. The state thus authorized, in 1852, the foundation of the *Crédit foncier*, funded with the purpose of supporting agriculture, but which ended up playing a determinant role in the financing of Paris' urban renewal. But it was the foundation, also in 1852, of the Pereire brother's *Crédit mobilier*, an investment bank whose creation was directly authorized by the emperor that epitomizes the financial transformation initiated under the Second Empire.

We saw in Chapter 2 that experiments with investment banking had been attempted during the 1830s with the creation of Jacques Laffitte's *Caisse générale du commerce et de l'industrie*. The *Caisse générale*, which went under during the 1848 crisis, however, was a limited partnership in line with legal constraints of the time. The Second Empire liberalized finance and authorized the *Crédit mobilier*, as well as several new financial institutions, to form as a joint-stock bank. The *Crédit mobilier* realized Laffitte's vision on a much larger scale and broke new ground by issuing bonds and attracting deposits to provide long-term credit for the entire economy. The new financial institution sought to facilitate public and private loans and offer credit against exchangeable industrial shares and securities. A key goal was to support mergers and the consolidation of industrial firms.[22]

To launch such an ambitious project, the Pereires secured financial resources from key members of the *Haute Banque*. Yet, they also faced resistance, as illustrated by the feud between the Pereires and Rothschilds that made headlines for about 15 years. James Rothschild ensured that the *Banque de France* refrained from bailing out the *Crédit mobilier* in 1867, when, bogged down by too many financial ventures, it lacked liquidities and became unable to discharge its short-term debt obligations. Despite this failure, other investment banks were established, and some of the hitherto recalcitrant old bankers felt that they had to adapt to emerging practices. In 1864, for instance, a group of old *banquiers-négociants* founded the *Société Générale pour le Développement du Commerce et de l'industrie*, another investment bank that turned toward industrial financing.

Opposition to what was perceived as a potentially economically destabilizing scheme also came from within the government. While Benoît Fould was among the major bankers to follow the Pereires into their adventure, his brother Achille Fould used his function as Minister of State to oppose the creation of the new investment bank, defending financial orthodoxy against Interior Minister Victor de Persigny. Although the emperor intervened personally to authorize the Pereire brother's investment bank, this discord exemplifies the contradictory nature of the state discussed above. Fould later used his influence to rein in the further development of a Saint-Simonian banking system and, in 1855, prodded the government to forbid the *Crédit mobilier* to issue short-term bonds, thus denting much of the innovative edge of the investment bank and limiting its leverage.[23]

Meanwhile, after 1855, English investors in French railways sought partnerships with French bankers and attempted to import the model of deposit banking that had been spreading north of the Channel since the 1830s. This new project was met with hostility by the *Haute Banque* and conservatives within the government. But Napoleon III ignored this hostility and used his decree power to authorize the establishment of the *Crédit industriel et commercial* in 1859. While its name might suggest otherwise, the new bank planned to leave large and longer-term industrial credit to the *Crédit mobilier* and focus on short-term operations such as discounting commercial papers and on small personal transactions and credit. The *Crédit industriel et commercial*, a deposit bank, drained small individual savings. This model diverged from the traditional mobilization of the private wealth of banking dynasties. The state, however, limited and regulated transactions, capped the volume of deposits and gave the emperor the power to name the bank's president and vice president.

The government liberalized deposit banking after 1860, spurring the creation of new banks, such as the *Crédit Lyonnais*, in 1863, and the *Société générale*, in 1864, the latter mixing short-term credit with industrial investment banking. Investment banks were also founded shortly after the fall of the Second Empire, including the *Banque de Paris et des Pays-Bas* in 1872 and the *Union Parisienne* in 1874. All these deposit and investment banks shied away from long-term industrial investment, especially during the crisis-ridden 1880s, and instead stuck to short-term commercial discounting.[24]

As the government liberalized legislation regulating finance and approved new financial institutions, it also increased its influence over the privately controlled *Banque de France*, which had been accused of an overly cautious credit policy curbing economic growth. The government persuaded members of the *Haute Banque*, which controlled the *Banque de France*, to facilitate money creation by reducing interest rates and relaxing credit policy. The success of these efforts increased the discounting activities of the *Banque de France*. Conservative financiers, such as the Rothschilds and their allies, however, had the *Banque de France* increase interest rates in 1856 and 1857.[25]

By 1860, these financial innovations doubled the money supply that had existed in 1835. The value of circulating bank notes quadrupled from 1860 to 1885 and nearly doubled again by 1910. The number of individuals with bank accounts went up from 730,000 in 1849 to 2.4 million in 1869. The total value of deposits increased from 800 million to 2.1 billion francs from 1860 to 1885 and reached 10.4 billion by 1910. Titles traded on the stock market diversified and their aggregate value substantially increased under the Second Empire. The banking and credit reforms introduced by the Second Empire laid the foundation for an integrated financial market.[26]

Nevertheless, these achievements should not be overstated. The *Crédit mobilier* played a decisive role in introducing investment banking, but it derived much of its profit from speculation, facilitated by the frantic expansion of the Paris stock market during the 1850s. The Pereire brothers' bank encouraged speculation by manipulating and inflating the value of the corporate structures that it created via its investments in railway and public works companies. The *Crédit mobilier* was thus often associated with speculative activities by contemporaries, who contrasted it with the industrial investments of banks on England and Belgium. French investment banks had limited holdings in manufacturing and mining companies under the Second Empire and their funding of industry only began to pick up from around the turn of the twentieth century. French banks remained substantially less involved in the funding of industrial activities than German banks before the First World War, and industrial firms waited until the 1890s before they started issuing shares and bonds on the stock market to fund their activities. French savings were mostly invested in government loans, domestic and foreign, to fund infrastructure and public works, in government-backed railroad bonds and in the ongoing frenzy of urban public works. The canalization of savings toward industrial investments remained limited.[27]

Important regional disparities endured within the financial market, and industrial branches were integrated unevenly in credit circuits. Banks had just begun to develop their branch networks, and "France still had one of the lowest 'bank densities' among the developed countries of the time,"[28] a handicap that limited the possibility of tapping into the savings of the peasantry. Bank deposits, though larger than they had been under previous regimes, were limited until the 1870s and most of the population still did not have a bank account on the eve of First World War. Small bank notes were only introduced toward the end of the Second Empire, and most citizens never saw one before 1870.[29]

The limited development of financial institutions and their reluctance to invest in industry did not result solely from the enduring weight of traditional banking. It was also related to the reluctance of industrial firms to invest in their facilities, a reluctance which limited demand for capital. Bonaparte's government resolutely tackled this issue. The regime needed to create an economic context of price competition which would compel firms to invest and modernize their facilities and organizations. In his 1860 letter to Fould, the emperor insisted that "without competition, industry stagnates."[30] Saint-Simonians had claimed for decades that a key step toward enforcing competition and avoiding industrial stagnation was to develop transport and communication networks. They sought to use the state to apply this program, building canals and roads, turning rivers into navigable waterways and investing in ports. Railways were their priority: trains accounted for 11 percent of all commodity transportation in 1851 and 63 percent in 1876.[31]

This accomplishment resulted from the government policy to mobilize funds. The 1842 law that had launched railway construction and the ensuing offer of concessions to private companies to build and operate the lines proved unsuccessful, and the development of France's network lagged behind that of other European countries. To remedy this situation, the government authorized rail companies to issue bonds (sticking to a measure already introduced under the Second Republic) and offer 99-year concessions to exploit the lines. After completion of the national network at the end of the 1850s, the government instructed the *Banque de France* to fund branch lines by continuing to back interest payments on bonds,[32]

The government and railway companies granted concessions—some of which guaranteed state subsidies—to establish regional companies with the understanding that the companies were not to raise dividends above certain levels. Decision-making over these concessions was restricted to small groups of ministers, civil servants and company directors, which made the process more rapid than under preceding regimes, when it had been slowed by parliament. The executive branch acted swiftly to grant lengthy concessions and financial guarantees in addition to financing part of the railway's construction and supporting the merger of smaller companies into larger entities.[33]

The policy met with success, and "the security these arrangements offered proved very attractive to investors."[34] Counting 1,931 km in 1850, France's railway network expanded to 4,100 km in 1860 and 23,600 km in 1880. All the main routes of the present-day network were built by 1869. France caught up with or surpassed other countries. Transportation costs fell from 12 centimes per *tonne-kilomètre* in 1841 to 5.88 centimes in 1881 and 4.8 centimes in 1900. Train freight rose from 100 million tons per kilometer in 1845 to 5,057 million in 1870, and rail traffic rose by 1,590 percent between 1851 and 1876. Railways contributed 101 percent to the growth of the volume of trade from 1851 to 1863 and 248 percent between 1851 and 1882. The upshot was a stunning "contraction of space."[35] At the start of the 1860s, freight moved from Lille to Paris in three days compared with eight days by road. This "space contraction" was consolidated by improvements to rail yards and locomotives, as well as by rural roads to train stations. The creation of a national electric telegraph network revolutionized the speed of information flows and became essential to commercial companies and banks. Telegraph stations connected every prefecture to Paris by 1855, and the construction of local stations had already begun.[36]

The overhaul of trade and marketing practices went hand in hand with this modern transport and communication networks. This overhaul was uneven, stretched over decades and left different trades unaffected in various regions and localities. Yet, for many industries, commodity trading became more rational with the consequences for production. The number of commercial intermediaries decreased and the long-standing strategies for profit-making in circulation disintegrated. Producers in various branches began to make systematic efforts to reach consumers, and contacts between them became more direct and continuous. A growing number of industrial firms had to adjust production to an ongoing flow of daily orders.

The new figure of the commercial commissioner personified these changes. Commissioner houses developed a type of distribution that gave consumers access to equivalent products manufactured by French and foreign firms. The spread of *grands magasins* in Paris and other cities deepened this price competition. The practice of fixed and marked prices, which few shops had adopted earlier in the century, began to replace the age-old practice of price bargaining that had until then been the rule in retail. Some shopkeepers had to engage in innovative marketing strategies and advertising to attract clients. Twelve thousand retail stores with multiple branches could be counted by 1914. The development of chain stores, however, was still modest, and overall, retailing remained traditional until the Second World War. The *grands magasins* counted for only 17 percent of value produced in the Parisian retail sector in 1914. Nevertheless, major changes in marketing and retailing had been initiated.[37]

Massive investments in railway building not only provided an impetus to metallurgy, engineering and mining, but above all transformed the circulation of merchandise and eroded the economic compartmentalization of France. Though this process was protracted and uneven, the multitude of local and regional economies, which had endured for decades after the abolition of internal customs barriers and tolls in 1789, were at last effectively integrated within a national market. Market opportunities increased, but producers were now also compelled to compete on prices. The "nationalization" of markets created increasingly frequent confrontations between equivalent products and their producers. The assured incomes of regional monopolies began to disappear. Whole regional industries were wiped out as a result of competitive selection, leading to rural deindustrialization in various parts of the country.

The industrial map radically changed, with concentration in the north and northeast, as well as in large cities such as Paris, Lyon and Lille, and towns such as Roubaix and Saint-Étienne. Commenting on these transformations, Caron asserts that the formation of a national market was as important a factor as the exposure to international competition in causing industrial modernization during the Second Empire and the decades that followed.[38]

Modern transport and communication networks also became a vector of foreign competition. It was the emperor's intention to integrate the national market into an emerging capitalist world market. Indeed, as Minister of Finance Fould explained in an 1862 speech, "the intensification of competition through improved communications and the reduction of tariff protection were ... the central features of a coherent policy designed to create a new environment for entrepreneurial activity."[39]

The government played a non-negligible role in the building of this world market by initiating a series of commercial treaties with other European states, starting with Britain in 1860. Part of the motivation was diplomatic, to strengthen the British alliance. But the main purpose was to modernize the economy. The lowering of tariffs, officials believed, would enhance competitive pressures and "stimulate material progress, after the initial dislocation," in a context in which "the most highly protected ... industries would be forced to equip themselves to world standards on pain of losing their home market, and thus their whole basis for existence."[40] As President of the Corps Législatif, Charles de Morny had stated in 1853, "what French industry particularly lacks is the pressure of competition," which would largely come from exposure to foreign trade.[41]

Napoleon III ruled out completely free markets but was convinced to liberalize trade by his Saint-Simonian advisors, who had been promoting the idea since the 1830s, arguing that competition on the domestic market was too weak and needed to be supplemented by foreign competition. Support for this policy also came from a group of producers and traders—wine producers, high-end textile manufacturers such as silk makers and other luxury-goods producers—already export oriented and interested in larger market shares. A solid majority of industrialists, however, organized in protectionist lobbies.[42]

During the 1850s, the regime opted for a progressive erosion of the protectionist wall. It reduced tariffs on coal, steel and iron to 20 percent to facilitate the building of railways and adopted other targeted reductions. The State Council, however, was divided over the issue of foreign trade liberalization, and protectionist lobbies mobilized their allies within the state and press. An 1856 bill to substitute a prohibition on textile imports with moderate tariffs sparked commotion among industrialists in the Conseil Législatif. The emperor backed down but seized the occasion to announce his intention to liberalize foreign trade within five years. Preparing for this liberalization, the government ordered prefects to deliver steady and thorough reports on the state of regional industries. While most entrepreneurs decried the plan, some firms had already taken their cue from previous tariffs reductions and invested in machinery. Others demanded the delay of further liberalization to proceed with the investments needed to compete against British firms.[43]

Meanwhile, Michel Chevalier began secret bargaining with Britain for the Anglo-French commercial treaty of 1860. The treaty was immediately denounced as a "coup d'État douanier" by industrialists and conservatives in the legislature. The treaty specified that Britain was to remove tariffs on the main French exports such as *article de Paris*, silk and wine, while French tariffs on British goods would not exceed 30 percent (25 percent from 1864). Separate conventions, also negotiated in 1860, fixed duties for other sectors.

The government had learned a lesson from the economic debacle that had followed the first commercial treaty with Britain in 1786. It formed a commission of enquiry to guide the negotiation of tariffs for different industrial branches by collecting exhaustive information on commercial exchanges with Britain and other states. The government instructed consular officials and foreign missions to inform on the production and transport costs of foreign firms. In assessing the impact of competition on industry, the state discovered that competitiveness was highly uneven between companies, branches and regions. It deemed a substantial portion of firms in sectors such as cotton and woollen textiles incapable of competing with British firms and likely to go under. Officials believed these firms needed to improve their productivity under competitive pressure from abroad. They therefore moved to support these sectors, offering low interest loans worth 38 million francs to support investments following the enactment of the treaty. Branches such as locomotive or steam engine construction were deemed to be more resilient and able to cope with tariffs as low as 10–15 percent, while smaller textile machine manufacturers necessitated higher tariffs to stay afloat.[44]

Following the initial Treaty of 1860, France and other European states, including the Ottoman Empire, negotiated over a dozen new commercial treaties in the following years. The emperor's decree power, coupled with the parliament's exclusion from trade agreements, meant that free traders retained the upper hand. Protectionists voiced opposition, and much of the business community (led by mining companies, cereal and wool producers and textile manufacturers) felt that its vital interests had been betrayed. As Roger Price put it, "the commercial treaty would prove to be a major factor in the rise of opposition to the authoritarian regime," specifically in the demand for parliamentary control over commercial treaties.[45]

The second half of the nineteenth century saw the rise of a European market, concomitant with that of national markets, and a continent-wide process of industrialization. In 1850, Europe counted 14,500 miles of railroads, but by 1880, there were 101,700 miles across the continent. This development of rail networks, together with the signing of commercial treaties, contributed to the emergence of a European market and indeed, with the development of steamship transport, to the rise of a single world market. The 1860 treaty between France and Britain initiated an era of freer trade. Even after the return of protectionist impulses in the 1870s, tariffs remained below levels of previous periods. This was certainly the case in France, even after the more restrictive Méline tariffs of 1892, which were "geared mainly to protecting domestic farmers by warding off cheap food imports in a bid to slow down much-feared structural change (in particular rural migration to the cities)," while "industry, by contrast, was left powerless to stop the pre-1914 trade boom from knocking at the country's door."[46] In any case, tariffs did not impede the exposure of French industry to foreign trade—which grew continuously even after the return of protectionist policies. The upshot was a sharp fall of commodity prices within an increasingly competitive context.[47]

In the new context of a unified national market exposed to international competition, French industrial firms had to take control over labor processes.[48] They were backed by the state, which acted, from the second half of the 1860s and into the Third Republic, to abolish the customary regulation of labor relations (discussed in Chapter 2). These actions were, as was the case for the other economic policies discussed above, met with resistance both within and outside the state—not just from workers, but also from traditional elites.

A widely publicised ruling made by the Cour de Cassation—the highest court of justice—in 1866 invalidated a previous ruling made by a *prud'hommes* council. The Cour de Cassation confirmed that an employer could retain two weeks' pay from a worker who had kept her clogs while working in violation of workshop rules established unilaterally by her employers. Similar decisions by the Cour de Cassation, granting arbitrary powers to employers, were issued during the 1870s under the Third Republic. Public indignation ensued, and the Chamber of Deputies proposed bills to limit the impact of these rulings. These bills, however, died in the Senate, which sided with the Cour and confirmed the employers' power over employees. Employers then redoubled their challenges to customary trade regulations and court decisions. The Cour de Cassation continued to back them, thus creating a crisis and resignations among *prud'hommes*.[49]

As these rulings eroded the *bon droit*, which worker struggles had consolidated before and during the Revolution of 1789, a new legal doctrine concerning labor relations emerged. This doctrine, systematized by jurists after the 1870s, introduced the notion of the "labour contract," which was subsequently incorporated into law around the turn of the century. The doctrine accepted that all labor contracts were *louage de service*—as opposed to *louage d'ouvrage*—and consequently implied the subordination of workers to their employers. In the words of jurist Marc Sauzet, written in 1890, a labor contract necessarily implied "subordination of the worker to the employer, in the execution of the work he agreed to."[50] This notion went against decades of legal decisions by *prud'hommes* councils, justices of the peace and commercial tribunals, but nonetheless came to prevail in law courts and scholarly journals.[51]

Legal rulings in adherence to this new doctrine and supporting the power of capital continued to roll in. A ruling by the Cour de Cassation in 1886, and a law on abusive rupture of *louage de services* contracts introduced in 1890, gave firms the right to dismiss workers unilaterally and thus undermined the reciprocity of labor relations implied by *louage d'ouvrage* contracts. A law on occupational injuries adopted in 1898 clarified the power of employers over the organization of production. Under *louage d'ouvrage* contracts, widespread until the last third of the nineteenth century, workers were hired for a specific task—they did *not* sell their labor power for a given period of time. This implied that they controlled their activities at work and were consequently considered responsible in case of injury. The new law, however, specified that employers were responsible in case of injuries and should compensate injured workers. By the same token, employers were given power over employees, who were freed from their responsibility in occupational injuries, but now had to submit to employers. A bill introduced in 1901 embedded into law the notion of the "labor contract" and confirmed the subordination of wage laborers to their employers.[52]

The definition of contracts, formalized in the Labor Code in 1910, consolidated the subordination of workers to their employer's directives. The salient characteristic of this new legal framework was "to no longer treat relationships of subordination [of workers to their employers] as an annoying epiphenomenon but to move it to its centre."[53] Whereas interpretations of the 1804 Civil Code had previously asserted that the employer "was not a judge," the new labor law implied that the employer was, in fact, the "only judge" when it came to the best ways of organizing work. The new definition of labor contracts also implied that workers did not belong to trade communities and became legal subjects individually hired by firms as part of a structure organized by bosses. Legally speaking, workers became individual sellers of their labor power or their capacity to work, the price of which was to be settled on a free and competitive market. Accordingly, the Cour de Cassation and other law courts challenged the validity of tariffs fixing wages and working conditions as part of the customary regulation of trade communities. Workers were able, on occasions, to convince judges to uphold existing tariffs, but the prevailing trend pointed toward their erosion.[54]

Capitalizing on this new legal framework, employers moved to assert their control over production, as they became exposed to the competitive imperative to enhance labor productivity. Attempts to impose new modes of management became more frequent in the closing decades of the nineteenth century as part of an effort to optimize investments in mechanization.[55] The new economic context required textile factory owners, for instance, "to interfere directly in the work process, to induce laborers to alter their habits, apply themselves more assiduously, and accept dramatic price cuts."[56] Labor productivity was the employers' new obsession, and they came to realize that "exactly how time was spent was often more important than how much."[57]

In the old hiring model, individual workers or, as was the case for textile mills, teams of workers, purchased raw material, rented access to workstations within factories, workshops and mines and sold their finished products back to the mill owners. This gave way to new practices in which bosses directly hired workers as wage laborers. Growing numbers of employers, who previously had to deal with group leaders of work teams, began to hire workers individually and to unilaterally fix piece rates and impose performance-based pay. The change amounted to a transition from a relationship between merchants and direct producers inside the enterprise, in which the worker retained her or his autonomy (at least regarding the organization of her or his labour), to a relation of subordination in which control over the organization of her or his labour was taken away from the worker.[58]

Put another way, with the rise of this new employer-employee relationship, industrial workers began to sell their *labor power*, which was commodified and consequently abstracted from their individual and collective control (via their trade's framework of customary regulation).[59]

This process of commodification of abstract labor was again uneven, varied according to branches and regions and significantly obstructed by the slow proletarianization of the population, much of which remained on the land well into the twentieth century, as discussed in Chapter 1. To be sure, in 1882, 84.7 percent of landholdings were smaller than ten acres and insufficiently large to feed their owners, who had to secure other sources of income in agriculture or industry. Moreover, the number of industrial workers increased over the last third of the nineteenth century. The combined effects, stemming from intensified domestic and international competition, of disappearing rural cottage production and, especially from the 1880s, of plummeting agricultural prices, pushed small holders away from the countryside and toward towns and cities. Meanwhile, falling crop and land prices allowed peasants in possession of holdings sufficiently large to sustain their families to remain on the land and even acquire supplemental holdings.

Some have described these processes as a "de-proletarianization" of the peasantry—the share of the waged workforce in agricultural production decreased steadily, going from 37 percent in 1866 to 26 percent in 1914. A side effect of this was an incipient, but still largely incomplete, stabilization of an industrial working class, instantiated by a reduction of the seasonal variation of industrial workforces—the typical industrial worker worked an average of 295 days per year toward the end of the nineteenth century. Still, seasonal rotation, mixed employment and enduring links between industrial workers, their family and rural life endured well after the Second World War, ensuring that the outline of the labor market remained blurry. Moreover, since these processes entailed the entrenchment of a large peasantry in the countryside, a "rural exodus" never gathered steam, involving mainly agricultural and "proto-industrial" wage laborers—a point that will be discussed in further detail below.[60] That said, the average yearly increase of the number of factory workers from 1866 to 1896 was 1.3 percent (but fell to 1.1 percent in the 1920s).[61] Much of this increase, as will be explained below, was linked to immigration and gave employers the power to impose factory rules during the Second Empire, and especially during the Third Republic.

In the wake of the laws of 1863 and 1867 that eased the procedures for a joint stock company, the number of firms managed by salaried executives grew, albeit at a slow pace. The number of executives running hierarchical structures and of supervisors acting as disciplinary agents over labor processes swelled at the beginning of the twentieth century. Still, as in the case of the rural exodus, these changes were gradual, and only a handful of large industrial companies developed full-blown modern, rationalized management hierarchies before 1914.[62] These changes were part of a broader process of industrial restructuring, to which we now turn.

The First Wave of Capitalist Industrial Growth from 1860 to 1930

Until the end of the Old Regime, many spinners and weavers hired by textile merchants worked from home or in small workshops, as opposed to large factories equipped with mechanical looms. The rarity of modern machinery and factories was true for all manufacturing at the time. When confronted with British competition in the wake of the 1786 commercial Treaty, only a handful of merchants possessed large manufacturing facilities—they consequently had relatively little fixed capital to defend competitively. Textile merchants, employing most of the industrial workforce, reacted to this competition either by reducing rates paid to factors and, in turn, to direct producers or by buying manufactured goods directly from British producers to sell in France. In the first half of the nineteenth century, however, several French merchants turned into industrialists, investing in facilities and mechanized production, seizing market opportunities in a deeply segmented domestic market protected from competitors. By the 1860s, a non-negligible portion of industrial firms had significant fixed capital. These firms, facing a newly competitive setting, had to systematically invest and rationalize their activities to preserve their prior investments. Market opportunities had turned into competitive imperatives. This was the beginning of an uneven but prolonged period of capital accumulation and industrialization.

As discussed above, the acceleration of railroad building, and the arrival of a national network, improved the efficiency of commodity transportation and reduced its costs. The upshot was a substantial reduction of regional price variations and an intensification of competitive pressures. Competition was amplified by a major reduction of custom duties causing a sharp rise in imports, especially of manufactured goods, which went from 4 percent to 11.3 percent of total imports from 1855–1859 to 1875–1879. A growing portion of French producers had to compete on prices fixed by more efficient foreign firms. Administrative reports of the 1860s revealed the efforts of entrepreneurs to re-equip their facilities in the face of British competition. Relatively cheap products from Germany enhanced competitive pressures over the following decades.[63]

A process of competitive selection ensued within French industry. Firms had to maximize profits. The competitive selection of firms, at the expense of those who maintained traditional production structures and failed to modernize their facilities, was obvious in textile manufacturing, where "a more capitalistic and concentrated structure" developed, entailing a strong tendency toward the disappearance of handloom spinning.[64] From 1860 to 1880, over half of Normandy's cotton manufacturing was wiped out by foreign competition, while the remaining firms adapted and modernized.[65] Describing the mechanization of weaving and the sharp decline of domestic hand weaving, Claude Fohlen writes of an "industrial revolution" in cotton manufacturing, unfolding from the 1860s, as British goods flooded the domestic market.[66]

Firms renewed their equipment and concentrated cotton spinning in larger urban factories. During the 1870s, production grew 1.9 percent annually, while the number of spindles remained the same, a sign of productivity gains. The number of mechanized looms exceeded the number of handlooms. The mechanization of cotton weaving was uninterrupted through 1914. The overall productivity of this sector improved by over 52 percent from the early 1880s to the early 1900s. Fixed capital investments increased at the turn of the century, as the industry saw the introduction of automatic power looms. Equipment permitting continuous weaving operated 3.2 million spindles out of a total of 7.2 million in 1913. Spindles went from an average speed of 4,000–11,000 spins per minute from 1880 to 1914. A team of three individuals, which could operate two mule jennies using 300–500 spindles around 1850, could work two looms using 1,000–2,400 spindles by 1914. These improvements allowed French cotton mills to recapture parts of the home market in the second half of the 1860s.[67]

The wool trade, which encompassed luxury goods, also went through competitive selection, concentration and mechanization. Hand spinning, which had persisted into the 1870s, rapidly declined. France totalled 62,000 handlooms in 1876, but only 28,500 in 1886. Handlooms essentially disappeared under the impact of competition and bankruptcy in the first decade of the new century. Linen spinning and weaving, using a fiber less amenable to power tools, declined after the 1870s, as production concentrated in the north. Survival in linen spinning and weaving became possible only on condition of concentration and mechanization.[68]

The success of the silk industry and its capacity to seize foreign market shares, we saw, had historically been based on the quality of its products, traditional artisanal production and sophisticated expertise. This changed rapidly as international competition intensified and new techniques were adopted, forcing producers to mechanize workshops and penetrate entry-level markets for cheaper goods to stay afloat. Factory silk spinning, still rare at the end of the 1870s, rapidly supplanted artisanal workshops in the two decades that followed. The number of mechanical looms increased from 7,000 in 1875 to 19,000 in 1880, 25,000 in 1894 and 42,000 in 1914. The number of handlooms declined from 80,000 in 1875 to 17,300 in 1914.[69]

Domestic labor declined in the textile trades, as production became concentrated in factories and towns. Mechanization also began to affect other traditional industries such as shoe manufacturing, leather processing and tailoring. Paper, construction and civil engineering and glass and porcelain production underwent profound transformations from the last three decades of the nineteenth century through to the 1920s. Waves of investments introduced machines and factories for every stage of porcelain production. The productivity of the spinning and pressing stages of porcelain manufacturing multiplied by a factor of five. In the glass industry, the introduction of new Siemens ovens in the mid-1880s marked a turning point, making possible uninterrupted production and the elimination of less efficient producers.[70]

Just as market-opportunity-driven industrialization became no longer viable for cheaper and mass-produced goods such as cotton, the market-opportunities, which had propelled the export of manufactured luxury goods such as silk, dried up in the 1870s. Although these exports had grown rapidly over the preceding decades, their yearly variability contrasted with British industrial exports. French products responded to frivolous desires—rather than the basic needs covered by British goods—and their consumption could more easily be delayed during periods of economic uncertainty.

French exports proved vulnerable to innovations that allowed for cost-efficient techniques, standardized production, and an evolution of taste toward silk fabrics and ribbons, and *articles de Paris*, mass manufactured by German, Swiss and Austrian competitors in the 1860s. During the "Great Depression" of 1873–1896, when economic demand sharply declined for luxury and semi-luxury commodities, cost-efficient competitors had an especially devastating effect on French producers. As Verley explains, in exclusive high-end branches, "the hard law of costs henceforth tended to prevail over marketing strategies." This called for a deep restructuring of manufacturing facilities and an acceleration of mechanization.[71]

The growing weight of capital-intensive sectors, concentrated factory production, the acceleration of the diffusion of technological innovations and the diminishing lifespan of industrial equipment—within an industrial economy still geared toward luxury production performed in relatively small workplaces—showed in the growth of horsepower from 9,500 additional horsepower on average each year from 1839 to 1869 to 32,800 from 1871 to 1894, 73,350 from 1883 to 1903 and 141,800 from 1903 to 1913.[72] The mechanization of industry and the attendant acceleration of the growth of horsepower were naturally paralleled by a rapid increase of labor productivity at an annual average of 2.4 in the 1890s, twice the rate of the rest of the nineteenth century.[73]

Denis Woronoff notes that the powerful upswing of horsepower preceded the arrival of the long depression from the mid-1870s to the mid-1890s.[74] The more remarkable fact is that this upswing persisted through the depression, save for a brief deceleration during the particularly sharp downturn of the 1880s. The growth of horsepower continued to accelerate as the depression receded before the First World War. The last third of the nineteenth century was a period of falling profitability until the mid-1890s. Rising international and domestic competition pushed down prices and profits and pushed up bankruptcies. The European price of iron, for example, fell by 50 percent from the early 1870s through the late 1890s, and overall industrial prices fell by about 35 percent in France from the late 1860s to the late 1890s.[75]

And yet, in spite or in fact *because* of price competition, falling profitability and decreasing market opportunities, many industrial firms did not diminish but actually *increased* investments aimed at mechanizing their facilities.[76] As Woronoff puts it, "the response was to invest to increase labor productivity. The Great Depression favoured the diffusion of equipment, it was the crossing point toward mechanization and generalized motorization." Caron stresses that industrial growth changed during this period, becoming "strongly capitalistic." Investments accelerated until the mid-1880s, decelerated in the second half of the 1880s—though the absolute value stayed much higher than it had been at any point before 1860—during the low point of the depression and accelerated again in the 1890s even before the end of the long depression. A decline of profitability thus unfolded at the same time as investment in fixed capital increased.[77] This was a clear indication of the capitalist conversion of the industrial sector. Firms had previously tended to pause production in times of economic slowdown, but they now steadily invested to cope with competition.

This represented an epochal break. The capital factor was increasingly replacing the labor factor in a growing number of firms and sectors.[78] Net investments in plant and equipment reached 72 million francs in 1835 but fell to 60 million francs in 1850. They then skyrocketed to 164 million in 1880 and reached 310 million in 1910.[79] The share of investments in GDP went from 12.1 percent in the 1850s to 13 percent from 1875 to 1889 and reached 14.2 percent from 1905 to 1913. The portion of industrial investments in total investments reached 38 percent from 1905 to 1913, up from 13 percent from the mid-1840s to the mid-1850s.[80]

This new capitalist pattern of investment fuelled the development of industrial branches and the transformation of older ones from the late nineteenth century through to the 1920s. Metallurgy was one of the older sectors that went through rapid and deep transformations. The reduction of tariffs on imported iron announced by the government in 1854 sent the clear signal that further trade liberalization was to come and accelerated investment in cost-cutting technologies by producers. The number of wood-fired blast furnaces continued to grow, from 230 in 1850 to 316 in 1860, but fell to 119 in 1869. The number of coke-fired furnaces rose from 176 in 1850 to 582 in 1860 and 1,262 in 1869. By the mid-1860s, around 90 percent of firms had been compelled to switch to this technique. This transformation stemmed from and reinforced a process of competitive selection that once again contributed to the deindustrialization of certain regions, such as the disappearance of metallurgic firms in Poitou and of steel production in Berry.[81] This

> deep structural evolution ... gained even further speed after the commercial treaty with Britain. By 1864, although the 'industrialization' of iron- and steel-making was not yet completed (some one hundred old 'Catalan forges' and 210 wood-fired blast furnaces survived), the modern mode of production had undoubtedly triumphed.[82]

The metallurgic technological revolution continued unabated in the decades that followed:

> the competitive pressures during the depression of 1876–1896, coupled with the advent of basic steel ... led to the demise of several of the leading firms of the 1860s that could not, or would not, change.[83]

The Bessemer process, rapidly adopted by firms during the 1870s, allowed steel production, which did not exceed 10,000 tons in 1865, to increase to 100,000 tons by 1873 and 283,000 tons in 1878. The Thomas-Gilchrist process developed in the second half of the 1870s, which improved the Bessemer process and brought a reduction of costs, was subsequently adopted by firms during the 1880s. This competitive process, fought with the "heavy artillery" of fixed capital, multiplied steel production by a factor of 12 from 1880 to 1913, and led to the domination of a small number of iron making and steelmaking firms, such as the giants Wendel, Longwy and Commentry-Fourchambault-Decazeville.[84]

The French played a limited role in developing the technological innovations at the turn of the twentieth century. The automobile industry was an exception. France was the only producer in the world until 1904, and remained second, behind the United States, until the 1930s. During the 1890s and the first years of the following century, French automobiles remained luxury items produced by highly qualified workers who controlled the pace and manner of their labor within a myriad of micro enterprises. Some larger firms, such as Renault and Citroën, emerged as leaders before 1914, thus announcing the initial stages of the concentration, mechanization and rationalization. The number of machine tools at Renault increased from 400 in 1905 to 2,250 in 1914.

State contracts during the First World War contributed to a rapid increase of mechanization and rationalization. Concentration also accelerated—there were hundreds of car producers before 1914, 155 in 1924, but only 20–40 in the 1930s, when the big three, Renault, Peugeot and Citroën, controlled three quarters of the domestic market. Efforts to standardize parts intensified—though success remained limited until after the Second World War—and employers sought to import the American Taylorist system. The "scientific organization of labor" remained sparse in France before 1914, and the only Taylorist innovation in car factories was time-keeping at Renault between 1909 and 1913. Assembly lines were exceptional before 1914. They were first introduced in 1919 and became normal during the 1920s. This entailed fixed capital investments, as well as a systematic rationalization and deskilling of labor. At Renault's car factories, unskilled workers composed a third of the labor force in 1913 and 53 percent in 1925. Over the 1920s, production was rapidly transformed and organized around mechanized assembly lines, capital constantly replaced labor and workers lost control over the conditions of their labor as management imposed tasks and rhythms. Labor productivity thus increased, as did the number of cars: 254,000 in 1929, five times the number of 1913.[85]

The automobile industry entailed the development of related branches. The Michelin tire company grew rapidly after the early 1890s, first by producing pneumatics for cycles and then to equip automobiles. Massive and ongoing investments in equipment allowed Michelin to become a world leader, investing in foreign firms and acquiring Citroën in 1935. As the car fleet grew from 150,000 in 1920 to 1,100,000 in 1930 and petroleum consumption rapidly increased, the state adopted a policy for energy autonomy and imposed quotas on imports of refined petroleum from foreign companies in 1928. Foreign oil firms had to build refineries on French territory, and the number of modern refining facilities grew from one to 15 over the following decade. The oil-refining capacity grew from 300,000 to 7.8 million tons a year.[86]

A process of concentration and modernization also took place in chemical production, as the sector diversified and expanded at the turn of the century. France held a dominant position in chemicals during the nineteenth century, but German firms caught up with, and overtook, their French counterparts by 1914. Many French firms became subsidiaries of German firms in which research and innovation were more dynamic. Nevertheless, from the mid-1880s and increasingly during the 1920s, French companies modernized older chemical product lines, such as fertilizers, cement, dyes and perfumes, and produced new products, such as industrial gases, artificial fibers and electrochemicals. The capital managed by the three largest chemical companies rapidly increased over the period. Pechiny saw its capital grow from 3.6 million francs in 1896 to 17 million in 1914 and 208 million in 1931. Ugine's capital grew from 600,000 francs in 1889 to 10 million in 1914 and 88 million in 1931. Kulhman managed a capital of 6 million in 1914 and 250 million in 1931. This capital accumulation implied larger factories and "scientific management."[87]

Capital accumulation was also propelled by the rise of the electricity industry in conjunction with the development of other new branches such as electrometallurgy and electrochemical production. Electricity played a leading role in the industrial transformation. Electricity production supplied the tramway systems and the Paris metro during the second half of the 1890s. Investors founded power and light companies in the first decade of the twentieth century and began to manufacture electrical equipment around 1908–1914. Electric power rapidly replaced hydromechanical power in the first third of the twentieth century.

Manufactures used 2.8 million kilowatt-hours in 1906, 9.8 million in 1926 and 12.8 in 1931. The average annual increase of kilowatt-hours used in industry over the period was 14 percent, while the use of electrical mechanical power per worker increased by an annual average of 10.6 percent. The number of kilowatt-hours available per worker in manufacturing grew from 0.56 in 1906 to 1.61 in 1931 if all employees are considered and 0.92–2.01 if one only considers employees in workplaces equipped with motor force. By 1931, electricity provided 62 percent of the energy for all industry, a proportion that reached around 75 percent in mining, heavy metallurgy, machine building and textile industries. The total production of electricity increased fivefold from 1900 to 1913, from 530 million kilowatt-hours to 1.8 billion. It then boomed during the 1920s, as the number of kilowatt-hours produced reached 17.2 billion in 1930. The rapid electrification of industry and the growth of general-purpose electrical power spurred the development of an electrical equipment branch, producing accumulators, batteries, cables, wires, lamps, motors and other materials.[88]

The spread of large managerial enterprises accompanied the process of capitalist industrialization and accumulation. Companies moved from personal to professional management and developed organizational capabilities to coordinate complex operations within and between facilities, often as part of processes of vertical integration of stages of production. Management swelled a "white-collar" workforce to oversee hierarchical chains of command, set tasks and enforce disciplined "scientific" labor. This type of modern enterprise did not develop as rapidly in France as it did in more advanced capitalist countries. The largest enterprises with the latest standards in management were in banking, transportation and mining in the early twentieth century.

Professional management developed in large manufacturing firms, which by this time became limited liability companies—as opposed to limited partnership companies—even when they continued to be controlled by a single family. A law passed in 1925 made it easier for small firms to become limited liabilities companies, leading a growing proportion to adopt this new form of ownership. During the 1920s, professionals managed around 25 percent of large firms against 11.5 percent for small and medium enterprises. The number of shareholders of some of the big industrial firms also expanded during the interwar period, though many firms avoided this form of financing. The number of shareholders reached 25,000 in the case of Thomson, an electrical equipment firm, and 50,000 at Saint-Gobain, a glass manufacturer. Even as industrial firms continued to favor self-financing, banking institutions increased industrial investments and began to offer financial expertise to firms. Most industrial firms, however, took only a partial or incomplete "managerial" turn and loose conglomerations of enterprises, such as ententes, were common across the industrial landscape prior to the Second World War.[89]

Enterprises began to experiment with the "scientific" organization of labor on the eve of the First World War, discovering Frederick Taylor's model of management. Henry Le Chapelier introduced Taylor's idea in 1904 and translated and published his *Principles of Scientific Management* in 1912. Henry Fayol, an engineer and director of a mine owned by the Commentry-Fourchambault-Decazeville Steel Company, became an influential proponent of rationalized management after 1900 and published a guidebook of management titled *L'administration industrielle et générale* in 1916. These ideas percolated within industrial circles, some of which hired American consultants to improve their organizations during the 1920s. The capitalist rationalization of labor and use of assembly lines first developed in the automobile sector, which functioned as a springboard for the projection of these methods to other sectors, such as electrical mechanics, aluminium production and even less mechanized branches like apparel confection, shoemaking and food processing. The rationalization of labor management, which began before the First World War, continued to unfold over the interwar period, imposing new rules and sanctions on workers, and causing a significant erosion of their qualifications in some branches of industry.[90]

These transformations of labor processes took place in increasingly larger workplaces. The percentage of workers belonging to a workplace of 1 to 10 employees fell from 32.2 in 1906 to 19.7 in 1931. Meanwhile, workplaces employing 11–100 laborers increased from 27.6 percent to 30.1 percent and those counting 101–500 from 21.7 percent to 23.6 percent. The percentage of workers employed by large factories with a workforce of 500 or more increased from 18.5 percent to 26.6 percent. The median size of industrial firms doubled from 1906 to 1931. Smaller establishments were concentrated in trades such as food processing, construction, woodwork and leather, while larger factories were in metallurgy, textile, automobile and chemical production.[91]

The rate of investment increased from the late 1890s to the 1920s, from an averaged 14.9 percent from 1896 to 1913, to 16.8 percent in 1913 and 20 percent in 1929, a rate similar to that of the 1950s. This level of investment was unprecedented, but so was the fact that it focused on capital equipment as opposed to facility investments. Investment in equipment more than doubled from 1905 to 1913 and increased by another 84 percent from 1913 to 1930. This is illustrated, for instance, by the fact that 86 percent of coal extraction in the north was mechanized by 1927 against only 4 percent in 1913. Substantial and sustained industrial investments to mechanize production drove gains in labor productivity. Productivity grew by a 2 percent a year from 1906 to 1931 and peaked at 3 percent during the 1920s.[92]

Industrial production grew at a rate of 2.4 percent per year from 1896 to 1913 and 2.6 percent from 1913 to 1929, with unprecedented annual growth rates peaking at 4–5 percent in 1906–1913 and 1924–1929. Between 1913 and 1929, industrial production grew by 40 percent. While industry represented around a third of the national physical output in 1852, this proportion grew to around three-fifth in 1912. In 1895, the value of industrial production, set at 8.2 billion francs, was only moderately superior to that of agriculture, which reached 7.7 billion francs. By 1913, however, total industrial production was worth 16.1 billion francs, well above the 11.9 francs created in agriculture. Within industry, value added in modern branches such as mechanical and electrical engineering began to outpace that added in older branches such as textiles, which, during the 1920s, never surpassed the level of production reached in 1913.[93]

The data presented so far in this section clearly demonstrates that industry transformed and grew at an unprecedented pace during the last third of the nineteenth century and the first third of the twentieth. While this represented a break with the previous period, the general evolution of the economy, and that of its industrial sector, can be properly appreciated only in comparison with other advanced capitalist countries. While industry grew, so did that of other capitalist economies and often at a significantly faster pace. Despite its rapid pace of industrialization after the late 1890s, the average annual growth of gross national product for 1900–1913 was 1.63 percent, behind Britain (1.9 percent) and Germany (2.83 percent). In 1914, the British and German shares of global industrial production were twice that of France and, around 1930, France's gross domestic product was only three-fourths Germany's and Britain's and a mere one-seventh of the United States.[94]

While several indicators point toward rapid growth, the industrial sector was still strongly "dualist" in the 1920s, with a large and entrenched share of small traditional enterprises alongside the larger modern firms. Motive power was still absent in three quarters of all factories. The standardization and interchangeability of industrial parts progressed remarkably slowly compared to advances realized in the United States and Germany and the Taylorization of production, while spreading, remained spotty and failed to penetrate much of the manufacturing sector.[95]

German firms in modern industrial branches—steel, chemicals, electrical engineering—surpassed and dominated their French competitors on the eve of the First World War, and France remained far behind at the end of the 1920s. The French steel industry never attained the levels of efficiency and rationalization of the German. While the automobile industry remained a world leader for several decades, Britain and Germany caught up and surpassed France in this sector by the 1930s. British manufactures used 17.8 million kilowatt-hours in 1930, around five million more than French manufactures, and this relatively limited production and distribution of electricity entailed, in turn, a relatively slower development of the electrical equipment sector.[96]

The growth and managerial turn of industrial firms, while non-negligible, were slow and limited compared to developments in other advanced capitalist economies. France, unlike the United States, Britain and Germany, did not have giant enterprises, and only a limited number of industrial firms fully adopted a managerial model with a professional bureaucracy. The steel sector proved incapable of developing equivalents to US Steel or Germany's Vereinigte Stahlwerke. The mean assets of the top ten steel companies in Germany were 3.2 times those of the top ten French steel producers in 1913 and 3.4 times in 1930. In 1913, French electrical equipment manufacturing employed 30,000 workers as against 140,000 in Germany. Around 1930, the American General Electric and German AEG companies had, respectively, assets ten times and three times larger than those of Thomson, the largest electrical equipment manufacturer in France. Similar gaps existed in chemical industries.[97]

The strongest indicator of the slow capitalist transition of French industry, in spite of its substantial development, was the country's continuous loss of world market shares. France was no match for more advanced capitalist economies. The country's share of world trade went from 12.8 percent in 1860 to 7.2 percent in 1913 and 3.7 percent in 1930. Not only did France lose part of its European trade to the much more dynamic German economy, but the latter's exports to France doubled from 1898 to 1913.

French exports grew slowly, 0.86 percent annually, from 1875 to 1895, but at a much faster 2.4 percent annual rate from 1895 to 1913. Manufacturing exports boomed from 1.9 billion francs in 1898, to 2.5 billion in 1905 and 4.2 billion in 1913. The value of industrial exports in 1929 was superior by two-thirds to that of 1913. This growth of exports gave a substantial boost to industrial production. Yet, the relative inefficiency of the industrial sector showed in France's share of global manufactured exports, which fell from 16 percent in 1880 to 12 percent in 1913. Much of the export growth of the 1920s was due to the undervaluation of the franc, and receded once the currency was revalued in the early 1930s. Moreover, in 1913, traditional luxury products such as silk goods and *article de Paris* formed the basis of French industrial exports, whose composition remained unaltered into the 1920s. France struggled to preserve its market share for luxury goods on the world market, and a growing portion of the high-end products traditionally associated with France were now manufactured in Germany. Significantly, France was largely absent from the capital goods, locomotive construction, electrical equipment and farm equipment world markets. The high investment rates of the period fuelled an industrial boom that would have been unsustainable without a continuous growth of capital goods imports, since France did not have the capacity to supply the machines needed by its factories.[98]

Beginning under the Second Empire, the state transformed the domestic economic context and favored its integration to the world market. This brought forth new rules of reproduction by which industrial firms had to abide. Competitive imperatives replaced market opportunities, and a capitalist process of industrialization and accumulation took shape. Increasing numbers of firms had to compete on prices, and thus had to continuously invest in productivity-enhancing technologies and to rationalize labor processes. This led to rapid and unprecedented industrial concentration, mechanization and growth. The industrial landscape, transformed by the time of the First World War, and this restructuring accelerated through the 1920s.

Yet, at the same time, this transformation was remarkably patchy and incomplete when compared to the accomplishments of other capitalist countries. The transition to capitalism had remained partial in France because of entrenched obstacles, which stemmed from the country's class structure and struggles and which eventually led to a momentous economic relapse. The restructuring of industry could only be accomplished through a deepening of capitalist social property relations and competitive imperatives, which, in turn, would entail a transformation of the agrarian sector.

Notes

1 Asselain 1984; Caron 1995; Carré et al. 1973; Dormois 2004; Roehl 1976.
2 Todd 2022, p. 20, 58, 234, 237–38.
3 Plessis 1985, p. 62; Kemp 1971, p. 172–73; Price 2001, p. 210.
4 Price 2001, p. 210.
5 Dansette 1976, p. 265, 372. Our translation.
6 Marx 2010, p. 238–40. Marx was, in fact, aware of this and insisted that

> The Bonaparte dynasty represents the conservative, not the revolutionary peasant: the peasant who wants to consolidate the condition of his social existence, the smallholding, not the peasant who strikes out beyond it. It does not represent the country people who want to overthrow the old order by their own energies, in alliance with the towns, but the precise opposite, those who are gloomily enclosed within this old order and want to see themselves and their small-holdings saved and given preferential treatment by the ghost of the Empire.

7 Aprile 2010, p. 433; Berenson 1987; Dansette 1976, p. 300–301; Gaboriaux 2010, p. 155–58; Vigier 1991, p. 10–11.
8 Aprile 2010, p. 396, 450; Dansette 1976, p. 266, 268.
9 Aprile 2010, p. 388–91; Dansette 1976, p. 89; Plessis 1985, p. 15–18; Price 2001, p. 41–48, 303; Wright 1998, p. 13–14.
10 Price 2001, p. 64.
11 Marx 2010, p. 173. Marx contends that Legitimists represented the rule of "big landed property" against Orleanists upholding the interests of "high finance, large-scale industry, large-scale trade, i.e. capital."
12 Mooers 1991, p. 181; Teschke 2005, p. 93.
13 Aprile 2010, p. 469, 474–75, 480–83; Price 2001, p. 37, 49–53.
14 Price 2001, p. 396; Plessis 1985, p. 166.
15 Price 2001, p. 37, 51–52.
16 Aprile 2010, p. 396; Dansette 1976, p. 78–81, 83, 90; Plessis 1985, p. 80.
17 Plessis 1985, p. 62. See also Kemp 1971, p. 161.
18 Aprile, 2010, p. 396; Mooers 1991, p. 86; Plessis 1985, p. 64–65; Price 2001, p. 227.
19 Plessis 1985, p. 65.
20 Gille 1970, p. 106. Our translation.
21 Hautcoeur 2011, p. 27; Landes 1956, p. 207–208, 210; Stoskopf 2010.
22 Plessis 1985, p. 76, 82; Greenfield 2020, p. 48–49; Kemp 1971, p. 163; Stoskopf 2010.
23 Hautcoeur 2011, p. 28; Landes 1956, p. 219, 222; Stoskopf 2010.
24 Hautcoeur 2011, p. 28–29; Stoskopf 2010.
25 Price 2001, p. 228.

26 Dansette 1976, p. 269; Hautcoeur 2011, p. 32; Plessis 2001.
27 Hautcoeur 2011, p. 30; Kemp 1971, p. 168, 190; Landes 1956, p. 215; Plessis 1985, p. 81.
28 Plessis 1985, p. 78.
29 Asselain 1988, p. 1242; Hautcoeur 2011, p. 25, 38; Plessis 1991.
30 Quoted in Dansette 1976, p. 372.
31 Anceau 2012, p. 351; Léon 1993, p. 293, 295; Perez 2012, p. 3; Plessis 1985, 82; Price 2001, 220.
32 Anceau 2012, p. 352; Perez 2012, p. 6; Kemp 1971, p. 170–71; Plessis 1985, p. 83.
33 Price 2001, p. 215–16.
34 Price 2001, p. 217.
35 Léon 1993, p. 266. Our translation.
36 Anceau 2012, p. 351, 353; Beltran and Griset 1994, p. 90; Léon 1993, p. 264–65, 268; Perez 2012, p. 7; Plessis 1985, p. 85, 87; Price 2001, p. 215–16; Verley 1996, p. 108; Woronoff 1994, p. 230.
37 Caron 1995, p. 92–93; Dormois 2004, p. 122–23; Folhen 1956, p. 149–57; Léon 1993, p. 285–90; Plessis 1985, p. 95.
38 Beltrand and Griset 1994, p. 90; Caron 1995, p. 91–92, 120; Charle 1991, p. 277, 280; Léon 1993, p. 304; Noiriel 1986, p. 85, 93; Price 2001, p. 211; Woronoff 1994, p. 231.
39 Price 2001, p. 233.
40 Kemp, 1976, p. 173–74, see also Dunham 1930, p. 6, 141.
41 Quoted in Price 2001, p. 231.
42 Hirsch 1991, p. 399–400.
43 Anceau 2012, p. 377; Dunham 1930, p. 20–22 ; Price 2001, p. 231, 234.
44 Anceau 2012, p. 379; Cadier 1988, p. 357; Dunham 1930, p. 139–41, 146–50; Kemp 1971, p. 175–76; Price 2001, p. 231–32, 234–35.
45 Price 2001, p. 236.
46 Dormois 2004, p. 33.
47 Asselain 1984, p. 89; Dormois 2004, p. 55; Ferguson 2000, p. 106; Gildea 2003, p. 150, 152; Woronoff 1994, p. 359.
48 Barjot 2014b, p. 385; Beltran and Griset 1994, p. 120; Caron 1995, p. 122.
49 Cottereau 2002, p. 1522–23, 1555; Lefebvre 2009, p. 50.
50 Quoted in Cottereau 2002, p. 1525–26: "Une certaine subordination de l'ouvrier au patron, dans l'exécution du travail promis."
51 Cottereau 1987, p. 115; 2002, p. 1521, 1524–26; Didry 2016, p. 43–44; Lefebvre 2009, p. 56, 62–64.
52 Chamerttant 2006, p. 220, 226; Cottereau 2002, p. 1523, 1555; Didry 2012, p. 85; Woronoff 1994, p. 367.
53 Cottereau 2002, p. 1555. Our translation.
54 Cottereau 2002, p. 1554; Didry 2001, p. 1260–62; 2012, p. 86, 90.
55 Moutet 1998, p. 103.
56 Reddy 1984, p. 241.
57 Reddy 1984, p. 245. See also Noiriel 1986, p. 94.
58 Lefebvre 2003, p. 161. Our translation.
59 Lefebvre 2003, p. 160–61; Noiriel 1986, p. 94; Reddy 1984, p. 251.
60 Asselain 1984, p. 27; Caron 1995, 107–109; Dormois 2004, p. 85; Gaboriaux 2010, p. 321; Marchand and Thélot 1991, p. 90, 93–94, 139; Verley 1996, p. 106–107; Woronoff 1994, p. 430, 445.
61 Marchand and Thélot 1991, p. 99.
62 Beltran and Griset 1994, p. 120–21; Charmettant 2006, p. 215; Fridenson 1997, p. 216; Fureix and Jarrige 2015, p. 82; Lefebvre 2003, p. 172, 197–98, 207, 238; Lequin 1983, p. 428; Perrot 1983, p. 6; Price 2001, p. 214; Tombs 1996, p. 289.
63 Caron 1995, p. 95, 127; Price 2004, p. 238, 244, 246; Woronoff 1994, p. 353.

64 Caron 1995, p. 136; Woronoff 1994, p. 355.
65 Reddy 1984, p. 298–99. As discussed below, cotton firms also sought to survive through privileged access to the Algerian colonial market, which partly deadened the imperative to invest and increase productivity, in turn, compromising the long-term competitiveness of these firms.
66 Fohlen 1956, p. 441, 445, 452, 458, 461.
67 Caron 1995, p. 127, 129–31; Woronoff 1994, p. 355.
68 Caron 1995, p. 131–34; Woronoff 1994, p. 355.
69 Caron 1995, p. 135–36; Noiriel 1986, p. 93; Verley 1989, p. 70; Woronoff 1994, p. 351, 355, 412.
70 Caron 1995, p. 412; Charles 1991, p. 283; Woronoff 1994, p. 356.
71 Todd 2022, p. 111, 145, 237; Verley 2013, p. 696, 700, 709, 719. Our translation.
72 Barjot 2014b, p. 384; Beltran and Griset 1994, p. 97, 100–101, 115; Rioux 1989, p. 89.
73 Caron 1995, p. 120, 123, 130; Marchand and Thélot 1991, p. 143–44.
74 Woronoff 1994, p. 356.
75 Caron 1995, p. 122; Ferguson 2000, p. 83; Hobsbawm 1994, p. 35–37.
76 Broder 1993, p. 59; Beltran and Griset 1994, p. 125.
77 Caron 1995, p. 120, 122.
78 Caron 1995, p. 115, 123, 129; Broder 1993, p. 59; Plessis 1996, p. 149.
79 Plessis 1996, p. 134. Considering amortization costs, total firm investments are set at 153 million francs in 1835 and 192 million in 1850. They then rose rapidly to 428 million francs in 1880 and 778 million in 1910.
80 Asselain 1988, p. 1232; Caron quoted in Broder 1993, p. 216–17.
81 Beltran and Griset 1994, p. 96; Caron 1995, p. 92; Dansette 1976; Gille 1968, p. 69. See also Caron 1995, p. 124; Bergeron 1978, p. 73–74; Rioux 1989, p. 89.
82 Plessis 1985, p. 90.
83 Smith 2006, p. 344.
84 Beltran and Griset 1994, p. 108; Smith 2006, p. 333, 337–41.
85 Asselain 1984, p. 76; Caron 1995, p. 99, 153, 244; Noiriel 1986, p. 131; Smith 2006, p. 400, 404, 406–407, 412; Vigna 2012, p. 41, 43; Woronoff 1994, p. 387–97.
86 Smith 2006, p. 415–16, 427–31; Woronoff 1994, p. 372, 468.
87 Asselain 1984, p. 76–77; Caron 1995, p. 153, 234; Moutet 1998; Smith 2006, p. 432–33, 439; Woronoff 1994, p. 418, 421, 461.
88 Caron 1995, p. 164; Noiriel 1986, p. 128; Smith 2006, p. 374, 382; Woronoff 1994, p. 376, 380, 382, 385, 413–15.
89 Caron 1995, p. 241; Fridenson 1997, p. 213, 227; Smith 2006, p. 326–28, 467; Woronoff 1994, p. 424–27.
90 Charles 1991, p. 285; Fridenson 1987; Moutet 1998, p. 104, 109; Smith 2006, p. 462, 479–82; Vigna 2012, p. 41–42; Woronoff 1994, p. 415–17, 437–38, 443.
91 Caron 1995, p. 241; Dormois 2004, p. 115; Woronoff 1994, p. 418.
92 Caron 1995, 164, 190–92; Noiriel 1986, p. 128; Woronoff 1994, p. 411.
93 Asselain 1984, p. 27, 77, 105; Caron 1995, p. 34, 156, 190, 309; Noiriel 1986, p. 120; Woronoff 1994, p. 459, 460, 464–65.
94 Dormois 2004, p. 12; Smith 2006, p. 483; Woronoff 1994, p. 461.
95 Caron 1995, p. 193; Dormois 2004, p. 114; Kuisel 1981, p. 27–28; Moutet 1998, p. 110; Woronoff 1994, p. 417.
96 Caron 1995, p. 153; Smith 2006, p. 366, 386, 400; Woronoff 1994, p. 415, 481.
97 Fridenson 1997, p. 213–14; Moutet 1998, p. 105; Smith 2006, p. 328, 366, 371, 398; Woronoff 1994, p. 382.
98 Asselain 1984, p. 24, 26; Caron 1995, p. 99, 101; Kuisel 1981, p. 28; Woronoff 1994, p. 360–61.

4   The Agricultural Revolution of the Fifth Republic after the End of the 1950s

The conclusive evidence that French agriculture did not grow rapidly in the second half of the eighteenth century, or undergo a revolution in the nineteenth century, is the consensus among academic specialists on the rural transformation after the late 1950s. Describing this transformation in a manner typical of historians of postwar France, Venus Bivar remarks:

> Nowhere was the transformation of the agricultural sector effected so quickly and so thoroughly as in France. At the close of the Second World War, the agricultural sector was … a backward holdover of the nineteenth century, and yet by the mid-1970s, France had become the world's second largest agricultural exporter.[1]

This revolution would not have taken place had the market opportunities of remunerative prices continued to set the agriculture sector in motion as they had for the previous two centuries. We argue instead that the agricultural revolution resulted from the reorganization of the rural social structure overseen by administrators working under Charles de Gaulle. These administrators excluded the landed notables, who had dominated the parliamentary regimes of the Third and Fourth Republics (lasting from 1870 to 1940 and the end of the Second World War to 1958, respectively), so as to ration land to farmers with a plan to take out loans and purchase the latest implements needed to produce for competitive markets. In the early 1960s, once the farmers' solvency, and thus possession of the land, depended on matching or beating the prices of other farmers facing the same competitive imperatives, France embarked on a trajectory, which turned it into a world agricultural leader by the beginning of the next decade.

Prior to this epoch-making transition, rural inhabitants had focused on satisfying the subsistence needs of their households. At the beginning of the twentieth century, 50–70 percent of the population worked in agriculture. Over 50 percent of the national population continued to live in communities of fewer than 2,000 inhabitants until the 1930s. If one increases the size of a town from 2,000 to 3,000 or 4,000, the rural population would have comprised the overwhelming majority. In the decade after the Second World War, some of these rural inhabitants lived as artisans or day laborers, but most sought to assure their livelihood from about five

DOI: 10.4324/9781003092896-5

million farms, each with an average surface area of 10–15 hectares. Above all, as Marc Bloch observed in his cartographic study of 1931, farms consisted of scores of discrete parcels of land, each about a tenth of a hectare. The extraordinary number of plots resulted from the millennia-old practice of partible inheritance, from the fact that when a farmer had savings, the available plot might not be contiguous, and from the preference for holding different types of land—arable, woods, pasture and vineyards—to maximize self-sufficiency and safeguard against natural catastrophe.[2]

Each one of these millions of farms was unique yet analogous. Farm-owning families gathered around a fire, pot of food and table to eat the products of their lands in the 1950s, the same way they had since the Middle Ages. They made their own bread or exchanged their grain at the local bakery for it. The cattle ate fodder grown in the fields and returned manure to the soil. Family members knew how to make or repair wooden wheels, work with metal and put tools, wagons and carts back together. They thus spent little on their farms. Cultivators used money instead to buy a tool, save and buy land or pay off brothers and sisters at the time of inheritance. Otherwise, they only used money to buy rice, oil, coffee, sugar and meat for the holidays.[3]

Roussillon, for instance, a village in Provence in the southeast, had 92 farms, a quarter smaller than 25 acres, half 25–50 acres and a quarter 50–100 acres in 1951. Although many of the farms had land around a house, they all consisted of scattered fields separated from one another by plots belonging to other farmers. Cost-effective capitalist agriculture with machinery proved impossible. But that was not the villagers' goal. They grew wheat and dried vegetables on about a third of the land, the same way they had at the beginning of the nineteenth century. They knew that other crops were better suited to the soil around Roussillon. Yet they also knew that wheat could be consumed or bartered, and thus represented a form of disaster insurance. Households made many of their clothes, grew much of their food in gardens or on rented land and bartered crops for services, such as home repairs, from neighbors. They used common land to collect mushrooms, twigs and branches for heating and grass for their chickens and rabbits. Villagers raised silkworms in their homes and worked in the cherry, asparagus and grape harvests. The money they earned was used to buy parcels of land, which allowed them to put family members to work, hand down an inheritance and protect against unknown menaces.[4] In these ways, the noncapitalist rationality of community-based subsistence farming, existent since the Middle Ages, predominated even in the decade following the Second World War.

Progress had no doubt taken place. Nearly all farmers replaced the swing plow with improved varieties, such the Brabant, by 1929. Farms had horse-pulled tedders, rakes and harvesters. Hundreds of thousands of farmers acquired mechanical seeders and balers and over 10,000 used tractors. The tonnage of chemical fertilizer used in agriculture doubled from 1913 to 1938. Engineers provided electricity to the countryside, thereby reducing the gap in lifestyle between town and country and offering a new means to power farm machines. Agricultural growth amounted to over 1 percent a year in the interwar period, whereas it had remained below this rate in the nineteenth century. The national population classified as agricultural declined by 1,800,000, from 42 to 36 percent of the total from 1921 to 1936.[5] These simultaneous trends of agricultural growth and population decline demonstrate improved labor productivity.

The more complex and expensive implements, such as tractors and combine harvesters, belonged to a minority of the largest agricultural enterprises. But by far, the largest, and growing, part of the agricultural sector consisted of medium-sized farms of 10–50 hectares. These agriculturalists went on seeking self-sufficiency through the purchase of small pieces of land or several supplementary hectares. Two-thirds of the farm debt, contracted in the 1920s and 1930s, went to the purchase of parcels of land. Households borrowed little to acquire modern implements. If one examines the dimensions of, and norms of work on, the typical farm in relation to the equipment, one notices the pervasiveness of underemployment in the 1950s. Households did not find it worthwhile to part with money for labor-saving implements when family members could perform the same work at no cost. They instead relied on household labor and animal traction. Buying machinery, fertilizer and seed all entailed risk. They could all prove useless and compromise the income of a field and all the work it required. Peasants needed the crops from the field for their animals and family, and preferred not to gamble on their livelihood.[6]

One must bear in mind that the progress of the nineteenth and early twentieth centuries took place before the imposition of capitalist social property relations. Like the French owners of cotton mills, who used British technologies and seized market opportunities in the first half of the nineteenth century (see Chapter 2), farmers of the 1920s saw the gains afforded by industrial fertilizer, enhanced productivity and market production. They took up the better practices observable on neighboring farms. Yet they did not make any determined efforts to educate themselves in agriculture. Prior to the 1950s, nine-tenths of farmers learned about agriculture solely from their parents. Markets fluctuated and did not impose competitive imperatives. They did not force farmers down a path of continuous improvement. Although farmers used more industrial fertilizer in the 1920s and 1930s, the application of it varied from sharecropper to sharecropper, farm to farm and even year to year for the same cultivator. In the economic depression of the 1930s, as industrial and agricultural capitalists around the world refused to draw down production—constrained instead to try to augment their share of the dwindling market, wait for competitors to desist and thereby defray the costs of previous investments with whatever income they could recoup—French farmers reverted to subsistence agriculture, cut back on capital outlays and experienced technical regression.[7]

Scholars often assume that the large-scale farms around Paris in the Beauce and Picardy, as well as the vineyards of Languedoc constituted exceptions to the foregoing traditional norm. Indeed, the value, adjusted for inflation, of mechanized inputs doubled from 1910–1914 to 1938, as tens of thousands of the largest farms had tractors and hundreds of thousands had mechanical seeders and balers. Fallow land declined by half during these years. Large beet farms in Picardy using wage labor achieved yields as high as, or even higher than, those achieved in England.[8]

These large farms, however, did not display much economic dynamism. Why otherwise would 1,000 farms larger than 100 hectares have disappeared between the late 1800s and 1929? These farms had relied on the labor of landless peasants and micro-proprietors, who migrated to the towns, attracted by a partial capitalist transformation of certain sectors of manufacturing, such as textiles, after the 1860s (see Chapter 3). Beet farms, for instance, relied on the intensive labor of rural artisans and smallholders for hoeing and weeding. Once these local laborers began to migrate to manufacturing districts after 1910, many of the beet farms, rather than replace their labor with machines, disappeared with the artisans and smallholders. In areas of growing viticulture specialization, such as Aude or around Avignon, farms became smaller, as peasants—holding down costs by relying on family labor rather than purchasing machines—bought parcels from large estates. It wasn't until the late 1970s that viticulturists, using scientific inputs and methods, produced enough wine to cover the national market.[9]

And so it went, during the interwar years, as large landholders, in all economic lines, sold strips of land to peasants rather than cut costs through intensification and mechanization. They took out few loans to purchase industrial inputs. Networks joining agricultural industries to capitalist farmers did not exist in the 1920s and 1930s. Though the area of fallow declined, 1,700,000 hectares of uncultivated arable land remained in 1938. Farmers did not use modern methods to reconstitute soil fertility. Wheat yields, from 1921 to 1928, stayed what they had been prior to 1914. The government therefore had to lift tariffs, instituted in the late nineteenth century, and have massive recourse to overseas suppliers of foodstuffs, especially cereals, during the First World War. The state increased tariffs once again in 1927–1928 and raised them even higher during the 1930s. Nevertheless, in spite of the incentive of favorable prices guaranteed thanks to the tariffs on imported foodstuffs, French growers, even in the best years, covered less than 90 percent of the nation's alimentary needs.[10]

Overall, it suited the political and economic interests of the landed elites to maintain a large rural population, traditional methods of production and protected markets. Large landowners, often lawyers and doctors—notables, in a word—resided in the towns and focused on their lives there. They created the Society of French Agriculturalists (*Société des agriculteurs de France*) in 1867 to promote technical progress but focused especially on combatting agrarian reform (see Chapter 1). They relied on rural votes to dominate the Chambers of Deputies of every regime until the founding of the Fifth Republic in 1958. Joseph-Marie-Auguste Caillaux, for instance, a well-known statesman of the left-of-center Radical Party prior to 1914, only joined this party when the monarchist duc de Doudeauville would not allow him to inherit the seat in the Chamber of Deputies from the Sarthe department in western France. After adopting republican slogans and seizing this political opening in 1898, Caillaux held the seat from the Sarthe for decades. The way Caillaux referred to his constituents, "my peasants," as if on a fief, reveals much about how politics and elections functioned under the Third Republic. Politicians lauded the peasants as independent proprietors of a patrimony, like other members of the bourgeoisie. They extolled the values of the countryside, vaunted their familiarity with the rural inhabitants and trumpeted the peasants as the essence of the national identity. Landed elites advocated protectionism and price supports as the means to preserve small farms and the salutary traditions they supposedly embodied.[11]

Of course, protectionism and price supports principally benefited the proprietors with saleable surpluses. The ubiquity of small farms meant an abundance of cheap labor, sharecroppers and tenants. Notables, in charge of the judiciary, adopted an extremely liberal interpretation of property laws, allowing landlords to retake their holdings regardless of any investment made by the actual farmer. In 1946, they used their influence in the legislature of the Fourth Republic to prevent the extension of medical coverage and workers' compensation to farmers. These social insurance laws would have strengthened the rural population's bargaining power against large landowners in negotiations over employment and tenancies. The notables—thanks to favorable commodity, labor and leasing policies—maintained their social standing without having to submit to the capitalist compulsion to make investments year in, year out to cut costs and match the competitive prices of productive growers at home and abroad. Although landholders of the Paris basin and viticultural businesses spent on fertilizers and mechanical implements to capitalize on obvious opportunities, they did not part with funds for machines, such as the combine harvester, which would have eliminated the need for rural labor. Rather, they continued to rely on peasant households to squeeze in bales, transport millstones, thresh and perform other tasks. Because of the guaranteed prices and lack of investments, the total wheat harvest did not regain the level of 1907 until 1954. At this time, the average yield for grain amounted to 16 quintals per hectare compared to as high as 30 in Denmark and 29 in Belgium. Statistics for other staple commodities such as beets and potatoes demonstrate a similar lag far behind the more efficient farmers in Denmark, Belgium and the Netherlands.[12]

The political left had challenged the notables' control over agriculture at the time of the Liberation. The National Resistance Council chose Pierre Tanguy-Prigent, a young Breton Socialist, as minister of agriculture in 1944. He vowed that henceforth true rural inhabitants, to the exclusion of nonfarming landowners, would control agricultural policy. The leadership of the farm organizations was taken over by socialist militants from the CGA (Confédération nationale paysanne) or union of agricultural technicians formed in 1936 during the Popular Front and later outlawed under the Occupation. The CGA criticized the archaic subsistence economy and called for investment and technical progress. Tanguy-Prigent sought to expand cooperatives, encourage family farmers to join operations together, create a network of state marketing agencies, establish a statute for farm leasing and sharecropping to limit exploitation by landlords and form a national office to buy land and sell or rent it to small farmers on favorable terms.[13]

Within a year, however, the Radical Party of the previous Third Republic regained influence, denounced the CGA's control over the farm associations, portrayed the CGA as out of touch with rural realities, highlighted the peasants' bitter life and firsthand knowledge of the needs of agriculture and rejected the socialists' plans for structural reform. Nonfarming landowners formed their own national federation of agricultural property to oppose Marxism and protect rights of inheritance. When the new National Federation of Farmers' Unions (FNSEA or Fédération nationale des syndicats d'exploitants agricoles) held elections in January 1946, large landowners and conservatives won a crushing victory over the political left of the CGA.[14]

During the 1950s, the FNSEA offered rural inhabitants a newspaper with information on prices, farming techniques and federation policy statements, advice on taxes and other legal matters, assistance in filling out forms necessary for subsidies and building permits, mediation with the bureaucracy and low prices for services such as disinfecting stables in livestock areas. The main way the FNSEA drew support from virtually all rural France was by fighting against state officials to make them support commodity prices. The well-endowed growers in charge of the FNSEA made their case by emphasizing the plight of marginal farmers. Large growers, to be sure, benefited the most, reaping assured profits from the prices set at the survival costs of the poorest farmers. In the summer of 1957, in the midst of the Algerian war and inflation, the government sought to hold the line on agricultural prices. The FNSEA launched nationwide demonstrations, and the Minister of Finance defused the unrest by issuing a decree indexing seven major commodities to the general price level and thus protecting farmers from inflation.[15]

During these years, from 1954 to 1962, the workforce in agriculture fell from 31 percent to 20.5 percent of the total active population. The rural exodus accelerated after 1950 when industrial growth lured labor to construction sites and factories. The rising wages outside of agriculture (see Chapter 5) contrasted with the stagnation and then fall in commodity prices, and thus contributed to the departures from rural areas. The number of farms smaller than 20 hectares declined. The number of salaried agricultural workers declined more rapidly.[16]

The exodus of agricultural workers and of the farming population more generally resulted from the motorization of agriculture financed thanks to the support of the Fourth Republic. State subsidies for cereal prices mounted from 50 million francs in 1954 to 300 million, or 10 percent of the value of production in 1958. The sugar beet market cost the state 40 million in 1954, 90 million in 1956 and 68 million in 1958. Half of the state subsidies went to these two commodities, associated with large farms of the north and Paris basin. The landowners invested in tractors, combine harvesters, pickup balers, selected seeds, precise fertilizing practices and advanced mechanization. These well-equipped farms saw regular gains in productivity and enjoyed prosperity. By 1955, they increased yields and output beyond national needs, while they employed fewer agricultural workers.[17]

The rural exodus among small holders took place especially in Limousin (center), the departments in the south of the Alps and the forest of the Landes (the southwest below Bordeaux). The stagnation and then the fall in agricultural prices made it difficult for households with the smallest properties to make ends meet. In market gardening and vinicultural areas, however, small holders earned enough income to round out their subsistence. These peasant households, often indebted, resisted the rural exodus. Indeed, during the 1950s, rural households with 20–50 hectares continued to make land purchases and covered even more of the agricultural surface than they had in the 1940s. The number of family farms hardly declined from the 1940s through to the 1950s. Very few of them used credit to finance implements. Seventy percent of farms did not have a tractor, and the cooperative use of tractors only involved 2 percent of farms. Even fewer farmers had combine harvesters and pickup balers. Peasants ate bread and soup at most meals in the 1950s. Observers of the countryside described technical backwardness and few signs of progress. Overall, the postwar transformation remained limited.[18]

Forces for change reemerged toward the end of the 1950s—at the very moment the FNSEA rallied rural France to force the government to support commodity prices. Modernization and improvements in the standard of living in urban areas were obvious to everyone. Rural youths hoped to adapt their work and leisure to the better life visible in the towns. Testimonies show that many young women in the rural areas did not want to become a peasant's wife. They wanted to be like the city women who vacationed in the countryside. The men had difficulty finding women to marry and worried about passing their farms on to offspring. Peasants, in short, felt humiliated by their social situation and mediocre standard of living.[19]

These attitudes animated the Agricultural Catholic Youth Association (JAC or Jeunesse Agricole Catholique). The JAC made the case that the family farm, far from embodying the sacred intangible values of France, crushed couples with work and worry. Couples could hardly enjoy their relationship. Children and women labored in the fields rather than obtain an education. Fifty percent of rural children did not accede to a certificate of studies. The family farm thus constituted an extraordinary means of oppression. The leaders of the JAC argued that the traditional farm organizations and the preservation of small farms did nothing to alleviate isolation and poverty. The slogan of price supports seemed deceitful to these reformers. Price supports did nothing to stimulate innovation. Rather, they significantly augmented the income of the largest landowners but scarcely ameliorated the condition of most rural inhabitants.[20]

Members of the JAC sought to free young farmers from subordination to local notables so they could educate themselves about new techniques and become protagonists of modernization. The JAC grew into the National Circle of Young Agriculturalists (CNJA or Cercle National des Jeunes Agriculteurs), which called for local self-help, especially pooling resources in autonomous, technically advanced cooperatives. The JAC and CNJA called for new habits of thought, financing and investment to raise the social and economic level of the rural population. The JAC and CNJA encouraged farmers to master the circuits of distribution, standardize products, learn advertising and create and impose brands. This focus on productivity and profit would no doubt accelerate the decline of the rural population. It challenged one of the FNSEA's fundamental principles, that all family farms could be saved through price supports.[21]

The JAC and CNJA nevertheless brought new members into, and gained leverage within, the FNSEA. The traditional heads of this organization argued that the reform proposals amounted to state dictates. They opposed any regulation of the free land market. The FNSEA alleged that the real agenda of the CNJA, in promoting reforms, was to furnish directors to kolkhozes (Soviet collective farms). Conservative deputies in the National Assembly raised their voices in favor of sacrosanct rights of property and trumpeted the fact that "90 percent" of farmers did not support the CNJA proposals.[22]

Small producers had complained in vain during the Fourth Republic that they did not receive sufficient training and education in the techniques of industrial agriculture. But after 1958, under de Gaulle, the political logic of the state changed. It became better to know well-placed civil servants than deputies in the National Assembly. The bureaucrats of the Ministry of Agriculture recognized the CNJA, even though disgruntled opponents argued that the CNJA did not have the credentials to represent the farming population. Indeed, despite the growing number of rural inhabitants interested in structural reform, the majority may still have hoped for price supports to save their farms. Even within de Gaulle's own party, the Union for the New Republic (UNR or l'Union pour la nouvelle République), many deputies fretted over the alliance with the CNJA. They preferred the traditional leaders of the FNSEA. Conservatives trusted the time-tested wisdom that a large population in the countryside offered a social and electoral bulwark against the dangers of the working class apparent in 1848, 1871, 1936 and the Liberation.[23]

Consider Roussillon, where the mayor, since the Second World War, had vaunted his personal relationship with the departmental deputies to the national legislature, Charles Lussy of the Socialist Party and Édouard Daladier of the Radical-Socialist Party. Gaullist candidates, however, defeated them around 1961, and the mayor's reputation for connections suffered. The underlying reason for the electoral shift was a new awareness among the commune's farmers of their professional status and dignity. They came to understand the difficulty of using their lands to live better than their forefathers had. They rejected the traditional lot of the peasant and insisted that their hard work entitled them to a share of the national lifestyle seen on television and in magazines. The farmers of Roussillon joined the agricultural organizations and increased their solidarity in the same way farmers did across France. By the end of the 1950s, they felt superior to local squabbles and to village and regional politics.[24]

De Gaulle and his ministers hoped to use these aspirations to raise agricultural productivity. They did not, however, intend to put forth the requisite funds. When they took power in 1958, finances were in disarray, and their budget covered only about a tenth of the program advocated by the CNJA. De Gaulle's ministers abrogated the price indexing, just resolved in 1957 at the end of the Fourth Republic, in the hopes that this measure would suffice to force smallholders to put their finances in order.[25]

Farmers responded, however, with the most extensive and violent jacquerie in the history of modern France. From 1959 to 1961, rebels took over subprefectures, burned ballot boxes, barricaded the roads and destroyed factories. What was different about these waves of protests was that they were led by the reformers of the new generation. The rebels wanted sweeping structural reform and would not be placated with price supports. Gaullist ministers renewed negotiations with the CNJA and came forward with a program, known as the Orientation Laws, covering agricultural education, advisory services, land reform, improvements to distribution networks and amendments to property rights. By couching the Laws in the rhetoric of a work ethic and economic independence, the government response to the rural unrest helped alter the conservative majority with a reassuring message. The discourse legitimized the young farmers and disqualified their social and ideological submission to the elders of the FNSEA and traditional legislators. The CNJA thus helped purge Gaullism, give it a modernizing hue and lay the basis for a renewed right-wing electoral base in the countryside.[26]

The Orientation Laws, implemented from 1960 to 1962, augmented the budgetary financing for agriculture nearly six times over, while the entire state budget barely doubled. They focused on two age-old problems of the rural social structure. First, the peasant household had relied on partible inheritance among offspring, or sales of strips of land, as a sort of retirement fund or insurance when the elder generation became too frail to work and support itself. The result was an uneconomic division of the soil. To tackle this problem, the Orientation Laws accorded life annuities to farmers over 65 once they relinquished their holdings for the government to install capitalist growers. Additional funds were added to retirement incomes for farmers ready to cede their lands at 60. The retirement annuities were readily snapped up by the older generation, liberating 35 percent of the agricultural surface from what had been a rational system of land use from the peasants' perspective, but not one amenable to capitalist development.[27]

Second, well-to-do farmers and speculators customarily hoarded land to extract rent and work from poor peasants with holdings insufficient to support a household. Landed notables thus avoided the relentless capitalist imperative to reinvest earnings into labor-saving implements to match the prices of growers facing the same price competition. The Orientation Laws, aiming to exclude these rentier notables, created the Societies of land reorganization and rural installation (Sociétés d'aménagement foncier et d'établissement rural or SAFER) to preempt sales, group plots together, make farms suitable for the latest technology and then resell them to enterprising growers. The SAFER proved less successful than did the pensions for the older generation of farmers. Conservatives imposed limitations to the exercise of preemption. Speculators, backed by the judiciary, found ways to circumvent the intervention of the SAFER.[28]

Still, the SAFER took part in 15–25 percent of the land market every year. When it did so, the technical committee of the district SAFER discussed which potential purchaser had the best chance of economic success. The determination might be based on a farmer's experience growing a crop suited to local soils. The SAFER especially helped farmers to round out their holdings and only secondarily to set up new growers. Some of these growers, who obtained farms from the SAFER, especially from the pensioned-off retirees, emigrated from North Africa with cash in hand thanks to compensation after the end of the Algerian War in 1962. A wave of Algerians also obtained generous credit from government sponsored agencies for farms in the early 1960s.[29]

The vetting process of the state administrators and district SAFER, to determine which applicants would obtain land, especially focused on the investment capital deemed necessary for viability. State administrators and district SAFER favored farmers who took out loans to finance the latest implements. The Orientation Laws charged the Crédit Agricole with promoting 30-year loans at 3 percent interest to allow farmers to expand and modernize. The Crédit Agricole opened bank branches in small towns across the country. Farmers took out loans from the Crédit Agricole under pressure from competitors who made investments to improve production, increase output and thereby match or beat the prices of other growers. But to secure the loans, the farmers had to have a minimum farm size and a plan for market production. Half of the farmers could not meet the minimum farm size and thus found themselves deprived of the opportunity to obtain a tractor, increase productivity, dispense with the need for family labor and perhaps see their children secure a better future outside of agriculture. Marginal landholders disappeared, as the average size of farms, shaped as a result of SAFER intervention, grew from 26.1 hectares to 38.1 hectares from 1963 to the 1970s.[30]

The new generation of farmers in the JAC and CNJA embraced the necessity of farm concentration but did not necessarily want it to result from capitalist debt and competition. They envisioned the grouping together of small farms in vast units of production to facilitate the industrial division of labor under the control of the people actually doing the work. Leaders of the CNJA maintained that cultivators of rationally laid-out farms would surmount the misery of the peasantry. They hoped to give rural inhabitants control over these inhabitants' economic future. However, as the Fifth Republic distributed land to farmers with a plan for financing, specialization and market production, their lives changed in ways they had not envisioned.[31]

Farmers able to finance a tractor, for instance, plowed in a matter of days an area that used to take weeks. However, to get the full value from the tractor, farmers had to finance new arable lands and often chop down ancient orchards, which yielded less revenue than did the precious land added to the harvest. They had to buy tools and attachments to enhance the tractor's versatility, renovate farm buildings and roads to accommodate the tractor and purchase new fertilizers and special seed strains to resist crop disease and augment the harvest, all of which required further loans from the Crédit Agricole. One input required a whole slew of other changes, which ripped rural households out of their self-sufficient routines and rendered them dependent on obtaining the highest monetary return from every hour of the day. This capitalist logic obliged farmers to continually increase output even though it caused a steady decline in commodity prices. Farmers therefore had to generate even more output with greater efficiencies with the aim of creating the margins to make debt payments and stave off bankruptcy. In this way, the banks appropriated an ever-greater share of the agriculturalists' labor beyond the proportion needed to cover the costs of reproducing the farmers' capacity to work.[32]

At the end of the Second World War, financing of this sort—to buy the tractors and follow-on implements and specialize production for the market—would have shocked older farmers fearful of debt. But by the 1980s, all of them had an account with the Crédit Agricole. They needed financing to increase output and stave off competition. Farmers had to allocate more and more of their income to raising what Karl Marx referred to as the organic composition of capital: the value of implements, or perpetually improving technology, relative to labor. Farm debt increased 14-fold from 1960 to 1973. The credits of the Crédit Agricole grew eight times over to 804 billion francs by 1965. Farmers used these loans first and foremost to buy tractors. In the 1950s, horses and bovines still accounted for most of the energy used in agriculture. But by 1973, the number of tractors had grown more than five times over.[33]

The number of combine harvesters rose from 43,000 in 1959 to 185,000 in 1973. This machine drastically diminished the seasonal harvest workforce. The prolonged work of threshing in the autumn and winter ceased to exist, and it thus became more difficult for the owners of parcels of land to scratch out a living by supplementing their farm resources with wages from seasonal labor. From 1960 to 1967, 160,000 people left the countryside every year. The agricultural population declined from about 35 percent of the active population in 1945 to 8 percent in 1980 and 4 percent in 2000. All the peasant festivals related to harvesting and threshing disappeared. The remaining rural inhabitants instead spent more time working to raise the income needed to remain solvent.[34]

This work became far more productive thanks to mechanized inputs. In Roussillon, the cooperative of village farmers augmented its stock of implements from one tractor and two plows in 1950 to three tractors and three full-time employees in 1959. By 1961, the cooperative added a big new garage and had 225 members, up from 48 members in 1950. The cooperative had a variety of plows for different types of soils and crops. Government-backed loans helped the cooperative to acquire a bulldozer, a caterpillar tractor for plowing and a caterpillar tractor for vineyards, all of which ran on diesel. The cooperative had three diesel wheel tractors of different horse powers. It had a gasoline tractor for towing, two asparagus earthing machines, a gyro pulverizer, three rotavators, one forage press, one grain harvester and one rotor for subsoiling the earth. Private farmers owned an additional 57 tractors. In 1950, the commune scarcely had a single tractor.[35]

In France, as a whole, growers not only snapped up tractors and combine harvesters but also used more than five times as much fertilizer in 1978 as they had in 1946. The number of lawn tractors, moto-mowers, pickup balers and mechanical seed drills rose by the same proportions. Whereas average wheat yields hardly grew, from about 13.5 to 15 *quintaux* per hectare from the mid-1850s to the 1930s and 1940s, they jumped to 42.7 *quintaux* per hectare in 1970–1974. Labor productivity grew over 8.1 percent a year in agriculture between 1963 and 1967, whereas it grew at 5.1 percent in the rest of the economy. Prior to 1938, labor productivity in agriculture had only increased about 2 percent a year.[36]

Food expenses declined from 42 percent to 19 percent of household budgets from 1950 to 1988, thus liberating income for the purchase of nonagricultural commodities and services. After members of the European Economic Community (EEC) signed the Common Agricultural Policy (CAP) in 1962, French exports to member states grew 22 percent a year for the rest of the decade. Export earnings from agriculture skyrocketed 1,600 percent, increasing their share of the national exports from 14 percent to 20 percent from 1962 to 1967. By the 1970s, France had become the second agricultural exporter in the world after the United States, a stunning accomplishment for a country where farming, at the end of the Second World War, still had much in common with its medieval past. For rural inhabitants, success facilitated the building of new homes, or the remodeling of old ones, in the 1960s. The farmers' buying power grew every year from 1965 to 1973, as their lifestyle aligned with the rest of the country.[37]

However, the growing wealth generated in the countryside did not afford the farmers any additional leisure. The couple Françoise Bernier and François Dufour, for instance, joined the JAC in the hopes of making their farm, near Saint-Malo in Normandy, viable. They learned that to secure the allowance available to young farmers, they had to sell their horses, buy extra cattle and specialize in milk. The plan for the financing entailed 40 cows, the acquisition of six more hectares and the construction of concrete sheds for feeding. Although these investments allowed Dufour to generate more output in less time, he ended up by the 1970s doubling the hours he spent on the tractor, plowing up the natural meadows, mowing the colored clover fields and harvesting beetroot and cabbage as fodder. Dufour smothered the ground in nitrogen to give maize a kick-start and then covered it with more nitrogen to grow grass in the spring. He and Bernier followed the normal practices of the time, what was necessary to receive backing from the development committee and cooperative. All managerial decisions stemmed from fear of error which could ruin the family farm. The bank manager planned the economic cycle without regard for the quality of Dufour's and Bernier's products or how they were produced. In this way, by the 1970s, the notion of a head of a business—enjoyed by farmers across France such as Dufour and Bernier—led them to accept the instructions of the syndical directors of the agricultural organizations. Plans for financing entailed more hours of work than what was needed to generate the revenue to support the farmer. The banks collected the profits or surplus labor by dint of interest on loans.[38]

Nowhere was this transformation of technology, work, time and environment starker than in Brittany. Breton peasants had farmed millet, rye and buckwheat for centuries. They put in backbreaking work preparing shale, sandy loam and other inauspicious soils for grains. The Breton soil should have been left in grasses, but the inhabitants thought first and foremost about having enough bread for their families. Strong communities continually resisted the efforts of nobles, religious establishments and bourgeois landowners to monopolize woods and extend the arable onto common lands. The peasants needed the commons to graze cattle and maintain the ecological/agricultural balance of their subsistence farming. They made subsistence farming even more secure in the nineteenth century by clearing scrubland and adding potatoes to their rotations with rye. In the 1940s and 1950s, Brittany remained a province with a particularly large number of small farms. The peasants did as many tasks as possible with family labor to avoid having to part with household resources for agricultural equipment. They put excess family members to work, for instance, farming potatoes, a labor-intensive crop, which yielded more subsistence calories per hectare than did wheat, though less market income per hour of work.[39]

Astonishingly, Breton farmers, by specializing in animal rearing, generated the most rapid pace of rural development in France in the 1960s. In one generation, Brittany became the country's most important agricultural region. One would have expected investors interested in the animal-rearing business to concentrate operations near ports, such as Bordeaux, Nantes or Lorient or near areas supplying feed in the Ile-de-France, Picardy, Haute-Normandy or Champagne. Agricultural publications made the case that as poultry rearing industrialized, factories producing eggs and chickens would naturally cluster around cities. No one thought that they would develop in the interior of Brittany.[40]

The JAC, however, won many adherents in Brittany in the late 1950s. These farmers saw their opportunity when the state financed the bulldozing of embankments of what is known as the bocage and thereby created 200,000 hectares of farmland, fertilized with 700,000 tons of lime, a year. The state sponsored agricultural centers and schools in Pontivy, Guingamp, Combourg, Lanivisiau and Plélo. It thus helped organize farmers into large dynamic cooperatives and associations to revolutionize the production of maize and soy as fodder. Above all, from 1962 onward, through sanitary standards, instruction and financing, the state rationalized animal rearing by closing small obsolete facilities, ones with modest budgets, and by subsidizing standardized and specialized operations equipped with the latest technologies.[41]

From the early 1960s onward, Breton agriculturalists used academic research in genetics, nutrition and medicine to improve animal husbandry. Dairy farmers aimed to control costs per liter of milk. Those specializing in poultry invested in large chicken coups. Pork farmers used selective breeding to foster rapid growth of muscle in the carcass relative to the expense of pig feed. Brittany assured 35 percent of the tonnage of poultry reared in France, as well as 90 percent of its poultry exports, by the early 1960s. Poultry farmers brought in 17–18 percent of the agricultural revenue of the region, even though they made up just 7 percent of the farmers. By the end of the decade, Brittany took the lead on other regions of France in pig rearing.[42]

Breton farmers, specializing in poultry and pork, fueled regional development. Animal feed and slaughtering industries grew rapidly in Breton towns in the 1960s. Lamballe and Loudéac, for instance, had been stagnant market towns in the 1950s before hundreds of jobs opened in meat processing and agro-alimentary factories. The expansion of cattle rearing, using feed purchased from outside the farm, facilitated the modernization of Breton ports. Brest became the biggest port in the world for the export of poultry by the early 1980s. The slaughtering and agro-alimentary industries, once developed, further stimulated agricultural output by loaning funds to Breton farmers to augment animal production.[43]

Breton farmers, however—having embraced the Orientation Laws, perfected techniques and combined and improved the structure of their operations—soon faced crises of overproduction. Pork and poultry prices declined relative to the price of other agricultural commodities in the 1960s and 1970s. Like in Normandy, moreover, intensive dynamic agriculture came at the cost of the natural environment. Industrial pig rearing on duckboard, rather than on straw, piled up excrement equivalent to a human population of 35,000 million, dangerously polluting the air and ground water of Brittany by the end of the 1990s.[44]

In this way, the capitalist logic unleashed in the early years of the Fifth Republic, with the support of young farmers determined to escape isolation and poverty, has led to financial anxiety and environmental degradation. Real farm revenue grew regularly before plateauing in 1979 and falling ever since, despite the historic decline in the number of agriculturalists. The spectacular growth of productivity has overrun demand in France, Europe and the world. The CAP changed in the late 1980s and early 1990s—from subsidizing exports so that they obtained the prices prevalent within the European Economic Community—to promoting the reduction of the agricultural surface. The new policy accorded aids in proportion to the lowering of revenue occasioned by the reduction in farm sizes. It thus benefited the growers with the most capital and flexibility to take less productive land out of cultivation and raise yields on their best fields. The policy of the French government has also encouraged farmers to keep up or embellish the territory, to expand forests, attract tourism and develop "environmental agriculture."[45]

Indeed, activists such as André Louis, Mattéo Tavera and José Bové have captured the reality of the farmers' lives by calling attention to the way in which industrial agriculture has increased debts and diminished incomes. They have pointed out the harm done to the natural topography and drainage, to the flattening of slopes, the excessive use of water in irrigation and the loss of biomass through heavy plowing machinery and soil erosion. Farmers know that as their land loses soil and nutrients, it requires evermore fertilizer to maintain yields, that crops and livestock have been infused with chemicals and antibiotics and that grains, vegetables and cattle have lost their quality and taste. Activists have encouraged organic sustainable farming as an alternative. The capitalist logic proves, however, that once embarked on the path of industrial agriculture, it is nearly impossible for farmers to change course. Debts make the conversion to organic methods seem too risky, whereas financing more land and new inputs to increase output and cover financial obligations seems a more rational means to stay afloat. Needless to say, this logic only compounds the economic and environmental problems.[46]

In sum, this capitalist logic, which has brought on the current glut, depressed farm income and degraded the natural environment, is traceable to the late 1950s, when agriculturalists became dependent on market production in competition with their peers to hold on to their farms. Previously, dating back to even before the year 1000, France had millions of small farms, each one embedded in a rural community and divided into scores of discrete fields. Plots dispersed over the territory of a village, each with a distinct crop, allowed farmers to avoid seeing their sustenance imperiled by adverse weather, blight or a collapse in prices.

Improved implements and tillage, and the slow reduction of the rural population in the late 1800s, allowed the remaining farmers to purchase parcels of land. Growing grain, gathering wood and animal feed on common lands, working for compensation in the harvests of various crops and engaging in handicrafts, such as silkworm rearing in their cottages, allowed millions of farmers to eke out a living in the twentieth century. Farmers relied on household labor at no cost to perform agricultural tasks rather than deplete their income by spending on machines, which would leave family members with less to do. They found it more rational to save their earnings, purchase parcels of land and put family members to work making their existence more secure.

These traditions suited the notables who dominated the political institutions of the Third and Fourth Republics. Landed elites counted on a large industrious population in the countryside for tenants, sharecroppers and farm laborers, not to mention the votes to return year after year to the Chamber of Deputies. The notables, who held sway in government, offered platitudes about the national values embodied by the peasant farmers and historic regions. They enacted protective tariffs and price supports to preserve family holdings. Price supports, of course, benefited the landowners with the largest surpluses to sell. They also helped sustain rental incomes. Agriculture improved and output increased in the nineteenth and twentieth centuries, thanks to the opportunities to gain revenue by capitalizing on the latest tools and methods available at the time. Yet, neither the millions of peasants nor the notables faced the capitalist compulsion to make their husbandry more productive every production cycle so as not to lose their lands to more competitive growers. Large proprietors remained free from the unrelenting pressure to plow gains back into expanding production to match the competitive prices of other growers.

At the time of the Liberation in 1944, reformers sought to exclude the notables from agricultural policy. They hoped to carry out structural reform, improve the quality of life in the countryside and augment the output of foodstuffs. However, the traditional political groupings of the pre-Liberation era succeeded in isolating these dissenters and reasserting control over the newly created Fourth Republic and FNSEA (the national farm organization) by denouncing communism and by championing property rights and price supports for *all* farmers. It wasn't until the late 1950s that an insurgent movement of small holders, perceiving the growing gap between their lives and what was manifest in the towns, again exhorted rural inhabitants to cooperate and modernize, to raise the standard of living in the countryside, even if an agricultural revolution would eliminate family farms. The change of regime in 1958, which brought de Gaulle and his administrators to power, loosened the notables' grip on the legislative process and made it possible for the new generation of farmers, through violent demonstrations, to force the government to advance the funds needed for structural reform.

The reforms intervened in the land market to prevent peasant retirees from dividing the land among offspring and to prevent notables from accumulating property and extracting rent and labor from peasant small holders in need of land and work. The reforms accorded the land to capitalist growers with a plan to take out loans, invest in the latest implements and produce for the market. Once agriculturalists focused on market production, rather than on household and community needs, they constantly had to take out additional loans to finance the technology needed to keep pace with the productivity and prices of other growers. Farmers unable to match the prevailing price-cost ratio faced bankruptcy. The result of this capitalist transition was spectacular increases in the use of fertilizer and machinery, in labor productivity and rural incomes, as the number of farmers rapidly diminished during the 1960s.

The remaining farmers, since that time, have had to work ever longer hours to generate the revenue needed to cover their growing debts. Commercial counselors and technicians instruct farmers, like workers in the wider economy, on how they must produce. The farmers must follow the instructions in order obtain the capital required to stay in business. The ultimate beneficiaries are the financial capitalists of the banks.

At the beginning of the 1950s, household farms and villages across France produced grains and livestock for local needs. But since that time—under the guidance of technicians overseeing the flows of capital—animal breeding has concentrated in the West and Center, industrial pig and poultry production in Brittany, large-scale grain farming in northern France and fruits, vegetables and wine in the center and south. Such monoculture inevitably attracts pests and diseases, and requires evermore chemical and industrial inputs, which have detracted from the quality of the soil and food and damaged the natural environment. Agriculture, moreover, like the rest of the economy, has failed to improve living standards since the 1970s, as glut prevents farmers from raising prices and increasing incomes. Although organic sustainable agriculture stands as a potential alternative, recurrent impending financial obligations compel farmers to seek additional loans to secure better implements and more lands to augment output and remain solvent. Farmers are left with no choice but to aggravate the current problems.

Notes

1 Bivar 2018, p. 1. Sarah Farmer:

> In the 1950s and 1960s, in the course of a single generation, the impact of the mechanization of farm labor shifted the French agricultural sector from one based on ... a peasant economy to one sustained by the massive production and financial yields of a globally competitive agro-food industry.

Farmer 2020, p. 2. Armand Frémont: "The transformation of the 1960s modified nearly every human and economic element of the systems of animal rearing, the landscape, and society, and turned peasants into agricultural entrepreneurs in one or two generations." Frémont 2006, p. 125.

2 Bloch 1966; André and Delorme 1983, p. 303; Bivar 2018, p. 24–25; Herviaud and Viard 2011, p. 62–63; Frémont 2006, p. 131; Lefebvre 2022, p. 26.
3 Mendras and Fresney 1988, p. 31; Miquel 2004, p. 194.
4 Wylie 1974, p. 21–23, 126, 158–59, 161, 164, 180.
5 Gervais, Jollivet, and Tavernier 1977, p. 58, 60–61, 63, 68, 83; Barral 1980, p. 827.
6 Mendras 1970, p. 37; Pautard, 1965, p. 76–77; Gervais, Jollivet, and Tavernier 1977, p. 60–61, 69–70, 557–58; Moulin 1991, p. 142–43.
7 Amann 1990, p. 196–97; Lafrance 2020, p. 71, 75; Thier 2020, p. 166–67; Barral 1980, p. 828, 836; Gervais, Jollivet, and Tavernier 1977, p. 558–59; Moulin 1991, p. 148.
8 Gervais, Jollivet, and Tavernier 1977, p. 57, 60–62; Pinchemel 1957, p. 86–87, 92–93; O'Brien and Keyder 1978, p. 122; Barral 1980, p. 840–41; Heywood 1981, p. 367.
9 Pinchemel 1957, p. 95; Gervais, Jollivet, and Tavernier 1977, p. 57, 60–61, 71, 145; Barral 1980, p 840–41; Levine Frader 1991, p. 24 26; Heath 2014, p. 212; Moulin 1991, p. 140–41.
10 Gervais, Jollivet, and Tavernier 1977, p. 57, 60–61, 71, 74–75; Barral 1980, p. 827, 831, 839; Moulin 1991, p. 136, 140–41.
11 Augé-Laribé 1959, p. 94; Barral 1968, p. 79–81, 289; Mendras 1970, p. 218; Mendras and Fresney 1988, p. 31; Bivar 2018, p. 16–18; Keeler 1987, p. 44; Bruneteau 1994, p. 70; Gervais, Jollivet, and Tavernier 1977, p. 261; Herviaud and Viard 2011, p. 50–51; Berenson 1992, p. 47–48.

12 Keeler 1987, p. 44; Mendras and Fresney 1988, p. 29; Bivar 2018, p. 16–18, 43–44; Jessenne 2006, p. 225; Miquel 2004, p. 209–10, 235–36; Gervais, Jollivet, and Tavernier 1977, p. 618–19.
13 Barral 1968, p. 285, 287; Keeler 1987, p. 38–39.
14 Barral 1968, p. 289–90; Keeler 1987, p. 41, 43–44, 48, 50–51.
15 Keeler 1987, p. 43–44, 48, 50–51.
16 Gervais, Jollivet, and Tavernier 1977, p. 154; Miquel 2004, p. 197; Moulin 1991, p. 183, 185–86.
17 Gervais, Jollivet, and Tavernier 1977, p. 126–27, 161; Moulin 1991, p. 167–68; Jessenne 2006, p. 224.
18 Miquel 2004, p. 197–98; Gervais, Jollivet, and Tavernier 1977, p. 158, 165–66; Moulin 1991, p. 162–63, 168; Jessenne 2006, p. 224–25.
19 Mendras 1970, p. 207, 216–17; Farmer 2020, p. 20–21.
20 Keeler 1987, p. 59; Gervais, Jollivet, and Tavernier 1977, p. 498.
21 Bess 2003, p. 46; Keeler 1987, p. 60; Barral 1968, p. 314; Gervais, Jollivet, and Tavernier 1977, p. 500.
22 Barral 1968, p. 314; Keeler 1987, p. 61; Bruneteau 1994, p. 77; Gervais, Jollivet, and Tavernier 1977, p. 502.
23 Bivar 2018, p. 90–91; Keeler 1987, p. 62; Bruneteau 1994, p. 31–32; Bonneuil, Campagne, and Humbert 2017.
24 Wylie 1974, p. 353, 359, 374–75.
25 Bivar 2018, p. 90–91; Keeler 1987, p. 65.
26 Bivar 2018, p. 91–92; Keeler 1987, p. 65; Mendras 1970, p. 216–17; Bruneteau 1994, p. 61.
27 Alphandéry, Bitoun, and Dupont 1989, p. 182; Brenner 2005, p. 218; Gavignaud-Fontaine 1996, p. 143–44; Wright 1964, p. 170–71; Miquel 2004, p. 244; Barral 1968, p. 320, 323; Wylie 1974, p. 313–14.
28 Wright 1964, p. 170–71; Miquel 2004, p. 237–38, 240–41; Gervais, Jollivet, and Tavernier 1977, p. 657–59.
29 André and Delorme 1983, p. 337; Gavignaud-Fontaine 1996, p. 143–44; Bivar 2018, p. 102–103; Amann 1990, p. 206, 208; Bonneuil, Campagne, and Humbert 2017; Barral 1968, p. 320, 323; Moulin 1991, p. 171, 174–76.
30 Moulin 1991, p. 175–76; André and Delorme 1983, p. 339; Gavignaud-Fontaine 1996, p. 144.
31 Gervais, Jollivet, and Tavernier 1977, p. 500, 503–505.
32 Moulin 1991, p. 171; Barral 1982, p. 1433; Bess 2003, p. 43–44; Jessenne 2006, p. 228.
33 Moulin 1991, p. 182; Duboys, Fresney, and Mendras 1988, p. 30; Jessenne 2006, p. 228; Bess 2003, p. 43–44; Bivar 2018, p. 39; Thier 2020, p. 75; Allaire 1995, p. 372.
34 Gavignaud-Fontaine 1996, p. 150; Jessenne 2006, p. 228; Bess 2003, p. 46; Barral 1982, p. 1433–34; Bivar 2018, p. 39, 110–11; Gervais, Jollivet, and Tavernier 1977, p. 158, 161, 165–66; Campagne, Humbert, and et Bonneuil 2017; Frémont 2006, p. 131.
35 Wylie 1974, p. 360.
36 Barral 1982, p. 1429–30; Jessenne 2006, p. 225–28, 234; Moulin 1991, p. 170–71, 181–82; Fourastié 1979, p. 208–209; Gervais, Jollivet, and Tavernier 1977, p. 157–58, 161.
37 Barral 1982, p. 1459; Jessenne 2006, p. 233, 239; Moulin 1991, p. 170–71, 181–82, 194; Allaire 1995, p. 347; Bivar 2018, p. 111, 172.
38 Bové, Dufour, and Luneau 2002, pp. 44–46; Gervais, Jollivet, and Tavernier 1977, p. 173, 669–71; Alphandéry, Bitoun, and Dupont 1989, p. 132, 137. Pascal Dibie documents a similar phenomenon by which independent farmers of Upper Burgundy became increasingly productive workers on behalf of the banks; Dibie 2006, p. 255.
39 Mulliez 1979, p. 28–29, 32, 40; Meyer 1966, p. 538–39, 554, 566, 578; Bossis 1972, p. 136; Plack 2005, p. 45; Moulin 1991, p. 49; Clout 1983, p. 80–81, 145; Pautard 1965,

p. 76–77, 90; Gachon 1955, p. 43; Mendras 1988, p. 34; Diry 1985, p. 454–55, 457; Gaveau 2021, p. 283.
40 Diry 1985, p. 212, 228, 445, 448; Moulin 1991, p. 197.
41 Gervais, Jollivet, and Tavernier 1977, p. 661; Diry 1985, p. 248–49, 294, 456; Miquel 2004, p. 189; Allaire 1995, p. 352, 357; Gavignaud-Fontaine 1996, p. 145.
42 Allaire 1995, p. 352; Diry 1985, p. 115–16, 199, 427, 434.
43 Diry 1985, p. 212, 247, 452–55, 462–63; Allaire 1995, p. 357.
44 Gervais, Jollivet, and Tavernier 1977, p. 661; Diry 1985, p. 296, 298; Bové, Dufour, and Luneau 2002, p. 109–110.
45 Gavignaud Fontaine 1996, p. 149, 154–55, 192; Alphandéry, Bitoun, and Dupont 1989, p. 201.
46 Bové, Dufour, and Luneau 2002, p. 48, 53–54, 65, 67, 85–86; Bivar 2018, p. 136–37.

5 Slow Growth, Relapse and Rapid Capitalist Industrialization from the Interwar Period to the 1970s

Economic historians tend to explain economic growth by analyzing supply and demand. Carré, Dubois and Malinvaud used econometric methods to provide such an analysis of France in the early 1970s.[1] Jean-François Eck offers a more recent study of this sort. Caron also adheres to this procedure. He encapsulates a broadly shared view on the causes of sustained economic growth in France, explaining that the rising productivity of supply factors caused a long-term fall of industrial prices. Decreasing prices then allowed peasants to turn away from autarkic subsistence production toward the consumption of manufactured goods, which, in turn, stimulated industrial investment and demand for capital goods. A "previous accumulation," *à la* Adam Smith, according to Caron, caused both ends of this process, as merchants turned their circulating capital into fixed capital, thus generating productivity gains, while peasants redirected their swelling monetary mass toward an increasingly attractive consumer market.[2]

The problem with this type of explanation is that it is entirely circular: soaring productivity and falling prices depend on rising demand, which itself is said to derive from productivity gains and decreasing prices. The only way out of this circularity is to identify variables external to, and causing, this virtuous economic circle. Merchants decide at some point to redirect their circulating capital toward productive industrial investments, thus providing incentives for peasants to opt for market consumption. But why merchants would suddenly decide to *systematically* reinvest profits in fixed industrial capital, and peasants to become market consumers, is not explained.

What is missing from the picture is the fact that the virtuous economic pattern identified by Caron rests on a radical transformation of social property relations. These new relations create a mass of market dependent workers compelled to sell their labor-power and to buy goods and services on markets. They also compel firms to invest systematically in productivity-enhancing means of production to compete against rival companies so as to offer the lowest prices to the mass market. Put another way, we need a sociopolitical explanation of sustained growth, not simply an "economic" one. While the latter dimension of this transformation of social property relations (market imperatives compelling firms to systematically seek productivity gains) began to emerge in France from around the 1860s, the emergence of the first aspect (a class of market dependent wage laborers), as we

DOI: 10.4324/9781003092896-6

explained in the previous chapter, proceeded slowly and was at times stopped or even reversed, until the 1950s. This had momentous consequences for capitalist industrialization.

Only by considering the social-political basis of economic development—the effects of social property relations and rules of reproduction—can we explain the breakdown of the 1930s, namely the stalled industrialization, with no signs of recovery, which contrasted with the more advanced capitalist economies. Only by using this analytic framework—studying a capitalist restructuring of society—can we explain the sustained and dynamic industrialization of the 1950s.

We begin this chapter by explaining how, under the sociopolitical context of the Third Republic, industrial firms secured political support to control and divide markets and thereby mute competitive imperatives. We show how this eventually led to an industrial relapse during the 1930s. We then present the ways in which the deepening of capitalist social property relations and imposition of competitive imperatives upon reluctant employers after the Second World War transformed patterns of industrialization and led to sustained economic development.

Obstacles to the Capitalist Transition
and the Industrial Relapse of the 1930s

In his seminal paper of 1963, from which stemmed a historiography, Stanley Hoffmann presented the Third Republic as a "republican synthesis." The stabilization of the regime stemmed from a class alliance of the bourgeoisie, as the dominant partner, with the peasantry and middle classes ("independents," nonwage earners). This synthesis sustained a "stalemate society" which was "neither dynamic nor static," and was tied to an equilibrium between industry and the preservation of an agrarian order. Allying with the peasantry, the bourgeoisie held "beliefs" that favored "permanence" over "competition" and implied a "resistance to the machine age." This made for slow progress and sub-efficient firms that exacerbated the proletariat's discontent with a capitalist economy "which was not even productive." A social synthesis was thus reached through a class alliance that rested on the political exclusion of the industrial working class and its confinement to a "social ghetto."[3]

Hoffman was a liberal (Raymond Aron was his mentor), but similar approaches to the social composition, and ensuing state policies, of the Third Republic have been proposed by Marxists. Sanford Elwitt explains that to assume national leadership in the face of a growing proletariat, the bourgeoisie had to forge an alliance with "substantial farmers" and "petty producers." To maintain stability, the bourgeois republic had to adopt policies that "produced sympathetic vibrations among petty producers."[4]

Both Hoffmann and Elwitt, and authors with similar approaches, correctly identify the social logic—which shaped the economic evolution—of the Third Republic even though their work is at times too schematic. Elwitt, like most Marxists, assumes that the industrial bourgeoisie was composed of capitalists *en puissance*, who naturally sought economic modernization, but were compelled by circumstances to make an alliance with conservative social forces. Hoffmann correctly

stresses the bourgeoisie's lingering tendency to stick to the "practices of mercantilism" and to mimic the aristocracy and notables, investing in land and seeking state
offices, but he imputes this tendency to values and beliefs.[5] Our argument, by contrast, is that the social and economic conservatism of the industrial bourgeoisie was
rational behavior—not an atavistic cultural trait—in a sociopolitical and economic
context shaped by specific class relations. We agree with the prevailing thesis that
the state sacrificed economic expansion to the preservation of the existing social
equilibrium (the "republican synthesis"). Our argument is that not only did a large
section of the capitalist class support this conservatism, but also that this support
stemmed not from character deficiencies ("Malthusianism") but from concrete social property relations and attendant rules of reproduction and class conflict.

If the bourgeoisie aspired to join the notables seeking land and offices, notables
also invested in industry. The evolution of investment patterns illustrates this interest in capitalist investment and business careers. "In 1848 only about 5 percent
of money left at death was in [company] shares while 58 percent was in land or
houses. By 1900, 31 percent was in shares and only 45 percent in land or houses."
Moreover, "in the upper echelons more and more graduates of the *grandes écoles*
abandoned public service to go into industry and business. Young men of good
family became inspectors of finance only as a preparation for careers with large
companies."[6] On the eve of the First World War, capitalists accumulated wealth on
a scale that no landowning notables and state officials could pretend to reach.[7] As
Theodore Zeldin explains,

> at this period [1901] only a thousand civil servants were earning over 15,000
> francs a year, and the highest salary was only 35,000. But the department
> stores of Paris ... were paying over 250 of their employees' salaries of 20,000
> to 25,000, equal to that of most prefects, and in business many could hope to
> earn 50,000, 100,000, or more.[8]

Under the Second Empire, as we saw, the executive branch gained autonomy
from the legislature (compared to preceding regimes). The state, however, was
simultaneously an "extra-economic" tool of appropriation for notables who used
revenue from state positions to complement those obtained from land and other
forms of rent.[9] Notables preserved much social and political influence and the pro-
grammatic coherence of the executive branch—which sought to trigger a capitalist
process of industrialization—was, as we saw in Chapter 3, partly dissolved within
the wider state form.[10]

Things evolved in a new direction under the Third Republic. The maturation of
capitalist industrialization launched under the Second Empire, while comparatively
constrained, was associated with the emergence of an "economic" sphere in which
the appropriation of surplus value emerged as an alternative to state-mediated and
rentier forms of exploitation. *Direct* control over state power became decreasingly
imperative for the surplus appropriation schemes and material reproduction of
elites. In other words, surplus appropriation (gradually relocated toward an "economic" sphere and operating through private property and competitive markets)

and class domination (assured by state power) were now dissociated. It was in this evolving class context, and taking advantage of dynastic divisions within the notability, that popular pressures from below gave rise to a new Republican regime.

The differentiation of "economic" and "political" spheres could theoretically have given the state—now increasingly free from the notables' power and conservatism—a degree of autonomy sufficient to support, guide and accelerate the capitalist transformation of the economy. A great paradox of the Third Republic, however, is that just the opposite happened. This was because the elite's move toward industry and the pace of industrialization were restricted by the propensity of the new regime's leaders and institutional setting to favor social and economic conservatism as a way to avoid social conflict and stabilize the regime. This was partly due to the lingering power of notables, who, albeit in decline, endured and regained power with the Vichy Regime. It was also due to the entrenchment of peasant property in the wake of 1789, discussed in Chapter 1. It stemmed, finally, from the country's history of political turmoil and revolutionary outbreaks. The 1870 defeat at the hands of Germany would have shown the urgency of improving France's economic prowess propping up its military might. Yet, the Paris Commune the following year served as a reminder of the need to prioritize the social question. The answer was socioeconomic conservatism, and it was within this over-determining context that entrepreneurs forged their strategies.

In the initial phase of the Republic, Monarchist notables capitalized on their social status and local influence to seize a decisive majority in the legislative elections of 1871. Mainstream republicans sought a compromise with notables and local elites, attempting to win them over to a moderate form of republicanism. After debilitating internecine conflicts over rival royal and imperial dynasties, many notables came to accept a republican regime. They had already had to adapt to constitutional monarchy and then to the Empire. The stabilization of the Republic was attributable to a partial process of "republicanization" of the notability. A new republican elite gained prominence after its electoral successes during the legislative elections of 1876 and 1877, though notables retained influence in national politics and power within the state. The Republic began to take a harder stance toward the notables, purging many of them from the administration, toward the late 1890s.[11]

Both the initial compromising posture and the later harsher stance toward the notability were tied to the republicans' commitment to the rural world and small industrial producers. Even prior to the advent of the regime, leading republicans appealed to the peasantry, and this eventually turned into a concerted effort to drive a wedge between peasants and traditional elites. If the countryside generally accepted the republic after the 1870s, it was because republicans had to move toward the peasantry to consolidate a regime in which the rural and agrarian world played a decisive role.

The figure of the small landowning peasant, depicted as materially and morally independent, already occupied a central role in the republican ideal from the first half of the nineteenth century. This idealization receded when republicans saw the electoral behavior of the peasant masses, who voted for Bonaparte under the Second Republic and Second Empire. Leading republicans such as Léon Gambetta and Jules Ferry, however, rehabilitated the peasants, along with petty proprietors and producers more broadly, turning them into the pillars of the Third Republic.

As Alain Chatriot puts it, the republicans' relationship with the rural and artisanal worlds resulted from the heritage of political crisis that punctuated the nineteenth century. Ferry claimed that "the Republic will be the Republic of peasants or will not be at all." He celebrated the peasants' "antique love for the land," an "entrenchment" and "immutability" that preserved them—and the regime—against both "feudal reaction" and "social revolutions." He depicted landowning peasants—together with small employers, petty traders, manufacturers, and liberal professionals (Gambetta's *nouvelles couches sociales*)—as economically autonomous and politically independent, a proper social foundation for the Republic. Laborious peasants and small owners and producers were allegedly absorbed by their economic activities and happy to delegate politics to responsible representatives. The preservation and wheedling of these classes thus represented the solution to the instability of the era of agitated urban crowds.[12]

This political posture was forged by "opportunist" republicans, who dominated national politics from the late 1870s until the turn of the century, and was pursued by "radical" republicans during the interwar period. Partisan politics, especially after 1902, was dominated by Radicals, a center-left formation "who appealed to the median voters (les 'petits') whom they pledged to protect against 'les gros' (the fat cats)." With the socialist, and later communist, conquest of working-class voters, the Radicals "supported the preservation of the status quo, a position which entailed promoting policies aimed at sheltering certain activities and relieving specific constituencies."[13]

This concern for social stability expressed by conservative and republican politicians was replicated by the political engagement of the capitalist class. Employers' associations sought to bring together large and small bosses alike and to synthesize their interests. Chambers of commerce, which grew in numbers, also pursed this goal, which was reflected in the ways large and small firms divided public contracts amongst themselves. A large share of industrialists aligned themselves politically with conservative notables, small producers and the peasantry. This was seen in the ongoing collaboration between the Association de l'industrie française and the Société des agriculteurs de France around a protectionist program in the 1880s, a prelude to the fusion of the two organizations in the early 1890s.[14]

The political institutions of the Republic consolidated this conservative logic. Reacting to the experience of the Second Empire, republicans successfully fought against the creation of a powerful president elected directly by the people. The President of the Republic, elected by parliament, was a weak political figure. The Chamber of Deputies formed the stable core of the regime and commanded its politics. Its membership was remarkably stable, and it exercised constant control over—and regularly toppled—governments. The electoral system granted overrepresentation to rural regions and deputies. The latter offered patronage to constituents and were constantly bogged down in local affairs. The Chamber of Deputies was partially held in check by the Senate, which also overrepresented the rural world and had been designed "to give weight to the stable rural backbone of the country against the impetuousness of the towns." During the interwar period, the Senate "came to be the bastion of conservative republicanism against the demands for modernization." Zeldin characterized the Third Republic as the "acceptance of the *status quo*" and "institutionalization of inefficiency," a regime "sustained by the enormous strength of inertia."[15]

The combination of the class basis of the regime and its political institutions resulted in slow socioeconomic transformation. The dominant political tendencies favored the preservation of traditional structures. Forces for economic modernization had to contend with pressure groups allied to parliamentarians who exercised tight control over legislation and government. The Republic no doubt pursued modernization. It established a national public education system, completed the construction of the national railway system, undermined the customary regulation of work by laborers and granted control over the labor and production processes to bosses. It also reformed corporate law to facilitate the establishment of limited liability companies and preserved (until 1892) the liberal foreign trade agreements signed by the Second Empire.[16] The crux of the state's initiatives, however, prioritized social stability and economic moderation.[17]

Gambetta created the ministry of Agriculture in 1881 as a way to defend small landed property against large landowners. The republican leader hoped to undercut the political influence of notables in the countryside and to prop up the peasants' support for the regime.[18] Likewise, the ministry of Commerce and Industry explicitly claimed to "prioritize the rise of the middle class [...], the preservation of which was necessary for the conservation of social equilibrium." The aim was political, to secure the support of shopkeepers and small industrial producers—the *couches nouvelles*—at the expense of the interests of the working class.[19] This entailed policies aimed at sheltering small producers and enterprises from market pressures, namely fiscal schemes favorable to small firms and inimical to larger ones, easy credit and subsidies, trade restrictions and eventually, protection from foreign competition (a point discussed in more detail below).[20]

This reaction to the destabilizing effects of industrialization appeared in other European states, where political discourse and policy favored the preservation of small producers and peasants. In Germany, the emerging continental economic powerhouse, however, the tendency was to develop these policies only to a point and came with a countertendency to roll these policies back when they hindered industrial development.[21] In France, by contrast, the equilibrium tended to tip toward the preservation of peasants and small producers.

This was, again, a conservative strategy of social integration, aimed at limiting the growth of the *classes dangereuses*—urban wage laborers.[22] The threat posed by the latter social class became increasingly urgent with the growing strike activity and socialist electoral successes of the 1890s. In Germany, by contrast, the balance of class power between Junkers and industrial capitalists led to a mixed approach: social conservatives put forward policies to benefit the *petite bourgeoisie* but rolled them out within a broader capitalist agenda of economic growth and social integration. A swelling German proletariat experienced rising real wages supplemented by welfare programs mixed with repressive politics. In France, social reforms, though not inexistent, came relatively late and were often blocked or severely curtailed—while repression intensified around the turn of the century—by a ruling class that saw them as a threat to privilege and social stability.[23] The solution was not to ease the birth of the working class through reforms but to prevent or delay it.[24]

As Jean-Philippe Dumas explains, "the conceptions of French politicians and senior officials were quite different from those held in foreign countries. In Germany, the state addressed industrial issues, be it social questions or those related to industrial property." The state supported heavy industry by way of government contracts, fiscal exemptions, export premiums, and preferential rail tariffs. This enabled "spectacular industrial development, but at the price of important social turbulences, with dramatic consequences after the defeat of 1918." France, meanwhile, enjoyed decades of relative political stability under the Third Republic, but sacrificed a more rapid pace of economic restructuring and growth in the process.[25]

The upshot was comparatively slow processes of urbanization and proletarianization. The population grew slowly from 1870 to the Second World War—its growth rate below the western European average. The share of the population living off agriculture was computed at 45.5 percent in the early 1890s and 41 percent in 1911. In 1913, 55 percent of the population lived in districts of fewer than 2,000 people. The official census of 1931 was the first to register an urban population larger than the rural. As discussed at length in the previous chapter, under the Third Republic, France was one of the least urbanized western European countries and unlike most other countries on the continent, it preserved a comparatively large and constant labor force in agriculture even after the beginning of industrialization.[26]

In Germany, by contrast, mass migration from agrarian regions, together with foreign immigration, to industrializing cities led to one of the most rapid rates of urbanization in the world from around the mid-nineteenth century. The percentage of the total population engaged in agriculture had already declined to 35.8 percent by 1895 and dropped to 27 percent in 1911. Two-thirds of the population lived in villages and towns of fewer than 2,000 inhabitants in 1875, but this proportion decreased to less than half of the population by 1900. The urban population, which accounted for 36.1 percent of the total in 1870, increased to 60 percent by 1910. Furthermore, over 80 percent of the country's demographic growth (which was faster than France's) took place in cities larger than 20,000 inhabitants. In 1911, Germany had 45 cities with over 100,000 inhabitants, Britain 49, but France only 15.[27]

The limitations of proletarianization and, consequently, of the home market in France compared with Germany implied that the former had a much less adequate basis for capital accumulation than did the latter.[28] The matter, it should be noted, is not simply one of quantity but also of qualitative change. Once the mass of market dependent workers (who must purchase everything they need) has reached a certain threshold, changes in class relations of exploitation (of social property relations) cause economic mechanisms to kick in. These mechanisms tend to increase productivity and real wages, thus further fueling demand, which will, in turn, attract investments and productivity gains as part of an ongoing "virtuous" circle of growth—though one that is recurrently upset by crises. This is because first the growth of consumption will lead firms to invest and to seek the employment of growing numbers of waged workers, leading wage levels to rise as employers compete to hire employees—a tendency sometimes reinforced by organizing efforts and struggles waged by workers. Second, the adoption of new techniques and rationalization of production under the auspices of capitalist competition tends to reduce prices and increase real wages.[29]

A larger domestic consumer market, combined with the capacity of industrial firms to sell on foreign markets, created growth mechanisms in Germany which did not develop in France, where the working class and consumer market were less developed. The result, historians agree, was that real wages rose consistently in Germany by an average of 1.4 percent a year or just as fast as the economy as a whole between 1880 and 1913. The real incomes of industrial workers nearly doubled between 1870 and 1913.[30] In France, real wages grew less rapidly and inconsistently, and nearly stagnated from the end of the nineteenth century through to the 1920s. Wages, moreover, did not grow as fast as the economy as a whole and did not increase working-class consumption in any significant way. In 1930, most (72.6 percent) of the average working-class family budget was still dedicated to food and clothing, and this percentage had hardly declined since 1890 (77.6 percent).[31] Steadily rising real wages in Germany and slow and inconsistent wage growth in France, of course, only amplified the disparity between these countries' domestic markets and consequently between their pace of industrialization.

A comparatively stable peasantry and limited proletarianization limited the size of France's labor market. In the absence of a mass of market-dependent workers compelled to sell their capacity to work in exchange for a wage, capitalists found it arduous to subject labor to factory discipline. The production of surplus value and capital accumulation were therefore restricted.[32] Additionally, the reserve army of labor—produced and reproduced by the process of mechanization within the capitalist mode of production—hardly grew in the second half of the nineteenth century. This was because peasants, shopkeepers and artisans adopted "Malthusian" strategies, restricting their family size to limit the number of disinherited offspring compelled to migrate in search of employment. Means of production (land, tools and skills) could thus pass to the next generation. These Malthusian strategies allowed part of the population to avoid proletarianization, with the result that the "insufficient numbers of young, single, and mobile workers blocked the development of new and often more productive industries."[33]

Even when laboring in factories, much of the workforce continued to till the land part-time, made their own bread, retained gardens and bred animals. These workers did not fully depend on the labor market. Turnover remained high in most factories, and harvest work still paralyzed recruitment and production. Bosses complained about the lack of available labor and widespread indolence on the job. The scarcity and indiscipline of workers was their employers' "number one anguish." Employers developed "paternalist" schemes, offering housing and benefits (such as pensions and family allowances) to their employees in the hopes of attaching workers to factory routines. Feminine labor was another employer strategy. The percentage of women in the active workforce increased from 31 to 37 from 1866 to 1906, but remained constant during the interwar period and even fell slightly in the industrial sector.[34]

Prioritizing social stability, successive republican governments fixed peasants on the land and assuaged the competition for labor between modern industrial firms and traditional artisan workshops. Since the labor market in these circumstances could only grow slowly, immigration became the main means of providing firms with workers. Beginning in the 1880s, employers demanded and obtained an expansion of immigration. Foreign workers took up occupations in heavy industries: "in 1906, while they constituted only 3 percent of the economically active population, they represented 10 percent of the workforce employed in the chemical industry, 18 percent in the metal industries, and 9 percent in the construction industries."[35]

When labor-supplying countries began to impose restrictions on emigration, especially in the wake of the devastating casualties suffered by France in the First World War, the state intervened to ensure a steady influx of workers. Governments rationalized immigration processes to create a noncitizen and permanently monitored workforce, depriving immigrants of rights and freedoms enjoyed by native workers, and directing them to regions and sectors, where employers needed a malleable industrial workforce. Mining companies recruited Belgian and Polish workers to the north. Italians dug the iron mines of Lorraine and toiled in the steel factories of Longwy. Italians were also common in Lyon's industry, as were Spaniards, Czechs, Armenians and Chinese workers. The large modern industrial facilities of Paris received laborers from North Africa, Russia and other countries. Industry would not have grown as rapidly as it did without the arrival of nearly two million foreigners, representing 75 percent of the country's demographic growth during the 1920s.[36]

This influx of immigrants supported industrial modernization while partially limiting the decline of the artisanal (and agricultural) workforce, which industrialization would otherwise have required.[37] The remarkable endurance of small artisanal enterprises also resulted from the niches in France's peculiar market structure. Some small enterprises, to be sure, had to adapt to the competitive context of the last decades of the nineteenth century. This entailed an alteration of their functioning, if not always of their size. Michel Lescure presents, for instance, the case of a Parisian cookie factory, established in 1920, that counted 100 employees under a Taylorist division of labor. The firm created an administrative apparatus to calculate cost prices, organize production, focus on advertising and develop a commercial network.[38]

Lescure also explains, nonetheless, how the limitation and segmentation of the domestic market led differential scales of production series. Although the larger industrial firms submitted to the competitive pressures of an increasingly integrated national (and world) market through mass production and standardization, large numbers of small workshops continued to produce non-competitively for local markets, answering the episodic orders of clienteles. Companies avoided each other's competition by selling distinct products on distinct markets. Citing again cookie manufacturing, Lescure explains that, while three large firms shared the national market for superior quality cookies, a number of firms produced medium quality goods for regional markets, and several firms continued to produce low-end traditional cookies locally and sporadically.[39]

The gap between mass standardized production and small-scale customized production existed in other branches. Summarizing Lescure's argument, Woronoff explains that "small and medium firms" benefited from "differentiated products that did not entirely enter in competition from one part of the territory to the other." In such cases, firms "did not, in fact, share the same market." Indeed, because of a "slower progression of urbanization," and since the market was much smaller than in Britain or Germany, "demand was segmented, fragile and did not incite lengthy production series."[40] In addition to capital-intensive units, and traditional firms producing and selling locally, one could also find specialized firms manufacturing luxury goods for the slim higher end of domestic and international markets. Competing on quality more than on price, the latter mechanized production to a lesser extent than did larger industrial firms producing mass consumption, semi-finished or capital goods.[41] These market constraints on the development of large-scale production series and on standardized manufacturing restricted industrial growth before the Second World War.

Consider the automobile industry, in which, by the 1920s, firms had evolved from artisanal carmaking to concentrated production in mechanized factories. Most firms, however, had stopped short of the large buildings, complex machinery, and interchangeable parts required for the mass production of small and affordable cars like the T model introduced in 1908 by Ford in the United States. Renault and Peugeot dropped their plan to produce a unique and cheap model in the early 1920s and delayed it again in the mid-1930s, realizing that the number of potential buyers was too small. In 1929, industrial workers counted for only 2 percent of total car owners, and, in a context of nearly stagnant real wages, this percentage was unlikely to rise sufficiently to support production *à l'américaine*, even if the fall in car prices accelerated. Citroën thought otherwise, invested to produce a single model on a mass scale, but the firm's sales proved insufficient and ended in bankruptcy in 1934.[42]

The inadequate depth of the domestic market meant that carmakers lacked the base to develop facilities and to reach productivity levels that would have allowed them to succeed abroad. Predictably, they began to lose foreign market shares during the interwar period. This process was replicated in other branches. Deprived of a sufficiently large market, firms could not produce on the scale needed to reduce costs, and they "never attained the critical mass to challenge the American and German first movers in international markets."[43] They were not able to penetrate the much larger British market, which German firms began to achieve in the 1890s, thus gaining an even larger base to standardize and massify production.[44]

France could not follow suit and, as mentioned in the previous section, its share of global exports of manufactured goods declined after 1880. As also mentioned above, the country's firms remained largely excluded from capital goods export markets, and its industrialization was in large part dependent upon technological imports. While international competition called for investments that brought about economies of scale, firms were reluctant to sink capital into plants in the absence of sizable market outlets. The context tended to drive firms into adopting conservative investment practices, thus contributing to the perpetuation of existing structures or to their slow industrialization.[45]

German industrialists penetrated the British market by combining relatively cheap labor with advanced means of production. Likewise, Japanese textile manufacturers became competitive on world markets by capitalizing not just on low labor costs, but also by adopting, diffusing and constantly renewing advanced productive technologies.[46] In both rapidly industrializing countries, growing sales on home and foreign markets paid for the import of—but also for the development of domestic capacities to produce—state-of-the-art capital goods.

French administrators were aware of the need to secure access to capital goods and technology. The government pursued the liberalization of foreign trade in the latter part of the nineteenth century to lower the cost of these goods and provide competitive incentives to introduce them in production. Governments of the Third Republic generally stuck to this strategy, at least until 1892, but failed to act and compel firms to adopt new strategies even after it became clear that the adoption and diffusion of modern industrial techniques and penetration of foreign markets proceeded at a slower pace than in Germany, Japan, the United States, and other countries.

Governments actually moved in the opposite direction. We have already seen the Republic's inclination to retain peasant farms and artisan shops, as well as how this restricted the extent of the domestic markets and, in turn, the economies of scale in industry. Unable to compete on international markets for consumer or capital goods—and having to rely on protected colonial markets—much of the industrial sector stuck to luxury goods aimed at rich consumers. High quality products remained by far the most dynamic and important category of exports during the Belle Époque and interwar period.[47] The state contributed to this situation by adopting legislation aimed at ensuring the quality of goods, perpetuating a policy that could be traced back to the Old Regime.[48]

As the growth of imports accelerated and the rise of exports decelerated, industrialists intensified their demand for tariff protection. Unable to compete on foreign or domestic markets, they opted to safeguard profits through tariffs. The first sustained protectionist reaction against the liberal trade policy of the 1860s emerged between 1868 and 1873 and was followed by 20 years of parliamentary and public disputes punctuated by a first round of modest tariffs in the early 1880s that largely preserved the liberal framework.[49] The Méline tariffs of 1892, by contrast, brought a significant swing toward protectionism.

Fundamentally, the "split between free traders and protectionist," which structured debates over tariffs during this period, "was a split between outwardly directed *commercial* capitalists [including many luxury goods manufacturers] seeking international economic integration and inwardly directed *industrial* capitalists seeking national self-sufficiency."[50] Industrialists formed an "iron and wheat" alliance with agricultural producers to avoid competition. They worked in tandem with parliamentary representatives for tariffs. The falling agricultural prices and depression of the 1880s, general's Boulanger threat to the regime, and the rise of strike activity and socialism in the following decades created a context in which the state became increasingly responsive to protectionist demands in its effort to secure the peasantry's support. Besides pleasing industrialists, higher tariffs also had the advantage of showing French workers the regime's protection of "national labor."[51]

A similar "iron and rye" alliance between industrialists and agrarians had led Bismarck to shift to protectionism at the end of the 1870s in an effort to stabilize the Second Reich in Germany. From the start of the 1890s, however—when France made a decisive turn to protectionism—industrialists broke with agrarians during debates over the Caprivi trade treaties and again, definitively, over the Bülow tariffs during the opening years of the new century. It turned out that

> neither light industry, nor the likewise export-oriented West-German heavy industry [...] were ready to support the drastic rise of agricultural protectionism that the agrarian pressure groups vigorously called for and that would have had the potential to ruin German export opportunities by provoking foreign retaliations.[52]

Moreover, industry sought inexpensive foodstuffs to hold down wages and production costs and pushed against protectionist landowners whose interests were threatened by foreign competition and falling prices.

Since industrial products accounted for 70 percent of exports, interest in free trade came to dominate the economic policy of the Reich. Contrary to the French Republic, the German Reich's trade policy was aimed at consolidating its class basis and ensuring its sociopolitical stability without sacrificing its export-led industrial development. The regime sought to preserve the support of landowning Junkers by other means than tariff barriers. It offered export subsidies and tax cuts while also actively promoting the modernization of agriculture through credits, the dissemination of know-how and technology.[53]

In France, by contrast, the iron and wheat alliance endured, and the stronger tariff protection established in 1892 was renewed in 1910. As we have seen, industrialists—given the limited home market, which did not require product standardization and economies of scale—judged that the effort to penetrate foreign markets was too risky and costly. The state, as also discussed above, did not attempt to modify this judgment, nor the economic context out of which it emerged, for fear of destabilizing the social basis of the regime.

Moreover, *within this static socioeconomic context*, it was rational for industrialists to support agrarian tariffs to protect peasants against the threat of price-cutting competition. Having given up on international markets, and seeking protection of the home market, large sectors of industry did not regard low wages through cheap food as such an urgent necessity as did their German counterparts. To the contrary, and more to the point, in an economy in which agrarians still formed the largest consumer group, it made sense for industrialists to support the income of rural customers through tariff protection, since these customers would then be able to buy more manufactured goods. Higher food prices cut into industrial profits, to be sure, but "at least the family firm, the *patrimoine* was safe."[54]

The Méline tariffs, enforced to safeguard the Republic by securing the iron and wheat alliance, ended the period of liberalization that had begun in 1860. The tariffs shielded the peasants from foreign competition by subjecting farm imports to average tariffs increasing from 3.3 percent in the early 1880s to 21.3 percent in the early 1890s. These were significantly higher than tariffs imposed on industrial imports which, after over 40 targeted legislative amendments, were set at a 9 percent average in the wake of the overall legislative revision of 1910—significantly below the levels of the first half of the nineteenth century and of the 1930s. Tariffs on industrial goods varied greatly according to sectors and countries of origins, but their limited increase—compared to tariffs on agricultural products—offered a compromise between the interests of the outwardly oriented commercial and luxury sectors, and the inwardly oriented industrial sectors. Varying by sector and increasing moderately, industrial tariffs did not eliminate exposure to the international trade boom, which was fueled by the global recovery, as well as by the modernization and cheapening of transportation, of the mid-1890s.[55]

Exposure to foreign competition, causing falling prices and compressed profit margins, did, however, lead industrial firms to join forces, forming ententes and cartels, at an accelerated pace from the 1880s, and especially over the years preceding the First World War. By 1914, most industrial branches included forms of ententes, and participation in international cartels became increasingly frequent in the 1920s. While cartels were typically formalized and administratively well-organized, ententes consisted of (written or verbal) agreements between independent firms to regulate markets, fix prices and avoid or temper competition. Ententes could adopt different aims and functions, from setting quality standards to allocation of orders, patent management and technological development and diffusion, but their core and most frequent *raison d'être* was price fixing.

Article 419 of the Penal Code adopted in 1810 prohibited coalitions aimed at interfering with markets and prices. Many judges and public officials, however, were suspicious of market mechanisms and fearful of their disruptive effects on social order, and jurisprudence tended to weaken the impact of Article 419. The Waldeck-Rousseau law of 1884, which decriminalized labor unions, also permitted the formation of business associations. Its effect was to reinforce leniency toward ententes and to pave the way for a distinction, which emerged during the 1890s, between "good" ones, regulating "anarchic markets," and "bad" ones, leading to patent abuses and excessive prices and profits. A 1926 law gave legal content to this distinction, fully legalizing "good" ententes.

Ententes sometimes could not fully curtail competition. They constantly formed, dissolved and resurrected, and firms always had incentive to cheat. A firm could join an entente, only to leave or encroach on it as soon as it developed a new production technique that gave it a competitive edge over its partners. Some firms simply decided not to join an entente in their sector. Internal rules on price fixing, order sharing, or production quotas were hard to enforce and monitor. Export cartels, such as the one formed for cast iron tubes, could fix high prices at home to "subsidize" lower export prices. When effective, ententes provided a competitive edge on foreign markets and facilitated the diffusion of modern technologies (as was the case in the aircraft sector). But they could also, on the contrary, stifle competition and curtail innovation (as happened for iron and steel products and in coal mining).

The effectiveness of ententes varied according to the size of the market, the number of firms, and the presence (or absence) of a large firm able to play a leading role in organizing a given sector. The Saint-Gobain firm, for instance, primarily produced glass plates, a branch which it dominated nationally and internationally, and was able to act as a regulator in alliance with smaller firms (in France). Saint-Gobain, however, also had a smaller chemical division active on other markets over which it exerted no hegemonic control and where large numbers of firms made ententes notoriously unstable. Another key variable that determined the efficacy of ententes was the level of exposure to, or protection from, foreign competition. After 1892, higher tariffs, which varied according to goods, provided "the necessary degree of protection to allow ... producers ... to take control of their domestic and colonial markets and to apportion production for this market among themselves without fear of foreign competition."[56]

Relying on the protected colonial market was another tactic used by industrial firms to escape foreign competition and imperatives to modernize. The informal imperialist strategy that had emerged after 1815—involving coercively-imposed unequal commercial treaties for the export of luxury goods conspicuously consumed by foreign elites—brought diminishing returns after the 1860s. The stagnation and relative decline of luxury exports made a turn to territorial and protected colonies increasingly tempting during the closing decades of the century. Territorial expansion had been revived with the acquisition of Senegalese territories after the mid-1820s, followed by the penetration of Algeria in 1830, and its division into three departments integrated into metropolitan France by 1848. But the expansion of France's "second colonial empire" really took off in the wake of the 1878 Congress of Berlin. Tunisia was captured in 1881. Morocco was occupied by French troops after 1907 and became a protectorate in 1912. Formal control over Madagascar began in 1885, French West Africa was formally established in 1895, and French Equatorial Africa in 1910. France began its conquests of Southeast Asia in the early 1860s and united the territory in a singly colony, Indochina, in 1887. By 1931, 64.3 million people, extending over 12.4 million square kilometers, populated France's colonial empire.

Algeria had already served as a last refuge for cotton producers under Napoleon III, and this pattern was reproduced on a larger scale as the empire expanded in the closing decades of the nineteenth century. The share of the colonies in France's total trade grew steadily after the 1870s. Colonial markets, falling under the protection of the Méline tariffs after 1892, offered opportunities and a safety valve to industrial firms struggling to break into the markets of advanced economies, as illustrated by the sale of electrical goods in the colonies. This was a gain for industry representatives, who had already convinced the government to bring Algeria, Réunion, Guadeloupe and Martinique under the metropolitan tariff legislation in 1885, and Indochina in 1887. The empire also provided a life raft to older sectors—already in 1906, it absorbed over 85 percent of cotton fabrics sold abroad, 80 percent of metal structures, 73 percent of locomotives, 57 percent of steel rails, and 54 percent of shoes.

Extraction of primary resources was certainly profitable for individual firms, whose profit rates were often well above the metropolitan average, but economic development in the colonies did not ensue. Extractive and industrial companies announced business plans for various colonies, attracting funds from enthusiastic investors and fueling speculation in their shares. These plans, however, were often fraudulent and rarely followed by direct investments—the construction of productive infrastructures did not ensue, particularly in sub-Saharan Africa.[57] During the interwar period, colonies provided a mere 6.1 percent of textile raw materials transformed in metropolitan France. Except for phosphate and rubber, figures for other raw materials, including mineral resources, were similar. Moreover, imports from colonies were frequently directly or indirectly subsidized and acquired at a price superior to comparable goods sold outside the imperial zone.

Overall, the empire was (often highly) profitable for individual firms but reinforced the relative backwardness of the aggregate economy. The empire allowed firms and whole sectors to escape or assuage competitive imperatives and provided them with outlets that compensated for the limited metropolitan consumer market. Counting on safe and protected colonial market outlets, large sectors of industry stayed afloat while avoiding the costs of modernizing their productive capacities. Colonial markets slowed the development of high added-value industries, and supported the preservation of older branches, such as cotton manufacturing, which, following the First World War, started to decline as a share of the aggregate industrial structure of economically advanced countries. Access to the colonial markets favored the persistence of less concentrated and less "capitalistic" industrial structures. The empire therefore contributed to the preservation of small property, safeguarding small industrial firms by alleviating competition, and offsetting the maintenance of a large underproductive peasantry with colonial food stuff imports. It was recurrently presented by elected officials and industrial spokespeople as a means to protect factories and hold down unemployment. In these ways, imperial expansion fitted the strategy of social reproduction adopted by the regime, while also feeding nationalistic pride.[58]

The Great Depression of the 1930s reinforced ententes, protectionism, and the economic function of the colonies. The effects of the global crisis, delayed by an undervalued franc, hit France in 1931, when the devaluation of the pound sterling, followed by the US dollar in 1933, caused a sharp decline of exports. Industrial employers reacted by redoubling their demands for protection from competitive pressures. From 1931 to 1935, right-wing governments put forth a deflationist economic program that entailed public budgetary austerity and a Malthusian industrial policy aimed at reducing and realigning supply with demand in the hope of increasing prices and, eventually, profits and investments. The actual policies and impact of this program were, however, less significant than the dominant economic spirit they revealed.[59]

Governments adopted new fiscal and regulatory measures to protect small shops from large stores and retail chains. To "organize markets," they also became increasingly lenient toward, and often actively supportive of, ententes formed by industrial firms.[60] Commercial judges became lenient toward encroachments on price competition to the point of facilitating corporate scandals. In 1935, the chamber of deputies adopted a law to make ententes mandatory in all struggling industrial branches. Many industrialists resisted the initiative, not out of opposition to ententes but in defense of their autonomy from the state, and the legislation was ultimately blocked by the Senate. Sectorial initiatives were subsequently launched. The government made ententes compulsory in sugar refining, milling, shoemaking, and industrial fishing, while encouraging ententes for exports and in all sectors protected by tariff barriers.[61]

Attempts by the state to facilitate ententes, or even to impose them in some branches, should not make us forget that this remained a laissez-faire liberal era without industrial policy.[62] Successive governments left industrial firms largely free to collaborate within a protected home market. Indeed, the state indirectly supported the collaboration of private companies by adopting, after 1931, a strongly protectionist trade policy that enabled control over the domestic market. The government increased tariffs from an average level of under 10 percent in the mid-1920s to around 35 percent by the mid-1930s. It also subjected most commodities to a quota system by 1933. The upshot was a drastically reduced ratio of total exports and imports to the national income, falling from 14.4 percent in 1930 to 8.6 percent in 1934–1936, amounting to the lowest degree of economic openness since the mid-nineteenth century. This closure to foreign trade eased competitive pressures on industrial firms directly, but also indirectly, by facilitating the formation of ententes and improving their impact. After a short destabilizing period in 1931–1932, ententes spread again and allowed firms to divide markets and control prices.[63] Cartels and ententes covered 85 percent of French industrial production by the end of the 1930s, contributing to a reduction of "competitive forces."[64]

Meanwhile, the state reinforced the "imperial preference" with a law in 1928 that reserved colonial markets for French firms. If the narrowness of the domestic market limited the economic recovery, let alone an improvement of the productive forces, access to imperial outlets further delayed modernization by offering a safe shelter to noncompetitive firms. This pattern, as we saw, had already been established during preceding decades, but its importance was reinforced in the 1930s—the share of the colonies in total metropolitan trade rose from 13 percent to 30 percent from 1927 to 1936. Colonial outlets were crucial for declining branches. Slightly more than 3 percent of silk fabric exports went to the colonies during the 1920s, but as the turbulences of the 1930s set in, desperate firms sent a growing share of their output to the empire, which absorbed 50 percent of silk exports by the end of the Second World War. Access to colonial markets proved even more critical for cotton producers, a particularly uncompetitive branch. Whereas sales to the empire amounted to 34 percent of the industry's total before the First World War, this share skyrocketed to 90 percent by the end of the 1930s. Even in the more modern capital goods industry, the share of total sales absorbed by colonies reached 54 percent in 1940, up from 17.6 percent in 1928. The ratio of colonial to total exports of automobiles went from 16 percent in 1913 to 46 percent in 1938.[65]

The depression brought a severe drop in industrial production, its index falling by about a quarter from 1930 to 1935, and failing to recover after 1932, while the British index had by then already bypassed its 1929 level and the German index was rapidly filling the gap. By 1938, French industrial production was not only still below its 1929 level, but only slightly above that of 1913. After steady gains after

1913, the share of industry in aggregate added value fell from 46.7 percent to 41.4 percent from 1929 to 1938. Meanwhile, the share of agriculture in added value rose from 18.8 percent to 20.9 percent from 1929 to 1938. The Popular Front Government, in power in 1936–1938, intensely pressured by a massive strike wave in May and June 1936, broke with the Malthusian program of previous governments. It sought to stimulate demand by increasing wages and enacting a 40-hour week with the purpose of reducing unemployment. This policy, however, incited capital flight and fueled inflation. Industrial stagnation continued, and the government had to devalue the franc to stimulate exports before its fall in April 1938. Overall, the crisis of the 1930s set in train a process that "swept aside most of the gains in output and performance obtained in the 1920s."[66]

The evolution of the labor force highlights this economic relapse. While the country lost 1.8 million jobs during the Depression, industry alone shed around one million between 1931 and 1938. In the steel industry, the workforce declined by about a quarter and by up to 40 percent in Lorraine. The depression halted an already faint rural exodus. Agricultural employment vegetated at around 36 percent of the total labor force from 1931 to 1946. Moreover, while the crisis slowed industrial turnover, and stabilized a portion of the working class within factories, much of the rest of this class went back to the villages to rejoin the agricultural economy. Meanwhile, the state sent around a quarter of a million migrant workers back to their countries. The proportion of industrial workers dropped from 33.1 percent in 1931 to 29.5 percent in 1946, below its 1913 level and barely above the level of 1896. During the 1930s, it seemed as though "France had once again fallen back on its artisanal and rural ... values, as if it truly could not accept industrial mutations." On the eve of the Second World War, it was still the most agrarian of all large Western states.[67]

The atrophy of the industrial working class, together with falling real wages, had reduced effective demand. This, in turn, further reinforced the capacity of industrial firms to divide and manage limited and protected markets. Of course, industrial firms and governments in other states used cartels, protectionism and colonial markets, as was noted by analysts of the time. The effects of these economic institutions, however, varied according to the economic and class structures of the countries in question. Writing in Germany, Rudolf Hilferding described in his classic book, *Finance Capital*, published in 1910, how protectionism and cartelized industrial firms had been transformed

> from a means of defense against the conquest of the home market by foreign industry [into] a means of conquering overseas markets on behalf of home industries; from a defensive weapon of the weak [into] an offensive weapon of the strong.[68]

While fitting for Germany, where industries not only sought secured colonial markets, but also competed and penetrated the British and other markets, this analysis hardly applies to France.

In France, cartels thrived in a comparatively small and protected domestic market, which they could easily manage and divide. Cartels functioned more to safeguard profits than to maximize them through strategies to compete on foreign markets. The Great Depression severely decreased already weak competitive imperatives to invest, and firms had not only fewer opportunities, but also fewer resources to do so, as profits, and the issuing of shares, plummeted. The fall in the rate of investment was significant and prolonged. Set at 17 percent in 1913, this rate reached 21 percent in 1930, but collapsed to 13 percent by 1938. The investment drop in capital goods was severe, and the sector producing those goods saw its production fall 37 percent from 1929 to 1935. As investments declined, the pace of industrial concentration decelerated—after doubling in size from 1906 to 1931, the size of the median industrial workplace grew only 18 percent from 1931 to 1954. Another consequence of falling investments, which marked a momentous break with the preceding period, was that gains in labor productivity per hour in industry fell by more than half during the 1930s compared to the previous decade.[69] According to Eck, who references data provided by Carré et al., staff-hour labor productivity declined by 0.9 percent on an average yearly basis from 1929 to 1938.[70]

The Depression of the 1930s "delivered a decisive blow to the modernization" of the economy, following over three decades of substantial if uneven and comparatively slow industrial growth.[71] After maturing slowly and incompletely, capitalist growth mechanisms abruptly failed—industry employed less labor and its productivity lagged as the capital it wielded grew at a much slower pace due to a weakening—and vanishing in many sectors—of competitive imperatives.

The defeat of 1940 and the establishment of the Vichy regime consolidated the economic stalemate and underlying structure. Though some top officials proposed plans to modernize the economy, the economic policy of Pétain's government consisted of a mix of statist and corporatist dirigisme as well as traditional calls to a return to the soil.

The regime set up a super Ministry of Industrial Production in 1940, which oversaw a vast system of economic controls. It established "organizing committees" to replace the dissolved employers' associations and labor federations. These committees, operated by employers under the Ministry of Industrial Production, played a key role in organizing industrial branches, conducting censuses and recommending price schedules. The committees had the power to impose sanctions on disobedient firms. The regime established the Office Central de Répartition des Produits Industriels (OCPRI) to coordinate industrial branches and allocate resources to them. While initiating state dirigisme over the economy, with consequences that outlived the regime and impacted postwar developments, Vichy's organizing committees and OCPRI actually completed the cartelization of the economy that had been under way during the 1930s. The economic controls exercised by these institutions overlapped and short-circuited one another, creating a "bureaucratic nightmare." The depression was consequently made worse by the dirigisme of Pétain's regime. Industrial production fell 35 percent from 1938 to 1941 and remained around that level until the end of the war.[72]

The Postwar Capitalist Boom

The Commissariat Général du Plan (CGP) published a statistical report on the economic situation in early 1946. The report revealed economic backwardness. The stock of machinery was 25 percent smaller than Britain's. French industrial equipment was also significantly older—25 years old on average in 1939, and was not updated during the war, whereas British and US machines were respectively seven years and five years old on average by the end of the war. In addition, 87 percent of industrial buildings in France had been built before 1914. Investments in equipment and technology had been lagging for years, with the result that a wide productivity gap separated France from competitors. In 1946, production in the United States was 75 percent above its 1929 level, and labor productivity (output per person-hour) had improved by 40 percent. In the United Kingdom, production had risen by 40 percent and productivity 10 percent during the same period. Meanwhile, in France, production had decreased by 20 percent and labor productivity by 5 percent compared to the 1929 levels.[73]

This data revealed an urgent need to modernize industry, a task undertaken by the state in the following years and decades. In 1946, however, this was still anything but a foregone conclusion. Evidence of backwardness, its geopolitical and domestic consequences and proposals to renew and improve industry had been voiced long before the end of the Second World War. The First World War had revealed France's inability to counter Germany without support from allies. The chemical industry, for instance, proved unable to produce explosives in sufficient quantities. France had to rely on foreign providers for raw materials, manufactured goods and food. Economic dirigisme had to be rapidly implemented to organize the war effort, and the executive was temporarily freed from normal parliamentary supervision. Some administrators had begun toward the end of the war to design schemes to reconstruct, reorganize and modernize the economy. Minister of Commerce and Industry Étienne Clémentel proposed a mix of corporatist structures and statist interventions to accelerate industrial concentration and improve standardization and productivity. The aim was to make industry fit to compete internationally while securing class conciliation through corporatist institutions. Clémentel faced stanch opposition from business associations, which organized to restore "industrial freedom" by the end of the war. Parliament and parties regained control over economic policy, and minister of Industrial Reconstruction Louis Loucheur neutralized Clémentel and reinstated the liberalism cum foreign trade protectionism dominant before the war.[74]

Some political and economic elites gathered around groups like the X-Crise circle and Ernest Mercier's Redressement Français during the interwar period to propose schemes of economic modernization. They advocated for a powerful executive and administration relative to parliament, but were isolated, commanded no significant part of the electorate and consequently exercised scant political influence. The short-lived government of André Tardieu proposed a "prosperity policy" of industrial modernization in 1929. But the plan was subordinate to the more fundamental goal of curtailing the depopulation of the countryside and securing peasant votes. René Duchemin, head of the main employers' federation, praised the reluctance to follow the economic models of the United States and Germany and celebrated the prudent balanced economy of France.[75]

A few years later, Léon Blum, as leader of the Popular Front, envisaged liberal, interventionist forms of modernization. He hoped for state interventions and sustained growth to forge a class alliance of capital and labor, and stem the rise of fascist reactionaries. Productivity gains and wage increases seemed preferable to repressing strikes, such as the wave that swept the country upon the election of the Popular Front. The left government responded to strikers with a demand-side economic policy. But Blum's plan of economic modernization met resistance from high administrative officials and remained a dead letter.[76]

Leading administrators of the Délégation Générale à l'Équipement National later drafted two plans to restructure industry and maximize productivity under the Vichy regime. These plans targeted the elimination of bottlenecks in the energy and steel industries. A first ten-year plan underlined the necessity of technological renewal so that industry could compete on world markets and bring about higher living standards. Once again, however, the project was scrapped, as politicians sought to avoid strife by maintaining "peasant reserves" and "energies." Traditionalist administrators, in any case, opposed the plan, which was shelved in 1942. A second, two-year plan named "tranche de démarrage" was proposed in 1944. Influenced by the spirit of the mounting Resistance, which championed modernization and planning, this new project was resolute in its insistence on the need to renew capital equipment and modernize and reduce the agrarian sector—changes presented as unavoidable if France were to strive for prosperity and security. The Liberation and fall of Vichy did not allow the implementation of the new plan, which nonetheless served as an inspiration for postwar modernizers.[77]

The question, then, is why, in the wake of the Second World War, did neoliberal modernizers finally prevail against conservative state officials and capitalists? Why were reformist state officials and industrialists able to complete the transition to capitalism at this juncture, when their predecessors had consistently failed?

In a pioneering work on the postwar boom, first published in the early 1960s, Charles Kindelberger claimed that the economic resurgence was "due to the restaffing of the economy with new men and to new French attitudes." These "new men" took positions of command in the private economy and public sector, and new pro-growth attitudes, stemming "from the frustration of the 1930s and the war and the occupation," took hold, not just among leaders, but also among the public. Businesspeople displayed a "readiness [...] to compete" and "lost [their] inferiority complex *vis-à-vis* foreign competition." They came to accept that their "interests lied in lower prices, expanded output, and wider markets." Kindelberger insisted that the cause of these changes was "not an increase in domestic and foreign competition," and presents them as "the outcome of deep-seated social and value changes." Meanwhile, attitudinal transformations also brought faster population growth and a new drive toward consumerism among workers who had "become less revolutionary, more practical."[78]

Another influential account of the sustained growth of the postwar period is that of Hoffmann, who explains that the "stalemate society" of the Third Republic collapsed because of the "decisive impulse" for economic and social transformation provided by the state. The new perspective of state leaders is here explained by the urgency of regaining the geopolitical ranking of France in the wake of the 1940 disaster.[79]

Carré, Dubois and Malinvaud concluded their milestone econometrical analysis of postwar growth with an attempt to identify the sociohistorical factors that might explain it. The authors reject monocausal explanations and conclude that new growth patterns were due to a conjunction of multiple and cumulative factors, among which were the willingness of workers to intensify labor, the renewal and reorganization of productive units and the dynamism of administrators in charge of policies. The factors identified by Carré et al., however, are more effects than causes of sustained growth. Behind these factors, the reader finds once more an explanatory strategy focused on attitudinal change: the French came to prioritize work, embraced geographical mobility and showed a willingness to take on longer work hours; business leaders became conscious of the demands of modern production, came to understand the benefits of productivity and developed a will to expand their firms; and a group of statesmen was able to develop a sufficiently coherent strategy to support economic growth.[80]

Proposing an explanation similar to those of Kindelberger, Hoffmann and Carré et al., Richard Kuisel relates postwar economic performance to "a changing national consciousness" caused by dissatisfaction with an unproductive liberal order. Kuisel, however, argues that the quest for "social justice" and stability (to be generated by economic growth) constituted "a minor reason for economic overhaul." Kuisel also downplays the concern for geopolitical standing emphasized by Hoffmann. He holds that the new consciousness did not originate with the defeat of 1940 or the crisis of the 1930s: discontent with economic arrangements had been growing since the turn of the century and had accelerated after the First World War. Responding to Kindelberger, Kuisel claims that private entrepreneurs actually "had to be pushed toward adopting a more expansionist stance," but eventually "followed the lead of public officials."[81]

Michel Margairaz has produced a major study of the conversion of the Treasury, the Ministry of Finance and the state more generally, over two decades of the early 1930s to the early 1950s that develops the work on Kuisel. His analysis challenges Kindelberger's core thesis, showing that the Liberation led to few purges of senior officials. More than an institutional and personnel overhaul, it was a conversion of existing structures—along with the creation of new ones—and a reorganization of the hierarchy of ministries, which explain the dominance of a pro-growth perspective in the postwar era.

The mental conversion of governing and administrative officials, moreover, was not simply an endogenous process, but the consequence of exogenous sociopolitical shocks caused by the international context as well as massive labor mobilizations. As will become clear in the historical analysis presented below, the state "refracted" external shocks, as pro-growth administrators *converted* social pressures into economic expansion. Margairaz concludes that the state was as much the "object" as it was the "actor" of this conversion. The state played a crucial role to ensure the passage from stagnation to capitalist growth, and this, as stressed by John Zysman—and shown in detail by Margairaz and Kuisel—resulted not from a simple transformation of attitudes but from a political battle within and around the state.[82]

Our analysis is similar to Margairaz's. We situate, however, the balance of power between classes and battles internal to the state within the context of a broader study of social property relations and rules of reproduction. We also go further back than the 1930s (Margairaz) or the early twentieth century (Kuisel). We have shown that modernizers—inspired by capitalist models of development and responding to geopolitical pressure and resistance from below—had been active within the state since the mid-eighteenth century—though, of course, they championed different policies at different historical junctures. Until the postwar period, these modernizers faced intractable resistance from economic actors and political coalitions.

It is our contention that attitudes are not free-floating causal factors that can explain the persistence or demise of resistances to socioeconomic change. Indeed, to claim that attitudinal transformation explains sustained growth after the Second World War begs the question: why did attitudes change at that moment? More to the point: why would the populace suddenly accept market dependence and the risks it entails? Why would businesspeople embrace competition, ditch safe profits, and systematically invest to maximize productivity? Why would peasants and small shopkeepers leave their farms, shops and towns, relocate to cities and accept to sell their labor-power to survive? We have covered the capitalist transformation of the agrarian sector in the previous chapter. In the present section, we focus on the conversion imposed upon industrial firms, the transformation of class relations it entailed and the changes within the state that made the sustained growth possible.

To spearhead sustained growth, a state must have a coherent program capable of winning support for the creation and consolidation of new social property relations. The state's ability to develop an efficient administrative apparatus to coordinate the implementation of this program is also key, as is its ability to provide the institutional support for domestic firms to face international competition.[83]

These institutional considerations must then be situated within the broader context of class relations. As Vivek Chibber puts it, "the [developmental] state-building project is critically mediated by the nature of state-capitalist relations."[84] The ability of modernizers to develop and impose coherent policies and institutions within the state, on the one hand, and on industrial firms, on the other, depends on their insulation (especially within the executive and administration) from class coalitions and pressures. Capital's capacity for resistance and the balance of class forces further shape the ability of reformers to impose policies.

Power relations between classes, and between the state and classes (especially the capitalist class), must be located within the specific rules of reproduction—derived from specific social property relations—that shape economic rationality and orient the political strategy of social classes. A noncompetitive economic context will dispense employers from the obligation to systematically improve their operations and will facilitate their political mobilization in favor of the status quo against modernizers active within the state. Conversely, when capitalists must compete on markets against efficient rivals, their reproduction comes to depend upon efficiency gains and, increasingly, on their capacity to secure support from the state and willingness to satisfy its demands so as to compete against foreign firms.[85]

The defeat and humiliation of 1940 was a shock that forced the rulers to recognize the urgency of reforming the socioeconomic structure. This recognition had less to do with autonomously evolving values than with the recognition by a more perceptive section of the ruling class that the success of geopolitical rivals jeopardized their interests. The defeat made obvious that the matter was not simply one of military feebleness, but also of economic failure. During a trip to Washington in 1945, Jean Monnet, a key figure of postwar French economic modernization and leader of the CGP, warned de Gaulle, who talked about "grandeur" and the need to restore France's place among the great powers that "the French are a small people today." Monnet explained that France could not regain or maintain its international standing without a profound modernization of the economy.[86]

Meanwhile, the United States perceived the need for the development of the western European and Japanese economies as part of a strategy of "communist containment" in the emerging bipolar world. But the United States also understood that the growth of these economies was vital for the export and investment outlets of its own corporations. Washington consequently collaborated with—and put pressure on—foreign states to support economic reconstruction and growth, providing aid and access to its massive domestic market so as to facilitate their economic success.[87] French modernizers seized the groundbreaking opportunity offered by the new imperial hegemon.

A technocratic literature, which emerged in France after the Second World War, recurrently called for "modernization." Though conservatives had not yet said their last word, a consensus in key circles of state leaders stressed the need to bury the political economy of the Third Republic and Vichy and to uproot the "Malthusianism" of industrialists. Debates on socioeconomic structures and market mechanisms had raged within the Resistance and carried over at Liberation within the provisional government. Political leaders agreed on the need for state engagement and a dynamic industrial sector.[88]

Industrial employers were discredited and politically isolated at war's end, not only because of their collaboration with the Vichy government and Nazi occupiers, but also because of the poor economic performance of the period that preceded, and contributed to, the defeat of 1940. Capital's opposition to, and part in derailing, the Popular Front in 1936–1937 was still fresh in the working-class collective memory. The centrist and right-wing parties of the Third Republic were politically paralyzed. This was "the nadir of business influence in ... politics."[89] Business had lost its prewar national federation, and trade associations had been dismantled in favor of Vichy's corporatist institutions. Though business associations reorganized in the late 1940s and regained lobbying power under the parliamentary regime of the Fourth Republic, capital had extraordinarily little leverage at the time of the Liberation.

Industrialists held a series of unobtrusive reunions in the summer of 1944 in an attempt to recover influence and respond to the rise of the left. The disgrace and marginalization of business loomed so large, however, that prudence and patience seemed in order: "it was not until June 1946 that [employers] felt confident enough to launch a new ... association, the Conseil National du Patronat Français (CNPF)."[90] Employers tried to block or influence the sweeping legislative changes taking place but had little success. The parties that had represented their interests under the Third Republic were gone or weak, and most of the capital-friendly press was also temporarily lost.[91]

Meanwhile, working-class power and political influence was on the rise, a development that had begun with the massive strikes of May–June 1936. During these months, 2.4 million workers stopped production and occupied factories, extracting significant gains from employers (though eroded by the latter in the following months and years). Wildcat strikes demonstrated the workers' resolve. The membership of the Confédération Générale du Travail (CGT) grew fivefold, as the strikes reached sectors hitherto untouched by the union movement, especially new, large-scale industries. Even "white-collar" employees publicly voiced their "unqualified" support for industrial "comrades." Strikes resumed after a summer pause and broke out again in November 1938. The strike wave marked the birth of mass trade-unionism in France and launched a cycle of labor mobilizations that persisted into the postwar years.[92]

On 18 August 1944, the clandestine CGT and Confédération Française des Travailleurs Chrétiens (CFTC) issued a call for an insurrectional general strike. The strike, which began in Paris on August 10, played a decisive part in the Liberation. In the following weeks and months, "it became possible for workers to refuse to work under the supervision of a given foreman, to refuse an order, to reduce work rhythms, or take time off from work" as workers exercised "an authentic counter-power" in workplaces.[93] Workers formed factory committees to manage companies and maintain production. The government acted rapidly to defuse these initiatives. In February 1945, it adopted a law that made "enterprise committees" mandatory in all workplaces of 100 workers or more but deprived them of managerial power, apart for a right to access the firms' accounts.

The election of October 1945—in which the Communist Party (CP) won more votes than any other party and, with the socialists, an absolute majority in the Constituent Assembly—demonstrated the political weight of the working class and of the left more broadly. The same is true of the surge in union membership, leading to new records of unionization, as the CFTC claimed 700,000 adherents and the CGT 3.7–4.5 million, in 1946. The arrival of left parties in power, however, also contributed to the co-optation of trade-union leaders—whose organizations were organically tied to these left parties—within the government and administration.

The CGT supported the reconstruction of the economy through a "battle for production," a watchword of the CP that encouraged workers to take on longer hours. The union and party banned work-stoppages, though major strikes broke out nonetheless in 1945 and 1946. The CGT announced the great strike movement of November and December 1947, which resumed the mobilizing model of 1936, involved 1.5–2 million workers, and was followed by a massive miners' strike in the Fall of 1948. Strikers opposed government-mandated wage freezes (below the rate of inflation) and decried shortages of food and other basic goods.[94]

The 1947–1948 strikes faced violent repression, causing 24 deaths, and several mobilizations stretching over more than a decade made clear that repression would not suffice to maintain social peace. The more lucid sections of the state and business leaders realized that a new socioeconomic order was needed to ensure stability amidst industrialization, a "vertical alliance" between classes, made possible by sustained growth and rising real wages, an order envisioned by Blum's government in 1936 (and by Napoleon III, Michel Chevalier and other Saint-Simonians a century earlier).

Building the conditions for this new form of class co-optation and socio-political stabilization would take time, but the preconditions were laid at the Liberation. The shock of the 1940 defeat, the disorganization and political marginalization of business and its parties, together with the rise of the left carried by labor mobilizations and the Resistance during the war and Liberation, created a balance of class forces fundamentally different from the "prewar pattern of stalemated centrist politics." From 1944 to 1947, successive governments, in which communists and socialists enjoyed significant weight, enacted social security (including health insurance, retirement benefits and family allowances). The constitution of the Fourth Republic, adopted in 1946, obligated the state to uphold certain social rights.[95]

The nationalizations of this period proved vital to postwar industrial growth. A first wave of nationalizations occurred in 1944 and early 1945, as the provisional government selectively sanctioned the unilateral requisitions of factories by workers. The state nationalized the coal pits of Nord-Pas-de-Calais in December 1944 and Renault (blamed for collaboration) in January 1945. A second wave of parliamentary nationalizations took place in 1945–1946. The Bank of France was made public, followed by four large deposit banks in December 1945. The state completed its control over the financial system with the conversion of Vichy's Comité Permanent d'Organisation Professionnelle des Banques into the Conseil National du Crédit (CNC). The state nationalized electric power and gas in April 1946, establishing the Gaz de France and Électricité de France (EDF). The state took over coal companies and merged them into the Charbonages de France (CdF) in May 1946. A third wave came in 1948, touching terrestrial, maritime and air transport, including the creation of Air France.[96]

Polls showed in 1945 that a large majority supported nationalizations. No doubt part of the socialist left saw nationalizations, together with the establishment of social security, as steps toward a transition to socialism. A more widely shared goal was the fight against the industrial trusts that had managed the stagnant economy of previous decades. Private capital had failed to modernize key economic sectors and thus created major industrial bottlenecks. Though limited to basic sectors, nationalization was to serve as a tool to renovate and modernize industry. The CGP, founded in 1946, proved instrumental to economic renovation, as discussed in detail below. The government's task was also facilitated by the personnel trained at the École Nationale d'Administration (ENA)—and by the data and expertise provided by the Institut National de la Statistique et des Études Économiques—created, respectively, in 1945 and 1946.[97]

After enacting these changes, "political elites quickly and firmly pushed labor out of the ruling coalition."[98] The CP was expelled from the government in May 1947, days before state repression of the massive strikes of that year began. With the left out of the government, business interests rallied and intensified lobbying. Socialist ambitions entertained by the Resistance were ruled out, and the main contest over policy now opposed industrial firms to modernizers within the state. The latter aimed to use public institutions, enterprises and financial tools to invest and modernize the economy and to progressively impose competitive pressures on private capital.

This, however, was not a preordained success. The postwar state, to alleviate shortages, was forced to convert and preserve Vichy's distributive apparatus, including price and wage control mechanisms. The backwardness of the industrial sector, generally incapable of facing foreign competition, together with the heavy reliance on imports during the period of reconstruction and modernization, necessitated foreign trade management through quotas and tariffs.

The political influence of business over the parliamentary regime of the Fourth Republic reinforced the structural limits to market competition. Once capital's period of disorientation and marginalization had passed, its organizations multiplied and its tactics became more aggressive, ranging from lobbying to tax strikes. Toward the closing years of the Fourth Republic, "private interests staffed almost 5,000 consultative committees, councils, or tripartite boards."[99] Business capitalized on divisions between state ministries, using allies (such as the Industry Ministry) to curb competitive imperatives. Officials had to selectively subsidize precarious firms and sectors to defuse the opposition, even as they concentrated on building a competitive economic context.[100]

The transition to the Fifth Republic in 1958 limited parliamentary channels for business influence and provided executive power with more room to develop industrial structures. In the meantime, modernizers were increasingly able to impose their views within core, and politically insulated, segments of the bureaucratic apparatus. The upshot was that control over industrial policy began to shift from parliament toward part of the state bureaucracy.[101]

The creation of the CGP and the implementation of a modernization plan represented a first battle for the transformation of the state and economic policy. It was led by Jean Monnet, an international banker and influential broker with American and British allies on the eve of, and during, the Second World War. Pierre Mendès France, Minister of National Economy appointed by de Gaulle in 1944, put forward a project for planning. Mendès France recycled parts of Vichy's regulatory apparatus to control prices and imposed budgetary and monetary restrictions to curb inflation and liberate sums for structural reforms. Planning would involve nationalizations and austerity to support investments aimed at modernizing industry. Facing deep-seated and widespread opposition, including from Finance Minister René Pleven and de Gaulle—who feared that austerity would cause rural discontent—Mendès France resigned in August 1945.[102]

Monnet then became the head of planning, although he proposed a form that differed from Mendès-France's vision and pursued different tactics to achieve his ends. Monnet used his office, and contacts created as negotiator of international financial and military support during and after the war, to tie planning to aid provided by the United States. His aim was to ensure that reconstruction would simultaneously entail industrial modernization. France needed US aid to purchase basic imports and avoid the collapse of consumption at the same time as investments renovated industry and reconstructed the economy. This dependence on foreign support provided Monnet and his entourage with a lever to impose his vision within the state.

In February 1945, Washington agreed to issue low-interest loans for raw materials, capital equipment and military aid but the accord was cancelled in August of that year. The United States made any further financial aid conditional on strict accountability, productive use of funding and the elaboration of a modernization program. Monnet urged de Gaulle to prepare and implement a credible plan aimed at renovating industrial equipment. This plan, required to get US support, was urgently needed to avoid the reversion to traditional economic structures, which would seal the international decline of the country. In January 1946, a governmental decree established the CGP directed by Monnet. Washington agreed to supply a $900 million loan to support reconstruction and modernization in May 1946, a foretaste of the Marshall Plan of 1948.[103]

Monnet, to avoid the fate of Mendes France, insisted on attaching the CGP to the office of the President of the Council of ministers, insulated from ministerial jurisdictional battles and parliamentary supervision. The CGP invited representatives from labor, business and government to participate in modernization commissions and prepare its first plan. Although the support of labor helped to legitimize the planners' endeavors, most industrial employers proved refractory. The CGP then used its allies at the Treasury, and controls over financial levers, to devise selective alliances with specific firms and move its modernization program forward.[104]

Planners proselytized for modernization through persuasion, informal coordination and the circulation of information between state agencies. Their decisive instrument was the channeling of private and public credit. Far from challenging the precepts of a market economy, their aim was precisely to prepare the reinstitution and intensification of competitive imperatives. For this, the CGP used tools created by the reforms enacted from 1944 to 1946. They used state control over financial institutions and nationalized firms to direct investments toward equipment upgrades. The Monnet Plan, initially adopted for 1947–1950, was a program of investments and production targets in basic industries plagued by bottlenecks. The plan directed investments toward electricity, coal, transport and steel. US aid provided funds for the introduction of US machines in the chemical, automobile and metallurgic industries. France was thus able to secure access to the up-to-date and relatively cheap equipment and technology, necessary to compete on international markets, which its own capital-goods sector was not yet able to supply. The Americans also provided technological know-how, through "productivity missions" to facilitate information exchange between employers on both sides of the Atlantic.

The CGP faced opposition over its insistence on prioritizing modernization over consumption. This first plan was made possible by the financing of the Fonds de Modernisation et d'Équipement (FME), established in 1948 through the Marshall Plan, which led the CGT and CP to withdraw their support over opposition to US interference in French affairs. Fearing inflation, the government opposed the funding targets set by the plan in 1948 and again in 1950 and 1952. But funding was maintained, thanks to high officials in charge of the political agenda, and peaked in the following years, when the plan was renewed and expanded until 1952.

If the first plan, which updated basic sectors, was what one may call dirigiste, the second plan, directed by Étienne Hirsch and rolled out in 1954–1957, left more room for consultation with and among private firms that had by then been reexposed to competitive imperatives (as explained below). The Hirsch Plan aimed to accelerate productivity gains through the dissemination of new techniques, larger plants and product standardization in a larger number of sectors than under the first plan. The architects of both plans saw them as steps toward, and preconditions for, the fuller opening of the economy to competition within the European common market.[105]

The plans would never have been implemented without the transformation of the Ministry of Finance from the late 1940s to the early 1950s. The Ministry of Finance became the site of a second battle waged by modernizers within the administration. The Ministry of Finance absorbed the Ministry of National Economy in 1947 and confirmed its privileged position within the state apparatus. The responsibilities of the Ministry expanded beyond fiscal and budgetary matters to comprise economic financing, as well as regulatory power over the prices of several categories of consumer and capital goods.[106]

The evolution of the Ministry of Finance toward an expansionary and modernizing policy was undertaken under the leadership of the Treasury. The latter's own transformation was initiated in 1947–1948 under the direction of François Bloch-Lainé, who became a convert to the first plan by Monnet. This support of Finance and Treasury leaders was reinforced by the ENA, which produced graduates focused on using the state to renew the economic structure and foster industrial growth.[107]

The Treasury's influence over the Ministry of Finance and, indeed, the whole state loomed large. Zysman describes the Treasury as "the sanctuary inside the temple of the Ministry of Finance" and the "economic apex of a centralized state."[108] More than a bank for the state, it became the "banker of growth."[109] The Caisse Autonome de la Reconstruction (CAREC), the FME, and its successor, the Fonds de Développement Économique et Social (FDES), funded by the Marshall Plan, fell under the control of the Treasury, which used it to finance the investments targeted by the Monnet Plan, in collaboration with the CGP.[110]

Margairaz has shown how the Treasury experienced a double mutation during the late 1940s. The first was a massive increase of the proportion of its budget directed toward industrial investments, which went from below 5 percent before the war to over 30 percent in 1949. The second mutation, closely related to the first, had to do with the evolution of the Treasury's sources of revenue. The state imposed new taxes, which covered nearly 70 percent of public expenditures by 1947—by far the highest proportion of the previous 15 years—and between 84 percent and 88 percent from 1949 to 1951. State revenues multiplied by 13 in value and doubled in volume from 1945 to1952. Budget deficits, recurrent from 1932 to 1947, diminished as a result. Crucially, new revenues covered most of the ordinary expenditures and freed up revenue received from foreign aid, mostly to fund the extraordinary expenditures of economic reconstruction and moderni- zation established by the CGP's plan. Public funding of investments peaked in 1949–1950, which corresponds to a period of intense fiscal efforts to compress deficits.[111]

In addition to funds from Marshall aid, freed for investments by new tax rev- enues and administered and channeled through the FME, FDES and CAREC, mod- ernizers relied on the state's regulation of credit to enforce their agenda and provide loans to private firms. The reforms and nationalizations of 1944–1946 had brought the Bank of France and major deposit banks into the state's lap. The Treasury, to- gether with the CNC, the Bank of France and the CGP, framed and applied a credit policy of modernization. Inserted into the "Treasury circuit," banks functioned through a dozen public and semipublic financial institutions, which allowed of- ficials to tap into private savings, turning short-term deposits into long-term loans and subsidies.

The power of the state to turn private savings into public loans and to supervise the issuing of new stocks allowed it to avoid piling up debts through the issuing of bonds and to limit its need for new taxes. The Treasury thus had the capacity to reg- ulate the provision of credit and make it serve the plan. The state, moreover, turned the underdeveloped banking system of the prewar period—with its deposit banks focused on short-term commercial loans and underfinanced investment banks— into a financial system focused on investments and dynamic growth.[112]

The selective allocation of credit amounted to a tool through which Treasury officials could enforce their policy. Firms that refused to follow the plan and im- plement new techniques could see funds taken away and directed to competitors. Funds also subsidized struggling traditional sectors to pacify them and diffuse po- litical opposition while promoting structural change in modern and expanding sec- tors through other subsidies. The state, for instance, used this tactic to oversee the "orderly decline" of textile production in rural areas and thus dissipate obstruction of the economic renewal of the 1950s and 1960s. The complexity of the financial system supervised by the Treasury and its working at a distance from parliamen- tary overview and public debates allowed officials to make their credit policy and distribution of subsidies appear to be fair, "without *visibly* starving the traditional sectors" and privileging modernization.[113]

The state's control of key financial institutions and foreign aid allowed it to supplement private investments, which remained weak before the early 1950s, when firms lacked resources and still faced limited compulsion to contract loans and invest. State ownership of energy and transportation enabled development in other industrial branches by keeping costs low.[114] As Michel Loriaux explains, "be- tween 1959 and 1974, the prices of goods and services produced by the state sector actually diminished by 20 percent relative to the prices of goods and services as a whole. Energy prices fell by 30 percent."[115] Public officials thus freed up funds for private firms to reinvest.

Nevertheless, the subsidies, incentives and sanctions, made possible by state control over credit and public firms, did not transform the economy. Private firms, free from competitive imperatives, succeeded in limiting their dependence upon funding. Coordination problems emerged, as some firms and industries did not produce, at requisite levels of efficiency, the materials used in other branches. In the late 1940s and early 1950s, the state had to maintain tariffs, while upgrading basic sectors, before it could liberalize trade and force industrial firms to face foreign competition. The state also had to maintain price controls to cope with shortages, contributing to a context in which firms could still coordinate, manage and divide markets.

In the wake of the Liberation, the provisional government prioritized supplying the population with basic goods and services. It kept in place the system of economic management established under Vichy. "Organizing committees" renamed "professional offices" came under the leadership of new commissioners but continued to distribute materials and orders to companies with the help of administrative and statistical apparatuses. Although the law adopted in April 1946, under pressure from the CP, eliminated professional offices, their functions and personnel were taken over by private business. The Comptoir des Produits Sidérurgiques, for instance, centralized and allocated orders within the steel industry with the help of about 750 employees.[116]

Shortages abated in 1948 and 1949, as reconstruction was essentially complete and the country reached its prewar production level. Finance minister René Mayer abolished the OCPRI and began to lift price and wage controls as a means to "reestablish real prices" and enforce market competition.[117] A report on France's productivity lag, published in 1949 under the leadership of Monnet and CGP collaborator Jean Fourastié, emerged from a "productivity drive" pursued in collaboration with the Marshall mission in France. After management and labor representatives visited the United States in 1950, the government decreed the formation of the Comité National de la Productivité (CNP), which disseminated propaganda to promote productivity. By 1956, three billion francs had also been allocated as "productivity loans."[118]

Even so, price liberalization, propaganda and loans proved less than transformative in the face of business organizations, which reactivated the capacities of the former organizing committees and professional offices and used them to profit from high prices. In the second half of the 1940s, a private form of "professional dirigisme" replaced the former state dirigisme, ententes and stagnant economy of the 1930s.[119] Ententes of the 1940s often formed in response to the nationalization of formerly independent firms into a single public company. Suppliers coordinated to share the equipment orders issued by their newly formed public client. This strategy avoided price competition and kept low productivity firms afloat. The archives of EDF reveal an entente of firms producing aluminum cables, which allowed them to raise prices 25 percent over a period of three months in 1951.[120]

Notes produced for different ministries and agencies during the late 1940s and early 1950s by the Service Central des Marchés (SCAM) and the CNP attached to the Secrétariat d'État aux Affaires Économiques showed that private firms, through ententes, often reactivated former organizing committees. The notes identified disciplinary sanctions to impose on the firms. The SCAM and the CNP stressed the risks of "substituting state dirigisme for private dirigisme that distorts competition through illicit coalitions."[121]

The eradication of ententes and intensification of market competition became another major fight led by modernizers under the Fourth Republic. Public interventions in favor of the restoration of market competition multiplied. In 1948, the Commission des Affaires Économiques of the National Assembly called for anti-cartel legislation to reinstate price competition, including the formation of special tribunals to dissolve cartels. Such legislative acts, however, had little impact.

A governmental order, adopted in 1945, banned illicit price control practices. Laws adopted in 1946 and again in 1948 went in the same direction. The ambiguity of public institutions toward ententes endured, however, due to parliamentary interference and interministerial conflicts. While some firms opposed ententes, which inflated prices of industrial material, another section of business leaders and their representatives participated in parliamentary consultations on and obstructions of pro-competition legislation. These business representatives could also count on support from within the Industry Ministry.

The government established a Commission Techniques des Ententes (CTE) in 1953 to clamp down on illicit and detrimental coalitions between firms. However, according to the decree that established the CTE, ententes that "improved and expanded production" and contributed to the "development of economic progress" would be recognized as legitimate organizations. Working within this ambiguous legal framework, the CTE rarely intervened to curb the cartels' activities, and legislation to counter ententes had little effect.[122]

Facing parliamentary and ministerial obstruction, liberal officials sought to reactivate and intensify measures and policies legislated previously. Years before the creation of the CTE, nationalized firms had already begun to act against ententes on capital goods markets. Their aim was to eradicate coalitions that increased prices and restricted innovations, thus slowing down and making more expensive modernizing efforts spearheaded by the CGP and Treasury.

Claude Didry and Frédéric Marty have analyzed in detail how EDF targeted ententes between firms producing electric equipment. These firms had maintained prewar practices of dividing contracts, managing prices, limiting competition, guaranteeing profits and muting the compulsion to invest and innovate. Because of lagging innovation and dynamism, electric equipment was less efficient than equivalent goods imported from the United States. EDF responded by exercising its market power as unique buyer—as a monopsony—to break the coalitional market power of electromechanical firms. The nationalized firm centralized both the equipment order procedures and the information relative to the markets on which orders were placed. It also reduced its use of tenders based on price contests and privileged direct contracting with specific firms. This procedure was less transparent than open public tenders and made it more difficult for ententes to discipline members and provide safe conduits for "cheating" firms.[123]

Using this procedure to dismantle the ententes, EDF brought down prices of electric equipment and capacitors by 35–45 percent and 16 percent, respectively, in 1952. Other nationalized firms began to employ similar tactics and contributed to the eradication of ententes amongst their suppliers. In 1952, Antoine Pinay, as Minister of Finance and President of the Council of Minister, issued a note to all public agencies responsible for monitoring markets which stressed the negative impacts of ententes and instructed public officials to oppose any intent to form them.[124]

Meanwhile, the nationalized firms began to pursue the goal of rationalizing and optimizing production and investment. Public firms functioned increasingly on the model of capitalist enterprises, run by independent administrators, and "accommodated themselves to a market economy." Taylorism was implemented at the Société Nationale des Chemins de Fer, while mechanization and rationalization accelerated at CdF and EDF, which "led the way in applying econometric techniques."[125]

Monnet and Fourastié had concluded in 1949 that their country's lagging productivity growth was due to the narrowness of the domestic market and from the absence of market competition. Three years earlier, Fourastié had warned Monnet and the CGP that though necessary, public investment to modernize basic sectors would not suffice to level the balance of payment by 1952, as requested by the Marshall Plan. Competition and productivity growth had to spread throughout the economy, Fourastié explained. The CGP submitted an anti-cartel bill in 1949, arguing that coalitions formed to manage markets and inflate prices undermined the plan by artificially increasing the costs of equipment. Monnet and his aides could count on the support of Jean Constant, the leaders of the Syndicat Général des Industries Mécaniques et Utilisatrices des Métaux. Constant opposed ententes that swelled the prices of metallurgic products. But Georges Villiers, President of the CNPF, opposed the CGP's bill and defended "valid" ententes. Villiers had the support of high-ranking officials, such as Robert Burton, Director of the Secrétariat d'État aux Affaires Économiques, who responded to Monnet's proposal with counter-bills differentiating "good" from "bad" ententes and seeking to preserve the former. By 1950, it was clear that a strict prohibition of ententes would remain out of reach.

Facing domestic parliamentary barriers, modernizers turned to European trade, to the exposure of industrial firms to foreign competition, as a more efficient means to fight cartels. Matthias Kipping recounts how in 1950, following yet another Monnet imitative, Foreign Minister Robert Schuman issued the declaration that led to the establishment of the European Coal and Steel Community (ECSC) the following year.[126] Monnet directly intervened in negotiations preceding the signature of the Paris Treaty, which founded the Community, to ensure that it would include straightforward and strict pro-competition and anti-cartel sections and enforcement mechanisms.

Villiers, the CNPF and the Chambre Syndicale de la Sidérurgie Française ve-hemently opposed the project, challenged the myth of "ideal competition" and de-nounced the "hyper dirigisme" imposed by the ECSC. Monnet countered that the ECSC would, in fact, undermine dirigisme exercised through ententes. The Treaty was then signed over the objections of business, thanks to the intervention of the United States, which convinced Germany to accept anti-cartel measures, to divi-sions amongst French steel producers (the more modern firms supported trade lib-eralization to access larger markets) and to support from the council of ministers. In addition to targeting cartels, the ECSC reduced tariffs on coal and steel, and restricted subsidies to firms in these sectors. This tariff reduction enlarged market outlets and intensified competition, leading to a fall in coal and steel prices.[127]

The project of an Italian-French Customs Union had been defeated in parlia-ment in 1947, in large part due to the opposition of textile manufacturers. The adoption of the ECSC marked a reversal on foreign trade and paved the way for further liberalization and the signature of the Treaty of Rome of 1957, which estab-lished the EEC.[128] Various sectors of industry remained hostile to this new treaty, fearing foreign competition, but more dynamic and modernizing ones welcomed access to larger markets. Significantly, the electrical equipment industry, which had rationalized rapidly after the eradication of cartels, thanks to the action of EDF in the early 1950s, now welcomed the EEC.[129]

The EEC spread to other industrial sectors the competitive pressures that the ECSC had introduced on the coal and steel markets. Zysman summarizes the mo-mentous impact of the ECSC and EEC:

> These two treaties burst the insulation of the French economy and forced firms to compete, first in European and later in world markets. The presence of outside competitors made it harder for French firms to arrange markets, that is, to set prices or production by agreement. Whereas firms had once sought protection and state certification of private arrangements to control domestic markets, they now had to seek assistance for competitive adjust-ment. The modernizers had created market forces that could push the econ-omy in the direction they favored.[130]

The ECSC and EEC were used by French modernizers to open new markets for industrial firms, which had until then evolved on a narrow domestic market, and to eliminate inefficient firms in the process. Like the ECSC, the EEC curbed tariffs, quotas, subsidies and cartels. Both treaties created new obstacles to business lob-bying efforts and cartel coordination, as lobbies would now have to influence two levels of government and coordinate large numbers of firms across several coun-tries. Industrial firms still joined networks and ententes, but these efforts would now have to be geared toward penetrating international markets and coping with foreign competition as opposed to escaping the compulsion to upgrade productive capacities.

Members of the EEC reduced tariffs faster than required by the Treaty of Rome. Governments eliminated all quotas by 1962 and reduced tariffs by 40 percent instead of the scheduled 25 percent. The EEC eliminated all tariffs by 1968, 18 months ahead of the deadline, and reduced its common external tariff.[131]

The ECSC, the EEC and negotiations led under the auspices of the General Agreement on Tariffs and Trade contributed to the increasing exposure of industrial firms to imports. The latter increased by 78 percent from 1951 to 1957 and increased again by 147 percent from 1957 to 1963. The mean ratio of imports to consumption rose steadily from 8 percent in 1959 to 25 percent in 1980. For capital goods, the ratio increased from 7.6 percent in 1959 to 21.1 percent in 1972. The ratio increased by over 30 percent for shoes, knitwear and woven textiles and over 50 percent for household electronics and manufactured fibers.

Meanwhile, exports directed toward the EEC increased by 195 percent, while those directed toward countries outside the ECC increased by 140 percent from 1958 to 1964. The mean ratio of exports to total output went from 14 percent in 1959 to 27 percent in 1980, with a particularly sharp increase from the late 1960s. Among leading export sectors, electrical equipment rose by 20 percent, while business electronics, bulk organic chemicals and aerospace equipment increased by 23 percent, 30 percent and 37 percent, respectively.

International treaties also contributed to an exposure to foreign investments, especially after 1960. The mean value of direct foreign investment as a proportion of all manufacturing industries rose from 9 percent in 1962 to 25 percent in 1980. The nominal stock value of US direct investments in France went from $217 million in 1950 to $1,030 million in 1962 and $9,348 million in 1980.[132]

Overall, the share of international trade in the GDP went from 22.7 percent in 1950 to 34.1 percent in 1973. Evolving patterns of international trade led French manufacturers to depend significantly less on colonial markets and to redirect their exports toward the competitive economies of the Global North. The proportion of total exports that went to the French Overseas Union fell from 42 percent in 1952, to just 9 percent in 1972. Meanwhile, the share of exports directed toward the original EEC members increased from 15.9 percent in 1952 to 49.9 percent in 1972, while exports going to OECD countries increased from 43.2 percent to 76.5 percent, during the same period.[133]

The dependence of industrial sectors on colonial markets, the attachment of the population to the empire and geopolitical considerations had led France to cling to its colonies into the 1950s. But as the empire's weight on public budgets increased and industrial and foreign trade restructuring set in, modernizers began to question the usefulness of colonies. Mendès France declared in 1954 that France had to choose between Indochina and economic renewal. President de Gaulle assured, at a press conference in 1961, during the Algerian war of independence, that "decolonization is our interest and, consequently, our policy." Anti-colonial struggles, of course, helped to shape this perception of interest, but modernizers welcomed a shift away from the economic safeguard that colonies had offered to industrial firms.[134]

Increasing exposure to imports and foreign investments and greater penetration of the world market intensified the competitive imperatives faced by industrial firms.[135] As these changes took hold, the state acted to intensify domestic competition, specifically in retail, which had been at first less impacted by the evolving international environment and foreign competition. The government, in the face of parliamentary obstruction and countermeasures, passed legislative and fiscal reforms to favor innovation and concentration in the sector. In 1951, for instance, the government repealed the moratorium on new variety stores. A value-added tax progressively replaced the existing sales tax after 1954. Since the state levied the new value-added tax only on the retailers' markup (as opposed to the total commodity value as in the case of the sales tax), it represented an advantage for larger retail stores with low markups.

The measures introduced by the government rapidly intensified the development of large stores and chains. The first supermarket was established in 1957. By 1964, the country counted 1,441 of them and 2,719 in 1974. The number of hypermarkets went from five to 292 from 1964 to 1974. Supermarkets and chain stores contributed to tightening price competition in retail, squeezing a large portion of smaller boutiques and stores out of business in the process. This fueled the Poujadist movement of small shopkeepers, demanding protections for small commercial ventures and artisans. In spite of the adoption of measures to ease discontent, the arrival of foreign investors in the late 1960s—21 percent of net inflows of foreign investment took place in retail and wholesale from 1965 to 1978—intensified domestic competition and irreversibly undermined the time-honored world of French boutiques.[136]

The intensification of foreign and domestic competition contributed to a rapid acceleration of the proletarianization of the workforce—though, as stated above, this process was partially softened by subsidies aimed at slowing the erosion of traditional industrial and commercial activities. We saw in the previous chapter how the implementation of capitalist social property relations and competitive imperatives fueled a rural exodus. The share of agriculture in the total labor force fell from 36 percent in 1946 to 21 percent in 1962 and 9.5 percent in 1975. The rural exodus contributed to a sharp decline of self-employment and a rise of salaried employment. In 1954, less than two-third of the total workforce was salaried. The proportion of wage laborers increased to 71.6 percent in 1962 and reached 82.7 percent in 1975. This evolution also resulted from the attrition of small manufacturers and shops. The number of artisans decreased from 2 to 1.4 million between 1954 and 1975. In retail and wholesale, half the jobs were self-employed in 1954, but this proportion fell to a quarter in 1975. While some shopkeepers and small farm owners retired, significant numbers, along with their offspring, joined the wage labor force.[137]

As salaried employment rose from the late 1950s to the early 1970s, geographic mobility increased and remained high thereafter. Workers left villages and towns to seek employment in cities or other departments. A national labor market took shape. Meanwhile, from 1954 to 1975, the number of immigrants rose from 1.7 to 3.4 million, and the portion of industrial workers among them went from 53.4 percent in 1962 to 72.9 percent in 1975. The influx of immigrants accelerated during the 1960s. Women also massively entered the labor market from the late 1960s—from 1968 to the early 1980s, they accounted for three-quarters of the growth of the workforce. Overall, however, the country's workforce grew slowly—it totaled 20 million in 1968 compared to 20.4 million in 1931. The key difference between the two periods was that by the 1960s, large new layers of the workforce had been proletarianized.

The increasing commodification of labor, accompanied by an influx of migrant and women to the labor market, provided employers with a more stable and malleable workforce compared with earlier periods of industrialization. Crucially, proletarianization provided capital with cheap reserves of labor power, compensating for upward wage pressures stemming from the employers' competition to hire workers as they expanded capacities. Employers were thus able to combine state of the art technology, first provided by the United States, later developed domestically, with relatively low labor costs, gaining the ability to penetrate the US market and compete on the world market. After a meager growth of 500,000 between 1931 and 1954, the number of industrial workers increased by two million to reach 8.5 million in 1975. Access to a more stable workforce allowed employers to impose and intensify discipline and deskill jobs, as competition compelled them to mechanize production and maximize productivity. Of the new industrial jobs created from 1954 to 1975, 1.5 million were unskilled, held disproportionally by migrants.[138]

With the massification of the labor market came the massification of the consumer market. Like most Western countries, France experienced rapid demographic growth after the Second World War, its population increasing from 40.5 million in 1946 to 49.8 million in 1968. A considerable proportion of this population joined the salaried workforce, and real incomes rose rapidly as employers competed to hire workers and as workers organized to increase wages. Labor leaders accepted a trade-off whereby employers secured productivity gains—entailing intense work rates, deskilling and technological substitutions for labor—in exchange for regular wage increases. The scheme was aimed at buying "social peace" and avoiding work interruptions—it proved relatively efficient until the general strike of May-June 1968. The average monthly real wage of a full-time industrial worker multiplied by three between 1949 and 1976, increasing from 2,247 to 6,867 francs. The proportion of industrial workers owning a car rose from 8 percent in 1953 to 73.6 percent in 1975, while the share of television owners went from 0.9 percent to 88.4 percent over the same period. The share of households with vacuum cleaners grew from 14 percent to 55 percent from 1954 to 1972, 7.5 percent to 83.3 percent for refrigerators and 8.4 percent to 75 percent for washing machines.[139]

As the population became market dependent, industrial firms gained access to the mass domestic market outlets that made possible economies of scale and the acceleration of the standardization of production, a precondition to compete on, and penetrate, foreign markets. Market opportunities became sufficiently large to support the transition from labor-intensive industrial production, which had until then remained characteristically important in France, to higher value-added branches. And market imperatives compelled firms to merge activities, develop

new techniques and products, invest in research and development and design marketing strategies. The state encouraged concentration and oligopolies, which, in
the context of an economy opened to foreign competition, did not have the same
detrimental consequences as previously and, in fact, facilitated the capital leverage
and investments necessary to sustain this competition.[140]

Charles de Gaulle capitalized on the political crisis generated by the Algerian
anti-colonial struggle to make a political comeback and prepare a new constitution
for a new republic in 1958. Voters elected him President of the Fifth Republic in
December of that year. The new regime heightened the power of executive officials and limited the authority of the legislature. The institutional configuration
diminished party politics and collective action by private firms, thus limiting the
influence of industrial lobbies. Firms increasingly "presented their positions individually and in technical terms, instead of collectively in the more general political
terms of broadly based interests."[141]

The emergence of a competitive environment, moreover, encouraged firms to
defect from coalitions and accept state directives so as to secure the government
support needed to improve productivity and compete against domestic and foreign
rivals. The political reforms and economic restructuring of the Fifth Republic gave
the state the upper hand against industrial firms and coalitions. The state disarmed
economic ententes and disruptive political coalitions of the Third Republic, which
the Fourth Republic had reactivated, and thereby facilitated the pursuit of efficient
industrial policy.[142]

As tariffs declined within the EEC during the 1960s, the government reformed
planning to promote the efficiency of chosen firms—"national champions" set to
conquer world markets. The share of public investments in the state budget, and out
of total investments, had already begun to fall during the 1950s, and rising private
investments took over. The state actively sustained private investments through advantageous fiscal reforms, subsidies and private loans. The adoption of the valued-
added tax in 1954 encouraged investments in mechanization. Fiscal policy encouraged investment in industrial equipment. The state, moreover, supported research
and development investments, which grew from 1.14 percent of the GDP in 1959
to 2.23 percent in 1967. The state's share of these investments increased from 62
percent in 1963 to 68 percent in 1968. The "national champions," moreover, benefited from direct subsidies.[143]

The government devalued the Franc by 20 percent in 1957, the year of the signature of the Rome Treaty, by another 20 percent in 1958 and again by over 17
percent the following year. Hence, just as it began reducing tariffs and exposing
industry to foreign competition, the government also moved to provide an undervalued currency to industrial firms to support their competitiveness on international
markets. The state had already devaluated the Franc in 1950 and did so again in the
late 1960s and early 1970s, boosting exports on each occasion.[144]

The state thus intervened to reduce and socialize what it cost for domestic
industries to conquer foreign markets. Not all national champions, such as the
Compagnie Internationale pour l'Informatique (eventually taken over by American interests) and the Concorde plane, enjoyed success.[145] State-supported export

strategies largely succeeded, however, as illustrated by the automobile industry. Automobile makers developed cheap models on credit for mass consumption during the 1950s. They continued, however, to concentrate on the domestic market, while foreign markets played an auxiliary and restricted role in the firms' strategies. With the liberalization of foreign trade, the state required Renault to expand exports, offering fiscal advantages as well as technical and marketing support. The firm cooperated and the program proved successful. While exports represented 31.4 percent of car sales in the 1950s, this percentage fluctuated between 55 percent and 60 percent from 1970 to 1975. Car production grew 11 times over, exports over 19 times over, from 1950 to 1975. Because of investments and productivity efforts undertaken by private firms and supported by the state, overall industrial exports grew faster than the GDP during the second half of the 1960s.[146]

In summary, the balance of class power in the wake of the Second World War facilitated reforms which, together with US aid (and political pressures), gave the state the tools and resources necessary to substitute public for private investment. This took place over a first phase of development, from the late 1940s to the early 1950s, during which industrial upgrading was pursued behind protectionist walls. Planners directed these investments toward the elimination of industrial bottlenecks as a precondition for opening the economy to foreign competition. While modernizing industrial structures, the state used the same tools to buy off protests of declining manufacturers and proceed with a progressive and "orderly" erosion of traditional, under efficient, branches.

Meanwhile, nationalized enterprises framed public contracts to restore competition and break ententes, which came undone under the pressure of the Paris and Rome treaties at the end of the 1950s. International trade and domestic liberalization intensified competitive pressures, leading increasing numbers of small firms, workshops and stores to go under. This shakeout contributed to a rapid proletarianization of the workforce, already fueled by the capitalist restructuring of agriculture, and to a mass consumer market, as millions of people had to purchase basic items of necessity. Tapping into rural reserves of labor, industrial firms combined advanced industrial technology with relatively low labor costs. The rapid commodification of labor gave firms access a domestic market sufficiently large to standardize and concentrate production, which they were constrained to do— seeking public assistance in the process—by market imperatives.

The transition toward industrial capitalism, initiated under the Second Empire in the 1850s and 1860s, was thus completed, and locked-in, at the initiative of state officials determined to preserve the geopolitical interests of the ruling class and to disarm resistance from below through sustained economic expansion and real wage gains. These modernizers imposed competitive rules of reproduction on a class of industrial employers that had until then organized to avoid these rules.

The consolidation of capitalist social property relations and the imposition of competitive rules for reproduction brought rapid and sustained industrial development. This dynamic, of course, was not limited to France—all western European countries experienced sustained growth from the late 1940s to the early 1970s. What was remarkable is that whereas capitalist industrialization proceeded in France at a comparatively slow pace in the late nineteenth century and was reversed during the 1930s, the country experienced growth on par with other capitalist countries from the early 1950s and even above the average during the 1960s. This signaled the consolidation and deepening of capitalist socioeconomic relations.

French GDP grew at an average annual rate of 4.9 percent between 1949 and 1959, 5.7 percent between 1955 and 1968 and 6.1 percent between 1959 and 1974. GDP doubled between 1870 and 1902 and again between 1890 and 1929. After the Second World War, GDP doubled between 1950 and 1965 and again between 1959 and 1972. Compared with the prewar period, growth was not only much faster but also remarkably more stable—despite inflationary pressure and an often-precarious balance of trade. Whereas GDP had declined in absolute terms 12 times from 1870 to 1914 and on seven occasions between the world wars, it never contracted from one year to the next between 1945 and 1975. Total output increased by 168 percent and industrial output by 235 percent between 1959 and 1980.[147]

Intense investment efforts fueled rapid and sustained growth. The rate of investment was set at 18 percent for 1950–1954 and increased to 20 percent for 1954–1959, before reaching 26.5 percent for 1966–1973. Investments increased by an annual average of 8 percent between 1954 and 1974. Growing rates of investment translated into the substitution of capital for labor at an unprecedented pace in all branches of the economy. In industry, fixed capital grew at an annual pace of 3.1 percent from 1951 to 1957, 6 percent from 1957 to 1963 and 5.4 percent from 1963 to 1969. The ratio of fixed capital per worker progressed at an average annual rate of 5.2 percent between1950 and 1972. From 1950 to 1970, the average age of industrial equipment dropped from 14.5 years to eight years in intermediary industrial good sectors, from 14.5 years to six years in the capital goods sector and from 23 years to 11 years in the consumer goods sector.

French industry experienced a profound restructuring over this period as labor-intensive branches declined and higher valued-added sectors gained ground. During the mid-1950s, the number of workers in metal production and mechanical construction surpassed that of textile manufacturing for the first time. The output of capital goods grew by an annual average of 7.4 percent between 1952 and 1972, while that of the chemical branch grew at a rate of 8.1 percent from 1960 to 1972.[148]

Labor productivity growth followed suit. Labor productivity outside agriculture and housing services increased at a yearly rate of 5.5 percent from 1949 to 1961 and 6.7 percent from 1960 to 1973. The overall annual average of labor productivity growth between 1953 and 1973 reached 5.4 percent—0.4 percentage points above German growth. Productivity gains were remarkably high for capital goods and intermediate industrial goods. These productivity gains allowed France to become the world's third largest exporter in 1973, behind the United States and West Germany and slightly ahead of Japan.[149]

France regained the economic rank among states, which it had lost in the seventeenth century. It achieved this feat through the completion of the capitalist restructuring of its social property relations, which set the country on a path of spectacular economic growth that persisted until the global downturn of the 1970s.

Notes

1 Carré et al. 1973; Eck 2009.
2 Caron 1995, p. 87, 89.
3 Hoffmann 1963, p. 3–8. For works that develop theses similar to Hoffmann's, see Sauvy 1965–1967; Anderson 1977; Smith 1980; Lebovics 1988.
4 Elwitt 1975, p. 1, 9–10.
5 Hoffmann 1963, p. 5–7.
6 Zeldin 1993, p. 59, 124. See also Caron 1995, p. 91; Charle 1991, p. 236–37.
7 Charle 1991, p. 240–41.
8 Zeldin 1993, p. 122–23.
9 Mooers 1991.
10 We owe this phrase to Chris Isett.
11 Chamouard and Fogacci 2015; Charle 1991, p. 228–29, 291; Magraw 1986, p. 215, 220; Sick 2013, p. 372.
12 Chatriot 2013, p. 353–354; Elwitt 1975, p. 13–14, 18; Gaboriaux 2010, p. 26–27, 293, 309, 311–15, 321–23; Sick 2013, p. 366–69.
13 Dormois 2004, p. 55. See also Lebovics 1988, p. 192.
14 Lebovics 1988, p. 81–96; Sick 2013, p. 373.
15 Dormois 2004, p. 50, 102; Zeldin 1993, p. 572, 574, 576, 584, 587–88, 591–92.
16 Caron 1995, p. 51; Dumas 2016, p. 69–82.
17 Caron 1995, p. 48; Dormois 2004, p. 13–14; Woronoff 1994, p. 365.
18 Chartiot 2013, p. 355; Dumas 2016, p. 13–22.
19 Dumas 2016, p. 217. Our translation.
20 Caron 1995, p. 92; Zdatny 1984, p. 427, 436–37; Dormois 2004, p. 50–51, 55–56.
21 Sick 2003, p. 148; 2013, p. 365.
22 Dormois 2004, p. 33.
23 Anderson 1977, p. 27; Noiriel 1986, p. 115; Stone 1985, p. 179–180 ; Vigna 2012, p. 52–53, 61–62.
24 Lebovics 1988, p. 1; Noiriel 1986, p. 83.
25 Dumas 2016, p. 218. Our translation. See also Hardy-Hémery 1993, p. 326.
26 Dormois 2004, p. 3, 14, 102; Gaboriaux 2010, p. 15; Kemp 1971, p. 297; Marchand and Thélot 1991, p. 26; Noiriel 1986, p. 124; Woronoff 1994, p. 357.
27 Dormois 2004, p. 10; Gildea 2003, p. 144, 278; Lebovics 1967, p. 33–34; Tilly and Kopsidis 2020, p. 233–34; Torp 2011, p. 351; Verley 1996, p. 102–104.
28 Woronoff 1994, p. 354.
29 Brenner and Glick 1991, p. 65–66.
30 Tilly and Kopsidis 2020, p. 240; Torp 2011, p. 353.
31 Asselain 1984, p. 29; Caron 1995, p. 91; Noiriel 1986, p. 150; Vigna 2012, p. 66–67; Woronoff 1994, p. 444.
32 Brenner and Glick 1991, p. 62–63.
33 Cross 1983, p. 6–7. See also Noiriel 1986, p. 112, 117; Woronoff 1994, p. 440.
34 Noiriel 1986, p. 68, 90, 38, 113, 132, 144; Vigna 2012, p. 26, 32, 54–59, 65; Woronoff 1994, p. 445–47.
35 Cross 1983, p. 10. See also Noiriel 1986, p. 133; Vigna 2012, p. 33.
36 Cross 1983, p. 3, 9–11, 14–16; Dormois 2004, p. 2–4; Noiriel 1986, p. 112, 133–35; Vigna 2012, 32–4.
37 Lescure 1996, p. 87; Zdatny 1984, p. 422.
38 Lescure 1996, p. 82. See also Zdatny 1984, p. 427, 437.
39 Lescure 1996, p. 90–92, 100.
40 Woronoff 1994, p. 419. Our translation. See also Caron 1995, p. 91, 136; Fridenson 1997, p. 214.
41 Dormois 2004, p. 14, 114.

42 Moutet 1998, p. 110; Smith 2006, p. 402, 405, 409, 413; Vigna 2012, p. 66; Woronoff
    1994, p. 395, 398, 404, 409. As mentioned above, Citroën was acquired by Michelin in
    the wake of the carmaker's bankruptcy.
43 Smith 2006, p. 373–74. See also Woronoff 1994, p. 360, 482.
44 Cain and Hopkins 2016, p. 424; Hobsbawm 1989, p. 316.
45 For a general theoretical discussion of economic contexts leading capitalist firms to
    adopt conservative investment behaviors, see Chibber 2003, p. 16–17.
46 Chibber 2003, p. 237.

> Hence, by 1935, Japan accounted for 57 percent of all textile imports into the United
> States. Further, as evidence that success was not based on low wages, [...] by the
> 1920s, Japanese goods were displacing Indian competitors not only in India's key
> export markets but in the Indian domestic market as well.

47 Caron 1995, p. 96, 99, 180.
48 Dumas 2016, p. 69–82.
49 Smith 1977, p. 309–12.
50 Smith 1997, p. 307. Emphasis added.
51 Lebovics 1988, p. 93.
52 Torp 2011, p. 353.
53 Torp 2012, p. 423, 425–26; Schui 2004.
54 Lebovics 1992, p. 248.
55 Becuwe and Blancheton 2013; Blancheton 2020, p. 38–39; Dormois 2004, p. 29, 33;
    Smith 1977, p. 313; 1980, p. 24–25.
56 Smith 1980, p. 21, 238.
57 Indochina and during the interwar period, Morocco, were exceptions in this regard.
    Direct investments in Algeria remained limited.
58 Adams 1989, p. 145–47; Dormois 2004, p. 36–38; Dormois and Crouzet 1998, p. 340,
    343; Galissot et al. 1987, p. 62, 64; Lebovics 1988, p. 143–59; Marseille 1984, p. 64, 72,
    80, 105, 109–10, 117–19, 143–50; 165–69, 482–83, 500–503; Todd 2022, p. 145–46,
    239; Woronoff 1994, p. 362, 364.
59 Asselain 1984, p. 39–40.
60 Asselain 1984, p. 92, 244; Caron 1995, p. 196.
61 Chatriot 2008, p. 13–18; Daviet 1988, p. 275; Dormois 2004, p. 66.
62 Loriaux 1999, p. 251.
63 Asselain 1984, p. 41–42, 90; Dormois 2004, p. 29–30, 34, 55; Hardy-Hémery 1993, p. 332.
64 Kuisel 1981, p. 94; Didry and Marty 2016, p. 25.
65 Adams 1989, p. 147; Asselain 1984, p. 91; Galissot et al. 1987, p. 62; Lebovics 1988,
    p. 153; Marseille 1984, p. 52, 111–12, 200–202; Woronoff 1994, p. 480.
66 Dormois 2004, p. 115. Our translation. See also Asselain 1984, p. 10–11, 45, 55–59;
    Caron 1995, p. 173, 197; Woronoff 1994, p. 469.
67 Asselain 1984, p. 46, 75, 79–80; Caron 1995, p. 171; Dormois 2004, p. 85, 97; Noiriel
    1986, p. 173, 185; Vigna 2012, p. 68–69; Woronoff 1994, p. 469, 473.
68 Hilferding quoted in Colletti 1972, p. 58.
69 Asselain 1984, p. 47–50, 86; Caron 1995, p. 241; Marchand and Thélot 1990, p. 18–19;
    Woronoff 1994, p. 415.
70 Eck 2009, p. 51.
71 Asselain 1984, p. 10. Our translation.
72 Didry and Marty 2016, p. 27–28; Kuisel 1981, p. 131, 133–37, 140, 144; Kipping 1994,
    p. 432; Margairaz 1991.
73 Béracha 1947, p. 1261–62; Caron 1995, p. 203; Dormois 2004, p. 87; Kuisel 1981,
    p. 94, 299.
74 Kuisel 1981, p. 31–34, 42–44, 48, 50–52, 57.
75 Kuisel 1981, p. 88–93; Loriaux 1999, p. 256.

76 Margairaz 1991.
77 Kuisel 1981, p. 147–56; Margairaz 1991.
78 Kindelberger 1990, p. 185–86, 193–94, 197.
79 Hoffmann 1963, p. 62, 75.
80 Carré et al. 1973, p. 256, 259–62.
81 Kuisel 1981, p. 272–73, 275, 277–78.
82 Margairaz 1991; Zysman 1983, p. 105.
83 We have benefited from our exchanges with Chris Isett on the conditions necessary for the success of a developmental state.
84 Chibber 2003, p. 10.
85 Chibber 2003, p. 31–37. We should add to this that in a capitalist society, the state also become dependent upon the ongoing accumulation of private capital to maintain its legitimacy and access the economic resources needed to attain its own aims.
86 Kuisel 1981, p. 219.
87 Brenner 1999, p. 67.
88 Adams 1989, p. 47; Kipping 2001, p. 583–84; Kuisel 1981, p. 157–58; Loriaux 1999, p. 258.
89 Zysman 1983, p. 105.
90 Kuisel 1983, p. 191.
91 Kindelberger 1990, p. 193; Kuisel 1983, p. 209.
92 Noiriel 1986, p. 185–96.
93 Pigenet 2014, p. 427. Our translation.
94 Caron 1995, p. 209–10; Fontaine and Vigna 2014; Pigenet 2014, p. 428, 430–31, 433–37.
95 Zysman 1983, p. 105.
96 Caron 1995, p. 253–55; Woronoff 1994, p. 496–97; Zysman 1983, p. 111.
97 Kuisel 1981, p. 202–203, 215; Pigenet 2014, p. 428; Woronoff 1994, p. 498, 514.
98 Chibber 2003, p. 240.
99 Kuisel 1981, p. 258.
100 Caron 1995, p. 211, 228; Kipping 2001, p. 588; Kuisel 1981, p. 184; Loriaux 1999, p. 241; Zysman 1983, p. 112.
101 Zysman 1983, p. 136–37.
102 Bonin 1987, p. 68–69; Kuisel 1981, p. 191–98, 254; Margairaz 1991.
103 Kuisel 1981, p. 221–42, 232; Margairaz 1991, Chapter XXXIII; Woronoff 1994, p. 499–500.
104 Kipping 2001, p. 585; Kuisel 1981, p. 228; Zysman 1983, p. 107.
105 Caron 1995, p. 224; Eck 2009, p. 53; Margairaz 1991, General Conclusion; Kuisel 1981, p. 229, 253, 260–61; Woronoff 1994, p. 502–503, 514.
106 Kuisel 1981, p. 252; Margairaz 1991, General Conclusion; Zysman 1983, p. 106.
107 Margairaz 1991, Chapter XXX; Kuisel 1981, p. 255; Zysman 1983, p. 133.
108 Zysman 1983, p. 114.
109 Margairaz 1991, General Conclusion.
110 Caron 1995, p. 222; Kuisel 1981, p. 254; Margairaz 1991, General Conclusion.
111 Kuisel 1981, p. 262; Margairaz 1991, Introduction, General Conclusion.
112 Caron 1995, p. 219, 222; Eck 2009, p. 61; Kuisel 1981, p. 214, 254; Loriaux 1999, p. 245–46; Zysman 1983, p. 109, 111.
113 Adams 1989, p. 97, 113 14; Zysman 1983, p. 99–100, 135, 137–38, 154–57.
114 Eck 2009, p. 58–59.
115 Loriaux 1999, p. 244.
116 Kipping 1994, p. 433; 2001, p. 586.
117 Caron 1995, p. 220, 227–28; Kuisel 1981, p. 216.
118 Caron 1995, p. 231–32; Eck 2009, p. 45; Kipping 2001, p. 436; Kuisel 1981, p. 263.
119 Kipping 1994, p. 434.

120 Didry and Marty 2016, p. 32.
121 Didry and Marty 2016, p. 30, 33. Our translation.
122 Caron 1995, p. 261–62; Chatriot 2008, p. 20–21; Didry et Marty 2016, p. 28; Kipping 1994, p. 435; 2001, p. 586, 588.
123 Didry and Marty 2016, p. 32–35.
124 Didry and Marty 2016, p. 31, 34.
125 Kuisel 1981, p. 266–67; Caron 1995, p. 231, 233; Caron and Bouvier 1982b, p. 1099–101.
126 The founding members of the EEC were Belgium, France, West Germany, Italy, Luxembourg and the Netherlands.
127 Adams 1989, 123; Caron 1995, p. 225; Fridenson 1997, p. 226; Kipping 1994, p. 437, 439, 442, 448–53; 2001, p. 586–87; Margairaz 1991, Chapter XXXIII; Woronoff 1994, p. 519, 521.
128 The founding members of the EEC were the same as for the ECSC.
129 Caron and Bouvier 1982b, p. 1133.
130 Zysman 1983, p. 137.
131 Caron 1995, p. 274, 281; Adams 1989, p. 128, 134, 138, 145, 198, 200; Woronoff 1994, p. 522.
132 Adams 1989, p. 155–57, 159–61, 163–64, 192; Caron 1995, p. 181; Woronoff 1994, p. 522–23, 535.
133 Adams 1989, p. 178–80; Caron 1995, p. 274; Dormois 2004, p. 39–40; Woronoff 1994, p. 523.
134 Marseille 1984, p. 499–508. Our translation.
135 Adams 1989, p. 154, 177; Kipping 2001, p. 588.
136 Adams 1989, p. 208–209, 219–223, 236, 238–39, 241; Caron 1995, p. 250; Dormois 2004, p. 124; Zysman 1983, p. 101.
137 Adams 1989, p. 21, 27–29; Caron 1995, p. 171; Daumard and Willard 1982, p. 1534; Vigna 2012, p. 219;.
138 Adams 1989, p. 39; Brenner 1999, p. 67–68 ; Daumard and Willard 1982, p. 1536–37 ; Eck 2009, p. 50; Moutet 1998, p. 117; Noiriel 1986, p. 211–13; Vigna 2012, p. 219.
139 Armengaud 1982, p. 984; Brenner et al. 2010; Caron 1995, p. 178–79; Noiriel 1986, p. 214; Vigna 2012, p. 237.
140 Caron 1995, p. 255, 257–58; Zysman 1983, p. 152.
141 Zysman 1983, p. 103.
142 Kipping 2001, p. 591; Loriaux 1999, p. 259.
143 Caron and Bouvier 1982b, p. 1072, 1077–78, 1123–25; Eck 2009, p. 52, 60–61; Kipping 2001, p. 589; Loriaux 1999, p. 241.
144 Eck 2009, p. 47, 69–70.
145 Eck 2009, p. 42–43.
146 Eck 2009, p. 48, 56; Woronoff 1994, p. 527–28.
147 Adams 1989, p. 5; Eck 2009, p. 64–71; Caron and Bouvier 1982a, p. 1012.
148 Asselain 1984, p. 120–21; Caron 1995, p. 166–67, 175; Caron and Bouvier 1982a, p. 1015; Eck 2009, p. 53; Woronoff 1994, p. 542, 545.
149 Caron 1995, p. 165, 310–12; Eck 2009, p. 53–54; Giraud 1982, p. 1379; Woronoff 1994, p. 544.

Conclusion

This book set out from the premise of Adam Smith in *The Wealth of Nations* and Karl Marx in *Capital* that, for economic development, all factors of production—labor, materials, means of production, machines, land, credit, buildings, etc.—must be available for purchase on the market. A fundamental difference between the two theorists is that Smith, given the conditions of his country Britain in the eighteenth century, assumed that everyone and everything naturally appeared in the commodity form once market impediments were lifted and opportunities became available. Marx, in contrast, argued that Smith and other political economists assumed, what needed to be explained, that people appeared before capitalists as purchasable labor power bereft of land and communities to provide for their subsistence autonomously. Marx argued that it required processes, conflicts and sometimes violence to turn people into individual units of labor available for purchase and accumulation into capital.[1]

Although Smith believed that the appearance of market opportunities aroused the instinct to specialize production and compete for profit, he also held the contradictory belief that merchants and manufacturers tended to avoid market competition. Smith fretted over his observation that merchants sought to monopolize markets, avoid competition and raise prices and profits at the expense of the citizenry. The government therefore had to be in the hands of country gentlemen, devoted to the commonweal, who would discipline manufacturers by forcing them to do all their business in competitive markets. Only then, Smith argued, would nations see continuous cycles of technological development, abundance, falling prices and growth.[2]

We conclude that French history validates the insights of Smith and Marx that capitalism does not emerge naturally from the growth of trade and market opportunities. A *transition* to capitalism must take place—involving the separation of peasants from their lands and communities and the subjection of merchants to competitive markets—for sustained growth and economic development to ensue. Until the Second Empire (1852–1870), France remained a noncapitalist country, in which manufacturers made profits by monopolizing markets rather than by selling competitively on them. Even after the 1860s, well over half of the population lived in rural communities independently of capitalist social property relations. It was only at the end of the 1950s that the peasants, still accounting for nearly 50 percent

DOI: 10.4324/9781003092896-7

of the population, finally became part of the circuits of capital accumulation after accepting the program of the Fifth Republic to apportion farmland only to cultivators with a plan to take out loans, purchase the latest implements and specialize production for the market.

France had become a country of peasant communities in the feudal era around 1000 AD. From that time onward, through the nineteenth century, communities had vibrant festivals, religious rituals, collective responsibilities for tax quotas, common lands and resources and the bartering of goods useful to members.[3] Essential to the peasant community was the pattern of landholding comprised of scattered parcels usually smaller than a tenth of a hectare. Peasants dispersed their plots, in this way, across the territory of the village to prevent crop disease or adverse weather from wiping out their harvests and causing famine. Given this pattern of landholding, agriculturalists never considered fencing off their plots, rearing livestock separate from the common herd and farming individually. Moreover, as population recovered from the fourteenth-century crisis, villages always had more labor available than was needed in the agricultural cycle. Peasants therefore tended to eschew the outflow of resources on labor-saving technology when their family members could do the necessary tasks at no cost.

Most rural households did not have enough land to secure their subsistence. Peasants had to labor intensively on high-yielding subsistence crops such as maize and potatoes, turn plots over to money-making lines such as vines, market gardening and livestock, manufacture textiles in their cottages or rural workshops, rent land as sharecroppers and tenants and seek employment in the fields of other landholders. Although this surplus labor in the countryside bears resemblance to a rural working class, even to migrant farm workers of the present day—who are constantly replaced by technological innovations, such as mechanical pickers—the French peasants' existence in the rural community made them fundamentally different. Peasants eked out a living in myriad ways: handicrafts, bartering work and other useful items with fellow villagers, farming plots, availing themselves of common lands and renting fields. Because the peasants lived in communities, even if they frequently moved from one to another, they did not stand before the well-to-do classes individually as a labor cost or expense in the balance sheet of enterprises. Peasants did not disappear in the manner of employees, of a capitalist enterprise, liable to be rendered unnecessary through improved technology. They remained present in village communities regardless of the evolution to the wider economy.

Indeed, through the nineteenth century, nobles, clergymen and members of the bourgeoisie (notables in a word) preferred things this way. The growing population of peasants made it profitable for landowners, usually town residents, to take revenue from the work of sharecroppers, tenants and farm laborers. Merchants often found it profitable to put manufacturing out to peasants rather than to sink funds into factories. When merchants invested in mechanization, it was because they had already cornered markets and ensured profits. Thus, landowners and merchants in the towns lived comfortably from the work of rural inhabitants without having to submit to the capitalist pressure to constantly part with wealth for perpetually improving technology as the very condition for keeping this wealth. The upper classes remained free from the compulsion to plow profits back into improved implements and methods, cut labor costs relative to output and thus match the market prices of competitors, a cycle of reproduction through investment to which capitalists must submit if they wish to avoid bankruptcy.

Economic growth no doubt took place during the early modern period. The Bourbon dynasty could lay claim to be the most powerful in Europe. France had fertile and varied lands, and a large, spirited, and able population. Peasants had to make a living and pay taxes, seigneurial dues and tithes. They could hope to enlarge their holdings and improve the social status of their family. They rarely achieved all these aims. But their efforts to do so explain the wealth of the country.[4]

The French Revolution, far from transforming this economic pattern, actually consolidated it. The Revolution facilitated the creation of a rational administrative and legal organization of the country, a transformation no doubt beneficial to economic development. Yet the Revolution also entrenched artisan customs and peasant property. Urban workers, through struggles of the revolutionary period, consolidated their control over the labor process and thus sold commodities, rather than labor power, to manufacturers. Rural inhabitants intervened politically, from 1789 to 1793, to throw off the remaining feudal burdens and to appropriate and farm common and unused land. Peasants purchased tiny parcels of nationalized land. These purchases formed part of a longer trend in which peasants toiled intensively to scrape together funds and purchase plots.[5] Peasants thus extended their part of the agricultural surface from the 1740s until well into the twentieth century. The expansion of peasant proprietorship reinforced the upper classes' tendency to extract labor and rents from the growing and well-established rural population and to seek positions in the state funded by the taxation of household farms.

This persistence of the economic underpinnings of the early modern monarchy, characterized by peasant and artisan labor, did not prevent growth from accelerating in the nineteenth century. Farmers began to use draft animals, mechanical implements, fertilizers and nitrogen-restoring fodder crops. Manufacturing exports grew rapidly from the 1820s to the 1860s, thanks to the further development of France's reputation for quality luxury goods built up since the seventeenth century. Nevertheless, for all their success in winning markets among foreign elites, manufacturers did not develop the efficiency to compete with their British counterparts on mass markets. As this book has shown, improvements in agriculture and manufacturing resulted from one-off outlays, as entrepreneurs took advantage of the opportunities made available by new technologies observable in the agricultural and industrial revolutions in England. Investments did not result from a capitalist compulsion to reinvest surpluses back into labor-saving technology to compete with other agriculturalists and manufacturers.

As we have argued in the comparisons drawn with England, when capitalist social property relations take hold, the agriculturalists' efforts to retain their land by specializing their farms for the market and reinvesting surpluses to compete with other growers lead them not to respond to consumer demand in the towns, but to overrun this demand, generate excess staples and bring down food prices. By the late 1600s, farmers in regions unsuited to a particular economic line, such as bread grains in the English Midlands—where they had been major producers of grain for the market in the feudal period—could not endure this price competition and had to find alternative sources of income. Tenant farmers of the Midlands, Lancashire, and other northern counties began to specialize in pasturing livestock, an economic line which required far less labor than did arable husbandry. Inhabitants of these regions turned to manufacturing to make ends meet. By dint of specialized and competitive manufacturing, people turned these regions of England into the center of the industrial revolution and the most urban area in Europe in the nineteenth century.

No such regional specialization took hold in France until after the Second World War. Peasants continued to grow subsistence grains in every region. Artisans and peasants churned out textiles in villages and towns across the country. The upper classes—who had influence within the Old Regime monarchy and chambers of deputies of the nineteenth century—imposed tariffs on imports and protected the internal market rather than allow capitalist price competition to dictate their economic lives. France did not comprise an integrated national market until the 1860s and 1870s. Prior to this time, notables and merchants cornered markets, maintained lucrative prices in their areas or arbitrated between prices in different regions, buying cheap and selling dear. Farmers and manufacturers remained free from a social context in which price competition would mold their enterprises to the comparative advantage of their area.

One area of substantial growth was the Atlantic trade, especially Antillean commerce, during the eighteenth century. Shipbuilding, textile manufacturing, sugar refineries, distilleries and tobacco mills expanded in the hinterland of Marseille and the Atlantic ports. These developments resulted from the opportunities made available by American colonies and Atlantic trade. Nevertheless, because so much of the French population produced basic goods in communities, rather than purchase them on the market, effective demand did not develop to the point of inducing manufacturers to invest in mass production. In England, by contrast, communities had been dispersed at the end of the Middle Ages, inhabitants had to buy the items they needed to survive, and a mass market developed over the course of the early modern period. Thus, as the industrial revolution gathered steam, England relied on the Atlantic trade to import raw materials and export manufactured goods. France saw little to no increase in the percentage of manufactured articles relative to the total volume of exports and a significant rise of manufactured goods imports. England sold about 75 times more value in goods, than did France, to the newly created United States in the 1780s, and dominated other markets, including in South America, as it triumphed in the global commercial and industrial battle against France.

France's first transition to capitalism took place during the Second Empire and Third Republic (1870–1940), when Napoleon III and other political leaders, recognizing their country's weakness relative to Britain, sought to overhaul economic routines and instigate growth. Napoleon III's regime signed agreements with neighboring countries to lower tariffs. The regime formed a national market through roads, canals and especially railways. Businesspersons in some branches of industry could no longer corner markets, fix prices and profit from buying cheap and selling dear. They suddenly had to match prices determined by competitive markets across France and Europe. Administrators, legislators and judges, from the late 1860s to 1910, created a new legal context for industrial relations, which obliged workers to stand alone as individuals before employers. Manufacturers could then purchase labor on the market and accumulate it into capital. This process constituted France's first instance of primitive accumulation, or dispossession, as producers lost autonomy within workshops. The transformation of the labor process, combined with the competitive national and international market, accelerated economic growth from the 1850s to the early 1870s and from the 1890s to the 1920s.

And yet, this growth fell short of France's more dynamic industrial rivals. France retained an inordinately large sector of relatively poor low-productivity farm households, who remained, to a significant extent, independent of labor and consumer markets well into the twentieth century. The legislature of the Third Republic, dominated by landed notables, won the support of tenant farmers, sharecroppers and day laborers by raising tariffs on imports, protecting commodity prices and thus allowing this mass of citizens to eke out a living in the countryside. Legislators lent a sympathetic ear to the efforts of manufacturers to form industrial cartels, organize and allot markets, maintain price stability and profits and avoid the competitive capitalist compulsion to constantly reinvest profits back into improved technology and methods of production. For these reasons, many of the economic gains, made from the 1860s to the 1920s, were lost in the great Depression of the 1930s from which Germany, Britain and the United States recovered more rapidly than did France.

After the Second World War, high officials of the Fourth Republic (1946–1958) around the Commissariat Général du Plan and Treasury developed a coherent program and administrative capacity to transform the economy. They aimed to accelerate a capitalist restructuring of social property relations in the industrial sector. The regime, however, had a sovereign chamber of deputies nearly identical to the Third Republic. Manufacturers continued to find legislators tolerant of their efforts to form industrial ententes, coordinate market control, maintain prices and profits artificially high and avoid the discipline of capitalist rules of price competition and constant reinvestment of surpluses. Legislators and large landowners retained electoral backing after the Second World War through government-subsidized price supports, which particularly benefited growers with significant surpluses and which also won the allegiance of smallholders at the threshold of subsistence worried about maintaining their ancestral lands.

Administrators around Jean Monnet in the National Planning Board evaded parliamentary controls, as well as resistance within the executive, by leveraging negotiations over US financial aid. They restructured and augmented tax revenues to fund the government so that the aid could be used, not to enhance general consumption, but to invest in nationalized firms encompassing basic industries. The administrators also benefited from the state's takeover of key levers of the financial system.

The balance of class power at the time of the Liberation—characterized by a mass militant labor mobilization and the political disarray and isolation of industrialists—had made the state's capture of finance and the nationalization of industry possible. Industrial firms, though politically weakened for some years after the Second World War, furtively rejoined ententes. Administrators of the nationalized firms successfully dismantled several of these cartels by foisting competitive bidding for contracts on suppliers. Monnet, and likeminded politicians and advisers, moreover, subjected industries to foreign competition by negotiating the European Coal and Steel Community, followed by the European Economic Community in 1958. These agreements enlarged and intensified exposure to competition and compelled industrialists to invest in the latest technologies and achieve the highest standards of productivity of the time.

Meanwhile, in 1958, colonial wars lasting from the end of the Second World War until 1962—fought for an empire symptomatic of a lethargic economy reliant on closed noncompetitive markets—brought to power Charles De Gaulle and a team of politicians intent making France a leading power in Europe. By this time, many peasants—aware of the better life enjoyed by townspeople and no longer mollified by the stale slogan of price supports—launched a militant movement to obtain extension services, access to state-of-the-art implements, training, marketing networks, credit and farmland on reasonable terms. Leaders of the movement promoted peasant initiative to improve their lives and work by joining technically advanced cooperatives. The Gaullist regime, harried for over a year by this peasant militancy, came forward with legislation to retire the older generation of farmers with generous benefits and ration land to cultivators with a plan to seek financing for specialized market production using the latest technology. From the early 1960s onward, the government intervened in the land market to distribute farms to growers willing to take out loans and follow the guidance of technicians focused on maximizing commercial output. Once farmers thrust themselves into this capitalist logic—by which they had to make their time more productive in order to match or beat the prices of other agriculturalists and thereby earn the money needed to service loans and retain their lands—competitive selection forced many farmers out of business. Successful family farms shed the labor of children and spouses rendered unusable in a context of rapidly rising productivity.

The state thus accomplished France's second and most thorough instance of primitive accumulation through dispossession. The process constituted a veritable transition to capitalism, for although farmers nominally owned the land, they had to accept the directives of technicians to secure the loans needed to raise productivity, compete and stay afloat. Farmers enjoyed a higher standard of living, but also worked longer hours, during the 1960s than they ever had before. The beneficiaries were the financial capitalists who amassed the interest payments from the ever-growing volume of loans.

In one of the most rapid rural transitions in history, a peasant society, retaining characteristics of the Middle Ages, became one of most productive agricultural populations in the world over the course of a single generation. Farmers flooded the market with staples and brought down food prices to a small portion of household budgets. Employers could thus hold down wage costs and make their enterprises competitive, yet still allow for a massive growth in discretionary spending, which fueled a rapid expansion of the consumer market. Agriculture, in tandem with the forcing house of Gaullist industrial policy, facilitated growth rates of 6 percent a year across the economy, the fastest rates in Europe, during the 1960s and early 1970s.

The full proletarianization of the population, abolition of monopolies and imposition of a competitive market resulted in a rapid rise in real wages and an unprecedented growth in consumer spending. The overwhelming majority of households acquired appliances and automobiles by the end of the 1970s. Nevertheless, this second and thorough transition to capitalism bred problems of another magnitude. Despite the improvement of the standard of living, people had to return day after day to the employer's workplace, submitting to domination and pressure for productivity, in order to make a living. The full transition to capitalism resulted in a more starkly alienated form of labor on assembly lines. Rates of exploitation, measured in value appropriated by employers per hour of work, increased dramatically. Dissatisfaction erupted in the largest strike in world history in May 1968, a moment when millions of workers glimpsed the possibility of an alternative organization of social labor.

Above all, capitalism, like former modes of production, grows, blooms (to full radiance in France in the 1960s and early 1970s) and then begins to wilt. In France, each decade since the 1970s has seen worse economic performance than the previous one, with growth rates limping along before the 2020 Pandemic at between 0 percent and 2 percent. The unemployment rate has hovered for the last 30 years at around 10 percent, a rate twice as high for the youth and even higher for immigrants. One of the only growth industries is armaments. French corporations sold more than 11.7 billion euros worth of weapons and other military-related technology to foreign states in 2021, the industry's third best year on record in terms of exports after 2015 and 2016 which saw 16.9 and 13.9 billion, respectively. France is the world's third biggest exporter of armaments after the United States and Russia. Its military industries encompass 4,000 contractors and subcontractors and more than 200,000 workers.[6]

Since the Socialist Party turned to the right in 1983 during François Mitterrand's first term as president, every subsequent government, whether left or right, has pursued what is known as a neoliberal agenda. The neoliberal policies have included cutting budget deficits, laying off workers from nationalized firms, deindexing wages (to cut inflation but also lowering living standards), liberating financial markets, rising stock market valuations, increasing stock ownership among the citizenry, growing foreign ownership of the largest French companies, deregulating the labor market and raising the retirement age.[7]

Resistance to neoliberalism has had a lasting impact. France has an exceptional propensity for popular mobilizations, which have periodically paralyzed the country from the revolutions of the nineteenth century to the Popular Front of the 1930s and the events of May 1968. Recurrent mass strikes and demonstrations, since the early 1990s, have kept France at the top of the table for government spending as a share of GDP at nearly 55 percent, to the despair of domestic elites and high-ranking bureaucrats in the European Union and the Organization for

Economic Cooperation and Development (OECD). This spending ranks ahead of all Scandinavian countries and stands about 10 percent higher than the percentage in Germany and the OECD average.[8]

Despite the spirited defense of social rights, the average length of retirement peaked for the generation born in 1950 before shortening when neoliberal policies raised the retirement from 60 to 62 in 2010. This increase in the retirement age has surpassed the growth of life expectancy. It will not be until the retirement of the generation born in the 1980s that the regular increase in life expectancy will raise the number of retirement years to the number enjoyed by the generation born in 1950. But now, even the generation born in the 1980s will see fewer retirement years after President Emmanuel Macron raised the retirement age from 62 to 64, requiring 43 years of employee contributions for a complete pension by 2030. Poorer workers will enjoy very few or no years of healthy retirement in the decades to come.[9]

Neoliberal policies since the 1980s have come in the ideological garb of entrepreneurial ingenuity, profit-making, streamlining the mixed economy and rationalizing and upgrading technology to compete with the USA, Germany, Japan and other nations. Managers have tried to instill belief in the firm as the site for creating meaning, sharing goals, developing personal autonomy and contributing to a collective project. They no longer seek to command employees. Managers instead give workers autonomy to fulfill targets. They evaluate personnel according to workplace accomplishments. Employees in well-managed firms align their work with company goals out of internal dispositions. The use of phrases such as workforce participation and intrinsic mobilization is supposed to mean that the workers take pleasure in the tasks rather than face sanctions or earn rewards. Layoffs are to be accepted as a normal outcome of productivity and success. Morality and loyalty to employees is no longer reasonable. Making them redundant is legitimate. Mass layoffs, shocking in the 1960s, have become acceptable normal restructurings since the 1980s.[10]

But by 2020, as yellow-vest protesters on the roundabouts discussed their daily constraints and humiliations, wasted lives and the impossibility of reaching the end of the month with their earnings, Macron's "start-up-nation" lay in tatters. Voting patterns make clear that the discourse of freedom and fulfillment in the workplace, productivity, quality and profits has not appealed to the majority. Since Mitterrand's victory in 1981, nearly every cycle of legislative and presidential elections has ended in the defeat of the party pursuing neoliberal policies. After 2016, when President François Holland went beyond previous policies pursued by socialist governments since the 1980s, such as deregulating financial markets, and took the extraordinary step of deregulating the labor market, the popularity of the Socialist Party plummeted. Whereas the Socialist Party had alternated in government with the conservatives for 40 years, it now finishes a distant fifth in elections and has become irrelevant in national politics.[11]

In the place of the left, voters have moved steadily to the extreme right. In the former industrial basins of the North and East, where Communists had once done well, the Left has fallen away. Marine Le Pen's National Rally Party

(Rassemblement National or RN), which calls for halting immigration and aggressively imposing law and order, has built an electoral base in the working class, despite the decline in immigration relative to the high rates of the 1960s when workers voted for socialists and communities. France is similar in this regard to other Western democracies, where the center-left vote comes from the highly educated, low- and middle-income electorate. French workers, in the ballot booth, seem to have resigned themselves to the reality of capitalist social relations rather than vote as a class opposed to the wealthy. Having accepted capitalism, however unpleasant, as immutable, their strategy to increase, or at least prevent the further erosion of, their standard of living is to vote as white and native, and thus to keep immigrants out and non-whites down. Workers vote to put immigrants and non-whites at a disadvantage in a competitive labor market. The RN openly proclaims its intention to increase the value of "French" labor.[12]

Workers, however, have a paradoxical condition under capitalism. They compete for jobs yet share an interest in defending their energy, or leisure, against capital's impetus to use as much of it as possible to create more capital. In France, given the country's exceptional propensity for mobilizations, this paradox has facilitated massive militant opposition to Macron's legislation to raise the retirement age. This movement has brought together millions of white and non-white workers against neoliberal policies, despite the working-class vote for the anti-immigrant, "pro-French" (white), extreme right. In the years to come, it is likely that the economy will continue to grow slowly (if at all) and that the state will continue to cut public services to maintain business profitability. Workers will probably continue to vote in ever-larger numbers for the extreme right. But in France, one can never be sure that people will not rise above labor-market competition, band together and reverse the neoliberal drift. What seems certain is that a conscious transition to socialism has become the obvious way out of the general economic and political doldrums of the last four decades.

Notes

1　Michael Heinrich emphasizes this point that Marx in *Capital* accepted the arguments of the political economists of his time but critically evaluated their assumptions; Heinrich 2012, p. 9.
2　For Smith's argument that merchants seek high prices, through monopolies, for their commodities and that they should *not* therefore have political power; see Adam Smith 1986, p. 227. David McNally emphasizes Smith's anxiety over the efforts of manufacturers to create monopolies, avoid price competition and accumulate profit at the expense of the citizenry; McNally 1988, p. 214, 221–25, 250–51, 264. Vivek Chibber shows that the inability of the Indian state, unlike the South Korean one, to discipline investors, by subjecting them to competitive markets, explains why the South Korean economy performed better than did the Indian economy after the Second World War; Chibber 2003, p. 29, 34–35.
3　Delleaux 2022, p. 81.
4　Goubert 1970, p. 34.
5　Bodinier, Teyssier, and Antoine 2000, p. 220, 223, 368, 443.
6　Anderson 2004a; Zemmour 2023; Stetler 2023.

7 Jenson and Ross 1988; Anderson 2004b; Ettinger 2023; Zemmour and Stetler 2023; Escalona 2022a.
8 Kouvelakis 2019b.
9 Zemmour and Stetler 2023; Ettinger 2023.
10 Janson and Ross 1988; Boltanski and Chiapello 2018, p. 4, 63, 66, 69–70, 80, 89, 94, 97, 465–66.
11 Kouvelakis 2019a; Anderson 2004b; Escalona 2022a.
12 Escalona 2022b; Kuhn 2022; Riley and Brenner 2023.

Bibliography

Adams, William James. 1989, *Restructuring the French Economy: Government and the Rise of Market Competition since World War II*, Washington, DC: Brookings Institution.

Ado, Anatoli. 1996, *Paysans en révolution: Terre, pouvoir et jacquerie 1789–1794*, Paris: Société des études Robespierristes. Coll. Bibliothèque d'histoire révolutionnaire, no. 1.

Agulhon, Maurice. 1979, *La République au village: Les populations du Var de la révolution à la IIe République*, Paris: Éditions du Seuil. Coll. Univers historique.

Allaire, Gilles. 1995, 'Le modèle de développement agricole des années 60 confronté aux logiques marchandes', In *La grande transformation de l'agriculture lectures conventionnalistes et régulationnistes*, edited by Gilles Allaire and Robert Boyer, Paris: INRA, 245–380.

Allen, Robert C. 2000, 'Economic Structure and Agricultural Productivity in Europe, 1300–1800', *European Review of Economic History*, vol. 4, no. 1: 1–25.

Alphandéry, Pierre, Pierre Bitoun, Yves Dupont, and Pierre Bitoun. 1988, *Les Champs du départ: Une France rurale sans paysans?* Paris: La Découverte.

Amann, Peter H. 1990, *The Corncribs of Buzet: Modernizing Agriculture in the French Southwest*, Princeton: Princeton University Press.

Amsden, Alice H. 1992, 'A Theory of Government Intervention in Late Industrialization', In *State and Market in Development: Synergy or Rivalry?* edited by Louis Putterman and Dietrich Rueschemeyer, Boulder, CO: Lynne Rienner.

——— 2001, *The Rise of 'The Rest': Challenges to the West from Late-Industrializing Economies*, New York: Oxford University Press.

Anceau, Éric. 2012, *Napoléon III: Un Saint-Simon à cheval*, Paris: Tallandier. Coll. Texto: Le goût de l'histoire.

Anderson, Perry. 2004a, 'Dégringolade', *London Review of Books*, vol. 26, no. 17: 3.

——— 2004b, 'Union sucrée', *London Review of Books*, vol. 26, no. 18: 10.

Anderson, Robert D. 1977, *France 1870–1914: Politics and Society*, London: Routledge and Kegan Paul.

André, Christine, and Robert Delorme. 1983, *L'État et l'économie: Un essai d'explication de l'évolution des dépenses publiques en France: (1870–1980)*, Paris: Éditions du Seuil.

Antoine, Annie. 1999, 'Systèmes agraires de la France de l'Ouest: Une rationalité méconnue?', *Histoire, Économie et Société*, vol. 18, no. 1: 107–32.

——— 2006, 'L'élevage: un facteur de spécialisation des économies rurales anciennes', In *Acteurs et espaces de l'élevage, XVIIe-XXIe siècle: Évolution, structuration, spécialisation*, edited by Philippe Madeline and Jean-Marc Moriceau, Rennes: Association d'histoire des sociétés rurales. Coll. Bibliothèque d'histoire rurale, no. 9.

Appleby, Joyce. 2010, *The Relentless Revolution a History of Capitalism*, New York: W.W. Norton & Co.

Aprile, Sylvie. 2010, *La révolution inachevée 1815–1870*, Paris: Belin. Coll. Histoire de France/sous la direction de Joël Cornette.

Armengaud, André. 1982, '1945–1974 le renouveau démographique ?', In *Histoire économique et sociale de la France: L'ère industrielle et la société d'aujourd'hui (1880–1980): 1950 à nos jours*, edited by Fernand Braudel and Ernest Labrousse, Paris: Presses Universitaires de France.

Asselain, Jean-Charles. 1984, *Histoire économique de la France du XVIIIe siècle à nos jours: De l'Ancien Régime a la Première Guerre mondiale*, Paris: Éditions du Seuil.

——— 1988, 'Histoire économique de la France regards nouveaux sur le long terme', *Revue Économique*, vol. 39, no. 6: 1223–47.

——— 1991, *Histoire économique: De la révolution industrielle à la Première Guerre mondiale*, Paris: Presses de la Fondation des sciences politiques. Coll. Amphithéâtre.

Augé-Laribé, Michel. 1950, *La politique agricole de la France de 1880 à 1940*, Paris: Presses universitaires de France.

Autexier, Marie-Louise. 1947, *Les droits féodaux et les droits seigneuriaux en Poitou de 1559 à 1799*, Fontenay-le-Comte: P. & O. Lussaud frères.

Aymard, Maurice. 1998, 'Autoconsommation et marchés: Chayanov, Labrousse ou Le Roy Ladurie?', In *La Terre et les hommes: France et Grande-Bretagne, XVIIe-XVIIIe siècle*, edited by Gérard Béaur, Paris: Hachette littératures. Coll. L'histoire en revue, no. 919.

Bairoch, Paul. 1965, 'Niveaux de développement économique de 1810 à 1910', *Annales*, vol. 20, no. 6: 1091–1117.

——— 1976, 'Europe's Gross National Product: 1800–1975', *The Journal of European Economic History*, vol. 2: 273–340.

Ballot, Charles. 1978, *L'introduction du machinisme dans l'industrie française*, edited by Claude Gérel, Genève: Slatkine reprints.

Barjot, Dominique. 2012, 'Histoire économique et historiographie française: Crise ou renouveau?', *Histoire, Économie et Société*, vol. 31, no. 2: 5–27.

——— 2014a, 'L'économie, 1851–1914', In *La France au XIXe siècle, 1814–1914*, edited by Dominique Barjot, Jean-Pierre Chaline, and André Encrevé, Paris: Presses universitaires de France.

——— 2014b, 'L'économie française, 1815–1851', In *La France au XIXe siècle, 1814–1914*, edited by Dominique Barjot, Jean-Pierre Chaline, and André Encrevé, Paris: Presses universitaires de France.

Barral, Pierre. 1968, *Les agrariens français de Méline à Pisani*, Paris: A. Colin.

——— 1980, 'Les grandes épreuves: agriculture et paysannerie, 1914–1948', In *Histoire économique et sociale de la France: L'ère industrielle et la société d'aujourd'hui (siècle 1880–1980): Le temps des Guerres Mondiales et de la grande crise (1914–vers 1950)*, edited by Fernand Braudel and Ernest Labrousse, Paris: Presses Universitaires de France.

——— 1982, 'Le secteur agricole dans la France industrialisée (1950–1974)', In *Histoire économique et sociale de la France : L'ère industrielle et la société d'aujourd'hui (siècle 1880–1980): Années 1950–1980, le second XXe siècle. Vers quels horizons?*, edited by Fernand Braudel and Ernest Labrousse, Paris: Presses Universitaires de France, vol. 3:1425–63.

Bartolomei, Arnaud, Guillaume Calafat, Mathieu Grenet, and Jörg Ulbert. 2017, *De l'utilité commerciale des consuls: l'institution consulaire et les marchands dans le monde méditerranéen (XVIIe–XXe siècle)*, Rome: École française de Rome.

Baulant, Micheline. 1979, 'Groupes mobiles dans une société sédentaire: La société rurale autour de Meaux au XVIIe et XVIIIe siècle', In *Les marginaux et les exclus dans l'histoire*, edited by Bernard Vincent, Paris: Union générale d'éditions. Coll. Cahiers Jussieu 5 de l'Université de Paris VII, no. 1290.

Baulant, Micheline, and Arlette Schweitz. 2006, *Meaux et ses campagnes: Vivre et survivre dans le monde rural sous l'Ancien régime*, edited by Gérard Béaur and Anne Varet-Vitu, Rennes: Presses universitaires de Rennes.

Beaud, Michel. 2010, *Histoire du capitalisme: 1500–2010*, Paris: Éditions du Seuil, 6th ed. Coll. Points. Economie, no. 18.

Béaur, Gérard. 1984, *Le Marché foncier à la veille de la Révolution: Les mouvements de propriété beaucerons dans les régions de Maintenon et de Janville, de 1761 à 1790*, Paris: Éd. de l'École des hautes études en sciences sociales. Coll. Recherches d'histoire et de sciences sociales, no. 9.

———— 1991, 'Investissement foncier, épargne et cycle de vie dans le pays chartrain au XVIIIe siècle', *Histoire & Mesure*, vol. 6, no. 3/4: 275–88.

———— 1996, 'Les Chartier et le mystère de la révolution agricole', *Histoire & Mesure*, vol. 11, no. 3/4: 367–88.

———— 2000, *Histoire agraire de la France au XVIIIe siècle: Inerties et changements dans les campagnes françaises entre 1715 et 1815*, Paris: SEDES. Coll. Histoire moderne, no. 139.

Becuwe, Stéphane, and Bertrand Blancheton. 2013, 'Les controverses autour du paradoxe Bairoch, quel bilan d'étape?', *Revue d'économie Politique*, vol. 123, no. 1: 1.

Belhoste, Jean-François. 1994, 'La maison, la fabrique et la ville: L'industrie du drap fin en France (XVe -XVIIIe siècles)', *Histoire, Économie et Société*, vol. 13, no. 3: 457–75.

Beltran, Alain, and Pascal Griset. 1994, *La croissance économique de la France 1815–1914*, Paris: Armand Colin, 2nd ed. Coll. Cursus: Histoire.

Benoist, André. 1985, 'Vie paysanne et protestantisme en « Moyen-Poitou » du XVIe siècle à la Révolution', *Annales de Bretagne et des pays de l'Ouest*, vol. 2: 161–82.

Béracha, S. 1947, 'La production industrielle', *Revue d'économie Politique*, vol. 57, no. 6: 1245–73.

Berenson, Edward. 1984, *Populist Religion and Left-Wing Politics in France, 1830–1852*, Princeton, NJ: Princeton University Press.

———— 1987, 'Politics and the French Peasantry: The Debate Continues', *Social History*, vol. 12, no. 2: 213–29.

———— 1992, *The Trial of Madame Caillaux*, Berkeley, CA: University of California Press.

Berger, Gérard. 1985, '*Le Pays de Saint-Bonnet-Le-Chateau (Haut-Forez) de 1775 à 1975: Flux et reflux d'une société*', Saint-Étienne: Université de Saint-Étienne, Centre d'histoire régionale.

Bergeron, Louis 1978, *Les capitalistes en France, 1780–1914*, Paris: Gallimard. Coll. Collection Archives, no. 70.

Bianchi, Serge 1999, *La terre et les paysans en France et en Grande-Bretagne : Du début du XVIIe à la fin du XVIIIe siècle*, Paris: Armand Colin. Coll. U.

Bivar, Venus 2018, *Organic Resistance: The Struggle over Industrial Farming in Postwar France*, Chapel Hill: University of North Carolina Press. Coll. Flows, Migrations, and Exchanges.

Blackburn, Robin 2010, *The Making of New World Slavery From the Baroque to the Modern, 1492–1800.*, La Vergne: Verso. Coll. World History Series.

Blancheton, Bertrand 2020, 'La loi Méline de 1892', In *Histoire des faits économiques*, Paris: Dunod, vol. 3:38–39. Coll. Maxi Fiches.

Bloch, Marc 1966, *French Rural History: An Essay on its Basic Characteristics*, Berkeley: University of California Press.

Bodinier, Bernard, Eric Teyssier, and François Antoine 2000, *L'événement le plus important de la Révolution : La vente des biens nationaux, 1789–1867, en France et dans les territoires annexés*, Paris: Société des études robespierristes, 1st ed. Coll. Mémoires et documents d'histoire de la Révolution française.

Boltanski, Luc, and Ève Chiapello 2018, *The New Spirit of Capitalism*, Translated by Gregory Elliot, London: Verso, New updated edition.

Bonin, Hubert 1987, *Histoire économique de la IVe République*, Paris: Economica. Coll. Histoire.

Bonneuil, Christophe 2017, '1962. Le nouvel ordre agricole mondial', In *Histoire mondiale de la France*, edited by Patrick Boucheron, Nicolas Delalande, Florian Mazel, Yann Potin, and Pierre Singaravélou, Paris: Seuil.

Bossis, Philippe 1972, 'Le milieu paysan aux confins de l'Anjou, du Poitou et de la Bretagne, 1771–1789', *Études Rurales*, vol. 47: 122–47.

——— 1980, 'La foire aux bestiaux en Vendée au XVIIIe siècle: Une restructuration du monde rural', *Études Rurales*, vol. 78/80: 143–50.

Bouton, Cynthia A. 1993, *The Flour War: Gender, Class, and Community in Late Ancien Régime French Society*, University Park, Pennsylvania.: Pennsylvania State University Press.

Bouvier, Jean 1968, *Histoire économique et histoire sociale: Recherches sur le capitalisme contemporain*, Genève: Droz. Coll. Travaux de droit, d'économie, de sociologie et de sciences politiques, no. 62.

Bové, José, François Dufour, and Gilles Luneau. 2002, *The World is not for Sale: Farmers Against Junk Food*, London: Verso.

Boyns, Trevor, John Richard Edwards, and Marc Nikitin. 1997, 'The Development of Industrial Accounting in Britain and France before 1880: A Comparative Study of Accounting Literature and Practice', *European Accounting Review*, vol. 6, no. 3: 393–437.

Braudel, Fernand. 1980, *On History*, Translated by Sarah Matthews, Chicago: The Chicago University Press.

——— 1986, *L'indentité de la France. Les Hommes et les Choses. Seconde Partie: Une « économie paysanne » jusqu'au XXe siècle*, Paris: Éditions Arthaud.

Brennan, Thomas Edward. 2006, 'Peasants and Debt in Eighteenth-Century Champagne', *Journal of Interdisciplinary History*, vol. 37, no. 2: 175–200.

Brenner, Aaron, Robert Brenner, and Calvin Winslow, eds. 2010, *Rebel Rank and File: Labor Militancy and Revolt from Below During the Long 1970s*, London; New York: Verso.

Brenner, Robert. 1977, 'The Origins of Capitalist Development: A Critique of Neo-Smithian Marxism', *New Left Review*, vol. 104: 25.

——— 1985, 'The Agrarian Roots of European Capitalism', In *The Brenner Debate: Agrarian Class Structure and Economic Development in Pre-Industrial Europe*, edited by C. H. E. Philpin and T. H. Aston, New York: Cambridge University Press.

——— 1986, 'The Social Basis of Economic Development', In *Analytical Marxism*, edited by John E. Roemer, Cambridge/Paris: Cambridge University Press/Éditions de la Maison des sciences de l'homme.

——— 1989, 'Bourgeois Revolution and Transition to Capitalism', In *The First Modern Society*, edited by A.L. Beier, David Cannadine and James M. Rosenheim, Cambridge: Cambridge University Press.

——— 1997, 'Economic Relations and the Growth of Agricultural Productivity in Late Medieval and Early Modern Europe', In *Economic Development and Agricultural Productivity*, edited by Amit Bhaduri and Rune Skarstein, Cheltenham: E. Elgar.

―――― 1999, *Turbulence in the World Economy*, London: Verso.

―――― 2001, 'The Low Countries in the Transition to Capitalism', In *Peasants into Farmers?: The Transformation of Rural Economy and Society in the Low Countries (Middle Ages-19th century) in Light of the Brenner Debate*, edited by P. C. M. Hoppenbrouwers and J. L. van Zanden, Turnhout: Brepols. Coll. CORN publication series, no. 4.

―――― 2003, *Merchants and Revolution: Commercial Change, Political Conflict, and London's Overseas Traders, 1550–1653*, London; New York: Verso.

―――― 2006, 'From Theory to History: "The European Dynamic" or Feudalism to Capitalism', In *An Anatomy of Power: The Social Theory of Michael Mann*, edited by John A. Hall and Ralph Schroeder, Cambridge: Cambridge University Press.

―――― 2007, 'Property and Progress: Where Adam Smith Went Wrong', In *Marxist History-writing for the Twenty-first Century*, edited by Chris Wickham, Oxford: Oxford University Press.

Brenner, Robert, and Mark Glick. 1991, 'The Regulation Approach: Theory and History', *New Left Review*, vol. I/188: 45–119.

Brenner, Robert, and Christopher Isett. 2002, 'England's Divergence from China's Yangzi Delta: Property Relations, Microeconomics, and Patterns of Development', *The Journal of Asian Studies*, vol. 61, no. 2: 609–62.

Brenot, Édouard. 1980, *Documents pour servir l'histoire de Grigny-en-Lyonnais: Des origines à 1789*, Grigny: Œuvre municipale pour l'enfance et la jeunesse.

Broder, Albert. 1993, *L'économie française au XIXe siècle*, Paris: Ophrys. Coll. Synthèse: Histoire.

Brunet, Pierre. 1960, *Structure agraire et économie rurale des plateaux tertiaires entre la Seine et l'Oise*, Caen: Société d'impressions Caron.

Bruneteau, Bernard. 1994, *Les paysans dans l'État: Le gaullisme et le syndicalisme agricole sous la Ve République*, Paris: Ed. l'Harmattan. Coll. Alternatives rurales.

Cadier, Gabrielle. 1988, 'Les conséquences du traité de 1860 sur le commerce francobritannique', *Histoire, Économie et Société*, vol. 7, no. 3: 355–80.

Cain, Peter J., and Antony G. Hopkins. 2016, *British Imperialism, 1688–2015*, Abingdon, OX; New York, NY: Routledge.

Carlson, Chris. 2019, 'Rural Property Relations and the Regional Dynamics of Brazilian Capitalism', In *Case Studies in the Origins of Capitalism*, edited by Xavier Lafrance and Charles Post, Cham: Palgrave Macmillan. Coll. Marx, Engels, and Marxisms.

Caron, François. 1995, *Histoire économique de la France: XIX-XX siècle*, Paris: Armand Colin, 2nd ed.

Caron, François, Jean Bouvier, and René Girault. 1982, 'L'État et le capitalisme. Nouvelles structures. Nouveaux problèmes. 1949-années 1970', In *Histoire économique et sociale de la France: L'ère industrielle et la société d'aujourd'hui (siècle 1880–1980): Années 1950–1980, le second XXe siècle. Vers quels horizons?*, edited by Fernand Braudel and Ernest Labrousse, Paris: Presses Universitaires de France, 1009–1435.

Carré, Jean Jacques, Edmond Malinvaud, and Paul Dubois. 1973, *Abrégé de la croissance française. Un essai d'analyse économique causale de l'après-guerre*, Paris: Éditions du Seuil. Coll. Économie et société.

Chagnollaud, Dominique. 1991, *Le premier des ordres: Les hauts fonctionnaires, XVIIIe–XXe siècle*, Paris: Fayard.

Chamouard, Aude, and Frédéric Fogacci. 2015, 'Les notables en République: Introduction', *Histoire@Politique*, vol. 25, no. 1: 1.

Charle, Christophe. 1980, *Les hauts fonctionnaires en France au XIXe siècle*, Paris: Gallimard. Coll. Collection Archives, no. 82.

———— 1991, *Histoire sociale de la France au XIXe siècle*, Paris: Editions du Seuil. Coll. Points. Histoire, no. H148.

Charmettant, Hervé. 2006, 'Un modèle conventionnaliste de l'autorité dans la relation d'emploi', Doctoral Thesis in Economic Science, University Lyon 2.

Chassagne, Serge. 1979, 'La diffusion rurale de l'industrie cotonnière en France (1750–1850)', *Revue du Nord*, vol. 61, no. 240: 97–114.

———— 1981, *European Textile Printers in the Eighteenth Century: A Study of Peel and Oberkampf*, London: Heinemann Educational.

———— 1991, *Le coton et ses patrons: France, 1760–1840*, Paris: Editions de l'École des hautes etudes en sciences sociales. Coll. Civilisations et societes, no. 83.

Chatriot, Alain. 2008, 'Les ententes: débats juridiques et dispositifs législatifs (1923–1953). La genèse de la politique de la concurrence en France', *Histoire, Économie et Société*, vol. 27, no. 1: 7–22.

———— 2013, 'Les paysans au cœur de la République', In *Une contre-histoire de la IIIe République*, edited by Marion Fontaine, Frédéric Monier, and Christophe Prochasson, Paris: La Découverte, 353–63. Coll. Cahiers libres.

Cheminade, Christian. 1994, 'Libéralisme, corporatisme et dérogeance: À propos des édits sur le commerce de 1701 et 1765', *Dix-Huitième Siècle*, vol. 26, no. 1: 269–84.

Cheney, Paul Burton. 2017, *Cul de Sac: Patrimony, Capitalism, and Slavery in French Saint-Domingue*, Chicago; London: The University of Chicago Press.

Chevet, Jean-Michel. 1994, 'Production et productivité: Un modèle de développement économique des campagnes de la région parisienne aux XVIIIe et XIXe siècles', *Histoire & Mesure*, vol. 9, no. 1/2: 101–45.

———— 2014, 'The Growth of Plough Team Productivity during the Nineteenth Century in the Île-de-France', In *Measuring Agricultural Growth: Land and Labour Productivity in Western Europe from the Middle Ages to the Twentieth Century (England, France and Spain)*, edited by Jean-Michel Chevet and Gérard Béaur, Turnhout, Belgium: Brepols. Coll. Comparative Rural History of the North Sea Area, no. 15.

Chibber, Vivek. 2003, *Locked in Place: State-Building and Late Industrialization in India*, Princeton and Oxford: Princeton University Press.

———— 2017, 'Rescuing Class from the Cultural Turn', *Catalyst*, vol. 1, no. 1: 27–56.

Clapham, John Harold. 1921, *The Economic Development of France and Germany 1815–1914*, Cambridge: The University Press.

Clarke, Gregory. 1993, 'Agriculture in the Industrial Revolution, 1700–1860', In *The British Industrial Revolution: An Economic Perspective*, edited by Joel Mokyr, Boulder, CO: Westview Press.

Clough, Shepard B. 1946, 'Retardative Factors in French Economic Development in the Nineteenth and Twentieth Centuries', *The Journal of Economic History*, vol. 6, no. S1: 91–102.

Clout, Hugh D. 1983, *The Land of France 1815–1914*, London, UK: Routledge, Coll. Rural History.

Cocaud, Martin. 2016, 'An Early Form of Specialized Agriculture in Western France', In *Agricultural Specialisation and Rural Patterns of Development*, edited by Annie Antoine, Turnhout: Brepols Publishers. Coll. Rural History in Europe (RURHE), no. 12.

Colletti, Lucio. 1972, *From Rousseau to Lenin: Studies in Ideology and Society*, Translated by John Merrington and Judith White, New York; London: Monthly Review Press.

Collier, Frances. 1964, *The Family Economy of the Working Classes in the Cotton Industry, 1784–1833*, edited by R.S. Fitton, Manchester: Manchester University Press.

Comninel, George C. 1987, *Rethinking the French Revolution: Marxism and the Revisionist Challenge*, London; New York: Verso.

Coquelin, Charles. 1839, 'De l'industrie linière en France et en Angleterre', *Revue Des Deux Mondes*, vol. 19, no. 1: 61–96.

Cottereau, Alain. 1987, 'Justice et injustice ordinaire sur les lieux de travail d'après les audiences prud'homales (1806–1866)', *Le Mouvement Social*, vol. 141: 25–59.

——— 1993, 'Book Review: Work & Wages. Natural Law, Politics & the Eighteenth-Century French Trades', *Le Mouvement Social*, vol. 165: 129–34.

——— 1995, 'L'embauche et la vie normative des métiers durant les deux premiers tiers du XIXe siècle français', In *L'embauche: Objet du contrat, nature des engagements, pratiques de recrutement*, edited by Philippe Bernoux, Lyon: Glysi-Mrash, 47–71. Coll. Les cahiers des relations professionnelles, no. 10.

——— 1997, 'The Fate of Collective Manufactures in the Industrial World: The Silk Industries of Lyons and London, 1800–1850', In *World of Possibilities: Flexibility and Mass Production in Western Industrialization*, edited by Charles F. Sabel and Jonathan Zeitlin, Cambridge: Cambridge University Press, 75–152. Coll. Studies in Modern Capitalism.

——— 2002, 'Droit et bon droit: Un droit des ouvriers instauré, puis évincé par le droit du travail (France, XIXe siècle)', *Annales. Histoire, Sciences Sociales*, vol. 57, no. 6: 1521–57.

——— 2006, 'Sens du juste et usages du droit du travail: une évolution contrastée entre la France et la Grande-Bretagne au XIXe siècle', *Revue d'histoire Du XIXe Siècle*, vol. 33: 101–20.

Couturier, Henri. 1909, *La préparation des états généraux de 1789 en Poitou principalement d'après les cahiers des paroisses et des corporations: Étude d'histoire du droit*, Poitiers: Société française d'imprimerie et de librairie.

Crafts, N. F. R. 1984, 'Economic Growth in France and Britain, 1830–1910: A Review of the Evidence', *The Journal of Economic History*, vol. 44, no. 1: 49–67.

Cross, Gary S. 1983, *Immigrant Workers in Industrial France: The Making of a New Laboring Class*, Philadelphia, PA: Temple University Press.

Crouzet, François. 1964, 'Wars, Blockade, and Economic Change in Europe, 1792–1815', *The Journal of Economic History*, vol. 24, no. 4: 567–88.

——— 1966, 'Angleterre et France au XVIIIe siècle: Essai d'analyse comparée de deux croissances économiques', *Annales. Histoire, Sciences Sociales*, vol. 21, no. 2: 254–91.

——— 1985, *De la supériorité de l'Angleterre sur la France l'économique et l'imaginaire, XVIIe-XXe siècles*, Paris: Perrin. Coll. Pour l'histoire.

——— 1989, 'Les conséquences économiques de la Révolution française: Réflexions sur un débat', *Revue Économique*, vol. 40, no. 6: 1189–1203.

——— 2003, 'The Historiography of French Economic Growth in the Nineteenth Century', *The Economic History Review*, vol. 56, no. 2: 215–42.

Dansette, Adrien. 1976, *Naissance de la France moderne: Le Second Empire*, Paris: Hachette.

Daudin, Guillaume. 2011, *Commerce et prospérité. La France au XVIIIe siècle*, Paris: Presse de l'Université Paris-Sorbonne.

Daumard, Adeline. 1993a, 'Caractères de la société bourgeoise', In *Histoire économique et sociale de la France: L'avènement de l'ère industrielle (1789-années 1880)*, edited by Ernest Labrousse and Fernand Braudel, Paris: Presses universitaires de France, Vol. 3. Coll. Quadrige.

——— 1993b, 'La hiérarchie des biens et des positions', In *Histoire économique et sociale de la France: L'avènement de l'ère industrielle (1789-années 1880)*, edited by Ernest

Labrousse and Fernand Braudel, Paris: Presses universitaires de France, Vol. 3. Coll. Quadrige.

Daumard, Adeline, and Claude Willard. 1982, 'Bouleversements et adaptations des classes urbaines', In *Histoire économique et sociale de la France: L'ère industrielle et la société d'aujourd'hui (1880–1980): 1950 à nos jours*, edited by Fernand Braudel and Ernest Labrousse, Paris: Presses Universitaires de France.

Daumas, Jean-Claude. 2018, *La révolution matérielle: Une histoire de la consommation: France, XIXe-XXIe siècle*, Paris: Flammarion.

Daviet, Jean-Pierre. 1988, *Un destin international: la Compagnie de Saint-Gobain de 1830 à 1939*, Paris: Ed. des Archives contemporaines.

De Vries, Jan, and Ad Van der Woude. 1997, *The First Modern Economy: Success, Failure, and Perseverance of the Dutch Economy, 1500–1815*, Cambridge: Cambridge University Press.

Dehergne, Joseph. 1963, *Le Bas Poitou à la veille de la Révolution*, Paris: Centre National de la Recherche Scientifique. Coll. Commission d'histoire économique et sociale de la Révolution française, no. 16.

Delleaux, Fulgence. 2022, *Les Inquiétude dans les champs: Essai sur la gestion des exploitations agricoles dans l'espace francophone (vers 1730-vers 1830)*, Louvain-la-Neuve: Belgique PUL Presses Universitaires de Louvain.

Delsalle, Paul. 1987, 'Tisserands et fabricants chez les prud'hommes dans la région de Lille-Roubaix-Tourcoing (1810–1848)', *Le Mouvement Social*, vol. 141: 61–80.

Demangeon, Albert. 1905, *La Picardie et les régions voisines: Artois, Cambrésis, Beauvaisis*, Paris: Librairie Guénégaud.

Démier, Francis. 2000, *La France du XIXe siècle: 1814–1914*, Paris: Éditions du Seuil.

Désert, Gabriel. 2007, *Une société rurale au XIXe siècle: Les paysans du Calvados 1815–1895*, Caen: Centre de Recherche d'Histoire Quantitative.

Deyon, Pierre, and Philippe Guignet. 1980, 'The Royal Manufactures and Economic Progress in France before the Industrial Revolution - ProQuest', *Journal of European Economic History*, vol. 9, no. 3: 611.

Dibie, Pascal. 2006, *Le village métamorphosé: Révolution dans la France profonde: Chichery, Bourgogne nord*, Paris: Plon. Coll. Terre humaine.

Didry, Claude. 2001, 'La production juridique de la convention collective: La loi du 4 mars 1919', *Annales. Histoire, Sciences Sociales*, vol. 56, no. 6: 1253–82.

——— 2012, 'Du sujet de droit à la citoyenneté du travail, une autre histoire du salariat', *Le sujet dans la cité*, vol. 3, no. 2: 80–91.

——— 2016, 'L'apprentissage à l'épreuve du droit du travail', *Artefact. Techniques, histoire et sciences humaines*, vol. 3: 39–51.

Didry, Claude, and Frédéric Marty. 2016, 'La politique de concurrence comme levier de la politique industrielle dans la France de l'après-guerre', *Gouvernement et action publique*, vol. 5, no. 4: 23–45.

Dimmock, Spencer. 2014, *The Origin of Capitalism in England, 1400–1600*, Leiden: Brill. Coll. Historical Materialism Book Series, no. 74.

——— 2019, 'Expropriation and the Political Origins of Agrarian Capitalism in England', In *Case Studies in the Origins of Capitalism*, edited by Xavier Lafrance and Charles Post, Cham: Palgrave Macmillan. Coll. Marx, Engels, and Marxisms.

Dion, Roger. 1959, *Histoire de la vigne et du vin en France des origines au XIXe siècle*, Paris: Imprimerie Sévin et Cie.

Diry, Jean-Paul. 1985, *L'Industrialisation de l'élevage en France: économie et géographie des filières avicoles et porcines*, Gap: Éd. Ophrys.

Dontenwill, Serge. 1973, *Une seigneurie sous l'Ancien Régime: L'étoile en brionnais, du XVIe au XVIIIe siècle (1575–1778)*, Roanne: Horvath.

——— 2003, 'La mise en valeur des terres en Roannais Brionnais au dernier siècle de l'Ancien Régime (1670–1789)', In *Exploiter la terre: les contrats agraires de l'Antiquité à nos jours: actes du colloque international tenu à Caen du 10 au 13 septembre 1997*, edited by Anne Varet-Vitu, Mathieu Arnoux, and Gérard Béaur, Rennes: Association d'histoire des sociétés rurales. Coll. Bibliothèque d'histoire rurale, no. 7.

——— 2006, 'Élevage bovin et exploitation agricole en Roannais-Brionnais (XVIIe-XVIIIe siècle', In *Acteurs et espaces de l'élevage, XVIIe-XXIe siècle: évolution, structuration, spécialisation*, edited by Philippe, Madeline, Jean-Marc Moriceau, Pôle pluridisciplinaire Sociétés et espaces ruraux (Caen), and Centre international d'études des patrimoines culturels du Charolais-Brionnais, Rennes: Association d'histoire des sociétés rurales. Coll. Bibliothèque d'histoire rurale, no. 9.

Dormois, Jean-Pierre. 1996, 'La « vocation agricole de la France »: L'agriculture française face à la concurrence britannique avant la guerre de 1914', *Histoire & Mesure*, vol. 11, no. 3–4: 329–66.

——— 1997, *L'économie française face à la concurrence britannique à la veille de 1914*, Paris: Harmattan.

——— 2004, *The French Economy in the Twentieth Century*, Cambridge: Cambridge University Press. Coll. New Studies in Economic and Social History.

Dormois, Jean-Pierre, and François Crouzet. 1998, 'The Significance of the French Colonial Empire for French Economic Development (1815–1960)', *Revista de Historia Económica/Journal of Iberian and Latin American Economic History*, vol. 16, no. 1: 323–49.

Dumas, Jean-Philippe. 2016, *L'État, moteur du progrès: Le ministère du Commerce et de l'Industrie, 1870–1914, L'État, moteur du progrès: Le ministère du Commerce et de l'Industrie, 1870–1914*, Vincennes: Institut de la gestion publique et du développement économique.

Dunham, Arthur Louis. 1930, *The Anglo-French Treaty of Commerce of 1860 and the Progress of the Industrial Revolution in France*, Ann Arbor: University of Michigan Press. Coll. History and Political Science, no. 9.

——— 1951, *A New Perspective on the Industrial Revolution in France*, Ann Arbor, MI: Alumni Association of the University of Michigan.

Dupâquier, Jacques. 1956, *La propriété et l'exploitation foncières à la fin de l'Ancien Régime dans la Gâtinais septentrional*, Paris: Presses universitaires de France. Coll. Commission de recherche et de publication des documents relatifs à la vie économique de la Révolution, no. 11.

Dupâquier, Jacques, Alfred Sauvy, Emmanuel Le Roy Ladurie, Maurice Garden, and Pierre Chaunu. 1995, *Histoire de la population française*, Paris: Quadrige/PUF.

Dupeux, Georges. 1962, *Aspects de l'histoire sociale et politique du Loir-et-Cher, 1848–1914*, Paris: Mouton. Coll. Études, no. 4.

DuPlessis, Robert. 2016, 'Conclusion: Reorienting Early Modern Economic History: Merchant Economy, Merchant Capitalism and the Age of Commerce', In *Merchants and Profit in the Age of Commerce, 1680–1830*, edited by Pierre Gervais, Yannick Lemarchand, Dominique Margairaz, and Darla K. Rudy-Gervais, London: Routledge, 171–80. Coll. Perspectives in Economic and Social History, no. 30.

Durand, Georges. 1979, *Vin, vigne et vignerons en lyonnais et beaujolais: XVIe-XVIIIe siècles*, Paris: Édition de l'École des hautes études en sciences sociales. Coll. Civilisations et sociétés, no. 63.

Eck, Jean-François. 2009, 'Le temps du redressement (1949–1969)', In *Histoire de l'économie française: De la crise de 1929 à l'euro*, Paris: Armand Colin, 39–73. Coll. U. Histoire.

Elie, Jean. 2003, 'Note sur l'économie agricole en Haut-Poitou au XVIIIe siècle. La Chapelle Moulière: Un exemple ou un cas particulier?', *Revue Historique Du Centre-Ouest*, vol. 2: 231–48.

Elwitt, Sanford. 1975, *The Making of the Third Republic: Class and Politics in France, 1868–1884*, Baton Rouge: Louisiana State University Press.

Engrand, Charles. 1981, 'Les industries lillois es et la crise économique de 1826 à 1832', *Revue Du Nord*, vol. 63, no. 248: 233–51.

Escalona, Fabien. 2022b, 'France's Left Needs to Speak to All Parts of the Working Class', *Jacobin*. https://jacobin.com/2022/07/french-left-nupes-vote-demographics-rural-voters-base

——— 2022a, 'French Socialism Embraced Neoliberalism and Signed Its Death Warrant', *Jacobin*. https://jacobin.com/2022/01/french-socialist-party-francois-mitterrand-collapse

Ettinger, Marlon. 2023, 'Emmanuel Macron's Pension Reform Will Make Workers Toil Till They Drop', *Jacobin*. https://jacobin.com/2023/01/emmanuel-macron-france-pension-reform-retirement-age-working-class

Evans, Jessica. 2019, 'Colonialism, Racism, and the Transition to Capitalism in Canada', In *Case Studies in the Origins of Capitalism*, by Xavier Lafrance and Charles Post, Cham: Palgrave Macmillan. Coll. Marx, Engels, and Marxisms.

Fairchilds, Cissie. 1988, 'Three Views on the Guilds', *French Historical Studies*, vol. 15, no. 4: 688–92.

Farmer, Sarah Bennett. 2020, *Rural Inventions: The French Countryside after 1945*, New York: Oxford University Press.

Feinstein, Charles H. 1998, 'Pessimism Perpetuated: Real Wages and the Standard of Living in Britain during and after the Industrial Revolution', *The Journal of Economic History*, vol. 58, no. 3: 625–58.

Ferguson, Niall. 2000, 'The European Economy, 1815–1914', In *The Nineteenth Century: Europe 1789–1914*, edited by Timothy Charles William Blanning, Oxford; New York: Oxford University Press. Coll. The Short Oxford History of Europe.

Fohlen, Claude. 1956, *L'industrie textile au temps du Second Empire*, Paris: Plon.

——— 1973, 'France 1700–1914', In *The Fontana Economic History of Europe: The Emergence of Industrial Societies*, edited by Carlo M. Cipolla, translated by Robert Swann, Glasgow: Fontana/Collins.

Fombonne, Jean. 2001, *Personnel et DRH: l'affirmation de la fonction personnel dans les entreprises, (France, 1830–1990)*, Paris: Vuibert.

Fontaine, Marion, and Xavier Vigna. 2014, 'La grève des mineurs de l'automne 1948 en France', *Vingtième Siècle. Revue d'histoire*, vol. 121, no. 1: 21–34.

Fourastié, Jean. 1979, *Les trente glorieuses, ou la Révolution invisible de 1946 à 1975*, Paris: A. Fayard.

Fournial, Etienne, and Jean-Pierre Gutton. 1974, 'Introduction', In *Cahiers de doléances de la Province de Forez: Bailliage principal de Montbrison et bailliage secondaire de Bourg-Argental; états généraux de 1789*, Saint-Etienne: Centre d'Études Foréziennes. Coll. Recueil de mémoires et documents sur le Forez, no. 19.

Frémont, Armand. 2006, 'Élevage et vie rurale en Normandie: Un regard rétrospectif, 1954–2004', In *Acteurs et espaces de l'élevage, XVIIe-XXIe siècle: Évolution, structuration, spécialisation*, edited by Philippe Madeline and Jean-Marc Moriceau, Rennes: Association d'histoire des sociétés rurales. Coll. Bibliothèque d'histoire rurale, no. 9.

Fridenson, Patrick. 1987, 'Un tournant taylorien de la société française (1904–1918)', *Annales. Histoire, Sciences Sociales*, vol. 42, no. 5: 1031–60.

———— 1997, *Industrialisation et sociétés d'Europe occidentale, 1880–1970*, Paris: Paris. Coll. Mouvement social.

Frobert, Ludovic. 2009, *Les Canuts, ou la démocratie turbulente Lyon, 1831–1834*, Paris: Tallandier. Coll. L'histoire.

Fureix, Emmanuel, and François Jarrige. 2015, *La modernité désenchantée: Relire l'histoire du XIXe siècle français*, Paris: La Découverte. Coll. Écritures de l'histoire, no. 3.

Gaboriaux, Chloé. 2010, *La République en quête de citoyens: Les républicains français face au bonapartisme rural, 1848–1880*, Paris: Presses de Sciences po. Coll. Fait Politique.

Gachon, Lucien. 1955, 'L'évolution de l'agriculture française depuis 1940', *Revue Économique*, vol. 6, no. 1: 35–55.

Gallissot, René, Catherine Coquery-Vidrovitch, Daniel Hémery, Jacques Marseille. 1987, 'La colonisation a-telle été un fardeau ?', *Le Mouvement social*, no. 138 : 61-68.

Ganiage, Jean. 1988, *Le Beauvaisis au XVIIIe siècle: La campagne*, Paris: Presses universitaires de France. Coll. Travaux et documents de l'Institut national d'études démographiques, no. 121.

Garnier, Josette. 1982, *Bourgeoisie et propriété immobilière en Forez aux XVIIe et XVIIIe siècles*, Saint-Etienne: Centre d'Études Foréziennes.

Gaveau, Fabien. 2021, *Propriété, cadastre et usages locaux dans les campagnes françaises (1789–1960)*, Besançon: Presses Universitaires de France Comté.

Gavignaud-Fontaine, Geneviève. 1996, *La révolution rurale dans la France contemporaine, XVIIIe-XXe siècle*, Paris: L'Harmattan. Coll. Alternatives rurales.

Gay, François. 1955, 'L'Agriculture en Berry au XVIIIe siècle. Les enquêtes agricoles de 1762 et 1786', *Mémoires de l'Union des Sociétés Savantes de Bourges*, vol. 5: 25–46.

———— 1958, 'Production, prix et rentabilité de la terre en Berry au XVIIIe siècle', *Revue d'histoire Économique et Sociale*, vol. 36, no. 4: 399–411.

———— 1967, *La champagne du Berry: Essai sur la formation d'un paysage agraire et l'évolution d'une société rurale*, Paris: Tardy.

Gayot, Gérard. 1985, 'Les entrepreneurs au bon temps des privilèges: la draperie royale de Sedan au XVIIIe siècle', *Revue Du Nord*, vol. 67, no. 265: 413–45.

Gérard, Alain. 1990, *Pourquoi la Vendée?*, Paris: A. Colin.

Gerschenkron, Alexander. 1962, *Economic Backwardness in Historical Perspective*, Cambridge, MA: Harvard University Press.

Gervais, Michel, Marcel Jollivet, and Yves Tavernier. 1977, *La fin de la France paysanne depuis 1914*, Saint-Quentin: Éditions du Seuil.

Gervais, Pierre. 2004, *Les origines de la révolution industrielle aux États-Unis: Entre économie marchande et capitalisme industriel, 1800–1850*, Paris: École des hautes études en sciences sociales. Coll. Studies in History and the Social Sciences, no. 102.

———— 2008, 'Neither Imperial, nor Atlantic: A Merchant Perspective on International Trade in the Eighteenth Century', *History of European Ideas*, vol. 34, no. 4: 465–73.

———— 2014, 'Early Modern Merchant Strategies and the Historicization of Market Practices' *Economic Sociology (European Electronic Newsletter)*, vol. 15, no. 3: 19–29.

———— 2020, 'Capitalism and (or) Age of Commerce: The Peculiarities of Market Exchange in the Early Modern Era', *XVII-XVIII : Revue de La Société d'études Anglo-Américaines Des XVIIe et XVIIIe Siècles*, vol. 77: 1–19.

Gervais, Pierre, Yannick Lemarchand, and Dominique Margairaz. 2016, 'Introduction: The Many Scales of Merchant Profit: Accounting for Norms, Practices and Results in the Age of Commerce', In *Merchants and Profit in the Age of Commerce, 1680–1830*, edited by

Pierre Gervais, Yannick Lemarchand, Dominique Margairaz, and Darla K. Rudy-Gervais, London: Routledge. Coll. Perspectives in Economic and Social History, no. 30.

Gildea, Robert. 2003, *Barricades and Borders: Europe, 1800–1914*, Oxford; New York: Oxford University Press, 3rd ed. Coll. Short Oxford history of the modern world.

Gille, Bertrand. 1968, *La sidérurgie française au XIXe siècle: Recherches historiques*, Genève: Droz. Coll. Travaux de droit, d'économie, de sociologie, no. 66.

——— 1970, *La Banque en France au XIXe siècle: recherches historiques*, Genève: Droz. Coll. Travaux de droit, d'économie, de sociologie et de sciences politiques, no. 81.

Goubert, Pierre. 1970, *Louis XIV and Twenty Million Frenchmen*, translated by Allen Lane, New York: Vintage Books.

Goy, Joseph. 1987, 'Effets et limites de l'essor de l'agriculture nouvelle au dix-huitième siè-cle', In *Septième Congrès international des Lumières: rapports préliminaires, Budapest, 26 juillet-2 août 1987*, Oxford: The Voltaire Foundation.

Grantham, George. 1975, 'Scale and Organization in French Farming, 1840–1880', In *European Peasants and their Markets: Essays in Agrarian Economic History*, edited by William N. Parker and Eric Lionel Jones, Princeton, NJ: Princeton University Press. Coll. Princeton Legacy Library.

——— 1978, 'The Diffusion of the New Husbandry in Northern France, 1815–1840', *The Journal of Economic History*, vol. 38, no. 2: 311–37.

——— 1980, 'The Persistence of Open-Field Farming in Nineteenth-Century France', *The Journal of Economic History*, vol. 40, no. 3: 515–31.

——— 1996, 'The French Agricultural Capital Stock, 1789–1914', *Research in Economic History*, vol. 16: 37–83.

——— 1997a, 'Espaces privilégiés: Productivité agraire et zones d'approvisionnement des villes dans l'Europe préindustrielle', translated by Marie-Noëlle Sarget, *Annales. Histoire, Sciences Sociales*, vol. 52, no. 3: 695–725.

——— 1997b, 'The French Cliometric Revolution: A Survey of Cliometric Contributions to French Economic History', *European Review of Economic History*, vol. 1, no. 3: 353–405.

——— 2000, 'The French Agricultural Productivity Paradox: Measuring the Unmeasur-able', *Historical Methods: A Journal of Quantitative and Interdisciplinary History*, vol. 33, no. 1: 36–46.

Greenfield, Jérôme. 2020, 'Le Crédit mobilier avant la suprématie des Pereire', *Histoire, Économie & Société*, vol. 39e année, no. 2: 46.

Grenier, Jean-Yves. 1996, *L'économie d'Ancien Régime un monde de l'échange et de l'incertitude*, Paris: Albin Michel. Coll. L'Évolution de l'humanité.

Guicheteau, Samuel. 2014, *Les ouvriers en France 1700–1835.*, Paris: Armand Colin.

Guillaumin, Emile. 1983, *The Life of a Simple Man*, edited by Eugen Weber. Translated by Margaret Crosland, Hanover, NH: University Press of New England.

Guillemet, Dominique, Nicole Pellegrin, and Jacques Peret. 1981, *Le Haut-Poitou au XVIIIe siècle*, Poitiers: CNDP.

Gutton, Jean Pierre. 1971, *La société et les pauvres: L'exemple de la généralité de Lyon, 1534–1789*, Paris: Société d'édition les Belles Lettres. Coll. Bibliothèque de la faculté des lettres et sciences humaines de Lyon, no. 26.

Haggard, Stephan. 2015, 'The Developmental State is Dead: Long Live the Developmental State!', In *Advances in Comparative-Historical Analysis*, edited by James Mahoney and Kathleen Thelen, Cambridge: Cambridge University Press.

Haine, W. Scott. 2000, *The History of France*, Westport, CT: Greenwood Press. Coll. Green-wood Histories of the Modern Nations, no. 1096–2905.

Hardy-Hémery, Odette. 1993, 'Une limite au libéralisme intégral? Ententes et cartels dans le monde au XIXe et dans le premier tiers du XXe siècle', *Revue Du Nord*, vol. 75, no. 300: 319–41.

Harris, John Raymond. 1998, *Industrial Espionage and Technology Transfer: Britain and France in the Eighteenth Century*, Aldershot: Ashgate.

Hau, Michel. 1987, *L'industrialisation de l'Alsace (1803–1939)*, Strasbourg: Association des publications pres les Universites de Strasbourg.

Hautcœur, Pierre-Cyrille. 2011, 'Les transformations du crédit en France au XIXe siècle', *Romantisme*, vol. 151, no. 1: 23.

Heath, Elizabeth. 2014, *Wine, Sugar, and the Making of Modern France: Global Economic Crisis and the Racialization of French Citizenship, 1870–1910*, Cambridge: Cambridge University Press. Coll. New Studies in European History.

Heinrich, Michael. 2012, *An Introduction to the Three Volumes of Karl Marx's Capital*, New York: Monthly Review Press.

Herment, Laurent. 2013, 'Life Cycle and the Transfer of Small Farm Properties in Milly-la-Forêt During the First Half of the Nineteenth Century', In *Property Rights, Land Markets and Economic Growth in the European Countryside, Thirteenth-Twentieth Centuries*, edited by Gérard Béaur, Phillipp R. Schofield, Jean-Michel Chevet, and Maria Teresa Pérez Picazo, Turnhout: Brepols. Coll. Rural History in Europe, no. 1.

Hervieu, Bertrand, and Jean Viard. 2011, *L'archipel paysan: La fin de la république agricole*, La Tour d'Aigues: Éditions de l'Aube.

Heywood, Colin. 1981, 'The Role of the Peasantry in French Industrialization, 1815–1880', *The Economic History Review*, vol. 34, no. 3: 359–76.

——— 1992, *The Development of the French Economy, 1750–1914*, Cambridge: Cambridge University Press. Coll. New Studies in Economic and Social History, no. 17.

Hilferding, Rudolf. 1955, *Das Finanzkapital*, Berlin: Dietz.

Hills, Richard L. 1989, *Power from Steam: A History of the Stationary Steam Engine*, Cambridge: Cambridge University Press.

Hirsch, Jean-Pierre. 1985, 'La région lilloise: Foyer industriel ou place de négoce?', *Le Mouvement Social*, vol. 132: 27–41.

——— 1991, *Les deux rêves du commerce: Entreprise et institution dans la région lilloise, 1780–1860*, Paris: Éd. de l'École des hautes études en sciences sociales. Coll. Civilisations et sociétés, no. 82.

Hobsbawm, Eric J. 1987, *The Age of Empire: 1875–1914*, New York: Pantheon Books, 1st ed. Coll. History of Civilization.

——— 1996, *The Age of Revolution, 1789–1848*, New York: Vintage Books.

Hoffman, Philip T. 1996, *Growth in a Traditional Society: The French Countryside, 1450–1815*, Princeton: Princeton University Press. Coll. Princeton Economic History of the Western World.

Hoffman, Philip T., Gilles Postel-Vinay, and Jean-Laurent Rosenthal. 1999, 'Information and Economic History. How the Credit Market in Old Regime Paris Forces Us to Rethink the Transition to Capitalism', *The American Historical Review*, vol. 104, no. 1: 69–94.

——— 2001, *Des marchés sans prix: Une économie politique du crédit à Paris, 1660–1870*, Paris: Ed. de l'École des hautes études en sciences sociales. Coll. Civilisations et sociétés, no. 105.

——— 2019, *Dark Matter Credit: The Development of Peer-to-Peer Lending and Banking in France*, edited by Joel Mokyr, Princeton, NJ: Princeton University Press.

Hoffmann, Stanley. 1963, 'Paradoxes of the French Political Community', In *Search of France*, edited by Stanley Hoffmann, Charles P. Kindleberger, Laurence Wylie, Jesse

R. Pitts, Jean-Baptiste Duroselle, and François Goguel, Cambridge: Harvard University Press, 1–118.

Horn, J. 2012, '"A Beautiful Madness": Privilege, the Machine Question and Industrial Development in Normandy in 1789', *Past & Present*, vol. 217, no. 1: 149–85.

Horn, Jeff. 2006, *The Path Not Taken: French Industrialization in the Age of Revolution, 1750–1830*, Cambridge, MA: MIT Press. Coll. Transformations.

———— 2010, 'The French Path to Industrialization', In *Fertility and Public Policy: How to Reverse the Trend of Declining Birth Rates*, edited by Jeff Horn, Leonard N. Rosenband, and Merritt Roe Smith, Cambridge, MA: MIT Press, 87–106.

Hudson, Pat. 1986, *The Genesis of Industrial Capital: A Study of the West Riding Wool Textile Industry, c. 1750–1850*, Cambridge; New York: Cambridge University Press.

Isett, Christopher Mills, and Stephen Miller. 2017, *The Social History of Agriculture: From the Origins to the Current Crisis*, Lanham, MD: Rowman & Littlefield.

Jacquart, Jean. 1974, *La crise rurale en Île-de-France, 1550–1670*, Paris: Armand Colin. Coll. N.S. Recherches, no. 10.

———— 1975, 'La rente foncière, indice conjoncturel?', *Revue Historique*, vol. 253, no. 2: 355–76.

Jarrige, François, and Cécile Chalmin. 2008, 'L'émergence du contremaître. L'ambivalence d'une autorité en construction dans l'industrie textile française (1800–1860)', *Le Mouvement Social*, vol. 224: 47–60.

Jenson, Jane, and George Ross. 1988, 'The Tragedy of the French Left', *New Left Review*, vol. I/171: 5–44.

Jessenne, Jean-Pierre. 2006, *Les campagnes françaises entre mythe et histoire: XVIIIe-XXIe siècle*, Paris: Armand Colin. Coll. Enjeux de l'histoire.

John, A. H. 1965, 'Agricultural Productivity and Economic Growth in England, 1700–1760', *The Journal of Economic History*, vol. 25, no. 1: 19–34.

Johnson, Chalmers A. 1982, *MITI and the Japanese Miracle: The Growth of Industrial Policy, 1925–1975*, Redwood City, CA: Stanford University Press.

———— 1999, 'The Developmental State: Odyssey of a Concept', In *The Developmental State*, edited by Meredith Woo-Cumings, Ithaca, NY and London: Cornell University Press.

Jomand, Joseph. 1966, *Chaponost en Lyonnais*, Lyon: E. Vitte.

Jones, Eric Lionel. 1967, 'Editor's Introduction', In *Agriculture and Economic Growth in England, 1650–1815*, edited by Eric Lionel Jones, London; New York: Methuen ; Barnes & Noble. Coll. Debates in Economic History.

———— 1968, 'Agricultural Origins of Industry', *Past & Present*, vol. 40: 58–71.

Jones, Peter. 1995, *Reform and Revolution in France: The Politics of Transition, 1774–1791*, Cambridge: Cambridge University Press.

———— 2016, *Agricultural Enlightenment: Knowledge, Technology, and Nature, 1750–1840*, Oxford: Oxford University Press.

Kasdi, Mohamed. 2014, *Les entrepreneurs du coton: Innovation et développement économique, France du Nord, 1700–1830*, Villeneuve-d'Ascq: Presses universitaires du Septentrion. Coll. Histoire et civilisations.

Kasza, Gregory J. 2018, 'Gerschenkron, Amsden, and Japan: The State in Late Development', *Japanese Journal of Political Science*, vol. 19, no. 2: 146–72.

Keeler, John T. S. 1987, *The Politics of Neocorporatism in France: Farmers, the State, and Agricultural Policy-Making in the Fifth Republic*, New York: Oxford University Press.

Kemp, Tom. 1962, 'Structural Factors in the Retardation of French Economic Growth', *Kyklos*, vol. 15, no. 2: 325–52.

—— 1971, *Economic Forces in French History: An Essay on the Development of the French Economy, 1760–1914*, London: Dobson.

—— 1976, *Industrialization in Nineteenth-Century Europe*, London: Longman.

Kindleberger, Charles P. 1990, *Historical Economics: Art or Science?* Berkeley, CA: University of California Press.

King, Peter. 2006, 'The Production and Consumption of Bar Iron in Early Modern England and Wales', *The Economic History Review*, vol. 59, no. 1: 264.

Kipping, Matthias. 1994, 'Concurrence et compétitivité: Les origins de la legislation anti-trust française après 1945', In *Études et documents VI*, edited by Comité pour l'histoire économique et financière de la France, Paris : Ministère de l'Économie et du Budget.

—— 2001, 'Les relations gouvernement-monde des affaires dans la France de l'après-Guerre: Adaptations et adaptabilité d'un système original', *Histoire, Économie et Société*, vol. 20, no. 4: 577–96.

Koulischer, Joseph. 1931, 'La grande industrie aux XVIIe et XVIIIe siècles: France, Alle-magne, Russie', *Annales*, vol. 9 : 11–46.

Kouvelakis, Stathis. 2019a, 'The French Insurgency: The Political Economy of the Gilets Jaunes', *New Left Review*, vol. 116/117: 75–98.

—— 2019b, 'Emmanuel Macron Wants to End France's Welfare State', *Jacobin*. https://jacobin.com/2019/12/france-strike-welfare-state-pensions-emmanuel-macron

Kuhn, Raymond. 2022, 'Wither the French left?', *Modern & Contemporary France*, vol. 30, no. 4: 461–77.

Kuisel, Richard F. 1981, *Capitalism and the State in Modern France: Renovation and Eco-nomic Management in the Twentieth Century.*, New York: Cambridge University Press.

Labrousse, Ernest. 1944, *La crise de l'économie française à la fin de l'Ancien Régime et au début de la Révolution*, Paris: Presses universitaries de France.

—— 1954, *Aspects de l'évolution économique et sociale de la France et du Royaume-Uni de 1815 à 1880*, Paris: Centre de Documentation Universitaire. Coll. Les cours de Sorbonne: Histoire economique.

—— 1966, 'The Evolution of Peasant Society in France from the Eighteenth Century to the Present', In *French Society and Culture since the Old Regime*, edited by Evelyn Mar-tha Acomb and Marvin Luther Brown, New York: Holt, Rinehart, and Winston.

—— 1970, 'L'expansion agricole: la montée de la production' and 'Aperçu de la reparti-tion sociale de l'expansion agricole', In *Histoire économique et sociale de la France: Des derniers temps de l'âge seigneurial aux préludes de l'âge industriel (1660–1789)*, edited by Fernand Braudel and Ernest Labrousse, Paris: Presses universitaires de France.

—— 1984, *Esquisse du mouvement des prix et des revenues en France au XVIIIe siècle*, Paris: Éditions des Archives contemporaines.

Lafrance, Xavier. 2020, *The Making of Capitalism in France: Class Structures, Economic Development, the State and the Formation of the French Working Class, 1750–1914*, Chicago: Haymarket Books.

Lambert-Dansette, Jean. 1991, *Histoire de l'entreprise et des chefs d'entreprise en France: Genèse du patronat, 1780–1880*, Paris: Hachette, Vol. 1. Coll. Histoire.

Landes, David S. 1949, 'French Entrepreneurship and Industrial Growth in the Nineteenth Century', *The Journal of Economic History*, vol. 9, no. 1: 45–61.

—— 1956, 'Vieille Banque et Banque Nouvelle: la révolution financière du dix-neuvième siècle', *Revue d'histoire Moderne et Contemporaine (1954-)*, vol. 3, no. 3: 204–22.

—— 1969, *The Unbound Prometheus: Technological Change and Industrial Develop-ment in Western Europe from 1750 to the Present*, Cambridge, GB: Cambridge University Press.

Le Roy Ladurie, Emmanuel. 1974, *The Peasants of Languedoc*, Urbana: University of Illinois Press.

———— 1981, *The Mind and Method of the Historian*, Translated by Sian Reynolds and Ben Reynolds, Chicago: University of Chicago Press.

Lebovics, Herman. 1967, '"Agrarians" Versus "Industrializers": Social Conservative Resistance to Industrialism and Capitalism in Late Nineteenth Century Germany', *International Review of Social History*, vol. 12, no. 1: 31–65.

———— 1988, *The Alliance of Iron and Wheat in the Third French Republic, 1860–1914: Origins of the New Conservatism*, Baton Rouge; London: Louisiana State University Press.

———— 1992, 'Economic Positivism as Rhetoric', *International Review of Social History*, vol. 37, no. 2: 244–51.

Lefebvre, Georges. 1963, *Études sur la Révolution française*, Paris: Presses universitaires de France.

Lefebvre, Henri. 2022, *On the Rural: Economy, Sociology, Geography*, edited by Stuart Elden and Adam David Morton. Translated by Robert Bononno, Matthew Dennis, and Sîan Rosa Hunter Dodsworth, Minneapolis: University of Minnesota Press.

Lefebvre, Philippe. 2003, *L'invention de la grande entreprise: Travail, hiérarchie, marché (France, fin XVIIIe-début XXe siècle)*, Paris: Presses universitaires de France. Coll. Sociologies.

———— 2009, 'Subordination et « révolutions » du travail et du droit du travail (1776–2010)', *Entreprises et Histoire*, vol. 57, no. 4: 45.

Legal, Pierre-Yannick. n.d., 'Paysans Bas-Poitevins entre plaine, bocage, gâtine et marais (1730–1750)', *Recherches Vendéennes*, vol. 2: 317–53.

Lejosne, Raymonde. 1989, 'Champarts autours d'Étampes', *89 En Essonne*, vol. 2: 61–62.

Lemarchand, Guy. 1988, 'Du féodalisme au capitalisme: À propos des conséquences de la Révolution sur l'évolution de l'économie française', *Annales Historiques de La Révolution Française*, vol. 272: 171–207.

———— 1989, *La fin du féodalisme dans le pays de Caux: Conjoncture économique et démographique et structure sociale dans une région de grande culture, de la crise du XVIIe siècle à la stabilisation de la Révolution, 1640–1795*, Paris: Éditions du Comité des travaux historiques et scientifiques. Coll. Mémoires et documents.

———— 2008, *L'économie en France de 1770 à 1830: De la crise de l'Ancien régime à la révolution industrielle*, Paris: Armand Colin. Coll. U. Histoire.

Lemarchand, Yannick 1995, 'Style mercantile ou mode des finances: Le choix d'un modèle comptable dans la France d'Ancien Régime', *Annales. Histoire, Sciences Sociales*, vol. 50, no. 1: 159–82.

———— 2016, 'Revisiting the Birth of Industrial Accounting in France, a Return to the Actors Involved', *Accounting History Review*, vol. 26, no. 3: 351–71.

Lemarchand, Yannick, Cheryl McWatters, and Laure Pineau-Defois. 2016, 'The Current Account as Cognitive Artefact: Stories and Accounts of la Maison Chaurand', In *Merchants and Profit in the Age of Commerce, 1680–1830*, edited by Dominique Margairaz, Pierre Gervais, and Yannick Lemarchand, London: Routledge, 13–32. Coll. Perspectives in Economic and Social History, no. 30.

Léon, Pierre. 1960, *Les enquêtes de Grignon et de Binelli, 1778–1783; recueil de textes relatifs à la technique métallurgique dauphinoise*, Paris: Hermann.

———— 1993, 'La conquête de l'espace national', In *Histoire économique et sociale de la France: L'avènement de l'ère industrielle (1789-années 1880)*, edited by Ernest Labrousse and Fernand Braudel, Paris: Presses universitaires de France, Vol. 3. Coll. Quadrige.

Lequin, Yves. 1984, *Histoire des français XIXe-XXe siècles: La société*, Paris: Armand Colin, Vol. 2.

Lescure, Michel. 1996, *PME et croissance économique: l'expérience française des années 1920*, Paris: Economica.

Levine, David. 1976, 'The Reliability of Parochial Registration and the Representativeness of Family Reconstitution', *Population Studies*, vol. 30, no. 1: 107–22.

―――― 1977, *Family Formation in an Age of Nascent Capitalism*, New York: Academic Press. Coll. Studies in social discontinuity.

Levine Frader, Laura. 1991, *Peasants and Protest: Agricultural Workers, Politics and Unions in the Aude, 1850–1914*, Berkeley, CA: University of California Press.

Lévy-Leboyer, Maurice. 1964, *Les banques européennes et l'industrialisation internationale dans la première moitié du XIXe siècle*, Paris: Presses universitaires de France. Coll. Publications de la faculté des lettres et sciences humaines de Paris.

―――― 1968, 'La croissance économique en France au XIXe siècle: Résultats préliminaires', *Annales. Histoire, Sciences Sociales*, vol. 23, no. 4: 788–807.

―――― 1996, *Histoire de la France industrielle*, Paris: Larousse.

Lévy-Leboyer, Maurice, and François Bourguignon. 1985, *L'économie française au XIXe siècle: Analyse macro-économique*, Paris: Economica. Coll. Collection Economie.

Lipson, Ephraim. 1921, *The History of the Woollen and Worsted Industries*, Edinburgh: A. & C. Black.

Liu, Tessie P. 1994, *The Weaver's Knot: The Contradictions of Class Struggle and Family Solidarity in Western France, 1750–1914*, Ithaca, NY: Cornell University Press.

Loriaux, Michel. 1999, 'The French Developmental State as Myth and Moral Ambition', In *The Developmental State*, edited by Meredith Woo-Cumings, Ithaca, NY: Cornell University Press, 235–75. Coll. Book collections on Project MUSE.

Loutchisky, I. 1933, 'Régime agraire et populations agricoles dans les environs de Paris à la veille de la Révolution', Translated by N. Stchoupak, *Revue d'histoire Moderne*, vol. 8, no. 7: 97–142.

Lugnier, Antoine. 1962, *Cinq siècles de vie paysanne à Roche-En-Forez, Loire (1440–1940)*, Saint-Étienne: Dumas.

Maddison, Angus. 1982, *Phases of Capitalist Development*, Oxford; New York: Oxford University Press.

Magraw, Roger. 1986, *France, 1815–1914: The Bourgeois Century*, New York: Oxford University Press.

Marchand, Olivier, and Claude Thélot. 1991, *Deux siècles de travail en France: population active et structure sociale, durée et productivité du travail*, Paris: Institut de la statistique et des études économiques. Coll. Études.

Marczewski, Jean. 1965, *Introduction a l'histoire quantitative*, Paris: Droz. Coll. Bibliographies.

Margairaz, Dominique. 1986, 'La formation du réseau des foires et des marchés: Stratégies, pratiques et idéologies', *Annales. Histoire, Sciences Sociales*, vol. 41, no. 6: 1215–42.

Margairaz, Michel. 1991, *L'État, les finances et l'économie: histoire d'une conversion: 1932–1952*, Paris: Comité pour l'histoire économique et financière de la France.

Markovitch, Tihomir J. 1965, *L'industrie française de 1789 à 1964*, Paris: Institut de Science économique appliquée.

Marseille, Jacques. 1984, *Empire colonial et capitalisme français: Histoire d'un divorce*, Paris: A. Michel.

Marseille, Jacques, and Jean-Charles Asselain. 1997, *Puissance et faiblesses de la France industrielle, XIXe -XXe siècle*, Paris: Éditions du Seuil. Coll. Histoire, no. 241.

Martin, Bernard. 1988, *La vie en Poitou dans la seconde moitié du XVIIIe siècle: Mazeuil, paroisse du Mirebalais*, Maulévrier: Hérault.

Marx, Karl. 1990, *Capital. A Critique of Political Economy*, London: Penguin Books.

———— 1991, *Capital. A Critique of Political Economy*, London: Penguin Books.

———— 2010, 'The Civil War in France (1871)', In *The First International and After Karl Marx*, edited by David Fernbach, London; New York: Verso. Coll. Marx's Political Writings.

Marzagalli, Silvia. 2012, 'Commerce', In *The Oxford Handbook of the Ancient Régime*, edited by William Doyle, Oxford: Oxford University Press. Coll. Oxford Handbooks.

Massé, Pierre. 1956, *Varennes et ses maîtres: Un domaine rural, de l'Ancien Régime à la Monarchie de Juillet (1779–1842)*, Paris: S.E.V.P.E.N. Coll. Les hommes et la terre, no. 1.

Mathews, John A. 2016, 'Latecomer Industrialization', In *Handbook of Alternative Theories of Economic Development*, edited by Erik Reinert, Jayati Ghosh and Rainer Kattel, Cheltenham, UK and Northhampton, MA: Edward Elgar Publishing.

McNally, David. 1988, *Political Economy and the Rise of Capitalism: A Reinterpretation*, Berkeley, CA: University of California Press.

Menault, Ernest. 1991, *Histoire de l'agriculture en Berry: La condition paysanne du Ve au XVIIIe siècle*, Mayenne: Royer. Coll. Les Racines du terroir.

Mendras, Henri. 1970, *The Vanishing Peasant: Innovation and Change in French Agriculture*, Translated by Jean Lerner, Cambridge, MA: MIT Press. Coll. M.I.T. Studies in Comparative Politics Series.

Mendras, Henri, and Laurence Duboys Fresney. 1988, *La seconde Révolution française: 1965–1984*, Paris: Gallimard. Coll. Bibliothèque des sciences humaines.

Merle, Louis. 1958, *La métairie et l'évolution agraire de la Gâtine poitevine de la fin du Moyen Âge à la Révolution*, Paris: S.E.V.P.E.N. Coll. Les Hommes et la terre, no. 2.

Meuvret, Jean. 1987, *Le problème des subsistances à l'époque Louis XIV: La production des céréales et la société rurale*, Paris: Editions de l'Ecole des hautes études en sciences sociales. Coll. Civilisations et sociétés, no. 75.

Meyer, Jean. 1966, *La noblesse bretonne au XVIIIe siècle*, Paris: S.E.V.P.E.N.

———— 2016, 'Des origines à 1763', In *Histoire de la France coloniale: Des origines à 1914*, edited by Jean Meyer, Jean Tarrade, Anne Rey-Goldzeiguer, and Jacques Thobie, Paris: Armand Colin. Coll. Histoires.

Miller, Stephen. 2008, *State and Society in Eighteenth Century France: A Study of Political Power and Social Revolution in Languedoc*, Washington, DC: The Catholic University of America Press.

Milward, Alan Steele, and Samuel Berrick Saul. 1973, *Economic Development of Continental Europe, 1780–1870*, Totowa, NJ: Rowman and Littlefield.

Minard, Philippe. 1998, *La fortune du colbertisme: État et industrie dans la France des Lumières*, Paris: A. Fayard.

———— 2007, '"France colbertiste" versus "Angleterre libérale"? Un mythe du XVIIIe siècle', In *Les idées passent-elles la Manche?: Savoirs, représentations, pratiques (France-Angleterre, Xe-XXe siècles)*, edited by Jean-Philippe Genêt and François-Joseph Ruggiu, Paris: PUPS. Coll. Centre Roland Mousnier, no. 28.

———— 2008, 'Économie de marché et État en France: Mythes et légendes du colbertisme', *L'Économie Politique*, vol. 37, no. 1: 77.

Miquel, Pierre. 2004, *La France et ses paysans: Une histoire du monde rural au XXe siècle*, Paris: Éditions de l'Archipel.

Mireaux, Emile. 1958, *Une province française au temps du grand roi: La Brie*, Paris: Hachette.

Mokyr, Joel. 1999, 'Editor's Introduction: The New Economic History and the Industrial Revolution', In *The British Industrial Revolution: An Economic Perspective*, edited by Joel Mokyr, Boulder, CO: Westview Press.

Mooers, Colin. 1991, *The Making of Bourgeois Europe: Absolutism, Revolution and the Rise of Capitalism in England, France and Germany*, London; New York: Verso.

Morazé, Charles. 1947, *La France bourgeoise: XVIIIe-XXe siècles*, Paris: Armand Colin.

Moriceau, Jean-Marc. 1994a, 'Au rendez-vous de la "Révolution agricole": Dans la France du XVIIIe siècle : À propos des régions de grande culture', *Annales. Histoire, Sciences Sociales*, vol. 49, no. 1: 27–63.

——— 1994b, *Les fermiers de l'île de France: l'ascension d'un patronat agricole, XVe-XVIIIe siècle*, Paris: Fayard.

Moriceau, Jean-Marc, and Gilles Postel-Vinay. 1992, *Ferme, entreprise, famille grande exploitation et changements agricoles: Les Chartier : XVIIe-XIXe siècles*, Paris: Édition de l'École des hautes études en sciences sociales. Coll. Les Hommes et la terre, no. 21.

Morineau, Michel. 1976, 'The Agricultural Revolution in Nineteenth-Century France: Comment', *The Journal of Economic History*, vol. 36, no. 2: 436–37.

Morny, Charles, Auguste Louis Joseph. 1853, *Conseil supérieur du commerce, de l'agriculture et de l'industrie, Séance du 14 novembre 1853*, Paris: Archives nationales de France.

Moulin, Annie. 1991, *Peasantry and Society in France since 1789*, translated by Mark C. Cleary and M. F. Cleary, Cambridge: Cambridge University Press.

Moutet, Aimée. 1998, *Industralisation et sociétés en Europe occidentale, 1880–1970*, Paris: SHMC. Coll. Le bulletin de la SHMC: Spécial concours, no. 98.

Mulliez, Jacques. 1979, 'Du blé, "Mal nécessaire": Réflexions sur les progrès de l'agriculture de 1750 a 1850', *Revue d'histoire Moderne et Contemporaine*, vol. 26, no. 1: 3–47.

Napoléon III. 1860, 'L'Empereur a adressé au ministre d'Etat, la lettre suivante', *Le Moniteur universel: Journal officiel de l'Empire français*, no. 15: 1.

Nash, R. C. 2005, 'The Organization of Trade and Finance in the British Atlantic Economy, 1600–1830', In *The Atlantic Economy During the Seventeenth and Eighteenth Centuries: Organization, Operation, Practice, and Personnel*, edited by Peter A. Coclanis, Columbia, SC: University of South Carolina Press.

Newell, William H. 1973, 'The Agricultural Revolution in Nineteenth-Century France', *The Journal of Economic History*, vol. 33, no. 4: 697–731.

Nicolas, Jean. 2002, *La rébellion française: Mouvements populaires et conscience sociale, 1661–1789*, Paris: Seuil. Coll. L'Univers historique.

Noiret, Charles. 1836, *Mémoires d'un ouvrier rouennais*, Rouen: François.

Noiriel, Gérard. 1986, *Les ouvriers dans la société française, XIX–XXe siècle*, Paris: Éditions du Seuil. Coll. Points. Histoire, no. 88.

O'Brien, Patrick, and Çağlar Keyder. 1978, *Economic Growth in Britain and France 1780–1914: Two Paths to the Twentieth Century*, London: George Allen & Unwin.

Overton, Mark. 1996, *Agricultural Revolution in England: The Transformation of the Agrarian Economy, 1500–1850*, Cambridge: Cambridge University Press. Coll. Cambridge Studies in Historical Geography, no. 23.

Palmade, Guy P. 1972, *French Capitalism in the Nineteenth Century*, Translated by Graeme M. Holmes, New York: Barnes & Noble.

Paris, André. 1975, 'Les conditions du progrès agricole dans le centre du Bassin parisien: Droits seigneuriaux, jachère et vaine pâture dans la région de Montfort-L'Amaury (XVIIe-XIXe siècle)', *Ethnologie et Histoire*, 536–58.

Parker, David. 1996, *Class and State in Ancien Regime France: The Road to Modernity?*, London; New York: Routledge.

Pautard, Jean. 1965, *Les disparités régionales dans la croissance de l'agriculture française*, Paris: Gauthier-Villars. Coll. Série Espace économique, no. 3.

Pellegrin, Nicole. 1987, 'Ruralité et modernité du textile en Haut-Poitou au XVIIIe siècle: La leçon des inventaires après-décès', In *Actes du 112e Congrès national des sociétés savantes (Lyon, 1987): Section d'histoire moderne et contemporaine*, Paris: CTHS.

Peret, Jacques. 1976, *Seigneurs et seigneuries en Gâtine poitevine: la duché de la Meilleraye XVIIe-XVIII siècles*, Poitiers: Au siège de la Société. Coll. Mémoires de la Société des antiquaires de l'Ouest, no. 4.

———— 1998, *Les paysans de Gâtine poitevine au XVIIIe siècle*, La Crèche: Geste éditions. Coll. Pays d'histoire.

Perez, Yves André. 2012, '« Lendemains de fêtes impériales: retour sur la crise du mode saint-simonien de croissance polarisée en économie ouverte, en France, à la fin du XIX', *Humanisme et Entreprise*, vol. 310, no. 5: 1.

Perrot, Michelle. 1974, *Les ouvriers en grève, France 1871–1890*, Paris: Mouton. Coll. Civilisations et sociétés.

———— 1983, 'De la manufacture à l'usine en miettes', *Le Mouvement Social*, vol. 125: 3–12.

Peru, Jean-Jacques. 2003, 'L'évolution de l'outillage aratoire dans trios communautés au nord-est de Paris (1600–1850)', In *Jardinages en région parisienne du XVIIe au XXe siècle*, edited by Jean-René Trochet, Jean-Jacques Péru, and Jean-Michel Roy, Grâne: Créaphis.

Pigenet, Michel. 2014, 'La Libération: Les mobilisations sociales à l'heure de la Reconstruction', In *Histoire des mouvements sociaux en France*, edited by Michel Pigenet and Danielle Tartakowsky, Paris: La Découverte, 427–37. Coll. Sciences humaines et sociales.

Pinaud, Pierre-François. 1990, *Les Receveurs généraux des Finances, 1790–1865: Étude historique: Répertoires nominatif et territorial*, Genève; Paris: Droz; Champion. Coll. École pratique des hautes études, IVe section, no. 66.

Pinchemel, Philippe. 1957, *Structures sociales et dépopulaton rurale dans les campagnes picardes de 1836 á 1936*, Paris: Armand Colin. Coll. Centre d'études économiques: Études et mémoires, no. 35.

Pitié, Jean. 1971, *Exode rural et migrations intérieures en France: L'exemple de la Vienne et du Poitou-Charentes*, Poitiers: Norois.

Plack, Noelle L. 2005, 'Agrarian Individualism, Collective Practices and the French Revolution: The Law of 10 June 1793 and the Partition of Common Land in the Department of the Gard', *European History Quarterly*, vol. 35, no. 1: 39–62.

Plessis, Alain. 1985, *The Rise and Fall of the Second Empire, 1852–1871*, Cambridge; New York; Melbourne; Paris: Cambridge University Press; Éd. de la Maison des sciences de l'Homme. Coll. The Cambridge History of Modern France, no. 3.

———— 1991, 'Les banques, le crédit et l'économie', In *Entre l'Etat et le marché: L'économie française des années 1880 à nos jours*, edited by Maurice Lévy-Leboyer, Jean-Claude Casanova, and Jean-Charles. Asselain, Paris: Gallimard. Coll. Bibliothèque des sciences humaines.

———— 1996, 'Le financement des entreprises', In *Histoire de la France industrielle*, edited by Maurice Lévy-Leboyer, Paris: Larousse.

———— 2001, *De la fête impériale au mur des fédérés: 1852–1871*, Paris: Éditions du Seuil. Coll. Nouvelle histoire de la France contemporaine, no. 9.

Pollard, Sidney. 1965, *The Genesis of Modern Management. A Study of the Industrial Revolution in Great Britain*, London: Edward Arnold.

Post, Charles. 2011, *The American Road to Capitalism: Studies in Class-Structure, Economic Development, and Political Conflict, 1620–1877*, Leiden; Boston: Brill. Coll. Historical Materialism Book Series, no. 28.

Post, Charles. 2017, 'Slavery and the New History of Capitalism', *Catalyst*, vol. 1, no. 1: 173-192.

———— 2019, 'The American Road to Capitalism', In *Case Studies in the Origins of Capitalism*, edited by Xavier Lafrance and Charles Post, London: Palgrave Macmillan, 165–89. Coll. Marx, Engels, and Marxisms.

Price, Roger. 1975, 'The Onset of Labour Shortage in Nineteenth-Century French Agriculture', *The Economic History Review*, vol. 28, no. 2: 260–79.

———— 1981, *An Economic History of Modern France, 1730–1914*, New York: St. Martin's Press.

———— 1983, *The Modernization of Rural France: Communications Networks and Agricultural Market Structures in Nineteenth-Century France*, New York: St. Martin's Press.

———— 2001, *The French Second Empire: An Anatomy of Political Power*, New York: Cambridge University Press. Coll. New Studies in European History.

———— 2004, *People and Politics in France, 1848–1870*, Cambridge; New York: Cambridge University Press. Coll. New Studies in European History.

Reddy, William M. 1984, *The Rise of Market Culture: The Textile Trade and French Society, 1750–1900*, New York: Cambridge University Press.

Riley, Dylan, and Robert Brenner. 2022, 'Seven Theses on American Politics', *New Left Review*, vol. 138: 5–27.

Rioux, Jean-Pierre. 1989, *La Révolution industrielle, 1780–1880*, Paris: Editions du Seuil, 2nd ed. Coll. Points. Histoire, no. 6.

Rivoire, Hector. 1842, *Statistique du département du Gard*, Nîmes: Ballivet et Fabre.

Roehl, Richard. 1976, 'French Industrialization: A Reconsideration', *Explorations in Economic History*, vol. 13, no. 3: 233–81.

Rostow, W. W. 1960, *The Stages of Economic Growth: A Non-communist Manifesto*, Cambridge: Cambridge University Press.

Ruttan, Vernon W. 1978, 'Structural Retardation and the Modernization of French Agriculture: A Skeptical View', *The Journal of Economic History*, vol. 38, no. 3: 714–28.

Salomon, Jean-Jacques. 1991, 'La capacité d'innovation', In *Entre l'Etat et le marché: L'économie française des années 1880 à nos jours*, edited by Maurice Lévy-Leboyer, Jean-Claude Casanova, Jean-Charles Asselain, Maurice Lévy-Leboyer, and Jean-Claude Casanova, Paris: Gallimard. Coll. Bibliothèque des sciences humaines.

Sauvy, Alfred. 1965, *Histoire économique de la France entre les deux guerres: De l'armistice à la dévaluation de la livre*, Paris: Fayard.

———— 1967, *Histoire économique de la France entre les deux guerres: De Pierre Laval à Paul Reynaud*, Paris: Fayard.

Sauzet, Marc. 1890, *Le livret obligatoire de l'ouvrier*, Paris: Pichon.

Schofield, R. S., and Edward Anthony Wrigley. 1981, *The Population History of England 1541–1871: A Reconstruction*, London: Edward Arnold. Coll. Studies in Social and Demographic History, no. 2.

Sée, Henri. 1926, *Les origines du capitalisme moderne: Esquisse historique*, Paris: Armand Colin. Coll. Section d'histoire et sciences économiques, no. 79.

Sée, Henri-Eugène. 1942, *Histoire économique de la France*, Paris: Armand Colin.

Sewell, William H. 1980, *Work and Revolution in France: The Language of Labor from the Old Regime to 1848*, Cambridge; New York: Cambridge University Press.

———— 2021, *Capitalism and the Emergence of Civic Equality in Eighteenth-Century France*, Chicago and London: The University of Chicago Press.

Sick, Klaus-Peter. 2013, 'La République, des "nouvelles couches" aux "classes moyennes"',
In *Une contre-histoire de la IIIe République*, edited by Marion Fontaine, Frédéric Monier,
and Christophe Prochasson, Paris: La Découverte. Coll. Cahiers libres.

Sick, Klaus-Peter, and Daniel Argelès. 2003, 'Deux formes de synthèse sociale en crise. Les
classes moyennes patronales de la Troisième République à la lumière d'une comparaison
franco-allemande', *Revue d'histoire Moderne et Contemporaine (1954-)*, vol. 50, no. 4:
135–54.

Smith, Adam. 1986, *The Essential Adam Smith*, edited by Robert Heiolbroner, New York:
W. W. Norton & Company.

——— 2003, *The Wealth of Nations*, New York: Bantam Classic.

Smith, Michael S. 1977, 'Free Trade versus Protection in the Early Third Republic: Economic Interests, Tariff Policy, and the Making of the Republican Synthesis', *French Historical Studies*, vol. 10, no. 2: 293–314.

——— 1980, *Tariff Reform in France, 1860–1900: The Politics of Economic Interest*,
Ithaca; London: Cornell University Press.

——— 2006, *The Emergence of Modern Business Enterprise in France, 1800–1930*, Cambridge, MA: Harvard University Press.

Sonenscher, Michael. 1989, *Work and Wages: Natural Law, Politics and the Eighteenth-
Century French Trades*, Cambridge: Cambridge University Press.

Stearns, Peter. 1965, 'British Industry through the Eyes of French Industrialists (1820–
1848)', *The Journal of Modern History*, vol. 37, no. 1: 50–61.

Steinfeld, Robert J. 2001, *Coercion, Contract, and Free Labor in the Nineteenth Century*,
Cambridge, GB; New York: Cambridge University Press. Coll. Cambridge Historical
Studies in American Law and Society.

Stetler, Harrison. 2022, 'France's Weapons Industry Is Growing Rich off Dictatorships',
Jacobin. https://jacobin.com/2022/11/france-arms-exports-authoritarian-europe-military-
industrial-complex

Stokey, Nancy L. 2001, 'A Quantitative Model of the British Industrial Revolution, 1780–
1850', *Carnegie-Rochester Conference Series on Public Policy*, vol. 55, no. 1: 55–109.

Stone, Judith F. 1985, *The Search for Social Peace Reform Legislation in France, 1890–
1914*, Albany: State University of New York Press. Coll. SUNY Series on Modern European Social History.

Stoskopf, Nicolas. 1994, *Les patrons du Second Empire: Alsace*, edited by Dominique Barjot, Paris; Le Mans: Picard; Cénomane.

——— 2007, 'Se passer de la monnaie: la banque d'échange de Victor-Corentin Bonnard
(1849–1862)', *Revue Européenne Des Sciences Sociales*, no. 137 :167–75.

——— 2010, 'Morny et le système bancaire', In *Morny et l'invention de Deauville*, edited
by Dominique Barjot, Éric Anceau, and Nicolas Stoskopf, Paris: Armand Colin, 153–66.
Coll. Recherches.

Surrault, Jean-Pierre. 1990, *L'Indre: Le Bas-Berry de la préhistoire à nos jours*, Saint-Jean-
d'Angély: Bordessoules. Coll. L'Histoire par les documents.

Sutherland, Donald. 2014, 'Productivity and Farm Management: The Hospitals of Le Mans,
1661–1913', In *Measuring Agricultural Growth: Land and Labour Productivity in Western Europe from the Middle Ages to the Twentieth Century (England, France and Spain)*,
edited by Jean-Michel Chevet and Gérard Béaur, Turnhout, Belgium: Brepols. Coll. Comparative Rural History of the North Sea Area, no. 15.

Taylor, A. J. 1949, 'Concentration and Specialization in the Lancashire Cotton Industry,
1825–1850', *The Economic History Review*, vol. 1, no. 2–3: 114–22.

Taylor, George V. 1967, 'Noncapitalist Wealth and the Origins of the French Revolution',
The American Historical Review, vol. 72, no. 2: 469–96.

Teschke, Benno. 2003, *The Myth of 1648: Class, Geopolitics, and the Making of Modern International Relations*, London; New York: Verso.

—— 2005, 'Bourgeois Revolution, State Formation and the Absence of the International', *Historical Materialism*, vol. 13, no. 2: 3–26.

Thier, Hadas. 2020, *A People's Guide to Capitalism: An Introduction to Marxist Economics*, Chicago, IL: Haymarket Books.

Thillay, Alain. 2002, *Le faubourg Saint-Antoine et ses 'faux ouvriers': La liberté du travail à Paris aux XVIIe et XVIIIe siècles*, Seyssel (Ain): Champ Vallon. Coll. Epoques.

Tilly, Charles. 1964, *The Vendée*, Cambridge, MA: Harvard University Press.

Tilly, Richard H., and Michael Kopsidis. 2020, *From Old Regime to Industrial State: A History of German Industrialization from the Eighteenth Century to World War I*, Chicago, IL: The University of Chicago Press.

Todd, David. 2008, *L'identité économique de la France libre-échange et protectionnisme, 1814–1851*, Paris: Grasset.

—— 2022, *Un empire de velours. L'impérialisme informel français au XIXe siècle*, Paris: La Découverte.

Tomas, François. 1967, 'Alleux et parcellaire à Sury-le-Comtal (Forez): Un essai de reconstitution du cadastre ancien', *Cahiers d'histoire*, vol. 12, no. 4: 407–12.

—— 1968, 'Problèmes de démographie historique: le Forez au XVIIIe siècle', *Cahiers d'histoire*, vol. 13: 381–99.

Tombs, Robert. 1996, *France, 1814–1914*, London; New York: Longman. Coll. Longman History of France.

Torp, Cornelius. 2010, 'The "Coalition of 'Rye and Iron'" under the Pressure of Globalization: A Reinterpretation of Germany's Political Economy before 1914', *Central European History*, vol. 43, no. 3: 401–27.

—— 2011, 'The Great Transformation: German Economy and Society, 1950–1914', In *The Oxford Handbook of Modern German History*, edited by Helmut Walser Smith, Oxford: Oxford University Press, 336–58. Coll. Oxford Handbooks in History.

Toutain, Jean Claude. 1961, *Le produit de l'agriculture française de 1700 à 1958*, Paris: I.S.E.A. Coll. Histoire quantitative de l'économie française, no. 1–2.

Trebilcock, Clive. 1981, *The Industrialization of the Continental Powers, 1780–1914*, New York: Longman.

Tulippe, Omer. 1934, *L'habitat rural en Seine-et-Oise: Essai de géographie du peuplement*, Paris: Sirey.

Vandewalle, Paul. 1994, *Quatre siècles d'agriculture dans la région de Dunkerque 1590–1990: Une étude statistique*, Gand: Centre Belge d'Histoire Rurale. no. 110.

Vardi, Liana. 1988, 'The Abolition of the Guilds during the French Revolution', *French Historical Studies*, vol. 15, no. 4: 704–17.

Venard, Marc. 1957, *Bourgeois et paysans au XVIIe siècle: Recherche sur le rôle des bourgeois parisiens dans la vie agricole au sud de Paris au XVIIe siècle*, Paris: S.E.V.P.E.N. Coll. Les hommes et la terre, no. 3.

Verley, Patrick. 1989, *Nouvelle histoire économique de la France contemporaine: L'industrialisation 1830–1914*, Paris: Éd. La Découverte. Coll. Repères, no. 78.

—— 1996, 'La dynamique des marchés et croissance industrielle', In *Histoire de la France industrielle*, edited by Maurice Lévy-Leboyer, Paris: Larousse.

—— 1997, *L'échelle du monde: Essai sur l'industrialisation de l'Occident*, Paris: Gallimard. Coll. NRF essais.

Verley, Patrick, and Jean-Luc Mayaud. 2001, 'Introduction. En l'an 2001, le XIXe siècle à redécouvrir pour les historiens économistes?', *Revue d'histoire Du XIXe Siècle*, vol. 23: 7–21.

Vidalenc, Jean. 1970, *La société française de 1815 à 1848: Le peuple des campagnes*, Paris: Marcel Rivière et cie.

Vigier, Philippe Historien. 1991, *Paris pendant la Monarchie de Juillet (1830–1848)*, Paris: Association pour la publication d'une histoire de Paris. Coll. Nouvelle histoire de Paris.

Vigna, Xavier. 2012, *Histoire des ouvriers en France au XXe siècle*, Paris: Perrin.

Vignon, Louis. 1978, *Annales d'un village de France, Charly-Vernaison en Lyonnais, 1150–1610*, Vernaison: Vignon.

Vivier, Nadine. 1998, *Propriété collective et identité communale: Les biens communaux en France, 1750–1914*, Paris: Publication de la Sorbonne. Coll. Histoire de la France aux XIXe et XXe siècles.

Vovelle, Michel. 1980, *Ville et campagne au 18e siècle: Chartres et la Beauce*, Paris: Éditions sociales. Coll. Problèmes histoire.

Walton, Charles. 2014, 'The Fall from Eden: The Free-Trade Origins of the French Revolution', In *The French Revolution in Global Perspective*, edited by Suzanne Desan, Lynn Hunt, and William Max Nelson, Ithaca: Cornell University Press, 44–56.

Weber, Eugen. 1983, 'Introduction', In *The Life of a Simple Man*, by Emile Guillaumin, edited by Eugen Weber, translated by Margaret Crosland, Hanover, NH: University Press of New England.

Weber, Max. 1958, *From Max Weber: Essays in Sociology*, edited by Hans Heinrich Gerth and Charles Wright Mills, New York: Oxford University Press. Coll. Galaxy book, no. 13.

Wood, Ellen Meiksins. 1995, *Democracy Against Capitalism: Renewing Historical Capitalism*, Cambridge: Cambridge University Press.

———— 2002a, 'The Question of Market Dependence', *Journal of Agrarian Studies*, vol. 2, no. 1: 50–87.

———— 2002b, *The Origin of Capitalism: A Longer View*, London: Verso.

———— 2003, 'Globalization and the State: Where is the Power of Capital?', In *Anti-Capitalism: A Marxist Introduction*, edited by Alfredo Saad-Filho, London; Sterling, VA: Pluto Press.

Woronoff, Denis. 1994, *Histoire de l'industrie en France: Du XVIe siècle à nos jours*, Paris: Éditions du Seuil. Coll. L'univers historique.

Wright, Gordon. 1964, *Rural Revolution in France: The Peasantry in the Twentieth Century*, Stanford, CA: Stanford University Press.

Wright, Vincent. 1998, 'Le Conseil d'État et les changements de régime: Le cas du Second Empire', *La Revue Administrative*, vol. 51: 13–18.

Wrigley, E. A. 2000, 'The Divergence of England: The Growth of the English Economy in the Seventeenth and Eighteenth Centuries: The Prothero Lecture', *Transactions of the Royal Historical Society*, vol. 10: 117–41.

———— 1985, 'Urban Growth and Agricultural Change: England and the Continent in the Early Modern Period', *The Journal of Interdisciplinary History*, vol. 15, no. 4: 683–728.

———— 2006, 'The Transition to an Advanced Organic Economy: Half a Millennium of English Agriculture', *The Economic History Review*, vol. 59, no. 3: 435–80.

Wrigley, Edward Anthony, R. S. Davies, J. E. Oeppen, and Roger S. Schofield. 1997, *English Population History from Family Reconstitution 1580–1837*, Cambridge: Cambridge University Press. Coll. Cambridge Studies in Population, Economy and Society in Past Time.

Wylie, Laurence. 1974, *Village in the Vaucluse*, Cambridge, MA: Harvard University Press.

Young, Arthur. 1969, *Travels in France during the years 1787, 1788, and 1789*, edited by Jeffry Kaplow, Garden City, NY: Doubleday.

Zdatny, Steven M. 1984, 'The Artisanat in France: An Economic Portrait, 1900–1956', *French Historical Studies*, vol. 13, no. 3: 415.

Zeldin, Theodore. 1993, *A History of French Passions 1848–1945*, Oxford: Clarendon. Coll. Oxford History of Modern Europe.

Zemmour, Michaël. 2023, 'Emmanuel Macron's Plan to Raise the Pension Age Is Class War', *Jacobin*. https://jacobin.com/2023/02/emmanuel-macron-pension-reform-labor-market-wage-supression-tax-cuts-protest

Zmolek, Michael Andrew. 2014, *Rethinking the Industrial Revolution: Five Centuries of Transition from Agrarian to Industrial Capitalism in England*, Chicago: Haymarket Books. Coll. Historical Materialism Book Series, no. 49.

Zysman, John. 1983, *Governments, Markets, and Growth: Financial Systems and Politics of Industrial Change*, Ithaca, NY: Cornell University Press. Coll. Cornell Studies in Political Economy.

Bibliography

Index